ONE LAST READ

ONE LAST READ

THE COLLECTED WORKS OF
THE WORLD'S SLOWEST
SPORTSWRITER

◆ ◆ ◆

Ray Didinger

WITH A NEW AFTERWORD BY THE AUTHOR

TEMPLE UNIVERSITY PRESS

Philadelphia • Rome • Tokyo

TEMPLE UNIVERSITY PRESS
Philadelphia, Pennsylvania 19122
tupress.temple.edu

Paperback edition published 2023
Cloth edition published 2007

Library of Congress Cataloging-in-Publication Data

Names: Didinger, Ray, author.
Title: One last read : the collected works of the world's slowest
   sportswriter / Ray Didinger ; with a new afterword by the author.
Description: Paperback edition. | Philadelphia : Temple University Press,
   2023. | Includes index. | Summary: "A collection of columns and profiles
   by Philadelphia sportswriter Ray Didinger"— Provided by publisher.
Identifiers: LCCN 2023005266 | ISBN 9781592136018 (paperback)
Subjects: LCSH: Sports—United States. |
   Sports—Pennsylvania—Philadelphia. |
   Sportscasters—Pennsylvania—Philadelphia—Anecdotes.
Classification: LCC GV583 .D53 2023 | DDC 796.09748/11—
   dc23/eng/20230216
LC record available at https://lccn.loc.gov/2023005266

The paper used in this publication meets the requirements of the American National
Standard for Information Sciences—Permanence of Paper for Printed Library Materials, ANSI
Z39.48-1992

Printed in the United States of America

9 8 7 6 5 4 3 2 1

TO JACK WILSON

You opened the door. I'll always be grateful.

◆

Contents

Acknowledgments

If there is one theme to this book, it is how lucky—and grateful—I am. I have spent my entire adult life writing about, talking about, and making films about sports. It has been a labor of love in the truest sense of the word. There were a lot of people along the way who provided guidance, inspiration, assistance, and friendship, so this is a chance to say thanks.

I have to start with my family, especially my father and mother, who nurtured my love of sports, and my grandparents—in particular, my grandfather—who taught me what it means to be a fan. I grew up watching Eagles and Phillies games with him, and through all the lean years I never once heard him boo.

"Even good players have bad days," he would say.

I have to thank Sister Clare Ursula, my fifth-grade nun, and Donald Bell and John Mooney, my English teachers at St. James High School, for encouraging me to develop my writing skills. Also, thanks to Doug Perry and John Roberts, who taught the fine journalism and broadcasting courses at Temple.

Growing up in Philadelphia, I was fortunate to have great role models in the local media. Reading Sandy Grady and George Kiseda in the *Philadelphia Bulletin* and Stan Hochman and Bill Conlin in the *Philadelphia Daily News* was my introduction to the fine art of sportswriting. Listening to Bill Campbell call Phillies and Eagles games on the radio had the same effect. Their words, all passion and power, were the magnetic force that drew me from the bleachers to the press box.

I was fortunate to have editors such as Arthur Mayhew of the *Delaware County Daily Times*, Jack Wilson and Herb Stutz of the *Bulletin*, and Mike Rathet and Brian Toolan of the *Daily News* who gave me the freedom to express myself. I had colleagues such as Alan Richman, Jim Barniak and Mark Whicker at the *Bulletin* and Rich Hofmann, Jay Greenberg, Dick Weiss and Phil Jasner at the *Daily News* who made the long nights and tedious road trips bearable. Thanks to the public relations directors of the local teams who were always willing to help, in particular Jim Gallagher, Chick McElrone, and Derek Boyko of the Eagles, Larry Shenk and Gene Dias of the Phillies, Harvey Pollack of the 76 ers, and Joe Kadlec of the Flyers. Thanks to Steve Sabol, who brought me into his NFL Films family in 1996 and provided a wonderful second chapter to my life.

I also thank Tommy McDonald, who inspired me in so many ways, first as an athlete, then as a friend. I feel the same way about Dick Vermeil. Just being around Vermeil when he coached the Eagles, I learned lessons about loyalty and commitment that still resonate today.

Thanks to director Alex Holzman and editor Micah Kleit at Temple University Press for their confidence. The team that helped put *One Last Read* together—production editor Elena Coler of Temple University Press and freelance copy editor Susan Deeks—did a masterful job.

I offer a special note of appreciation to Pat McLoone and Michael Days of the *Philadelphia Daily News* and John Wiebusch, of NFL Publishing, for their help in acquiring the material for this book. Bob Vetrone Jr. spent many nights in the *Daily News* library, digging up the old columns. Thanks so much for your patience, Bob.

And speaking of patience, I thank my wife, Maria, and children David and Kathleen. It could not have been easy, living with the world's slowest sportswriter. I lost count of how many birthdays and holidays I missed because I was either in a press box or on an airplane. Your love and support over the years made this book possible.

Introduction

Writing a column is like opening a vein and letting the words bleed
out, drip by drip.
—Red Smith, *New York Times*

People ask why I never wear a wristwatch. They are surprised that someone who spent his life in journalism—a world defined by deadlines—would not want to know the time.

"Well," I say, "it's a long story."

That's my problem. Every story is a long story. Even short stories become long stories because that's how I write them.

I . . . write . . . verrry . . . slooooowly.

In twenty-seven years in the newspaper business, I never missed a deadline, but I teetered on the brink almost every night. My editors have the gray hairs and nicotine patches to prove it.

For a while, I did wear a watch, but it only made things worse. I would check the time and see that another hour had passed. I'd feel the sweat trickle down my neck. I could hear the sweep of the second hand as it cut through the stillness of a deserted press box.

Two hours to deadline. One hour to deadline. I would be all alone staring at a blank sheet of paper, hearing the tick, tick, tick of precious time slipping away.

I thought the watch was part of the problem. I felt if I did away with that distraction, I would write faster. I removed the watch, but when I sat down to write, nothing had changed. The words still came out in a slow, painful drip like molasses poured through a strainer. I had to accept the fact it was my own sluggish muse that was at fault, and, sad to say, it wasn't likely to improve.

Still, I left the watch at home. I learned to keep time by the rhythms of the stadium. The game would end. The clean-up crew would come and go. The security guards would change shifts. I knew their schedules by heart. I was the last writer to file every night, but I never missed an edition.

There was one night, however, when I almost didn't make it. It was the final game of the 1979 World Series. Willie Stargell had just led the Pittsburgh Pirates to victory in a dramatic game seven in Baltimore. I decided to take the press bus back to the hotel and write my story there. I had until 6:30 in the morning to file my column to the *Philadelphia Bulletin*. Plenty of time, even for me.

Stargell had just culminated the finest season of his Hall of Fame career with a Most Valuable Player (MVP) performance in the World Series. As he savored the victory in the Pirates clubhouse, his sister Sandra burst through the crowd to embrace him. "I'm so proud of you," she said. It was a wonderful moment that ended with brother and sister sobbing on each other's shoulders.

I took a long time writing that column, selecting just the right words to describe a memorable night. Hours passed. Then I noticed an odd glow in the room. It was the sun peeking through the curtains.

"Oh, my God," I thought. "What time is it?"

I didn't have a watch, and I was afraid to look at the clock. I just started writing as fast as I could. Of all the days to blow deadline: game seven of the World Series. As I wrote the last line, the telephone rang. It was Bob Wright, the assistant sports editor, calling from the office.

"Are you going to file soon?" he asked.

Bob had placed these calls before, tracking me down in hotel rooms from Clearwater to Calgary, checking on the status of my column. His tone was usually calm and comforting, although the mere fact that he felt the need to call suggested the hour was late.

This time I could hear the anxiety in his voice, which was a very bad sign.

"Yeah, Bob," I said. "I finished the column. I'm giving it one last read."

I tried my best to sound as though I had everything under control, but the guys in the office were not fooled. They knew me all too well. I could hear someone in the background shouting: "Right (expletive) now. Tell him he has to send it right (expletive) now. I don't care if it's finished or not."

I filed the column without looking at the clock. To this day, I don't know what time it was. I was too shaken to sleep, so I checked out of the hotel and drove back to Philadelphia. I still wasn't sure my story made it into the paper. There was always the chance the transmission was garbled or the editors tired of waiting and ran a wire-service story in my place. I would not have blamed them if they did.

It wasn't until I picked up a copy of the *Bulletin* that afternoon and saw my column ("Pittsburgh's Pops: Best of the Best") that I was able to breathe again.

I don't know why I was such a slow writer. To explain it would require taking apart my writing mechanism and inspecting it as if it were a faulty snow blower. That's not how writing works. There are no moving parts to oil, no valves to replace, no wires to connect. If it were that easy, I would have gone in for servicing years ago.

Writing is an art. It flows from the imagination, and it flows faster for some people than it does for others. The great Red Smith, the Pulitzer Prize–winning columnist of the *New York Times*, once said: "I love my job, but I find one of the disadvantages is the several hours I spend at the typewriter each day. That's how I pay for this nice job. And I pay dearly. I sweat. I bleed. I'm a slow writer."

Red was a slow writer, but I was slower. At my first Super Bowl in January 1971, I still was fumbling for a lead on my game story when Red filed his column. I was the last writer to leave the press box that night. In fact, I was the last writer the leave the press box at every Super Bowl from V to XXX, and I'm sure the streak would have continued if I had not left newspapers for my job as a producer with NFL Films in 1996.

I was locked in almost every stadium in North America. The security guards would assume that by 6 A.M., everyone was gone, so they would bolt the doors and turn out the lights. As a result, I often had to find my way out in the dark. After years in the business, I knew every fire escape and catwalk from Yankee Stadium to Candlestick Park. I scaled walls, crawled under fences, and outran guard dogs, all while carrying a briefcase and portable typewriter.

At Veterans Stadium, there was an elevator from the press box to the street level, which sounds very convenient, except, like many things at the Vet, it often broke down. If I finished writing in the wee hours of the morning, rather than risk being trapped on the elevator for hours, I would walk down the deserted ramps, listening to the rats scurry through the garbage.

Once after an Eagles Monday night loss in 1976, I was walking through the darkened concourse when I bumped into someone coming the other way. It was Dick Vermeil, then a rookie head coach, who was already notorious for working around the clock. He was so deep in thought he did not even recognize me at first. The pain of the 20–17 loss to the Washington Redskins was still etched in his face. He looked like he had been walking all night.

"I didn't know sportswriters worked so late," Vermeil said.

"Only me," I said. "It takes me a while."

I envied the writers who could dash off a readable column on deadline. Bill Lyon of the *Inquirer*, Stan Hochman of the *Daily News*, and Mark Whicker of the *Bulletin* (and later the *Daily News*) had the wonderful gift of writing both quickly and well. All three of them could knock out a column in less than an hour, and it would read as though they had labored over it for days.

I once shared a Florida condominium with Whicker during a Phillies spring training. One afternoon, Mark wrote his game story, a sidebar, and a two-thousand–word piece on college basketball while I was trying to finish my column. He played two sets of tennis, came back to the room, and I was still writing. He went to dinner, came back, and found me still hunched over my computer. I finished just in time to catch the end of the eleven o'clock news.

After three days, Mark stopped asking: "Are you almost done?" By then he knew the answer. It was always, "No."

Doug Todd, the former publicity director of the Dallas Cowboys, gave me the nickname "Dawn Patrol." Doug was in charge of media transportation at several Super Bowls, which meant he had to draw up two post-game itineraries: one for the two thousand or so accredited reporters assigned to cover the game; the other for me. I was at least one hour behind the next slowest writer, so Doug usually kept one bus waiting just for me.

Super Bowl XXI was the worst. The New York Giants defeated the Denver Broncos, 39–20, at the Rose Bowl. I spent nine hours laboring over a column about Giants quarterback Phil Simms. At 2 A.M., Pacific time, there were only three people left in the press tent—Doug, a very irritated bus driver, and myself—and I wasn't even close to being finished.

"Go ahead," I said, "I'll find my own way back."

"Are you sure?" Doug asked.

"Yeah, don't wait for me."

I finished my column an hour later and called for a taxi. The driver was thrilled when I told him I was going to Anaheim. That was a $95 ride from Pasadena, not counting the tip.

When I turned in my expense account, my editor asked about the cab fare. "Why didn't you take the press bus?" he asked. I told him I missed it.

"You missed *all* the press buses?" he said.

I nodded.

"You have to start writing faster," he said.

I promised to try, but I knew it was impossible. I had been trying to write faster for almost twenty years, ever since my first road trip with the Eagles in 1970. I was twenty-three years old, a wide-eyed rookie on the football beat, when the Eagles went to Buffalo for their pre-season opener. It was a nothing game between two nothing teams, but I was determined to compose a masterpiece.

By the time I finished writing—and it wasn't a masterpiece—they had turned off the lights in War Memorial Stadium. If it hadn't been for a compassionate security guard who stood behind me with a flashlight, I might still be there. "Why does it take you so long?" he asked. I explained I was new on the job, so I was taking great pains to make sure I got everything just right. I thought I would get faster with experience, but I never did.

Part of the reason, I suppose, is I spent most of my life working for afternoon newspapers. That meant I had all night to write. If an Eagles game ended at 4 P.M., I had twelve hours to file a game story and a sidebar. I used all of it—writing, rewriting, and polishing. I became a slow writer, basically, because the P.M. deadlines allowed it.

If I had worked for a morning paper, I would have been forced to write faster. I know I could have done it. There were times at the *Bulletin* and the *Philadelphia Daily News* when stories broke late at night, and I'd write a one-thousand–word column on deadline. I did it because I had to. But if I had more time, I'd use it.

It didn't always make the finished product better. At Super Bowl XX, I was assigned two stories: one was a column on Buddy Ryan, Chicago's defensive coordinator who was about to be named head coach of the Eagles; the other was a sidebar on Walter Payton, the great running back who finally won his first NFL championship.

I spent almost ten hours laboring over the Ryan column. It was 5 A.M., Philadelphia time, when I filed it. The editor said, "You know you're on the schedule for a Payton story, too."

"I'll start it right away," I said.

"We need a twenty-inch story, and we need it in twenty minutes," he said.

"I'll do it," I said.

I grabbed a few quotes from my notebook, a couple stats from the play-by-play sheets, and slapped them together. I hit the "send" button with two minutes to spare. The story was a total blur. I just knew it was done and on time.

The next day, I bumped into one of the *Daily News* editors. "Nice piece on Walter Payton," he said. Nothing about the column I spent the whole night writing. He liked the sidebar I had dashed off in eighteen minutes. There is a moral in there somewhere.

This book is a collection of my writings, mostly from the *Bulletin* and *Daily News*. It spans more than thirty years and represents countless hours spent at the keyboard. It isn't about one sport or one athlete. It is more like a portrait gallery, dozens of individual pieces, each one capturing a different face and a different moment in time. Some are heroic; others, tragic, but I remember them all. In many ways, they define my life.

I reread hundreds of columns to select the ones that appear in this book. It was like revisiting the old neighborhood, it brought back so many memories. I smiled when I saw a January 1981 column previewing the Eagles–Cowboys NFC championship game. I described sitting with Tex Schramm, the Cowboys' president, when his secretary handed him a wire from the NFL office. It read: "Please be advised the Philadelphia Eagles will wear their white jerseys in Sunday's championship game."

That meant the visiting Cowboys would have to wear their blue jerseys, which they considered bad luck. Schramm's smile dissolved into a "What-the-(expletive)?" scowl.

"How many times have the Eagles worn white at home this year?" he asked.

"This will be the first," I said.

Schramm growled, "White jerseys. Blue jerseys. I'm glad that's all they have to think about with a championship game coming up."

The final score was White Jerseys, 20; Blue Jerseys, 7. Did the colors make a difference? Probably not, but so what? The look on Schramm's face made it all worthwhile. I mentioned it to Dick Vermeil later and he smiled.

"That's what we were hoping for," he said.

There were painful memories, as well. For example, the July day in 1981 when I was writing the Jim Tyrer story in a Kansas City hotel room. Suddenly, the afternoon calm was shattered by the wail of sirens. I looked out the window and saw dozens of police cars, fire engines, and ambulances pulling into the Hyatt Hotel across the street.

I did what any reporter would have done. I grabbed my notebook and ran into the Hyatt. I will never forget the sight. A skyway had collapsed into the lobby. There were 114 people dead and more than 200 injured. I spent hours on the scene, interviewing rescue workers and survivors. That night I dictated a story to the *Daily News* city desk.

Just nine months earlier, I was in the same hotel, writing about the Phillies–Royals World Series. Now I was piecing together the details of the worst structural disaster in U.S. history. That is the nature of a reporter's life. It is unpredictable, often wrenchingly so. My journalism career was a long, winding journey across four decades, and the stories you will find in this book are like the oversize postcards I wrote along the way.

An older fan will find moments that are familiar but worth reliving. Garry Maddox catching the final out in the Houston Astrodome, lifting the Phillies to the 1980 World Series. The Eagles celebrating their championship win over Dallas. A younger fan who wasn't around for the Flyers' Stanley Cup parade or the Miracle of the Meadowlands can learn how it all unfolded. I was there, and I will give you the whole story.

But slowly, always slowly.

I can't tell it any other way.

The thought first hit me on August 1, 1998, while I was riding in an open convertible through Canton, Ohio. The sun was shining. There were two hundred thousand people lining the streets. There were twenty-three marching bands in front of me, twenty-one spectacular floats behind me, and my boyhood idol, Tommy McDonald, was sitting alongside me.

All I could think was, "How did I get so lucky?"

It should have occurred to me years before, when I was given the opportunity to do the thing I loved—write about sports—in the city where I was born and raised. It should have crossed my mind hundreds of times when I found myself in the company of people like Hank Aaron, Muhammad Ali, Michael Jordan, Jack Nicklaus, Gordie Howe, Joe Montana, Jim Brown, and Don Shula.

I'll never forget the day I sat with John Unitas in his kitchen talking about the 1958 NFL championship game. I was with NFL Films at the time, and we were working on a documentary about the Hall of Fame quarterback. The crew was in another room setting up the lights for the interview, so I was alone with Unitas as he ate his morning Wheaties. How could I not ask about the `58 championship, the historic game in which Unitas led the Baltimore Colts to their first world title and lifted pro football to the top of the American sports marquee?

I asked Unitas if he was nervous on the drive to the winning touchdown. It was, after all, football's first sudden-death overtime, uncharted water even for the great Unitas.

"You're only nervous if you don't know what you're doing," he said. "I knew what I was doing."

It should have dawned on me then—how lucky I was to be in that position, talking to a legend and seeing in his eyes exactly what it was that made him great. But at the time, I didn't see the bigger picture. I was in my reporter mode: This is my job, this is what I do. I meet people, I ask questions and for almost thirty years, one story just followed the next.

But that day in Canton changed everything. For the first time, I took a step back. I reflected on where I was and what I was doing. Tommy McDonald had asked me to be his presenter at the Pro Football Hall of Fame. I would stand on the steps of the hall and deliver a speech about the great receiver I once chased for an autograph at the Eagles' training camp in Hershey, Pennsylvania.

"How did I get so lucky?"

I asked myself that question a thousand times.

I grew up in Philadelphia, which meant I grew up loving the Eagles. They were there every Sunday when I awoke, like the church bells and Blondie. Our family would go to mass; then we would go to the Eagles game, and I couldn't tell where the religion left off and the football began. For me, it was all part of the same ritual.

I went to my first Eagles game in 1956. I was ten years old, and the team was playing at Connie Mack Stadium. We rode to the games on a bus chartered by my grandfather. He owned a bar on Woodland Avenue in Southwest Philadelphia called Ray's Tavern. He was the original Ray Didinger. The name was handed down to my father and me, along with a passion for sports. Each year, my grandfather ordered a block of Eagles season tickets for his patrons. My father, my mother, and I tagged along. Every Sunday morning, we piled aboard the bus with our hoagies and our hope.

There were usually about forty people on the bus. My mother, grandmother, and aunt were the only women, so they sat up front. My father and I sat a few rows back. The men who rode with us were all working-class guys from the neighborhood, burly cigar smokers with names like Big Don, Old Gus, and Whitey the Milkman. Some of them struggled to come up with the $18 for their season tickets (six home games, $3 per game), but they were always there, sitting in the same seats every Sunday.

One of the regulars was Johnny Hayes, a former boxer with a raspy voice and a cauliflower ear. He liked nothing better than needling my grandfather.

"You know, Ray," he'd say, "for a few more bucks, you could get a driver who actually has a license."

"Don't start, John," my grandfather would say.

The bus would rock with laughter.

I remember walking into Connie Mack Stadium for the first time, seeing the field, hearing the band, and feeling my heart leap. I fell in love with football at that moment. The Eagles won the game, 13–9, over the Washington Redskins, one of only three games they would win that season. It was played in a driving rain; we were soaked to the skin, and I didn't care. I was having the time of my life.

In 1957, the Eagles drafted Tommy McDonald from the University of Oklahoma. He was the smallest man on the field at five-foot-nine, 172 pounds, and he bounced around with the exuberance of a schoolboy at recess. I loved watching him.

Every Sunday, they would introduce the starting lineups. One by one, the players would jog through a gantlet of drummers and baton twirlers. Then the public-address announcer would say: "At flanker, number 25, from Oklahoma . . ." and Tommy would charge onto the field in a full sprint. We never heard his name announced because it was always drowned out by the cheers rolling down from the upper deck.

In the five seasons from 1958 through 1962, Tommy scored fifty-six touchdowns in sixty-three games, including the 1960 NFL championship game against Green Bay. The Eagles defeated the Packers, 17–13, and I was there in Section EE at Franklin Field. Tommy scored the first Eagles touchdown right in front of me, catching a thirty-five–yard pass from quarterback Norm Van Brocklin. I've carried that memory with me ever since.

Years later, after I became a sportswriter, I was named to the Hall of Fame selection committee. I began a personal campaign to get Tommy into the hall, not because he was my boyhood hero, but because I felt a player with eighty-four career touchdown receptions deserved enshrinement. Tommy heard about my efforts and called to say thanks.

"If I ever get in," he said, "I want you to be my presenter."

In 1998, thirty years after his retirement, Tommy finally was voted into the Hall of Fame. He kept his promise: He asked me to be his presenter. As we rode together in the parade, he said: "This never would've happened if it wasn't for you." He gave me a tearful hug, and that's when it struck me: what a billion-to-one shot this was.

Growing up, everyone has a hero, but for most people, that hero remains an image on a poster or a bubble-gum card. If you're lucky, you might get an autograph one day or maybe a quick handshake, but that's it. As a fan, you never expect to step across that line and into their world. Yet here I was, riding in the Hall of Fame parade with Tommy McDonald and sharing in his finest hour.

Lucky?

You bet.

On some level, I think I always felt it. That's one reason why I was such a slow writer. I was grateful for the opportunity to make a living writing about sports, so each time I sat at the keyboard, I wanted to do the best possible job. If that meant writing all night, so be it.

I grew up reading the *Philadelphia Bulletin*—in particular, Sandy Grady's sports columns and Hugh Brown's coverage of the Eagles. By the time I was in the eighth grade, I knew that was what I wanted to do. I wanted to be a writer; specifically, I wanted to be a sports writer for the *Bulletin* covering the Eagles.

Imagine my joy when in 1969 Jack Wilson, the sports editor of the *Bulletin*, called to offer me a job. At the time, I was working as a news reporter at the *Delaware County Daily Times* in Chester, Pennsylvania. That was my first job after graduating from Temple University. The *Daily Times* did not have any openings in sports, so I agreed to work on city side, covering county politics and school-board hearings for $100.25 a week. But, really, I was just biding my time, waiting for a chance to move up.

When Jack offered me a job covering high-school sports at the *Bulletin*, I almost leapt from my chair.

"Yes, absolutely," I said.

"Don't you want to know what it pays?" Jack asked.

"Whatever it is, I'm sure it will be fine," I said.

"You're easy," he said with a laugh.

Jack started me at $150 a week and gave me the desk next to Sandy Grady. I felt like a rookie called up from the minors and assigned the locker next to Babe Ruth. Sandy was the best sportswriter in America. He could take a ninth inning rally or a first round knockout and turn it into poetry. His writing was witty and graceful, and in my undergraduate days at Temple, I imitated him shamelessly. Now I was working alongside him.

In 1970, Hugh Brown was easing toward retirement, and Jack surprised everyone by assigning me to the Eagles. At twenty-three, I was handed my dream job. It was a huge leap of faith on Jack's part. I was the youngest writer on the staff. I had spent all of one year covering high schools. I was a rank amateur compared with the veteran reporters on the football beat. It was a wonderful opportunity, but also an enormous challenge with real crash-and-burn potential.

The day I left for my first Eagles training camp at Albright College in Reading, Jack asked how I felt. I answered honestly.

"I'm not sure I'm ready," I said.

"Then get ready," he said.

I'm often asked if it was hard to make the transition from life-long Eagles fan to beat reporter. It is a fair question, given the fact I went directly from the $3 seats at Franklin Field to the press box. But the truth is, I did not have a problem being objective, largely because the team was in such sorry shape.

The Eagles were 3–10–1 in 1970. They were on their way to their fourth consecutive losing season and their eighth losing season in nine years. They were a bad team. It was obvious to everyone, and I had to write that in one form or another every day. It would have been dishonest to do otherwise.

Besides, I knew there were people who questioned Jack's decision to put me on the football beat. It was the most coveted job in the sports department. Win or lose, the Eagles led the paper almost every day. There were a lot of shocked faces in the newsroom when Jack chose me to replace Hughie. I knew if I went soft on the team, there would have been pressure on Jack to put me back on high schools and promote someone else. I didn't want that to happen.

So I was pretty tough on the Eagles that season. It did not endear me to the players, especially the veterans. They asked what qualified me to critique their performance. Some, like quarterback Norm Snead and tight end Gary Ballman, were playing pro football when I was still in high school, yet here I was ripping them every day in the city's biggest newspaper. They saw me as a punk kid trying to make a name for himself at their expense.

Ballman sat next to me on the team charter to Dallas. He asked: "What do you know about pro football? I mean, what do you really know?" I said, "I know a losing team when I see one." Since the Eagles were 0–6 at the time—and the Cowboys would soon make them 0–7—there wasn't much he could say.

While I had no trouble maintaining my objectivity around the Eagles, that was not always true when I visited other teams. I remember walking into the Baltimore Colts clubhouse after they defeated the Eagles that season and seeing John Unitas standing alone at his locker. There were a dozen reporters in the room, but none were talking to the winning quarterback.

"Don't waste your time," one of the older reporters said. "Unitas is a terrible interview."

Impossible, I thought. I grew up watching Unitas. He was one of my earliest sports heroes. There he was just a few feet away. I had to talk to him.

I introduced myself. Unitas nodded but said nothing. I asked about his game plan for the Eagles. He shrugged and said, "We made enough plays to win; that's all I care about." I asked about one touchdown pass in particular. "Nothing special," he said. "We have that play in every week." I began asking another question, but he didn't let me finish. "It's one game," he said, pulling on his coat. "We have another one next week."

With that, he was out the door. I looked at my notebook. I had a few scribbled quotes, but really I had nothing.

Years later, when I was working on the Unitas documentary, I told him that story.

"Don't feel bad," he said. "I was that way with everybody."

"You knew you had a reputation as a terrible interview?" I asked.

"I'd rather be known as a bad interview and a good player than the other way around," Unitas said. "My job was winning games, not talking about them."

Unitas made me realize just how differently sports journalists and athletes view the same game. I always accepted the fact we had nothing in common off the field. They are wealthy, we're not. They are worshiped by millions, we're not. They live in a spotlight that we merely illuminate. I get it.

I thought the one thing we had in common was what happened between the white lines, but Unitas made it clear that's not true, either. The players, especially old-school types like Unitas, are defined by their performance, what they do on the field, good or bad. All we can supply are words, and no matter how lovely, they still are little more than tinsel on the athlete's tree.

"I wasn't trying to be a jerk, I just could never figure out what you guys wanted," Unitas said. "After the game, reporters would ask, `What happened on that play?' Or they'd say, `Describe that touchdown.' It didn't make any sense. You saw the game. Why do I have to describe it?"

"But people want to hear what you have to say," I said.

"What I say doesn't mean squat," Unitas said. "If we won, that's all that matters. If we lost and I played lousy, nobody wants to hear excuses. I just thought talking was a waste of time."

Unitas laughed. "I guess I was a terrible interview," he said.

My fondest memory of that 1970 season was the week three game against Washington at Franklin Field. I was shuffling through my notes at halftime when I felt a tap on the shoulder. It was Jim Heffernan, director of public relations for the NFL.

"The commissioner wants to meet you," Heffernan said.

"Yeah, sure he does," I replied.

Heff was a former *Bulletin* sportswriter, a friend, and a practical joker, so I assumed he was kidding. He insisted he was telling the truth.

"Pete likes to meet all the new beat guys," Heffernan said as he walked me to the far end of the press box. There, as promised, sat Pete Rozelle, dapper as always, extending his hand.

"Welcome to the NFL," Rozelle said.

I'll always remember that moment. The warmth of his smile, the ease in his manner. It wasn't at all what I expected from the man who was referred to as the czar of professional football.

He was eating a hot dog. His binoculars hung on a strap around his neck. I remember thinking he looked like a regular fan, which is what he was. He wasn't a lawyer, a politician, a former player or coach. He was an ex-sportswriter and publicist, but at heart, he was a fan. His greatest pleasure was kicking back on a Sunday afternoon and watching a game, even if it involved two winless teams, as that one did.

I asked Rozelle why he came to see the 0–2 Eagles play the 0–2 Redskins. He said he thought it would be a good game. It wasn't. The Redskins won easily, 33–21. But the stadium was full, the October sun was shining, and to Pete Rozelle, it was Camelot on the Schuylkill River.

That was the dawn of a golden decade for pro football. The NFL and the American Football League (AFL) had merged. *Monday Night Football* had debuted to blockbuster ratings on network television. The Super Bowl had become the world's biggest and most lucrative sports spectacle. Pro football was taking off like a NASA rocket, and Rozelle had his hand firmly on the throttle. I had hopped on for the ride.

We talked for about ten minutes. Rozelle asked about my background. He laughed when I told him I was the youngest beat man in the league. He reminded me that he was only thirty-three when he was named commissioner. He said: "I'll tell you the same thing the [team] owners told me, `You'll grow into it.'"

I spent seven years on the Eagles beat, then I became the sports columnist after Sandy moved to Washington, D.C., to cover politics, and his successor, Jim Barniak, left the paper for television. Again, I was lucky because Philadelphia was enjoying a sports renaissance. After decades of losing, all the local teams were arising. Julius Erving signed with the 76ers. Dick Vermeil resurrected the Eagles. The Phillies, led by future Hall of Famers Steve Carlton and Mike Schmidt, were on their way to five division titles in eight years.

As a sports columnist, it was like being a guest at a party where the good times never stopped. On any given day, you had your pick of winning teams to write about. At Broad and Pattison, where once there was a swamp, now was a land of milk and honey. It all began, really, with the Flyers. They taught Philadelphia how to win again by capturing back-to-back Stanley Cups in 1974 and '75. They were an irresistible story, a team known as the Broad Street Bullies brawling its way to the National Hockey League championship while a good-luck charm named Kate Smith sang "God Bless America."

There was a sweet, unspoiled quality to that first championship. When the Flyers won the deciding game, 1–0, over the Boston Bruins, the Spectrum security guards threw open the locker-room door. The players' families rushed into the room—wives and mothers included—along with reporters, photographers, fans, and what seemed like half the population of South Philadelphia. It was utterly out of control, yet utterly wonderful.

I was literally shoved into the locker of Dave Schultz, who earned the nickname "The Hammer" by pummeling every tough guy in the league. But on this day, Schultz was sitting with his arm draped around his father, Edgar. Father and son were sipping beer and enjoying the celebration.

The elder Schultz was a garage mechanic in Rosetown, Saskatchewan, and he had taken his vacation to follow the Flyers through the playoffs. "Last week, they told Dad to come home," Dave said. "They told him it was inspection time, and work was piling up. He said, 'No damn way I'm coming back now. My son is going to win the Stanley Cup, and I'm going to be there.'"

And so he was.

The city held a victory parade the next day. The police expected a hundred thousand people to attend. Instead, 2 million people filled the streets. Joe Watson Sr., the father of Flyer defensemen Joe and Jimmy Watson, could not believe his eyes. "I didn't know there were this many people in the world," said Watson, who rode a bus for thirty-three hours from Smithers, British Columbia, to see his sons drink from the Stanley Cup.

The crowd engulfed the cars carrying Flyers captain Bobby Clarke and goalie Bernie Parent, and the police pulled them out of the parade for their own protection. Andrea Mitchell, now an NBC news correspondent, was a reporter for KYW radio at the time. She filed a report quoting City Representative Harry Belinger as saying it was the biggest celebration in Philadelphia's history.

"All of this," she said, "for a hockey team."

Well, not exactly.

I never believed there were 2 million hockey fans in Philadelphia. But clearly in 1974, there were 2 million people in this area who were anxious to celebrate *something*. They wanted to point their index fingers to the sky and yell, "We're Number One." Other cities were doing it; why not Philadelphia?

The Flyers broke the cycle of losing, and their success seemed to energize the other franchises. It wasn't long before this was being called the "City of Winners," and lucky me, I had a front row seat to the whole thing.

Some people would say I was covering games, but I knew I was writing about something much larger than that. These athletes—beginning with the Flyers and soon including all of the local teams—were changing the self-image of Philadelphia.

As Red Smith once wrote: "Sports is not really a play world. I think it's the real world. Not in who wins or loses as it is reflected on the scoreboard, but in the people in sports who are suffering and living and dying and loving and trying to make their way through life just as bricklayers and politicians are. The man who reports on these games contributes his small bit to the record of his time."

This book represents my small bit to the record of a truly remarkable time.

Dick Vermeil arrived in Philadelphia in 1976. I was in my seventh year of covering the Eagles for the *Bulletin*, and Vermeil was the fourth head coach to come through owner Leonard Tose's revolving door.

It was easy to be cynical about the new hire, and most of the writers were. Jack McKinney of the *Daily News* took one look at the handsome, thirty-nine-year-old Vermeil and called him "California Slick."

"I wonder how long this one will last," Jack said as Tose and Vermeil posed for photographers.

We had witnessed this scene—smiles, flashbulbs, and promises—so often that by now we felt like guests at one of Tose's weddings. Those, too, started with the best of intentions, but they always ended badly. It was the same with Tose and his football coaches.

I had an advantage over the other writers because one month earlier I covered the Rose Bowl where Vermeil's UCLA team upset top-ranked Ohio State. The big story leading up to the game was the near-revolt among the UCLA players. They saw photos of the Ohio State players riding on floats with Mickey Mouse and frolicking at the pool with the Rose Bowl Queen. They could not understand why those guys were having so much fun while they were practicing three hours a day and studying film at night. So they went on strike.

That afternoon, Vermeil walked onto the practice field and found one player, quarterback John Sciarra. Sciarra told Vermeil the team would only return to practice if he agreed to lighten up. Vermeil told Sciarra the players had exactly fifteen minutes to get on the field. Anyone who did not report in that time was off the team.

"Tell them if they don't want to play, I'll go on campus and ask for volunteers," Vermeil said. "I won't have any trouble finding fifty kids who want to play in the Rose Bowl."

Fifteen minutes later, the entire varsity was assembled. Vermeil worked them for the customary three hours. When practice ended, he called the players together. "You want to have fun?" he said. "Win the damn game. Beat the number-one team in the country. That's what we're preparing to do."

On New Year's Day, UCLA shocked the mighty Buckeyes, 23–10, as Sciarra threw two touchdown passes to wide receiver Wally Henry. Afterward, the same players who had wanted to walk out on Vermeil were thanking him for a victory they would cherish forever. It was a masterful coaching job. I left the Rose Bowl thinking: "This guy Vermeil is going places."

Little did I know he was going to Philadelphia.

Vermeil walked into a bleak situation. There was precious little talent on the Eagles roster. The previous coach, Mike McCormack, had traded away most of the draft picks. Morale was at rock bottom. The fans were fed up. It looked like a hopeless cause, but Vermeil insisted there was no such thing.

"We'll just work until we get it turned around," he said.

Having seen what Vermeil did a month earlier at UCLA, I knew what to expect. Training camp would be hell. The Eagles practiced longer and harder than any team in the NFL. Vermeil brought more than a hundred players to camp—including Sciarra and Henry from his Rose Bowl team—and he drove them mercilessly. Three-hour practices in the sweltering heat. Full contact every day. Players were not permitted to remove their helmets or even unbuckle their chinstraps. The veterans grumbled about Vermeil's rules and called him "Harry High School." He knew it, but he didn't care.

"If they weren't bitching, I wouldn't be doing my job," he said.

My most vivid memory of that camp is Vermeil barking: "Again." When a play was not run to his satisfaction, Vermeil would make the players repeat it. He would stand with his arms folded, watching. If it still wasn't good enough, he would say it more sharply: "Again." It went on like this, every day for nine weeks.

The coaches studied film until three in the morning and were back on the field at eight. There were no days off, no time to rest. One afternoon I was interviewing Johnny Roland, the backfield coach, on a bench outside the cafeteria. Five minutes into our conversation, he fell asleep. I waited, hoping he would awaken. Instead, he began to snore. I nudged him, and his eyes fluttered open. He offered an embarrassed apology.

"I love Dick," Roland said, "but he's killing me."

On July 4, 1976, while America celebrated the Bicentennial, Vermeil stuck to his normal schedule: one practice in the morning, another in the afternoon, meetings at night. I asked why he did not give the players time off. It was the Bicentennial, after all, and the celebration was taking place at Independence Hall, just a short drive from the training camp at Widener University.

"The Fourth of July is just another block on the calendar," Vermeil said.

I thought he was missing the point.

As it turned out, I was.

Vermeil was building his kind of team. He wanted players who shared his commitment. All coaches talk about character, but for Vermeil it was a coat of arms. He believed in it as a way to live and a way to win. But for all of his passion and hard work, he did not have success overnight. It takes time to sweep away the cobwebs of nine straight non-winning seasons, and that's the kind of broken-down flop-house he inherited in Philadelphia.

The Eagles were winless (0–6) in their first pre-season under Vermeil and they were thumped by Dallas, 27–7, in the regular-season opener. I wrote an article about their lack of talent. I criticized Vermeil for not pursuing Larry Csonka, Jim Kiick, and Paul Warfield, the former Miami Dolphins who were free agents after the collapse of the World Football League. If Vermeil wanted any of those players, all he had to do was say the word, and Tose would have written the check.

"Why didn't you?" I asked.

"You can buy a player," Vermeil said, "but you can't buy motivation."

I'll never forget those words, because they were the foundation of what Vermeil built over the next six seasons with the Eagles and later in St. Louis, where he won the Super Bowl, and in Kansas City, where he won a division championship. He looked through each player's face mask, into his eyes, and, ultimately, into his heart. If he didn't like what he saw there, the rest of the package—the size, the speed, the muscle—didn't matter.

Vince Papale was a flesh-and-blood symbol of Vermeil's Eagles. He was a thirty-year-old schoolteacher who had never played college football—he attended St. Joseph's on a track scholarship—but he fought his way up from the local rough-touch leagues to the Eagles roster. He was the oldest rookie in NFL history and the most illogical, except he found in Vermeil a coach who was willing to give him the one thing he needed, and that was a chance.

Vermeil opened the door, and Papale did the rest, earning a place on the Eagles' special teams. In an era of long-term contracts and yawning superstars, he reminded everyone that football is still a game played by kids with scabby knees and sandlot hearts.

Since Papale made the team in 1976, the same year the film *Rocky* was released, his against-all-odds story was often compared to that of Sylvester Stallone's Italian Stallion. How fitting that thirty years later, Papale had a film of his own: *Invincible*, with Mark Wahlberg playing Vince and Greg Kinnear playing Vermeil. The film earned glowing reviews and was a $60 million hit for the Disney Studios.

Papale lasted three seasons with the Eagles, all on raw desire and determination. When Vermeil finally released him in 1979, Papale asked: "Is there anything else I could have done?"

"Die on the field?" Vermeil said.

It was his way of saying what Papale and everyone else already knew: He had given absolutely everything. By rising from rookie walk-on to special-teams captain, Papale had accomplished more than anyone thought possible. And it was that kind of passion, inspired by Vermeil, that eventually turned the Eagles around.

The team won only four games in Vermeil's first year and five the next. But by the third pre-season, the pieces were coming together. Vermeil had the attitude in place, and he was acquiring better talent. Wilbert Montgomery, a running back from Abilene Christian University, was a star in the making. Ron Jaworski was maturing at quarterback. The defense, led by linebacker Bill Bergey, was developing a snarl.

The Eagles concluded the 1978 pre-season with a 14–0 victory over the New York Jets. I could see the confidence growing. Vermeil still was barking at practice, but not as often. Most of the time, he stood with his hands on his hips, nodding as he watched the plays he designed come to life. "That's it," he would say. "That's what I'm looking for."

The week before the regular-season opener, I wrote a column saying the Eagles had the look of a winner. I had covered the team for nine years at that point, and it was the first time I had that feeling. In his first two seasons, Vermeil sometimes pulled me aside and told me I was too negative. He felt I dwelled too much on the years of losing and the ineptitude that characterized the Eagles for more than a decade.

I told him: "When I see something better, I'll write it."

In 1978, I saw it and wrote it in a Sunday column for the Bulletin:

"Dick Vermeil's plan, so painstakingly implemented over the past two seasons, has finally taken hold. . . . It is now possible to talk about the Eagles having a winning season and perhaps even competing for a playoff berth without feeling foolish."

Two days after the column appeared, I received a letter from Vermeil. "I appreciate your positive approach to what we're doing," he wrote. "Not that we've set the world on fire, but I do believe we cleaned up a real mess and have everything going in the right direction. . . Thanks. I know you are only doing your job."

The Eagles opened that season with narrow losses to the Los Angeles Rams (16–14) and the Washington Redskins (35–30), but they won four of their next five games, including a 17–3 upset of the Miami Dolphins. They carried a 6–5 record into the Meadowlands on November 19. What happened next was football history—and the most unforgettable day of my newspaper career.

It began when I arrived at Giants Stadium, and Jim Gallagher, the Eagles' publicity director, handed me a press release. It was a two-paragraph statement about Leonard Tose being in a Houston hospital following open heart surgery. The sixty-three-year-old owner was under the care of Denton Cooley, the world-renowned surgeon. Tose, we were told, was doing fine and would be listening to the game on a special radio hookup.

Perhaps the Eagles were unsettled by the news, or maybe, as some suggested, they were trying too hard to win one for the owner. Whatever the reason, they played miserably. With four minutes to go, they trailed the Giants 17–13, and when Jaworski threw his third interception, I headed for the elevator. I planned to watch the last few minutes on the field, then go to the locker room.

I was standing behind the end zone as the Giants ran out the clock. Quarterback Joe Pisarcik dropped to one knee as the seconds ticked away. One more snap and the game would be over. I was trying to decide what to write. Should I write about Tose? Should I write about the disappointing loss? Should I write off the post-season?

Then it happened.

Pisarcik took the snap, but instead of kneeling, he attempted a handoff to Larry Csonka. The ball hit Csonka on the hip and fell to the ground. It took a high hop off the artificial turf, and Eagles cornerback Herman Edwards caught it in stride. He was running right toward me, but it seemed like everything was in slow motion. I remember two things: the "Is this really happening?" look on Edwards's face and the stunned silence in the stadium.

The cop standing next to me said, "That won't count. The whistle must have blown." I checked the scoreboard. It read Eagles, 19; Giants, 17. It was, indeed, an Eagles touchdown, forever known as the Miracle of the Meadowlands.

I went inside and ran into a wave of reporters coming off the elevator. They had no idea what had happened. They had left the press box with the Giants leading. They thought I was joking when I said the Eagles had won. Then the teams came through the tunnel. The Eagles were whooping and hollering; the Giants were cursing and punching the wall. Suddenly, I was surrounded by reporters asking, "What happened?"

I saw the whole thing, but I still had trouble explaining it. It didn't make any sense. Why didn't the Giants just fall on the ball? I still don't have the answer. I just know that was a breakthrough for Vermeil's team. That was the day the players realized anything, even a trip to the Super Bowl, was possible. They made the playoffs that season, and two years later they were NFC champions.

General manager Jim Murray called Tose from the pay phone in the locker room. Murray handed the phone to Vermeil, who asked Tose, "How's your heart now?" Vermeil passed the phone to Jaworski, who told Tose the team was sending him the game ball.

"We won this one for you, boss," Jaworski said.

"You could've made it a little easier," Tose replied.

The next day, I flew to Houston and visited Tose at the hospital. Caroline Cullum, who would become his third wife, was at his bedside. Tose was on the phone, still talking about the game. "When Edwards picked up that ball," he said, "I let out a yell, and all the doctors came running into the room. They thought I was dying. I told them, 'Are you kidding? I never felt better.'"

We talked for more than two hours. The nurses were not happy. They wanted Tose to rest, but they knew he was going to do what he damn well pleased. On this day, with his heart thumping happily and his team in the playoff hunt for the first time, he felt like talking. So he talked, and I listened.

He talked about his father, Mike, the Russian Jewish immigrant who started the family trucking business with one horse and one wagon at the turn of the century. He talked about how his father became a millionaire yet never lost touch with his roots. Mike Tose was always reaching out, helping people and for all his playboy swagger, Leonard Tose was very much his father's son.

Stories of his generosity were legendary. In 1970, Tose donated $79,000 to keep extracurricular activities alive in Philadelphia's public schools. He wrote a $25,000 check to buy bulletproof vests for the police department. He pledged $1 million to launch Eagles Fly for Leukemia which helped build the bone-marrow-transplant laboratory at Children's Hospital of Philadelphia and funded the first Ronald McDonald House.

Those stories made headlines, but there were other acts of kindness that went unreported. Tose would see an item in the newspaper—a story about a family losing its home or a recreation center in need of repair—and he would circle it, hand it to one of his aides, and say, "Take care of this."

He once read about a young girl, a music prodigy, in North Philadelphia who was unable to continue her piano lessons due to a transit strike. Tose had a Steinway piano delivered to her home that afternoon. He did this sort of thing all the time.

Tose insisted on doing everything first-class. He had a fit when he arrived for a press conference and saw the staff putting out a tray of cold steak sandwiches for the media. "That's garbage," he said. "My team doesn't serve garbage." From then on, Tose treated the press like guests at one of his Main Line parties, bringing in tuxedoed caterers to serve filet mignon, lobster and even champagne for Monday night games.

When Tose traveled, he rode in a chauffeur-driven limousine, preferably with a police escort. On one trip to Los Angeles, Tose told Murray to arrange for his motorcycle escort. Murray called the Los Angeles Police Department who told him the LAPD had more important things to do than get some rich guy through rush-hour traffic on the Harbor Freeway.

But Murray was resourceful. He contacted a friend in Hollywood who lined up four actors, who were extras in the TV series *CHiPs* to serve as Tose's escorts. They had uniforms and motorcycles, so for three days they served as Tose's personal highway patrol, stopping traffic and waving him through. Tose had no idea the whole thing was a charade.

His reputation as a reckless spender made Tose an easy mark when the casinos came to Atlantic City. He lost an estimated $50 million gambling, and in 1984, in an effort to avoid bankruptcy, he negotiated a deal to sell a minority interest in the Eagles to the Arizona real-estate developer James Monaghan. The deal involved the Eagles' moving to Phoenix.

I was outraged that Tose would even consider taking the Eagles away from the fans who had supported them for so long. I wrote a series of columns that were sharply critical of Tose. As it turned out, he did not move the Eagles. Instead, he sold the team to Norman Braman, a Florida car dealer who kept the franchise in Philadelphia.

Most of the columnists in town let Tose down gently. They said in the end he did the right thing: He left the Eagles where he found them and where they belonged. I was not as forgiving. I wrote: "Tose and [daughter Susan] Fletcher turned off the city's sports fans with their disloyalty and they outraged nonfans with their greed." Rather than say goodbye to Tose and his daughter, I said good riddance.

The next morning, Tose called me at home and cursed me out. "If you ever see me coming," he said, "you'd better get out of the (expletive) way." He slammed the phone down, and we did not speak again for five years.

I felt bad about it. I didn't regret what I had written. I felt Tose's conduct was deplorable, and I said so. That's what columnists do. But I had known

Tose for a long time, and I had seen him do some very kind things. He had a good heart, but he also had a terrible weakness that was destroying his life.

He sold the Eagles for $65 million, but he netted only a fraction of that after his debts were paid. He swore he was set for life, but we knew better. It was only a matter of time before the casinos tapped him dry. In 1996, he was evicted from his Main Line mansion, and he lived out his final years alone in a center-city hotel room. Vermeil sent him money to keep him going.

Tose and I eventually repaired our relationship. We saw each other at a ten-year anniversary for the 1980 NFC championship team. It was held at Jaworski's golf club, the Eagle's Nest in Sewell, New Jersey. I was one of two media members invited; the other was Merrill Reese, the team's radio play-by-play man. It was a wonderful evening, with the coaches and former players hugging and reminiscing about that Super Bowl season.

At one point, Tose excused himself from the group and walked toward me. I was sure he would tell me to leave. Instead, he extended his hand. "I'm too (expletive) old to hold a grudge," he said. "Besides, I don't even remember what you wrote, it was so long ago." We shook hands, and that was that.

I've often thought back to that night and what it said about the 1980 Eagles. It was a collection of rather ordinary players, many of whom had been cast off by other clubs, but Vermeil molded them into something special. After dinner, Vermeil made a short speech, thanking the coaches and players for all they did.

"I'm as proud of you today as I was the day we beat Dallas," Vermeil said, referring to the NFC championship game that the Eagles won in a frigid Veterans Stadium.

Vermeil invited everyone to take the microphone. One by one, the players stepped forward. Wide receiver Charlie Smith, the quietest player on the team, spoke eloquently about the kinship he felt with the men in that room. He said: "You called me `Homeboy.' That was my nickname, and that's how it feels being with you again. It's like being home."

Tose was the last to speak. He, too, talked about the Dallas game. He talked about the fans' rushing onto the field to celebrate. That was the moment he cherished, he said, because he had delivered on his promise. He brought Philadelphia a championship. Tose turned to Vermeil and thanked him for making it happen.

"Dick Vermeil took us—all of us—from nowhere to somewhere," Tose said. "He taught us how to win football games and a helluva lot more. He left his mark on the city, and I know he sure as hell left his mark on me."

Over the next few years, I ran into Tose occasionally, usually at a Maxwell Club dinner or an Eagles Fly for Leukemia function. Sometimes he would call me at work just to talk. He was lonely and disconnected from the action. It was hard to accept for a man who lived so long in the spotlight. He would talk about the good times, hanging with Frank Sinatra, knocking back Scotches with Don Rickles, shuttling between Veterans Stadium and Bookbinder's restaurant in his private helicopter. Toward the end, those memories were all that kept him going.

A few years before his death in 2003, Tose was approached by a Hollywood producer who told the former Eagles owner he wanted to turn his life story into a movie. Tose called one day to tell me they had cast Alec Baldwin in the lead. "It's gonna happen," Tose said. He was delighted. He felt the movie would put him back on top. But the project wound up on the studio's back burner, then vanished altogether.

"It's their loss," Tose said. "It would've been one helluva movie."

I'll remember 1980 as the best—and worst—of times. It was the best of times for Philadelphia's professional sports franchises. All four teams went to the championship round, and the Phillies won their only World Series. Meanwhile, the U.S. hockey team shocked the world by winning an Olympic gold medal. Roberto Duran did the unthinkable, quitting in the middle of a championship fight with Sugar Ray Leonard. Jack Nicklaus won his fourth U.S. Open. Memorable stories were unfolding everywhere.

But it was the worst of times for many sportswriters because two of Philadelphia's four newspapers—the *Bulletin* and the *Journal*—were sinking in a sea of red ink.

Everyone who worked at the *Bulletin*—and I was there for a dozen years—was aware of the situation. Once the largest afternoon newspaper in the country, with a daily circulation over seven hundred thousand, the *Bulletin* was struggling to stay alive. It was the victim of what media analysts called a changing news cycle. The six o'clock news on TV made the afternoon paper obsolete. Folks came home from work, and instead of settling into an easy chair with the *Bulletin*, they flipped on the television.

Most people still wanted to read a newspaper in the morning, so the *Inquirer* gained strength as the *Bulletin* waned. Once upon a time, the slogan "Nearly Everybody Reads the *Bulletin*" was so well known it was quoted in motion pictures. In 1980, those words still graced the walls at 30th and Market streets, but those who worked there saw them for what they were: a melancholy echo of a bygone era, like the clippity-clop of the carriage horses in Old City.

The *Bulletin* was owned by the McLean family for more than eighty years, but in April 1980, with the circulation and advertising revenue plummeting, the paper was sold to the Charter Corporation, an oil conglomerate based in Jacksonville, Florida. The new owners talked about their commitment to the paper and the community, but it did little to ease our fears. We were like an ailing patient placed in the hands of total strangers. Anyone who said that he or she wasn't afraid was lying. We all felt it.

Three months after the sale, I was contacted by Mike Rathet, sports editor of the *Philadelphia Daily News*, who offered me a job as a columnist. It should have been an easy decision. The *Daily News* was offering more money and more security. It also was the best sports section in the city. I would be working with Stan Hochman, Bill Conlin, Tom Cushman, and other writers I knew and admired. It made all the sense in the world. Yet I agonized.

I felt a deep sense of loyalty to the *Bulletin*. That was where I got my start as a sportswriter. The *Bulletin* was very good to me, and I did not like the idea of abandoning the paper at a time when it was fighting for every breath.

I told Mike I'd give him an answer in a few days. A week went by. By now the word was out. Every night in the press box, people would ask: "What's up? Are you going?" I knew I couldn't keep the *Daily News* waiting forever. Finally, one evening I was at the *Bulletin* and saw Jack Wilson in his office. He was then editing *Discover*, the Sunday magazine.

Like everyone else, Jack knew about the *Daily News* offer. We talked for an hour. I expressed my misgivings about leaving. "I feel like I owe the *Bulletin* so much," I said.

"You owe your family," he said. "You have to do what's right for them."

We all knew the *Bulletin*'s future was tenuous. Whether I stayed or left was not going to make a difference. If I stayed and the *Bulletin* folded, I'd have to find another job. I wanted to stay in Philadelphia. My family wanted to stay here. The *Daily News* offer assured us of that.

I called Mike Rathet the next day and accepted the job. Clearly, it was the right move, but I'm not sure I would have done it if it hadn't been for Jack telling me it was OK. Seventeen months later, the *Bulletin* closed, and almost two thousand full-time employees lost their jobs. The *Journal* had gone out of business two months before that. It was a grim time for newspapers, but I was one of the lucky ones. I still had a job.

My first assignment for the *Daily News* was a Phillies doubleheader in Pittsburgh. It was August 10, and the Phillies trailed the Pirates by four games in the National League East. The team that had won the division three years in a row (1976–78) had slipped to fourth place in 1979 and appeared headed for another disappointing finish in 1980.

I was among the columnists who ripped the Phillies, characterizing them as a bunch of underachieving prima donnas who didn't have what it takes to win a world championship. In June 1978, I wrote a piece that predicted the Phillies would repeat as division champions, which they did, but I also predicted they would fall on their faces in the playoffs.

"They should start gathering their excuses now," I wrote. "That way they can avoid the last-minute rush in October." The piece ran with the headline: "The Phillies: Legends in Their Own Minds." I was the target of icy glares in the clubhouse for the rest of the season.

So it was almost fitting that on my first day as a *Daily News* columnist, the Phillies should lose both ends of a doubleheader to the Pirates, and manager Dallas Green should have the mother of all meltdowns. It happened after the

Phillies lost the first game, 7–1, slouching through nine lifeless innings. Green watched from the corner of the dugout seething.

After the game, we went to the clubhouse and found the door locked. Green had told the guard not to admit the press, but it didn't matter. He was so angry, his voice cut through the steel door like a blowtorch. We were in the hallway, yet we could hear every word.

"You've gotta stop being so (expletive) cool," Green roared. "Get that through your (expletive) heads. If you don't, you'll be so (expletive) buried, it ain't gonna be funny. Get the (expletive) off your (expletives). You're a good (expletive) baseball team, but you're not now, and you can't look in the (expletive) mirror and tell me you are.

"You tell me you can do it, but you (expletive) give up. If you don't want to (expletive) play, get the (expletive) in my office and (expletive) tell me, because I don't want to (expletive) play you."

Moments later, the clubhouse door opened. Most of the players were sitting at their lockers, staring at the floor. Green was in his office, his face still flushed from his tirade.

"I'm not gonna let these guys quit on themselves," Green said. "They're too (expletive) good. They can still win this (expletive) thing, but not playing like this. If I have to yell at them to get them going, I'll yell good and loud. The other way was tried with these guys, and that was unsuccessful. OK, now we'll try it my way."

"The other way" was the kinder, gentler approach of Green's predecessor Danny Ozark, who managed the team for six-and-one-half seasons. Under Ozark, the Phillies went to the playoffs three times but never advanced past the first round. Ozark coddled the players, protected them from criticism, and turned them into a bunch of spoiled children. He let them set their own rules. It was a culture of privilege and one of the reasons, I felt, the team always fell short.

The Phillies had never won a World Series, so they should have been the hungriest team in baseball, but they were not. They were arrogant to the point of nonchalance. They had enough talent to win a pennant, yet they melted on the October stage, and their failures did not seem to bother them as much as our writing about it.

In a town that loves scrappy overachievers, such as the Stanley Cup–winning Flyers and the Eagles under Vermeil, the Phillies were the exact opposite. They were seen as a team with an abundance of skill but a shortage of guts. The players hated the label and blamed the media for pinning it to their backs.

The Phillies' attitude toward the press was summed up in a brief exchange near the batting cage. Bill Conlin of the *Daily News* was telling several reporters about the *Bulletin*'s sale to the Charter Corporation. Bus Saidt of the *Trenton Times* noticed Bob Boone, the Phillies catcher, walking past.

"Did you hear that? The *Bulletin* was sold," Saidt said.

"Who gives a (expletive)?" Boone shot back.

For a reporter, the Phillies clubhouse was a miserable place. That would be hard for a baseball fan to understand. How could anyone not love going to the ball park? How could you not enjoy being around the players? It is easy. When you have a sweaty jock dropped on your shoe or a folding chair thrown into the wall behind you—followed by a smirking "Sorry, I didn't see you there"—the charm wears off in a hurry.

These things happened regularly in the Phillies clubhouse. It was the players' world, and they set the rules, so when we went in there, we were treated like trespassers or worse. There is a scene in the film *The Paper* where Robert Duvall, playing a newspaper editor, tells a reporter: "The people we cover, we move in their world, but it's *their* world."

It is so true, and as a reporter in a locker room of millionaire athletes, you are reminded of it every day. You gather around the players, and most of them either answer your questions with their backs turned or stare off into space so they never have to make eye contact. And with that Phillies team, those were the good days.

On an August day in 1978, I walked into the Veterans Stadium clubhouse to see Larry Bowa accost Ray Kelly Jr. of the *Courier-Post*. Bowa was enraged by a column Kelly had written in which he called the shortstop "an underclassed star" given to "immature tantrums." As Bowa pressed forward, screaming profanities, Kelly said: "Look at yourself. I wrote what you are."

Ron Reed, the hulking relief pitcher, grabbed Bowa around the waist as he tried to shove Kelly. As Reed pulled Bowa away, the shortstop's hand smacked Kelly in the face. Bowa denied striking Kelly—"I'll swear to that on a million Bibles," he said—and his teammates closed ranks around him.

I wrote a column describing what I had seen, thereby disputing Bowa's account of the incident. I wrote: "The Phillies aren't a baseball team anymore, they are a home for delinquent boys. . . . At their best, they are aloof; at their worst, they are degrading. We all know they are going to win the Eastern Division. The only thing we don't know is how many people they are going to step on along the way."

For the rest of that season, I was a pariah in the Phillies clubhouse. The veterans looked right through me. Occasionally, I'd be talking with a young player, such as Randy Lerch or Larry Christenson, and a teammate would shoot him a disapproving glance. That would end the interview. Peer pressure is a powerful force, and in that clubhouse, it was suffocating.

Interestingly enough, when Green took over as manager, he did not like the players any more than we did. He found them to be selfish and lacking in what he called "belly," his word for old-fashioned grit. He lashed the players, sparing neither their egos nor their eardrums. He said, in effect: "You think you're so good? Show me."

After Green's tirade in Pittsburgh, the Phillies won eight of their next nine games, then ten of thirteen to climb back into the pennant race. By late September, they were in second place, one-half game behind the Montreal Expos, but still there were problems. Several veterans—notably Boone, left fielder Greg Luzinski, and center fielder Garry Maddox—were slumping. Green replaced them with youngsters Keith Moreland and Lonnie Smith and veteran Del Unser.

Bowa accused Green of "talking out of the side of his mouth" by saying he believed in his veterans, then benching them. The Phillies pulled out a 6–5 win over Chicago in fifteen innings, and afterward I asked Green about Bowa's remarks. He had not heard them. I read Green the transcript. He thought a long time before answering.

"I get the feeling we're not all together in this thing," he said. "I wouldn't be surprised there aren't a few guys out there [in the clubhouse] rooting against us."

It was a stunning statement: a manager in the final week of a pennant race suggesting there were some players who did not want the team to win.

"I stayed with my veterans," Green said. "Hell, I stayed with them the whole month of September. It gets to the point where I felt I had to change. Damn it, I'm in this for one (expletive) thing, and that's to win it. I'm beyond the point of caring about people's feelings. I'll play the guys who I think can do the job.

"I could quit; that's what Danny did after seven years. He just threw it over to [the players]. He said, 'Here, do it your way.' Now I can see why. Well, these guys aren't giving me any ulcers. They might give a weaker guy an ulcer, but they won't give me a (expletive) ulcer. We've got six games left, and I'm gonna battle like hell to win those six games.

"What will straighten all this out," Green said, "is if we win the whole damn thing, and then we [the front office] are allowed to do what we want to do."

He was talking about a shakeup, hardly what you expect to hear from a manager whose team is scratching on the door to first place. My column was the lead story in the *Daily News* the next day. The headline was: "Bitter Taste to Phils Win." I closed with this line: "It would be fascinating to see the Phillies win the World Series now just to see that many players ordering champagne to go."

That afternoon I arrived at the ballpark early and went directly to the manager's office. It was already full of reporters asking Green about his comments. He saw me in the doorway. "Well, Ray," he said, "it looks like we really stirred up the (expletive) this time."

Once again, the Phillies responded to the sting of Green's words. They completed a four-game sweep of the Cubs, then flew to Montreal for the final weekend of the regular season. They met the Expos in a head-to-head showdown for the division title, and they won it by taking the first two games. Boone, back in the starting lineup, had a clutch hit to win one game and

Schmidt crushed a two-run homer, his forty-eighth of the season, to put the team in the playoffs.

In the National League championship series, Luzinski had two game-winning hits, and Maddox another, as the Phillies outlasted Houston three games to two. In the World Series, Boone batted .412, and Bowa was superb offensively and defensively as the Phillies defeated Kansas City to win their first world championship. The players Green rode the hardest were the ones who came through when he needed them most.

In the victorious locker room, Green wrapped his arm around Bowa and said: "You are a winner. You play my game." Bowa smiled and said, "Thanks, Dallas."

All the shouting and bitterness was washed away in the champagne spray of victory. That's usually how it works. In 2006, when Green was added to the Phillies Wall of Fame, he said: "We had our fights, we had our ups and downs, but that team finally came together and played as good a baseball as Philadelphia will ever see, in my opinion."

When the 1980 World Series finally ended, I was exhausted. I had worked every day for two months, covering the pennant race, then the post-season. The night the Phillies won it all, I wrote one last column on Dallas Green and filed it—typically—right on deadline.

"You know you're writing a piece for the special section," the editor said.

"The what?"

"We're putting out a special section, and you're supposed to write a column."

"A column on what?" I asked. "What's left to write?"

"You'll think of something," he said.

I felt like I had written every player on the roster at least twice in the final month of the season. By then, I had a decent relationship with most of them. Bowa and I made our peace during spring training in 1979. The arrival of Pete Rose, the most media-friendly of superstars, improved the mood of the clubhouse. Steve Carlton still was maintaining his vow of silence, but that was OK, because Tug McGraw was talking enough for the entire pitching staff. Still, by the end of the World Series, I had used up every quote, every stat, every scrap of information in my notebook.

I had nothing left except the mental snapshot of my grandfather in section 212, row 18, cheering the final out. So that's what I decided to write. I wrote about how my grandfather represented all the loyal Philadelphia fans who had waited a lifetime for that moment. I wrote that he "savored the final out in a way Mike Schmidt and Larry Bowa never could."

To me, that was the true bottom line. Long after I had forgotten the hits, runs, and errors of that night, I would remember how it felt. I would remember it through the sight of my grandfather turning toward the press box after the final pitch and looking up with that huge smile on his face. So I wrote that column, and in writing it, I brought my life full circle. I went back to the beginning, back to my earliest memories of watching games with him and lighting candles for the `64 Phillies as they slipped into their September coma.

The emotion I felt then was the same emotion that shaped and defined me as a sportswriter. It was all tied together. I finally realized it. As the only sports columnist in the city who was born and raised in Philadelphia, with all that pain and all that history, I could feel the moment in a special way. It took a World Series victory to bring it into focus.

I wrote: "My grandfather already had his tickets for the [1964] World Series opener at Connie Mack Stadium. He could have taken them back for a refund, but he never did. He just kept them in his desk drawer. He never said so, but I always suspected he thought that was as close as the Phillies were ever going to come to a world championship. He kept those worthless tickets around as a bittersweet remembrance, like rose petals from a summer romance that almost, but didn't quite, work out.

"That's why I know how much Tuesday's World Series triumph meant to him. It was his chance to reach out and embrace the moment he had waited for, the moment his Whiz Kids had promised but never delivered. I'm not writing this just for my grandfather, but for all the people in this baseball-happy town, all the people who have made the long, painful journey from the Baker Bowl to Shibe Park to Veterans Stadium and never lost the faith.

"Phillies fans lived on canned beans and stale bread for half a century. They rooted for a team that had seemingly made a pact with last place, yet they sat on their stoops with their transistor radios pressed to their ears and they rooted just the same. Those are the people I felt the happiest for on Tuesday night. All the people who wept in the stands, the people who danced and sang in the streets. The win belonged to them as much as it did to the mercenaries in pinstripes, maybe even more."

The column won a Philadelphia Press Association Award, which was nice, but it was almost too easy. How could I miss, writing about my grandfather? Forty years spent working behind a bar gave him a keen perspective on life. He didn't think there was any dispute that couldn't be settled with a firm handshake and a Ballantine draft.

He was the softest touch in town. I can't count how many times I saw him reach in his pocket, pull out a few bucks, and hand them to a guy on the street. Over time, I suppose, some of those people repaid him by filling his bar stools and drinking his beer, but mostly he was just doing what came naturally. He was helping out.

My grandfather loved sports. I must have watched a thousand Phillies games with him over the years, often sitting at the end of the bar, drinking a Coke, trying to see the black-and-white TV through the smoky haze. He was thrilled when I joined the *Bulletin*. He would tape my stories on the mirror behind the bar.

He had seen the Eagles win three world championships, and he often said he hoped to live long enough to see the Phillies win a World Series. The look on his face when Tug McGraw threw that final strike past Willie Wilson is a memory I will cherish forever.

My grandfather died in March 1982. The night he passed away, I sat down and started writing. I began stringing together memories, putting them on paper as a way of preserving them. I wrote about the last day we spent together. He was in the hospital, looking out the window at the sunshine. He talked about how he wished he was in Florida watching the Phillies. For years, that was his ritual. He would drive to Clearwater with my grandmother and they would visit the Phillies' training camp. They always came back predicting a pennant, that's how we knew it was spring.

I wrote the piece for myself, really, just sorting out my emotions. I sent it to the *Daily News* and told the editors, if they felt it was worth printing, go ahead. They ran it the next day, and it drew an enormous response. I received more than a hundred letters, most of which began: "Your column reminded me of my grandfather." Or father, or uncle, or someone. Clearly, it struck a chord.

A few weeks later, I covered a Villanova basketball game. The Wildcats pulled out a 76–72 win over Northeastern University. After the game, I had to interview Villanova coach Rollie Massimino. We had never met, so I introduced myself. When Massimino heard my name, he took my hand as if we were old friends.

"That was a beautiful column you wrote about your grandfather," he said.

I was stunned that, at a moment like that, he even remembered.

Then he said: "I'll bet it took a long time to write something like that."

Finally, someone who understood.

PART ONE

THE HOME-TOWN TEAMS

◆ ◆ ◆

THE EAGLES

Bednarik's Legend Etched in Concrete*

Chuck Bednarik and his wife, Emma, visited the former Soviet Union last month. One day, they boarded a bus in Kiev, and before they could take a seat, a woman called out, "Chuck Bednarik."

Think about that for a moment: Bednarik retired from pro football thirty-two years ago. Here he was, boarding a bus in Kiev, which is about as far from Franklin Field as you can get, and still someone recognized him.

That's fame.

The woman was a tourist from the Philadelphia area. She was stunned to see this Eagles great, the last of the sixty-minute men, on her bus. No doubt it was one of the first things she talked about when she came home.

"Guess who I met over there. No, not Gorbachev. Not Yeltsin. More famous than that . . . "

At sixty-nine, Chuck Bednarik is a living legend. Last year, *Sports Illustrated* devoted nine pages to a Bednarik profile, written by the former *Philadelphia Daily News* columnist John Schulian. A photograph of Bednarik's hands, gnarled by fourteen seasons of pro football, dominates the office of NFL Films President Steve Sabol in Mount Laurel, New Jersey.

Bednarik has not played football since 1962, yet people still talk about him. Mostly they remember two things. They remember his knockout hit on Frank Gifford in 1960. And they remember him playing both ways, offense and defense, in the championship game the same year that the Eagles defeated the Green Bay Packers, 17–13.

What Bednarik did that season borders on the mythical. At thirty-five, playing his twelfth pro season, the six-foot-three, 235 pound Bednarik was forced to play almost every down in four games, including the title game. He played center on offense and linebacker on defense. He also snapped on punts, extra points, and field goals.

The only time Concrete Charlie left the field in those games was on kickoffs. He played fifty-eight minutes in the championship game against the Packers, and it was his tackle of fullback Jim Taylor in the closing seconds that saved the Eagles' victory.

"It was twenty years before it dawned on me what I did," said Bednarik, now comfortably retired in Coopersburg, Pennsylvania. "I took it for granted. They told me to play, so I played.

"But as I got older, I thought about it. I said, 'Do you know what the hell you did?' No one will ever do it again, certainly not at the professional level. You don't even see [two-way play] in college anymore.

"I was the end of an era," Bednarik said. "No NFL player could do it today. These guys play three or four plays and come off sucking air. And they are making millions of dollars? It makes me sick."

Bednarik does not have much use for the modern athlete. He feels that the vast majority are overrated and overpaid. The former Penn All-America earned $15,000 in 1960, and his two-way heroics got him a $2,500 raise the next year, when he returned to offense exclusively.

"If I didn't have this knee replacement, I could still be playing as a long snapper," Bednarik said. "They pay guys a half-million and that [snap] is all they do."

An injury to linebacker Bob Pellegrini forced coach Buck Shaw to use Bednarik on defense in 1960. The Eagles had a backup linebacker, John Nocera, but he lacked experience. With the team in title contention, Shaw called on Bednarik, the starting center who had made the Pro Bowl seven times at linebacker in the 1950s.

Bednarik was the oldest player on the team, one year older than quarterback Norm Van Brocklin, but he played fifty-plus minutes in wins over Cleveland (31–29), New York (17–10, the Gifford game), and the Giants again (31–23). He did it again in the championship game against Vince Lombardi's Packers at Franklin Field.

"Defenses weren't as sophisticated as they are now," Bednarik said. "I got tossed in cold, but Chuck Weber [the middle linebacker] told me what to do on every down. It wasn't that hard. The game is half instinct anyway.

"I never got tired. It was late in the season, and the weather was cool, so I stayed pretty fresh. Besides, when you're winning, you don't feel the aches and pains. You feel like you can play all day."

"I was in awe of Chuck, I think we all were," said Maxie Baughan, who started as a rookie linebacker in 1960. "We [the defense] would come on the field and Chuck would be there waiting. He'd say, 'Let's go, let's get together.' If he was tired, he never let it show."

That was a strange team, the 1960 Eagles. Nineteen of the thirty-six players were let go by other teams. End Pete Retzlaff was signed for $100 as a waiver pickup from Detroit. Halfback Tim Brown was cut by Green Bay. Ditto defensive end Joe Robb, by the Chicago Cardinals.

The key acquisition was Van Brocklin, who helped lead the Los Angeles Rams to four NFL championship games. Van Brocklin, better known as the Dutchman, was traded to the Eagles in 1958 after clashing with Rams coach Sid Gillman.

"Van Brocklin turned everything around," Bednarik said. "It had become a depressing situation. I was disgusted personally. We were winning three or four games a year. The team had fallen so far from my rookie year [1949, when it won its second consecutive NFL championship].

"I kept hoping the team would get some decent players, and every year they got more guys who weren't worth a damn. But when they got Van Brocklin, I said, 'Finally, we have a quarterback who can take us someplace.'"

Van Brocklin's leadership, combined with Bednarik's inspirational play, lifted a very average team to amazing heights in 1960. The Eagles went 10–2 in the regular season, despite a sputtering ground game and a defense that ranked ninth among twelve teams in yardage allowed.

They trailed going into the fourth quarter of six games that season, yet they usually found a way to win. Van Brocklin would throw a touchdown pass to either Retzlaff or Tommy McDonald, and the defense would force a turnover.

That's how it was in the championship game. The Packers, with five future Hall of Famers on offense, out-gained the Eagles 401 yards to 296. They took a 13–10 lead in the fourth quarter, only to see the Eagles go ahead 17–13 on fullback Ted Dean's five-yard run.

The Packers got the ball back with one minute and twenty seconds left. They marched right down the field, reaching the Eagles' twenty-two–yard line with time left for just one play.

Quarterback Bart Starr looked deep, but his primary receivers were covered, so he dumped the ball off to Taylor, the bruising 215 pounder who accounted for 151 yards total offense that day.

Taylor lowered his head and drove toward the goal line. Baughan had the first shot at him but bounced off. Safety Don Burroughs, a spindly, six foot, four inch, 180 pounder, dove and missed.

Taylor made it as far as the nine-yard line. That was where Bednarik bear-hugged him and wrestled him to the ground.

"They didn't have any timeouts left, so I just sat on [Taylor]," Bednarik said. "I was watching the clock in the east stands, watching the seconds tick off.

"Taylor was squirming like hell, trying to get up. He was saying, 'Get off me, you so-and-so.' When the second hand hit zero, I said: 'You can get up now, you blankety-blank, this game is over.' Then I started jumping around like a cheerleader.

"That was the ultimate, winning that game. It was a great achievement because, man for man, we weren't that good. I still don't know how we won it.

"Look at the Packers. My God, it was the same team that dominated the league for the next eight years. And we beat 'em.'"

That was the only post-season game Lombardi ever lost as a head coach. The Packers won the league championship the next two years and six times in all, including wins in the first two Super Bowls.

Friends claim that Lombardi talked about the 1960 title game right up to his death. He could not understand how he had lost it.

It was simple, really. He lost because for fifty-eight memorable minutes, he had number 60 standing in his way.

*Originally published in the *Philadelphia Daily News*, September 14, 1994. Reprinted with permission by Philadelphia Newspapers, LLC.

Vince Papale Ain't Just Another Bum from the Neighborhood Anymore*

The February wind was blowing off the Delaware River like a hard, stinging sleet, lashing through the narrow streets of South Philadelphia. Men and women shuffled stiffly in the early morning cold, pulling scarves tightly across their faces, wedging themselves into doorways to wait for buses that never came on time.

In the distance, a man could be seen running on Broad Street, weaving gracefully through the rush-hour traffic. He was wearing a Philadelphia Eagles sweat suit and a green windbreaker with the number 83 stenciled on the back. He ran easily with the unmistakable stride of an athlete, his head high, his arms pumping rhythmically across his chest.

Last week's snow had frozen and was crunching under his feet. His breath trailed a streak of white vapor over his shoulder. Truckers honked their horns in recognition. He waved and quickened his pace as if spurred on by their encouragement. He ran past the row houses and cut through a schoolyard. He turned down a small side street and ran past five guys who had just finished night work and gathered at the corner bar for a beer.

They recognized the man with number 83 on his back and, in the damp chill of a winter morning, they began to cheer. "Hey, Vince," one man shouted. "We love ya, baby."

Vince Papale smiled and kept running. He completed his six-mile run back to Veterans Stadium, pushing hard the last few blocks, expending whatever energy he had in reserve.

"I try to do the last mile under six minutes," he said. "Today, I'd say I came in around 5:50."

Papale seemed pleased as he returned to the Eagles locker room. He poured a cup of coffee and peeled off his sweat suit. He slipped on a fresh T-shirt and walked across the hall to the weight room, where he pumped iron for the next two hours. He didn't stop until Otho Davis, the Eagles' trainer, finally ordered him to the showers.

"They worry about me working too hard," Papale said. "When the season ended, they told me to rest a while. I came back right after the Christmas holidays, ready to start again. Otho threw me out. He said, `I don't want to see you until February.' February first, nine o'clock in the morning, I was sitting here, waiting for them to open the door.

"I trained for the decathlon every day for four years, so now it's part of my nature. I don't feel like I'm punishing myself. Compared to the decathlon, this is easy."

Papale was sitting on the carpeted locker-room floor, his right leg extended, his left leg tucked beneath him. He looked like a hurdler frozen in mid-stride. He leaned forward, grasping his ankle and slowly bringing his nose down to touch his right knee. He repeated the process a dozen times until he felt the hamstring stretch. He pulled that hamstring in a game against Minnesota last season. He is determined not to let it happen again.

"Know what I love?" Papale said, changing legs and working on the other hamstring. "I love running through South Philadelphia. I could run twenty-five laps around the stadium, but it wouldn't be the same. I once read that Jim Ryun ran in the mountains, the farther away from civilization the better. Not me. I like the atmosphere in the streets. It gives me a chance to get out among my people.

"Cab drivers, truck drivers, lunch-pail guys, they identify with me. They know I'm one of them. We all grew up in Philadelphia rooting for the Eagles. Now I'm out there playing. It's my dream, sure, but it's their dream, too. When I run along Delaware Avenue and the longshoremen holler, `Go get `em for us, Vince,' they really mean it.

"Every time I tackle a number-one draft choice, it's the hard hats in the nickel seats who cheer the loudest. They feel like they got a piece of that rich so-and-so, too."

Papale pulled up a stool and began sorting through his fan mail. The season had ended two months ago, but the letters continued to pour in. Unlike most players, Papale answers every letter personally. He stuffed this batch in his equipment bag and headed upstairs to check his personal appearance schedule.

During the off-season, Papale averaged five speaking engagements a week. He was in such demand he was often forced to double up, appearing at a businessmen's luncheon and a boy's club dinner on the same day. In the past year, Papale has made more public appearances than the 76ers' Julius Erving, the Phillies' Mike Schmidt, and the Flyers' Bobby Clarke combined.

"Vince makes Bob Hope look like a recluse," said Jim Murray, the Eagles' general manager.

You're probably wondering what's so special about Vince Papale, a backup wide receiver who has yet to catch a pass in a regular-season NFL game. Why did the Eagles make him the central character in their 1976 highlight film? Why do Philadelphia's notorious fans—who once threw snowballs at Santa Claus—stop their cars to cheer him on the street?

Maybe it's because so many people associate Papale with last year's Academy Award-winning film, *Rocky*. The parallels between the movie's hero,

Rocky Balboa, and Papale are striking, indeed. Rocky was a small-time thirty-year-old Philadelphia club fighter who lucked into a crack at the heavyweight championship. Papale is a thirty-year-old sandlot jock who went from a two-hand–touch league to the NFL.

Like Rocky, Papale is a gutsy, street-tough Italian Stallion who took his million-to-one shot at the big time. And like Rocky, Papale took his lumps, hung on, and went the distance. As Rocky would say, Vince Papale ain't just another bum from the neighborhood anymore.

"When I was little, I wanted to be a daredevil," Papale said, sipping a soda in the deserted press box. "A human cannonball, trapeze flier, stunt man, something like that. My parents thought I had a death wish. I was always vaulting across streams, climbing barbed-wire fences, hanging from trees by one hand. There was a gym set in the playground, and I'd do double-somersault dismounts with nothing to land on but concrete.

"My father says I started bleeding when I was two years old and didn't stop until I was in college. He'd tell my mother, `Why waste money on clothes? Just dress him in Band-Aids.'

"When I got older, I wanted to be a professional athlete. My cousin is George Dempsey, who played basketball with the [NBA's Philadelphia] Warriors. He was my idol. Whenever there was a family gathering, I'd ask my mother: `Is Cousin George gonna be there?'

"I'd hang on his arm all night, listening to his stories. I thought that was the neatest thing in the world, playing ball and getting paid for it. George wore number 5, so I got that number when I started playing Little League baseball and basketball.

"I always had athletic ability. We lived in a housing project in Glenolden. In the middle of the project was a recreation area, a half-mile around. There wasn't a kid in Glenolden who could outrun me. Every night we'd have races, and the fathers would sit in their beach chairs, making bets. I was like Seattle Slew. I always went off one-to-five, and I retired undefeated. My only problem was size. I was little and skinny. When I was thirteen, I was four feet, eleven inches, and didn't weigh a hundred pounds."

When Papale enrolled at Interboro High School, coach George Corner said he was too small for football, so he turned to other sports. He hit .510 for the baseball team, but he didn't enjoy it much. "Baseball is boring," he said. "Too much standing around."

Papale joined the Interboro track team. Actually, he became the track team. He ran all the sprints and hurdles. He also competed in the high jump, the long jump, the triple jump, and the pole vault. He became one of Philadelphia's top schoolboy track stars, but he still longed to play football. When he was a senior, he grew to five-foot-five and 145 pounds, and he talked Corner into giving him another shot at the Interboro varsity. He won a starting position at offensive end.

Papale teamed with quarterback Jim Haynie, who later starred at West Chester State College and was drafted by the Minnesota Vikings, to give Interboro the top passing combination in Delaware County. Papale set the school record for receptions in a season and won all-league honors.

"Football was the only sport I really loved," Papale said. "Part of it was my identification with the Eagles. My father and I went to every Eagles game, sat together in the upper deck, lived and died with the team. My favorite player was Tommy McDonald. I saw myself in him, the little guy who'd run through a brick wall to catch a pass.

"When I made the team at Interboro, I wore Tommy McDonald football shoes, I wore a single-bar facemask, the same as he did. When I was tackled, I bounced right up just like him. During practice, I'd imagine myself catching passes for the Eagles. I could hear Bill Campbell [the Eagles' radio announcer] doing the play-by-play in my mind: 'There's Papale, he's in the clear, he spins away from two Green Bay tacklers, he's going all the way.' I was a fanatic.

"I met Tommy and Chuck Bednarik at a banquet. I got their autographs. I told Tommy I wanted to play for the Eagles, but everybody said I was too small. He said, 'Aw, they told me the same thing. Don't listen to them. Just keep working, kid. You'll make it.'"

The football recruiters weren't interested in Papale, and for awhile he did not think he would go to college. His mother was ill, and his father, a shift worker at Westinghouse, did not have enough money to put him through school. Finally, St. Joseph's College offered a track scholarship. Papale accepted. There was only one problem: St. Joseph's, a small Catholic school in Philadelphia, did not have a football team.

"I wasn't happy about giving up football, but I didn't have much choice," Papale said. "The thing that really frustrated me was the way I grew [six-foot-two, 190 pounds] once I got to St. Joe's. Suddenly, I had the size to play college football, but I had no team. I played in the intramural [touch-football] league, but the track coach made me quit. He was afraid I'd blow out a knee, and my track career would go out the window."

Papale was the outstanding performer on the track team, setting school records in the pole vault, triple jump, and long jump. He also high jumped and ran the 120 and 440 yard hurdles. He was twice the top scorer in the Middle Atlantic Conference championships, taking first place medals in three events: pole vault, triple jump, and high jump.

After graduation in 1968, Papale began teaching business administration and coaching track at Interboro. He continued his training, expanding his program to include the ten decathlon events. He increased his daily workouts to five hours and began pointing toward the 1972 Olympics. However, the harder he worked, the more frustrating his pursuit became.

"Since I was an independent, a lot of track people didn't want to be bothered with me; they treated me like a bum," Papale said. "I sent an application to the director of the Drake Relays. He sent back the most degrading letter you ever saw. He said, `Who do you think you are? Our meet is for world-class athletes. We don't let people just walk in off the street.'

"My first reaction was total rage. I crumpled the letter up and threw it away. A few minutes later, I dug it out of the trash and put it on my desk. I've had the damn thing for nine years. Every morning when I didn't feel like running, every day when I didn't feel like working out, I just reread that letter, and I'd say, `I'll show you who's not good enough, creep.' Zoom, off I'd go.

"Today, I've got that letter hanging on my wall, surrounded by pictures of me playing for the Eagles. I call it `the Last Laugh Department.'"

Four years of decathlon training can be pretty dull stuff. To break the monotony, Papale joined the Delaware County Rough Touch Football League. He signed up to play for a Chester bar named the Gross Place. The games were played on a glass-strewn field behind a local spaghetti-and-beer joint called the T-Bar.

The games were like demolition derby, but without the cars. Players wore no padding, and the hitting was vicious. Papale led the league in receiving, which was like painting a bull's-eye on his forehead. In three seasons, he suffered a broken jaw, two concussions, and three broken ribs. Once he was knocked unconscious just kicking off.

"Talk about cheap shots—I caught four elbows for every pass," Papale said. "The term `touch' football is a joke. We had more fights than touchdowns. But it was a dare from one of those guys that put me back in pads. They were ragging on me one day, saying: `Sure, you're great in a touch league, but you don't have the guts to play real football.' The next year, I tried out for the Aston Knights [a local semi-pro team] just to prove I wasn't chicken.

"Actually, I was a little apprehensive. I'd been away from the game eight years [since his senior year at Interboro]. I didn't know if I could take a good lick. In our first scrimmage, I caught a pass, and Harry Salk, our middle linebacker, belted me. When I survived that, I knew I'd be OK."

Papale led the Seaboard Football League with sixty catches in 1973. The following year, he was one of eight hundred players who showed up for a one-day tryout for the Philadelphia Bell of the World Football League (WFL). He ran the forty-yard dash in 4.45 seconds, and coach Ron Waller signed him on the spot. At twenty-eight, Vince Papale finally was a professional athlete.

Many players, particularly NFL veterans, joked about the conditions in the new league. They practiced casually; they laughed at training-camp discipline, but Papale worked tirelessly, running out every pass pattern, staying after practice for extra wind sprints. Through sheer determination, Papale not only made the team but was a starting wide receiver when the Bell played its first game in June 1974.

Papale stayed with the Bell until the WFL folded in 1975. He suffered the indignities silently. He didn't complain, for example, when a stadium guard refused to admit the dilapidated team bus because he mistook the players for migrant farm workers.

"How could I knock it?" he said. "Two years earlier, my dressing room was the T-Bar parking lot. If it wasn't for the WFL, I'd still be getting my teeth knocked out in some bar league."

When the WFL went under, Rich Iannarella, the Bell's general manager, became Papale's agent. He talked the Eagles into inviting Vince to last spring's three-day rookie camp. Once again, Papale impressed, running a 4.5 in high grass and catching every pass thrown his way.

"He had everything going against him," coach Dick Vermeil said. "He was a thirty-year-old walk-on with no college experience. But after the three days, I had him rated as our top rookie receiver. I didn't care if he was an eighty-year-old grandfather. He had earned an invitation to training camp."

Papale quit his teaching job at Interboro and spent the next three months working out at Veterans Stadium, preparing himself for the most important summer of his life. Friends and relatives told Vince he was nuts. They told him to give up this football craziness and look for steady work.

"After all, Vince," they said, "you're not a kid anymore."

"The one who stuck by me was my father," Papale said. "He suffered with me every step of the way. I told him, `Dad, I waited all my life for this chance. Playing for the Eagles is my dream. I don't care what the odds are, I've gotta see it through.' He understood. He wished me luck."

Papale hung on through Vermeil's grueling training camp. He was hazed by veterans who sneered at his sandlot background. He was roughed up by defensive backs who resented his efforts to take a job away from their buddy, third-year receiver Don Zimmerman. One day Papale caught a pass and was slammed to the ground by cornerback Clifford Brooks. He suffered a partial shoulder separation, but he taped up the injured area and returned for the afternoon practice.

"There were times when it was hard to go on," Papale said. "I'd be in my room, beat to death, and I'd start thinking: `What am I doing here, thirty years old, competing against a bunch of kids? Look at my friends. They've got jobs and security. They know where they're going. Where the hell am I going?'

"Then I'd go on the field and see my father sitting in the stands. It was like getting a shot of adrenalin. Here's a guy who worked his whole life, never took a day off, busted his gut to put a roof over my head. This was my chance to do something for him. If I made the Eagles, it would be the greatest thing that ever happened to him. How could I quit?"

Papale went an entire week of two-a-days without dropping a pass. When Vermeil tested his receivers in the nutcracker drill, Papale blocked fiercely. In a scrimmage against the New York Jets, Papale made a spectacular over-the-shoulder catch for the Eagles' only touchdown.

"I'm beginning to think this guy's for real," Vermeil said.

"I'll never forget arriving at the stadium for our first pre-season game," Papale said. "I walked in, and there was a jersey with my name on the back. There was my green helmet with the silver wings. I put the uniform on and got goose pimples. When we knelt to say our pre-game prayer, tears were streaming down my face. I kept thinking about all the days I pretended to play for the Eagles. Now here I was."

The Eagles played Miami, and Papale, starting the second half, caught five passes, including a leaping grab between two Dolphin defenders. He also threw an open field block that sent veteran cornerback Tim Foley into a backward somersault.

"At the next team meeting, Dick reran that block a dozen times," Papale said. "He said, `This is what I want to see. This is Eagle Effort. If we get more guys playing like this, we'll win some games.'"

Papale caught ten passes in the pre-season to lead the team. Still, there was no guarantee he would make the final roster. On the Monday prior to the regular-season opener, Vermeil had to cut five players to reach the forty-three–man limit. Shortly before noon, the coach emerged from his office and walked directly toward Papale. Without saying a word, Papale reached for his playbook.

"I figured it was all over," he said. "I had this uncontrollable urge to throw up."

Vermeil extended his hand. "Congratulations, old man," he said. "You're a Philadelphia Eagle."

"I was so happy, I ran right out to the pay phone to call my father at work," Papale said. "When I told him, he shouted: `Vince made the team.' I could hear all the guys at Westinghouse cheering."

The Eagles had two veteran receivers, Harold Carmichael and Charlie Smith, so Papale played little offense during the regular season. He was a ferocious special-teams player, however, excelling as the outside man on punt coverage. The combination of his speed and punter Spike Jones's hang time enabled Papale to reach most return men just as they were fielding the ball. He delivered some memorable hits, including one that helped the Eagles defeat the New York Giants in their home opener.

In the fourth quarter, Jones's punt drove the Giants' Jimmy Robinson back to his own twenty-yard line. Papale flew off the line, brushed past one blocker, and out-muscled another who tried to shove him out of bounds. Papale hurled himself at Robinson, hitting him in the chest and jarring the ball loose.

Papale recovered the fumble inside the Giants' ten-yard line, setting up the Eagles' final touchdown. He waved the ball triumphantly in the direction of his father, who was sitting in the upper deck with the gang from Westinghouse. The Veterans Stadium crowd gave Papale a standing ovation, and a hero was born.

"Biggest day of my life," Papale said. "As I left the stadium, the fans were cheering and slapping me on the back. One little kid, maybe ten years old, chased me into the parking lot, waving his program. He was shouting, 'Mr. Papale, sign this please?' I saw myself chasing after Tommy McDonald in 1958. I signed the program; we shook hands and talked for a while. It was a bigger thrill for me than it was for him."

Papale continued his fearless play, sprinting downfield with the shrieking recklessness of a blindfolded bobsledder. In the first six games, he made eighteen solo tackles, assisted on twelve others, and forced three fumbles. Coaches Rod Rust and Ken Iman created a "Who's Nuts?" award for the outstanding special-teams performer each week. The prize was a T-shirt with the Eagles logo and the words "Who's Nuts?" across the front. Of the first fourteen shirts awarded last season, Papale won four.

"I've never seen a man play with such intensity," Rust said. "Vince will get knocked down three times, bounce up, and still make a tackle."

"It's a funny feeling," Papale said. "I hear people talk about this guy Vince Papale, and it's like they're talking about another person. They say how courageous, how committed Vince Papale is. I think, 'Who, me? I'm just a football player.' It took more courage and more commitment to be a good schoolteacher, to work that hard for so little money.

"The March of Dimes honored me for the charity work I've done. Why the fuss? How much effort does it take for me to raise money for the March of Dimes? I make an appearance, sign a few autographs, talk football for an hour. For that, maybe I've helped some little kid learn how to walk. That's all the reward I need.

"A professional athlete can do so much good if he'll only take the time to get involved. People are sick of hearing about athletes holding out for millions of dollars. They think we're greedy, and maybe they're right. More athletes should be involved in charity work. After all, we're part of the community, too."

Papale paused. He seemed embarrassed by his outburst. "Listen to me," he said. "I'm talking like a schoolteacher again."

"How does it feel to be a celebrity?" someone asked.

"I can't get used to the idea," he said. "At this banquet in Lancaster, Dick and I sat on the dais with Jim Palmer, Tom Lasorda, Steve Garvey, and Billy Cunningham. Driving home, I said to Dick, 'I must've looked pretty silly sitting up there with all those superstars.' Dick said, 'You were the real superstar. Compared to what you went through, those guys had it easy.' Coming from Dick, that made me feel great."

"Is that the best thing that happened to you since the season ended?"

"No, the best thing was a boy from Chicago named Sean," Papale said. "He was flown to Children's Hospital for a bone-marrow transplant. He was so depressed, the doctor was afraid to operate. He said in his emotional state, he wouldn't pull through.

"The staff asked me to visit him. Sean didn't know me from Adam, but the doctor felt it was worth a try. I put on a white gown, introduced myself and gave him a football. At first he was quiet, but then we became buddies. We talked for two hours. I said I expected him to be running downfield with me next season. He liked that.

"As I left, the nurse ran after me. She said, `Sean wants to wave goodbye.' I looked through the window, and he was smiling at me. The nurse said it was the first time he had smiled in weeks."

He paused. "I just heard from the doctor a few days ago," he said. "The operation went fine. Sean's gonna be all right."

Papale stopped talking and bit his lip. There were tears in his eyes.

Epilogue: Vince Papale played three seasons with the Eagles (1976–78), and his teammates voted him special-teams captain in 1977. In 2006, Disney Studios turned his story into a feature film, *Invincible*, with Mark Wahlberg cast as Papale and Greg Kinnear as Dick Vermeil. "It is more than a sports movie," Vermeil said. "It's a great example of striving for what you can be and not giving up on your dreams."

*Originally published in *Pro Magazine*, 1977.

Wilbert Has a Mom Who Frets*

Wilbert Montgomery was stretched out on a table in the Eagles training room, his eyes closed, his hands folded serenely on his chest. His legs were sealed in the pneumatic massage unit, two balloon-like, yellow hip boots that pumped a steady current of cold water against his aching muscles.

This was last Tuesday, following the loss to St. Louis, and the Eagles' trainers, like all the king's men, were working frantically to put Wilbert Montgomery together again. The Green Bay Packers were coming to town in five days, and the Eagles were doing everything imaginable to get Wilbert, their Purple Heart halfback, ready for the big game.

For two whole days, Montgomery had been whirlpooled, massaged, stretched, and flexed, and still he was hobbling on his left leg. The ankle and knee were both strained, and everyone knows strains take time to heal. Wilbert, being rather impatient about such matters, disagrees.

"Most guys would be out for two, maybe three weeks," said Otho Davis, the head trainer. "This rascal wants to practice tomorrow."

For the moment, at least, Montgomery was relaxing. His head was propped on two leather cushions; his red golf cap was pushed down over his eyes. The room was quiet except for the hum of those yellow hip boots and the soothing beat of the training-room stereo. Three minutes of Linda Ronstadt singing "Ooh, Baby, Baby" is worth three hours in the whirlpool any day.

"If only my mother could see me now," Montgomery said. "All banged up, hooked up to this machine. She'd die, I swear.

"She never wanted me to play football. She told me it was craziness, a lot of fools ripping each other's arms and legs off. My older brother [Alfred] separated both shoulders playing in junior college, and my mother swore none of her sons would ever play football again.

"I wanted to play for our [Greenville, Mississippi] high-school team, but I knew my mother would be against it. Before you were allowed to play, your mother had to sign a paper giving her permission. I got a girl in class to sign my mother's name, and I made all my friends promise they wouldn't tell her what was going on.

"After practice, I'd come home, and she'd ask where I was. I'd say I was at a friend's house. We played our games on Friday night. I'd say, `Momma, I'm going out for a while.' When we played on the coast in Gulfport and Biloxi, we'd stay overnight. Those nights, I told her I was sleeping over at a friend's house.

"If I came home limping, I'd say we did it fooling around," he said. "She'd always say, `Wilbert, you know I don't like it when you play so rough.'"

As you might expect, Montgomery had trouble keeping his football career under wraps. He was playing both ways, rushing for one hundred yards every game, scoring touchdowns in bunches, making All-State on defense. For two years, Gladys Montgomery did not know that the Greenville *Democrat-Times* had a sports page. Wilbert ripped that section out of the paper every night before his mother came home from work.

He won dozens of trophies, but he stashed them in a closet at his grandfather's house. Finally, late in his junior year, Montgomery gave up the charade. His fame was spreading too rapidly, and he knew it was only a matter of time before his mother opened the door and found a man in a hound's-tooth hat standing there, saying: "Hello, Mrs. Montgomery. My name is Bear Bryant, and I'd like your son to play football at Alabama." (That really happened, incidentally).

"I finally told her I was playing football," Montgomery said. "She told me she didn't approve, and I said, `Momma, I could get killed walking across the street. Besides, I might get a scholarship to college playing football.' She said, `All right, but don't come running to me when you get hurt.' I never did. I still don't.

"I call her every Sunday night after we play. I have to tell her how I did and let her know I'm OK. When I got hurt [last week], I didn't call, and she was worried. She called the first thing Monday, wanting to know what happened. I told her I sprained my ankle, but it wasn't serious. She kept saying, `Are you sure you're all right?'"

He glanced down at the gruesome-looking contraption pumping against his battered legs. "When you see my mother, please don't tell her about this," he said. "Tell her the last time you saw me, I was fine. Tell her I was going dancing."

"I still remember the night Wilbert told me," Gladys Montgomery said. "He said his conscience was bothering him. I can understand that. He was always a truthful child. I knew football must have meant a whole lot to him, because he never lied to me before. What could I say? I had already said no, and that didn't stop him.

"I never liked football. A few years ago, a boy on the next street broke his neck and died playing football. What mother in her right mind can watch all those boys pile up on her child and not worry? I never stop worrying. I worry every Sunday because I know Wilbert is playing, and I worry every Friday about these two."

She pointed to her two younger sons—Jerry, seventeen, and Leonard, fifteen—seated on the living-room sofa. Both have followed in Wilbert's cleated footsteps, excelling as running backs at Greenville High. Jerry was Greenville's star tailback until an ankle injury (sound familiar?) finished him for the year. With Jerry in the lineup, the Hornets were 5–0 and favored to win the state title. Without Jerry, they are 0–3 with games left against Yazoo City and Greenwood.

Jerry is taller and leaner than his seven brothers. He is five-foot-ten and a wiry 155 pounds. He runs, according to coach Fred Washington, "with fluid speed, not power." Leonard, however, is a carbon copy of Wilbert, a short, stocky back who darts around with a slashing recklessness that defies coaching and often defies logic. The only thing Leonard lacks, Washington said, is experience. Both are major college prospects.

If you've heard that Wilbert is quiet, you ought to meet Jerry and Leonard. Compared with his brothers, Wilbert is Henny Youngman. "I've never seen kids as quiet as the Montgomerys," Washington said. "When they get hurt, they don't even say ouch."

Gladys Montgomery, much to her dismay, has raised nothing but running backs. There were Alfred, Wilbert, and Cleotha, and now there are Jerry and Leonard, soon to be followed by John and Willie. "Why," she asks, "do they all have to play a position where they get tackled on every play? Out of seven boys, wouldn't you think I'd have at least one punter? Even a quarterback wouldn't be so bad."

Every autumn, she watches her seven running backs go off to practice with the dread of a mother watching her sons march off to war. She says the highlight of her year is Christmas, not for the caroling and gift giving, but because it marks the end of another football season.

"Two of Wilbert's games were televised here this year," she said. "The Miami game and the New Orleans game. I tried not to act too nervous because I know it distracts everyone else. The boys tell me not to worry, but all I can think is 'That's my Wilbert down there with all those giants jumping on him.' I think 'Why couldn't he have been better in basketball?'"

"It's the same thing with Jerry and Leonard. All the Greenville games are on the radio, and I listen. When the announcer says, 'Montgomery is down on the field,' I hold my breath. I hold it until he says he's up and on the sidelines. Then I say, 'Thank you, Jesus.' The night Jerry got hurt in Meridian, I sat up until he got home. He came in at two in the morning, his foot all swollen. Thank goodness nothing was broken."

Jerry was sitting on the sofa, staring glumly at his injured foot. "He's sorry to be sitting out," his mother said. "I'm not."

Gladys Montgomery is a remarkable woman. Her husband took off some time ago, leaving her alone to raise her seven sons and one daughter. She went to work at the Broadway Laundry, then landed a better-paying job as a machine operator at the Greenville Mill, a local rug factory. Business has fallen off sharply in recent months, and just last week, several employees, including Montgomery, were laid off. She took the news philosophically.

"I'll get unemployment for a while," she said. "If I'm not called back, I'll find something else. We'll get by. We always have."

The family lives in a modest, one-story brick house at the north end of town, a short distance from the airport. Greenville is a quiet community of fifty thousand tucked away on the western edge of Mississippi, next to Lake Ferguson and the Arkansas border. It is in the heart of the delta, with lush cotton and soybean fields sprawling for miles on the edge of town.

In the past decade, the Greenville area has shown a significant growth in industry. In fact, a large gypsum plant sprouted up less than a half-mile from the Montgomerys' front door. Still, whenever folks talk about Greenville's leading exports, they usually wind up discussing football players.

The Richardsons—Willie and Gloster—were the first brother combination ever to appear in the Super Bowl. Willie played for Baltimore in Super Bowl III; Gloster for Kansas City in Super Bowl IV. The Richardsons are Greenville natives, although segregation laws prevented them from attending Greenville High in the 1950s. Jimmy Giles, the starting tight end for Tampa Bay, is a Greenville High graduate, and, of course, there is Wilbert Montgomery.

Most of the townfolk agree that Wilbert is the finest athlete ever to come out of the area. That's pretty high praise considering George Scott, the Boston Red Sox first baseman, was also born and raised in Greenville. All of this fuss has made Gladys Montgomery a reluctant celebrity. She can't go window shopping on Washington Avenue now without someone asking her if Wilbert is still leading Tony Dorsett in rushing. Usually, Gladys comes back with a question of her own, like, "Who is Tony Dorsett?"

"When I go to church on Sunday," she said, "all of my friends ask what team the Eagles are playing that day and are they going to win. I'll admit, it is exciting. I'm real proud of Wilbert. I'm keeping a scrapbook on him. I've got all of his awards hanging on the walls. I'm happy for him because I know how much he wanted this.

"I remember him dragging home these old, beat-up tires and putting them in the back yard. Every night, he'd run through those tires for hours. He said he was going to make it in professional football, and he did."

"There isn't a kid out there who doesn't think about Wilbert," Fred Washington said, nodding toward the Greenville High practice field. "He's an inspiration to these kids. When he scored those four touchdowns against Washington, I thought we were going to declare a holiday. The thing is, Wilbert is someone the kids can identify with. He's not big, he didn't go to a big college, he just worked his butt off, and now he's up there with the [Walter] Paytons and Dorsetts.

"We [coaches] knew Wilbert would be something special. In gym class, he ran past the other kids like they were standing still. He could run a 9.6 hundred, and he set a school record in the broad jump [twenty-five feet, six inches]. Attitude-wise, you couldn't ask for a better kid. It made my day just to coach him. Nothing flashy or cocky. He never displayed any emotion. We named him captain, figuring it would make him talk. He didn't.

"But he could run. One game against Meridian, he ran back a kickoff. He went to one side, stopped, and cut back. When he cut, he left one shoe planted in the ground. He ran to the other side, stopped, and cut back again. He left the other shoe there. He ran out of both shoes. Unbelievable. He has more acceleration than any back I've ever seen. All he needs is the slightest opening and, pffft, he's gone.

"I felt he could play at any college he chose," Washington said, "and he had about a hundred fifty offers. He started at Jackson State, but he transferred when he saw all the other backs they had there at the time. [Walter Payton, Ricky Young who played for the Minnesota Vikings, Rod Phillips who played for the Los Angeles Rams].

"I wish Wilbert would have stayed at Jackson State. He would have given all of them, including Payton, a run for their money. Wilbert has that kind of ability. When he went to Abilene Christian, he didn't just set school records, he set national records. He scored thirty-seven touchdowns his freshman year. Some good backs don't score thirty-seven touchdowns in a career. To the people in Abilene, Wilbert was a god. He could've been elected mayor if he wanted it."

Gladys Montgomery smiles when a visitor tells her about Wilbert's celebrity status in Philadelphia. She shakes her head when she thinks about her son facing dozens of reporters after every game. She giggles when she hears he is now besieged by requests for speaking engagements. Somehow she cannot shake the vision of a painfully shy seven-year-old clinging to her apron strings at the kitchen stove.

"Of all my children, I was probably closest to Wilbert," she said. "He stayed around the house more than the rest. He'd sit with me while I cooked the dinner. He'd help me clean up. He was a wonderful influence on his younger brothers. He looked over them when I wasn't here. He worked [as a bricklayer] to help pay for his school clothes. He never complained. I still remember the day he left for Abilene. Lord, how the two of us cried.

"I can't see Wilbert as a big star. What does he say to all those reporters, anyway? Poor child, he must be scared to death. He lived here last winter, and it didn't seem like any of this went to his head. He never even mentioned football unless one of the boys asked him about it. He spent most of his time visiting old friends and reading his Bible. Wilbert loves his Bible. He reads it every night.

"Wilbert did say he wants me to come to Philadelphia and see him play," she said, her fingers tapping nervously in her lap. "I haven't done it yet. I'm afraid to fly."

She thought a moment and laughed. "One of these days, I'll do it just to surprise him," she said.

You won't have any trouble spotting Gladys Montgomery in the Veterans Stadium crowd. Just look around each time Wilbert carries the ball. She'll be the one covering her eyes.

Epilogue: Wilbert Montgomery played eight seasons with the Eagles (1977–84) and broke Steve Van Buren's club record for career rushing yards with 6,538. He won a Super Bowl ring as an assistant coach on the St. Louis Rams staff under Dick Vermeil in the 1999 season.

* Originally published in the *Philadelphia Bulletin*, November 6, 1978.

"A Real Philadelphia Kind of Win"*

On Saturday night, Jimmy Murray was in the back of a chauffeur-driven limousine, gliding down the Schuylkill Expressway toward Center City. The lights were shining brightly along Boat House Row; the downtown skyline was glowing warmly in the distance.

Murray had just finished a show at the WPVI-TV studios, a one-hour football special beamed live back to Dallas. The program was called *Shootout in Philly*, and it was a preview of the National Football Conference (NFC) championship game between the Eagles and the Cowboys.

Much of the hour was spent discussing the Philadelphia fans. A Dallas film crew spent a week in our town, shooting daytime scenes in the Italian Market, nighttime scenes at Mary's Irish Rose Pub on Two Street. "Real Real People," you might call it.

They interviewed a bunch of teenagers standing around a trash-barrel fire in South Philadelphia. They were typical street-corner kids, decked out in leather jackets, their collars turned up, their shoulders hunched stiffly against the wind.

The kids talked, they sang, but mostly they sneered. They sneered at the Dallas Cowboys the way they sneer at the cold every winter night. These kids learn early to size up strangers, figure out who can survive in the alley and who can't. The Cowboys, they agreed, were a team in short pants and Buster Brown collars.

"We're gonna beat you, Dallas," one kid shouted, jabbing his finger at the camera. "We're gonna beat you baaaad."

Drew Pearson was on the panel with Murray. He watched the videotape a while, his eyes bulging. "Is this for real?" he asked in a whisper. "Man, these people are crazy."

An hour later, Jimmy Murray was riding back to town, shaking his head. He could just imagine the people in Dallas watching all this Philadelphia footage. Surely, they thought they were tuned into a National Geographic special about lost civilizations. I mean, people like that don't exist anymore, do they?

"No way those people can understand any of this . . . no way," the Eagles' general manager said. "In Dallas tonight, they're all talking about how many head of cattle they're gonna ship to market. They're saying, 'I hear the price of crude is going up another five cents a barrel.'

"Those people are into oil barrels; we're into trash barrels. They're wearing Gucci everything, and we've got guys with no shirts on in zero degrees. But, hey, this is Philly. Unless you're from here, you can't appreciate what this game means.

"Playing Dallas here for the NFC championship? Are you kidding me? This is the Super Bowl. The indoor game [in New Orleans] is nice, but for Philly, this is the Super Bowl."

Murray looked out the window at the icy city, all white and glittering like something you'd see on a model-train platform. It was quiet for the moment, but Murray could feel the emotion rumbling beneath his feet, a geyser that had waited two decades to erupt.

"This town is gonna explode tomorrow," Murray said. "Absolutely explode. This is like Christmas Eve. I can't wait."

Jimmy Murray drifted slowly through the Eagles locker room yesterday afternoon, moving from one embrace to another like a man in a dream. His hat had been smashed down on his head by too many playful hands. His tie was pointing due east.

Tears were trickling down his cheeks and dripping into this great rain barrel of an Irish smile. The way the little guy was glowing, you would've thought he spent the day standing in a reactor puddle at Three Mile Island.

Every so often, Murray would roll his eyes and say the magic word. Champions. The Eagles dragged themselves to the top of the NFC, burying the Cowboys, 20–7, at Veterans Stadium. It was a great moment for the players who worked like galley slaves to get here, but it was an even greater moment for Jim Murray because, well, this was his valentine to Philadelphia.

Jimmy Murray grew up in West Philly, went to West Catholic High School, and fell in love with this town's sports teams back when they had trouble tying their shoes. For years, he sat in the upper deck at Franklin Field, rooting for the Eagles. He'd get heartaches that lasted all winter.

He went away for a while, working for a Minor League baseball team in Atlanta, then running a restaurant in Malibu, but he always knew he'd come back to Philadelphia. When he joined the Eagles in 1969, it was with the thought that someday he would give the old gang from the upper deck something to cheer about.

Yesterday, it all came together. The Eagles and the City of Philadelphia tossed twenty years of bitter memories over their shoulders and floated off into a bright, if frigid, new day.

"I never experienced anything like this, ever," Murray said, his voice still trembling. "I looked around before the game today. There's seventy thousand people in the stands, all singing 'God Bless America.' There's the Bishop McDevitt band unfurling that flag. People were crying, holding hands. That's what Philadelphia is all about.

"No way the Cowboys were gonna beat us. Not here, not today. We threw the Polish American string band at them. We threw Andrea McArdle at them.

The Cowboys weren't only playing the Eagles today, they were playing this whole town, and they just weren't prepared for that.

"There's no words to describe what this win means to Philadelphia," Murray said. "There's no words to describe how good this is gonna make so many people feel. All over this whole area, people are dancing in front of their TVs right now, feeling proud. Dinners are burning on the stove, and nobody cares.

"Do you think there will be some people smiling on the streets here tomorrow?" Murray said. "It's been twenty years since the Eagles gave this city a championship, but these fans hung in there. This is their moment; they deserve it."

Leonard Tose did not always have the warmest relationship with the Philadelphia fans. In the early '70s, his limousine was pelted regularly in the Veterans Stadium parking lot. Air-traffic controllers booed his helicopter. Three straight playoff seasons have changed all that.

Yesterday, as Leonard Tose enjoyed his finest moment, he spoke first of the fans.

"I'm thrilled that we could do this for the people of Philadelphia," Tose said, "and I'm thrilled with the way our fans responded. Today they showed the rest of the country what real fans are like. These people are the best, just like the guys in this [locker] room."

"The fans," strong safety Randy Logan said, his eyes glowing, "were like nothing I ever heard before. The only thing I could compare it with was the Michigan–Ohio State game at Ann Arbor. That was 105,000 people, but even then . . .

"We could feel it when we went down the tunnel to the field today. It was more than just the noise; it was the feeling, the emotion in the air. It was almost a spiritual thing, where the players and the fans were drawing strength from each other.

"The very first play, it was unbelievable. [Tony] Dorsett carried the ball. We hit him for no gain, and the stadium just shook. I knew then what kinda day it was gonna be."

"They stuck with us, too," linebacker Jerry Robinson said. "We had some tough breaks, but they picked us right up. I was thinking, 'I can't let these people down.' I wasn't here all those bad years, but I know what it's like to be hungry. I can relate to that.

"The Cowboys might be America's Team," Robinson said, "but we're Philadelphia's Team, and that's better."

"This is a special day," Jimmy Murray was saying. "My old friend Bobby Ellis picked me up this morning. We drove past our old parish, Our Mother of Sorrows, [at] Forty-Seventh and Lancaster. We couldn't resist, we had to stop.

"We asked the nuns to let us in. We walked in, said a few Hail Marys. Then Bobby drove past Franklin Field. He said, `I can see where I sat for the [1960] championship game.' I was getting goose bumps.

"Things flash back to me, like all the tough times. I thought about Joe Kuharich. I talked to him the other day, before he went back in the hospital. He looked at me, a twinkle in his eye. He said, `You're gonna do good against Dallas.' I feel like we won for him, too.

"This win didn't come easy. We had a touchdown called back, we had opportunities we failed to convert, but these guys never quit, they never lost their faith. They just kept battling back and battling back. It was a real, a real . . ."

Jimmy Murray paused, then smiled. "A real Philadelphia kind of win," he said. It was the ultimate compliment. The kids on the street corner, the ones standing around the trash barrel, sneering, they would understand.

Epilogue: The conditions that day—the bitter cold, the emotion in the stadium, and maybe even the White Jersey versus Blue Jersey mind game—gave the Eagles an overwhelming home-field advantage. When Wilbert Montgomery scored the first touchdown, the Veterans Stadium press box literally shook. I really believe the Eagles played their Super Bowl that day. When they went to New Orleans to face Oakland two weeks later, they looked—and played—like a drained football team.

*Originally published in the *Philadelphia Daily News,* January 12, 1981. Reprinted with permission by Philadelphia Newspapers, LLC.

The New Dick Vermeil—Who Is He?*

On Sunday afternoon, when Mark Moseley's game-winning field goal disappeared into the hushed Veterans Stadium crowd, Dick Vermeil displayed no emotion.

He removed his headset, then walked back and placed it carefully on the Eagles' bench. He went onto the field, shook hands with Washington coach Joe Gibbs, and chatted briefly with a few Redskin players.

He walked up the tunnel to the Eagles locker room, staring straight ahead, like a guy heading for the office elevator at 5 P.M. A few fans shouted at him, but Vermeil never looked up, never reacted.

Later, when the coach reappeared to meet the press, he was calm and even gracious.

"Give credit to the Redskins," Vermeil said. "They came back and played well. They deserve the victory."

The newsmen were surprised. They came to the interview room expecting Vermeil to explode. After all, his team had just blown a thirteen-point lead in the fourth quarter, a most inauspicious way to open the 1982 season.

Vermeil was annoyed, yes. He criticized wide receiver Ron Smith for lining up off-sides. And he wasn't too thrilled with Frank LeMaster for failing to check off the fake punt in the fourth quarter.

But basically, the coach was pretty cool. He was not nearly as overwrought as he had been following tough losses in other years.

There was a time when sudden death was like the real thing for Dick Vermeil. It was like washing down a cyanide capsule with hemlock. No more.

Yesterday, Vermeil went through his weekly press briefing with almost clinical dispatch.

There was no fire, no soul searching. The 37–34 defeat was discussed in simple, straightforward terms.

"It's a disappointing loss," Vermeil said, "but it's not the end of the world."

Again, the reporters were puzzled. Where was the old Vermeil passion? Where was the brimstone, for criminy sakes?

The last time the Eagles gave up thirty-seven points in a game, it was against Cincinnati in 1979. After that loss, Vermeil threatened to "kick some [players'] butts up into their throats."

Here he was, three years later, coming off the same kind of defeat, shrugging his shoulders and saying, in effect, "That's the way it goes."

What's with the Little Dictator, anyway?

"I keep thinking I'm gonna coach for a while longer," Vermeil said, "but, hey, if I can't learn to handle the ups and downs of this profession, I won't last more than this year. I'll be out of it.

"If I don't do a better job handling the pressure this year, I will get out of it. It's just not worth it to my wife, my family, to my coaches and myself."

The audience listened in stunned silence. The implications of Vermeil's remarks were staggering, indeed.

Was Dick Vermeil, at forty-five, actually thinking about walking away from the Eagles at the end of this year? If not this year, then how soon?

Did this have anything to do with the $2.5 million offer he received a week ago from the Phoenix franchise in the United States Football League (USFL)?

Vermeil said he had no immediate plans to leave the Eagles ("the best coaching job in the country"), and he had no desire to jump to the USFL.

He said he merely was talking in the abstract—what he might do if he did not get a better grip on his emotions.

This was his way of expressing a promise he made to himself and his wife, Carol. He wanted to restructure his priorities, to give more of himself to his family and less to his two-tight-end offense.

Personally, Vermeil said he felt the need to unwind. He didn't want to carry the franchise around in his gut twenty-four hours a day anymore.

These were all compromises Dick Vermeil made with the perfectionist that rages inside him, the force that last year drove him to work eighteen-hour days and watch films until dawn.

Vermeil has maintained his new, low-key approach through training camp and the opener. He hopes he can stick to it, no matter how the season unfolds.

"I'm just trying to keep on a more even keel emotionally, with my staff and everyone else, so I can do a better job through sixteen games," Vermeil said.

"I did not handle the pressure as well as I should have last season, I told the squad that a long time ago. I let the [four-game] losing streak get to me. I became totally drained.

"I realize now, to stay in this business, you've gotta be able to handle pressure better than I handled it last year. Now that I've been through it, I'm gonna handle it better. I'm not gonna make the same mistake again.

"I don't get as excited now. On the field [Sunday], I was probably the calmest I've been since my first job as a high-school coach. What good does it do to yell at an official?

"I'm not gonna do it, that's all there is to it."

The "new Dick Vermeil" is partly the result of his own sapping experience last season and partly the result of family influence.

Carol Vermeil has been after her husband to ease up for years, dating back to their UCLA days. Dick finally got the message when he burned out in the stretch last year, then came down with hepatitis in the off-season.

Dick's brother, Al, had some input, as well. Al is the San Francisco 49ers' conditioning instructor. He convinced Dick he could actually work more efficiently if he took some time off during the season.

Dick realized they were right. He was a victim of his own intensity. Even when he did go home to Carol and the kids, he wasn't much fun to be around. He'd stare off into space, thinking about a new play he could run against the Dallas flex.

"Someone would talk to me, and I'd tear their head off," Vermeil said. "At times, I was just a big ass."

Finally, he decided enough was enough.

Vermeil eased off this summer due to the hepatitis and the nagging of owner Leonard Tose. ("I didn't want to see the guy kill himself.")

He's working harder now, but he's still miles off the pace he set en route to Super Bowl XV.

That raises a question: Are the Eagles' current problems a byproduct of Vermeil's new work habits? Is he easing off too much?

This team is used to feeling a coach's whip across its flanks every fifteen minutes or so. Maybe, just maybe, these guys don't know how to react, suddenly living in Mr. Rogers' Neighborhood.

"In terms of discipline with the squad, I haven't changed," Vermeil said.

"If anything, I'm a little tougher on them. What I have to say to the team will be said in the normal Vermeil fashion.

"No, I haven't changed that way at all. The [changes] I'm talking about pertain to me. I don't want to blame myself for everything that goes wrong to the point where I become hesitant and ineffective in making decisions, that's all.

"There are times things will go wrong and I'm at fault," Vermeil said, "but I guarantee you, I'm not always gonna be the (expletive) crutch, either."

At last, a glimpse of the old Dick Vermeil. You know, it was kinda nice.

Epilogue: This was the first indication of where things were headed with Dick Vermeil. It was the first stage of the burnout that would force him to resign at the end of the 1982 season. Fourteen years later, he returned to coaching and won a Super Bowl with the St. Louis Rams. He was inducted into the Pro Football Hall of Fame in 2022.

*Originally published in the *Philadelphia Daily News*, September 14, 1982. Reprinted with permission by Philadelphia Newspapers, LLC.

Introducing Tommy McDonald at the Pro Football Hall of Fame*

Tommy McDonald is here today for one reason: He followed his heart. He had a passion for the game of football and a desire to be the best, and he wouldn't let anything stand in his way.

That's why he is here today. Not because it was easy. For Tommy, it never was. Not because it was destiny. Then it wouldn't have taken this long.

Tommy is here because he refused to listen to all the people who told him it was impossible. The high-school and college coaches who told him he was too small. The pro teams that ignored him in the 1957 draft. They did not realize that inside that jackrabbit body beat the heart of a lion.

Tommy McDonald was a great football player, but he is much more than that. He is an inspiration to every young person who's ever been told he wasn't big enough or fast enough or good enough. He is proof that the greatest strength is still the strength of the human will. He is proof that you don't have to stand tall to stand for everything that's good—in life as well as athletics.

Tommy was five-foot-nine and 172 pounds when he played in the National Football League. Today he becomes the smallest player enshrined in the Pro Football Hall of Fame, and that makes his accomplishments all the more remarkable. Four hundred and ninety-five receptions. More than nine thousand total yards. Those are imposing numbers. When Tommy retired in 1968, he was second only to the great Don Hutson with eighty-four touchdown catches.

Tommy averaged one touchdown for every 5.8 receptions, a figure that ranks among the all-time best and eclipses every current receiver, including Jerry Rice. But those numbers—compelling as they are—don't tell the story of Tommy McDonald. You had to see him play to know how truly special he was.

If I had one wish for the NFL today, in this era of billion-dollar TV deals and million-dollar contracts, it would be that more players played the game the way Tommy McDonald played it—that they gave as much, cared as much, and loved it as much as he did. We'd all have a lot more fun.

Tommy didn't just play the game, he embraced it. He played the game the way we played it as kids at recess, afraid that at any second the bell would ring, and we would have to go back to class. He savored every second, and so did we.

He played most of his career without a face mask. He had his jaw broken in the 1959 league opener, but he played the next week with his jaw wired shut and still scored four touchdowns to beat the New York Giants. That was Tommy McDonald.

He was the smallest man on the field, yet in the fourth quarter with the game on the line, there wasn't a better receiver in all of football. That's not just my opinion. Norm Van Brocklin himself said it, and if the Dutchman were here today to see Tommy join him in the Hall of Fame, I'm sure he would say, "It's about time."

Vince Lombardi once paid Tommy the ultimate compliment. He said: "If I had eleven Tommy McDonalds, I'd win a championship every year." Tommy scored a touchdown to beat Lombardi's Packers in the 1960 championship game. Tommy never won another championship after that, but he played like a champion every week for twelve seasons.

Growing up in Philadelphia, I saw every game Tommy played as an Eagle. They were the best Sundays of my life, going to Franklin Field and watching number 25 make catches that seemed like something out of a dream. I know there are thousands of people my age in the Philadelphia area who are pro football fans today because—like me—they grew up watching Tommy McDonald.

He was our hero. He is my hero still. Words cannot describe what a thrill it is for me to be a part of this very special day. It is now my great honor to present at long last, the newest, the smallest and surely the most grateful member of the Pro Football Hall of Fame, Tommy McDonald.

Epilogue: This is the speech I delivered when I presented Tommy McDonald for induction into the Pro Football Hall of Fame. It remains one of the great thrills of my life. I later wrote a stage play about our friendship and shared journey to Canton. In 2016, *Tommy and Me* was produced by Theatre Exile in Philadelphia. It was named the best regional theatre production by Broadway World.

*Text of a speech delivered at the Pro Football Hall of Fame in Canton, Ohio, August 1, 1998.

Reggie White*

We were standing in his driveway, Reggie White and I. We had just finished an interview for NFL Films, and we were saying our goodbyes. I still remember my parting words.

"I'll see you in Canton in 2006," I said, referring to White's no-doubt-about-it first-ballot selection to the Pro Football Hall of Fame.

Reggie gave me a big smile. "It's a date," he said.

A month later, Reggie was gone. He died of respiratory failure one week after his forty-third birthday. I remember hearing the news the morning of December 27, 2004. I couldn't believe it. I have trouble believing it even now.

On Monday, the Eagles will honor White at halftime of their game against Seattle. They will retire his number 92, a fitting tribute to the greatest defensive lineman ever to wear an Eagles uniform. He holds the club record with 124 career sacks, and he was voted NFL Defensive Player of the Year in 1987 and 1991. When he left the Eagles to sign with Green Bay in 1993, it marked the end of an era in Philadelphia.

"There is only one Reggie White," teammate Seth Joyner said, and it was so true.

As a football player, he was unique. No one else had his combination of speed and strength. He was six-foot-five and three hundred pounds, yet he had the quickness of a martial artist. He could lift an offensive tackle off the ground and literally throw him aside—the players called it "the Reggie toss"—and on the next play, he could beat the same guy with a spin move.

He also was an ordained minister who worked tirelessly to help the poor and disadvantaged. He often spoke about his athletic ability and how he felt it was a gift given to him by God for the purpose of spreading the Gospel.

"If I'm the best [in football]," Reggie once said, "then I'll have a platform to preach, and more people will listen."

I never questioned his sincerity. On Fridays after practice, he met Herb Lusk, the former Eagles halfback who is now pastor of the Greater Exodus Baptist church in North Philadelphia, and they delivered food and hope to the people in that community. I once asked Reggie if I could tag along. He said OK, but only if I promised not to write about it. God's work, he said, was not a photo op.

So one Friday I left my notebook at home and followed Reggie through a crumbling neighborhood near Temple University. I still remember an elderly woman taking his hand and saying: "I've been praying for something like this." She had no idea who he was—she had never even heard of the Philadelphia Eagles—but it did not matter. "So few people care," she said, "but he cares."

I had not seen Reggie since he retired from football following the 2000 season. I had heard his life had taken on a new direction. I was told he was not going to church anymore and he was questioning his faith. I wasn't sure what I would find when I went to North Carolina in November 2004 to interview him for our NFL *Films Presents* show on religion in football.

Reggie talked for almost three hours that day. It was true, he had gone through some profound changes. Since he retired from football, he had more time for reflection. He was no longer preaching. Rather, he was spending all of his time at home, learning Hebrew. He wanted to study the Bible in its original text. He felt that was the only way he could get a true understanding of God's word.

"I look back on all the years I was playing football and preaching," he said, "and I realize I was more of a motivational speaker than a teacher of the Word. People asked me to speak at their churches because I was a football player, not because I was a great theologian. They came to see Reggie White, but what was I really offering?

"I gave the perception that I understood what I was talking about, but I really didn't. All I was doing was preaching what somebody else wrote, or quoting what somebody else said. Yet [ministers] kept inviting me to speak at their churches. As I got older, I got sick of it. I felt like I was being prostituted. I realized if I was going to find the Lord and do His work, I had to go find Him for myself."

For Reggie, that meant spending long hours in his den, studying Hebrew with the long-distance assistance of a young Israeli scholar who coached him on the language. "I feel like I've been in seclusion," he said. "I heard people are spreading rumors about me: that I've converted to Judaism, that I've become a Muslim, all sorts of crazy stuff. I've become an outcast among some people in the church. They don't understand."

Reggie began rethinking his beliefs one year into his retirement. He was reading a book about the apostles. He always thought of himself as a modern-day apostle, but in reading the book, he saw a difference. "They lived their doctrine," he said. "I was just some guy talking."

He felt the need to read the Old Testament in its original text, not some eighth-generation translation, so he could form his own conclusions about his faith. He did not turn his back on religion, as some people suggested. Indeed, he was more deeply committed than ever. He could not wait to get out among the people and spread the message. But this time, he wanted it to be a message he understood and truly believed.

"This is the hardest thing I've ever done, much harder than playing football," he said. "I was never disciplined when it came to reading. I hate reading.

So to make myself to sit there for ten hours a day and practice my Hebrew is hard, but I'm excited because every day I get deeper into it. I understand so much more. I've never felt so much at peace."

Looking back, Reggie admitted his views had changed. The idea that God wanted him to use his NFL platform to preach the gospel, he said, was silly. "God doesn't need football to glorify His name," he said. He also said that while he felt God gave him certain "signs" about his career path, God did not actually tell Reggie to go to Green Bay in 1993. He said as much as the time.

"There's a lot of things that I said God said that I realize now, He didn't say anything, that's what Reggie wanted to do," he said. "I never heard God's voice the way the prophets did. I'm hoping I will hear His voice now when I'm reading the original scripture."

Reggie walked me through his home, which resembled a castle on a lake. The walls were lined with photos, highlights from his football career next to scenes of he and wife, Sara, opening Hope Palace, a home for unwed mothers. Despite his ambivalent feelings, there was no doubt Reggie helped a lot of people over the years. That's what I'll remember.

Epilogue: During the 2005–2006 football seasons, I wrote a weekly column for the Comcast SportsNet website in Philadelphia. This is a piece I wrote the week before the Eagles retired Reggie White's jersey number 92.

* Originally published on the Comcast SportsNet website, December 2, 2005.

THE PHILLIES

Maddox Takes Ride of His Life*

When they immortalize the Phillies' 1980 pennant clinching on canvas, when they chisel the whole crazy scene in stone or squeeze it onto a postage stamp, it will come down to Garry Maddox's victory ride.

It will come down to Garry Maddox bouncing along on the shoulders of his teammates, his fists clenched above his head, the outline of his sideburns bristling against the bright Astrodome roof.

It was a game that decided perhaps the greatest post-season series in baseball history, a game that turned on one sudden flick of Garry Maddox's bat.

With two out in the tenth inning, Maddox stroked a Frank LaCorte fastball to center field. Terry Puhl charged the ball but couldn't come up with it. It skipped past him; Greg Gross scored the decisive run; and Maddox streaked into second base like a cheetah sniffing a fresh kill.

Then, in the bottom of the tenth, the final two Houston Astro batters hit fly balls to Maddox. He watched them both disappear into his Gold Glove and then, in an uncharacteristic display of emotion, Garry Maddox danced with joy.

He rushed toward the infield, toward the mob of Phillies who had come streaming from the dugout. He leaped into the arms of Larry Bowa, then into the arms of manager Dallas Green.

A moment later, Garry Lee Maddox was up on their shoulders and riding toward the dugout, a man who had just been reunited with his destiny.

Remember, it was Garry Maddox who dropped the fly ball that brought the curtain crashing down on the Phillies in the 1978 National League Championship Series.

Remember, it was Garry Maddox who lost a critical fly ball in the sun against Montreal two weeks ago, then vanished from the starting lineup in circumstances that could only be described as puzzling.

Now, when the Phillies came face to face with their final hour, when they would either win their first pennant in three decades or surely be cast to the baseball winds, Garry Maddox delivered the hit that delivered a franchise from bondage.

In the clubhouse later, Maddox looked like a man who had just fought his way through a long, dark tunnel into the daylight. He drank his champagne gently, respectfully. He didn't guzzle it; he didn't spray it like the other players.

Garry Maddox had struggled with this cork too long. He was entitled to take a nice, mellow sniff.

"I've never had a feeling like it," Maddox said. "This was such an emotional series; there were so many turns, so many comebacks. You just ached on every pitch.

"I can't say enough about this team. These guys never quit. They never let down. When Houston came back to tie us [in the eighth inning], the guys on the bench encouraged us, told us to get our heads up.

"I got the winning hit," Maddox said, "but I'll tell you, this was a real team effort. We got great clutch hitting, we got some great defensive plays, and Dick [Ruthven] did a super job in relief.

"When we got to the playoffs, we dedicated ourselves to one thing, and that was going all the way. We knew we wouldn't be satisfied—and our fans wouldn't be satisfied—by anything less than a National League pennant.

"We adopted the motto, 'Whatever it takes.' That means, whatever it takes to win, that's what we're gonna do.

"Coming back to win that crazy game on Saturday, then coming back to win again tonight, I think we proved something to a few people. I think we showed we have a lot of character on this ball club."

Coach Bobby Wine edged through the group of newsmen around Maddox, and he embraced the centerfielder. "Great job," Wine said.

"Thank you," Maddox said. His voice was weak, filling with emotion.

"I've never felt this way before . . . never in my life," Maddox said. "I'm elated but I'm almost limp. I'm tired from playing, I'm exhausted from jumping up and down in the dugout, yelling.

"The [winning] hit? I don't suppose I'll ever forget it. I was just looking to make good contact. I was trying to hit the ball back through the middle.

"Even when we scored the [go-ahead] run, we knew the game was far from over because they had come back so many times before. When we went back in the field, we were thinking, 'We can't let up. We can't let them get [a rally] started.'

"I wasn't really praying they would hit the ball to me," Maddox said, smiling, "but when they did, I was glad. I felt confident in my ability to make the plays. They weren't that tough."

"Will this make up for the [dropped] ball in Los Angeles?" someone asked.

"That's in the past," Maddox said, gracefully handling the painful memory. "This [win] is what's important now—this team and what it has accomplished.

"I'm elated. All the disappointments, all the frustrations I felt [in years gone by] are washed away. Hey, I can't tell you how it felt to have those guys pick me up and carry me off that field.

"I didn't know they were gonna do that. In fact, I didn't know what they were doing at first. When I realized, I thought, 'This must be a dream. This all has to be a dream.'"

So a season of conflicting emotion, a season tinted with controversy—perhaps real, perhaps imagined—ended happily for Garry Lee Maddox. The memory, like the bottle he sipped from, had no jagged edges.

The relationship between Dallas Green and Garry Maddox has not always been an easy one. There have been clashes of pride, clashes of wills, differences of opinion often more semantic than genuine.

However, it is worth noting that as Garry Maddox rode off the Astrodome field last night, the man clutching his left leg and hoisting him toward the ceiling was Dallas Green.

It was, indeed, a moment for all to cherish.

*Originally published in the *Philadelphia Daily News*, October 13, 1980. Reprinted with permission by Philadelphia Newspapers, LLC.

Walking into the Series Spotlight*

The first time the Phillies made it to a World Series was 1915. Their starting pitcher in the series opener was Grover Cleveland Alexander, a future Hall of Famer coming off his greatest season. Alexander won thirty-one games that year, pitched twelve shutouts, worked 376 innings, and compiled an astonishing 1.22 earned-run average. His strikeout total (241) was impressive even by today's slider-aided standards.

The next time the Phillies made it to the World Series was 1950. Their starting pitcher in that opener was Jim Konstanty, the wondrous palm baller who wore thick glasses and looked like a high-school physics teacher. Konstanty was the National League's Most Valuable Player that season, appearing in seventy-six games, winning sixteen and saving twenty-two. In a one-month period (July 23–August 23), Konstanty pitched in fourteen games and did not allow a single run.

Tonight, the Phillies return to the fall classic against the Kansas City Royals at Veterans Stadium. Their starting pitcher will be Bob Walk, a rookie who has won just two of his last thirteen starts, a kid who was working in a California service station this time a year ago.

From Grover Cleveland Alexander to Jim Konstanty to Bob Walk . . . from Hall of Famer, to MVP, to Mr. Goodwrench. I've heard of the generation gap, but this is ridiculous.

The Phillies get to a World Series once every three decades, and they hand the ball to some kid just off the bus from Sticksville? What's going on?

Well, it seems that Dallas Green asked for volunteers to pitch this game, and Bob Walk was the only one who was able to lift his arm up over his head. He was the only one who could pick up a baseball without using two hands.

Dallas Green burned out his pitching staff in that savage five-game championship series with Houston. He used six pitchers on Saturday and six again on Sunday. He wore out more arms than a little old lady on a slot-machine binge.

Green originally had planned for Dick Ruthven to open the World Series. But he needed Rufus to put away the last six outs in the Astrodome on Sunday. That move, though successful, left Green's starting rotation in a shambles. His only choice was to pitch Walk against Kansas City tonight. But sending a kid just one year removed from Double A ball into the heat of a World Series opener is like shoving a toddler into the middle of Market Street.

Walk, you might recall, got off to a sensational start after being called up from Oklahoma City on Memorial Day. He ran off eight wins in less time than it took to sew his name on the back of his jersey.

He was 8–1 on August 1 and he was considered a prime candidate for National League Rookie of the Year.

Since then, however, Walk has won only three games, lost six, and failed to survive the fourth inning in five of his starts. He went almost a month between victories (September 4–October 2), and he was the one eligible pitcher Green did not use in the Houston series.

But yesterday, Dallas Green dusted the twenty-three-year-old Walk off and introduced him to the assembled media as his game one starter. When someone asked Green if he had any qualms about pitching Walk, the Phillies' manager bristled.

"No, I don't have any qualms about pitching Bob Walk," Green said. "He did a heckuva job when we really needed help early in the season. He helped us get over the hump in June and July. I don't know where we'd be without him.

"He struggled for a while [later], but he pitched a real big game for us the final week, beating Chicago when we were trying to keep pace with Montreal.

"He's a tough kid, a competitor," Green said firmly. "He'll give us everything he's got [tonight]; I know that."

Bob Walk did not seem particularly overwrought by the news of his starting assignment, but, then, he never seems overwrought by anything.

The rookie the other Phillies call "Whirlybird" (he always seems to have his head in the clouds) handled his first World Series press conference as if it were, well, just another tire change and lube job.

"I guess it will probably hit me when I go home," Walk said. "I'll be watching television, and I'll think about it. Right now, I'm still emotionally drained from the Houston series . . . from the party and the trip home.

"I didn't even think about pitching this game until [Sunday] night when a few people said, `Hey, are you gonna start the opener?' My first reaction was, `Why would [Green] start me?' Then I thought about it, and I realized, hey, he might need me, after all.

"I didn't find out for sure until an hour ago," Walk said. "Dallas came over and told me I would pitch the first game."

"What did you say?" someone asked.

"I said, `OK, fine,'" Walk replied. He looked at his questioner curiously. "What was I supposed to say?" Walk asked. "No?"

Walk feels confident he can do the job, despite his shaky regular-season finish. Like Green, he points to his last appearance, a strong seven-inning effort against the Cubs, as proof that he has overcome his control and concentration problems.

"My problem this year has been inconsistency," Walk said, his 4.56 earned-run average reflecting that. "I'll throw one game well, then I won't even feel like the same pitcher the next time out. I'll feel clumsy, sluggish. It's all mental, I'm sure.

"Stuff-wise, there's no adjustment going from the Minor Leagues to the big leagues. The same stuff that wins for you in the Minors will win for you up here.

"The adjustment you have to make is mental . . . coping with the fans and the media.

"I feel pretty confident now," Walk said. "I haven't pitched in a while, so I can't go out there and try to muscle the ball past these guys. I'll just have to stay loosey-goosey and work it like it's just another ballgame."

Of course, this is not just another ballgame. This is the first game of the World Series, the ultimate showcase where players become national celebrities overnight, where guys appear out of nowhere to become superstars.

There will be some 60 million people tuned in when Bob Walk winds up to throw his first pitch tonight. Most of those people never heard of the Whirly-bird, the kid who started this season ticketed for a summer in the Minors, then rode in to rescue Green's tattered staff.

If Bob Walk pitches a terrific game, he could wind up as part of our World Series lore, right there with Don Larsen and Whitey Ford and all the rest. He might even wind up on a beefcake poster, like Bucky Dent.

Walk isn't thinking about any of that. He is basically the same easygoing kid who pitched last season in Reading, then went home to Newhall, California, and worked pumping gas at the local filling station.

He is not much for pretense. He cares little for mystique. When someone asked what he knew about the Royals' George Brett, Walk shrugged.

"I saw him hit in one [playoff] game against the Yankees," Walk said. "I was in a bar, and the game was on the TV. I glanced up, and he was at bat. That was when he hit the home run off [Goose] Gossage."

"What will you be thinking when George Brett steps in to hit against you?" someone asked, clearly expecting the rookie pitcher to hold the game's top hitter in the proper awe.

"I'll probably think, `Hey, that's George Brett,'" Walk said, smiling. "`Then I'll think, `I'm gonna get him out.'"

Grover Cleveland Alexander and Jim Konstanty couldn't have said it any better.

Epilogue: Bob Walk pitched seven innings and earned the victory as the Phillies defeated Kansas City, 7–6, in game one of the World Series. It was the last game he pitched in a Phillies uniform. Following the season, he was traded to Atlanta for outfielder Gary Matthews.

*Originally published in the *Philadelphia Daily News,* October 14, 1980. Reprinted with permission by Philadelphia Newspapers, LLC.

Winning Makes It All Worthwhile*

At 11:45 P.M., with the stadium erupting around him like a concrete volcano, with the entire city reeling along the banks of the Delaware like a sailor on shore leave, Dallas Green retired to his office to talk to the president.

No, not Ruly Carpenter, the Phillies' president. Hell, Dallas Green talks to him all the time. On this night of the Phillies' deliverance into the Promised Land, Dallas Green had a direct line to the Oval Office, where Jimmy Carter himself was waiting to extend his congratulations.

Dallas Green was standing behind his desk, his head tilted to one side, his eyes closed, the phone pressed against his ear. He had one hand on the World Series trophy, the other on a freshly opened bottle of Great Western champagne.

Flashbulbs were popping all around him. Mayor Bill Green was edging through the crowd to shake his hand. The White House was on hold. God, if only Gene Mauch could see Dallas Green now.

It was Gene Mauch, you might recall, who said Dallas Green, a big right-hander with the pop-gun fastball, would never make it in the big leagues. Well, Gene, Dallas made it last night, and he wept as he finally staggered onto the mountaintop.

Dallas Green was there in the jubilant clubhouse, wiping away the tears with his wife, Sylvia, and their four children. Suddenly, his weary eyes snapped to attention. The president was on the line.

"Well, thank you, Mr. President," Dallas Green said. "Yes, we're all thrilled. The City of Philadelphia has waited a long time for this moment, and we're all enjoying it.

"There were a lotta people who said we couldn't do it, but I think we proved ourselves in this series. We played our hearts out to win this thing."

Green paused, allowing the chief executive to get in a few words. Green laughed that big, thunderous laugh. Surely, Jimmy Carter hadn't heard anything like it since the day the silo blew up back in Plains.

"Well, I understand you're more of a football buff," Green said, "but one of these days we're gonna get you up here and show you how to play baseball."

Dallas Green hung up, shaking his head. Someone asked him what the president had said.

"He congratulated us," Green said. "He said he watched as much of the series as he could between briefings and enjoyed it."

"What did he say that made you laugh?" a newsman asked.

"Oh, he said he didn't play much baseball," Green said. "He said softball was his game. That's when I told him to c'mon up here. We'll show him what good, old-fashioned hardball looks like."

Good, old-fashioned hardball—that's the game Dallas Green taught the Phillies this summer. He took over an elitist team that played baseball in a tuxedo and turned it into a street-corner gang that rolled up its sleeves and scrapped its way through September and October.

He took a team that had all the fire of a string quartet and made them play hard rock. The Phillies were once a team of royal Lipizzaner stallions, all polished brass and heads held high. Under Dallas Green, they became Cossacks shrieking through the playoffs and World Series.

Dallas Green brought this team to its first World Championship. In truth, he dragged it by its earlobe, like a father tugging a whining toddler to the dentist's office.

But, last night, in the heady rush of a 4–1 victory over Kansas City, a summer of bruised feelings washed quietly away. It was an evening when the manager's "We, Not I" philosophy settled gently over this team, an embrace rather than a hammerlock.

Watching Dallas Green leave the celebration and run down the tunnel to take a bow for the crowd, watching him hug his players as they now returned, dripping champagne, to the field: It was like watching a farmer harvest the crop he had waited a lifetime for.

Philadelphia and Dallas Green, they had seen a lot of tough times together. But last night, the city and the manager took a long swig of champagne and washed thirty years of ashes from their mouths.

"What do I feel now?" Dallas Green said later, slumping against the wall, grabbing weakly for a beer. "I feel drained. I feel as if I've given everything I've got to give, but, it feels good to be on top.

"I know the players are happy, and I'm happy as hell for them. But in their own way, they can't appreciate this the way I can. I've been a Phillie for twenty-five years. I've been through so many lean years, it's been like a damn famine.

"I made a stop at every level in the organization—player, coach, manager, farm director. I have a feel for what this win means for all the people behind the scenes, like the secretaries and the front-office staff. I know how they feel right now.

"It was a very emotional moment when I came in here [the clubhouse] and saw Paul Owens," Green said.

"He was standing there on the [TV] platform, and he had tears in his eyes. I thought about all the nights when we felt like we were beating our heads against the wall. Now it was finally paying off.

"I love the man, and I believe he loves me, and we hugged each other there for a while, and I guess that's when it really sank in. We had won this damn thing. We accomplished what we set out to accomplish way back when."

Dallas Green gave his press conference in stages, pausing to answer a question or two as he made his way through the cluttered locker room. "I gotta see my players," Green kept saying. "Where are my players?"

Every time Green spotted one of the Phillies in the middle of a swarm of newsmen, he would work his way through the crowd to hug him and personally thank him for the season. He hugged them all, even the ones he had wanted to drop off the Walt Whitman Bridge just a few weeks ago.

"I'm proud of all these guys, every one of them," Green said. "You talk about courage, you talk about character. This team showed more guts the last month of this season than any team ever. You look at all the games we won by one run, all the `must' games we won.

"I take my hat off to them. I'm including guys like Larry Bowa and Garry Maddox; guys I had my differences with during the season. When we needed them down the stretch, they busted their butts for this team.

"I can't say this surprises me that much," Green said, "I felt at the start of spring training that we had the talent to go all the way. I told the players that at our very first meeting in Clearwater.

"I said, `We've got the personnel to win this thing, but we're gonna do it my way.' There were some doubters in the group; there were those who resisted, but I just had to show them that my way was the best way.

"I had help. Pete Rose pretty much exemplified the kind of spirit I'm talking about. He was sliding on his belly, breaking up double plays. Pretty soon, even our cool guys were sliding on their bellies. Our bench? You never heard so much noise in all your life.

"This team was juiced. Once we hit September, I knew we were gonna win it. I could feel it; the electricity was in the air. I think Larry Bowa said it best. He said this team had some ghosts to put to sleep, and these guys were anxious to do it.

"Along the way," Green said, "I made a few guys unhappy. I probably made a few guys miserable, in fact. But it was all for a reason. This [nodding toward the celebration] is the reason.

"I don't see any miserable people in here now, do you?" he asked.

Someone raised the question of 1981. Would Dallas Green now step down as manager and return to the front office? He had raised the possibility more than once.

Now, as only the fourth man in Major League history to win a World Series in his first year as manager, would seem a perfect time. After all, what is left to accomplish?

Green moved his head to one side, as if to let the question whiz harmlessly past.

"I don't know what I'm gonna do next year," he said. "Gimme a break, will ya? We just won the World Series. Let me savor it for one night, please?"

After waiting twenty-five years, Dallas Green is entitled to at least that much.

Epilogue: Dallas Green managed the Phillies through the 1981 season. He left to become general manager of the Chicago Cubs in 1982. He later returned to the Phillies' front office as a senior adviser. He died in 2017.

*Originally published in the *Philadelphia Daily News*, October 22, 1980. Reprinted with permission by Philadelphia Newspapers, LLC.

McGraw's Retirement Tugs at Heartstrings*

There will be other relief pitchers, guys who are bigger and throw harder, guys who make more money, but there will never be another Tug McGraw.

I mean, can you see Goose Gossage reciting "Casey at the Bat" with the Philadelphia Orchestra? Can you see Bruce Sutter doing his Elvis Presley impersonation between games of a doubleheader?

Can you see Jesse Orosco fluttering his hand over his heart when a four-hundred-fifty-foot fly ball curves foul? Can you imagine Willie Hernandez talking about his "Bo Derek fastball?"

No way. As the Phillies' assistant to the president, Paul Owens, said after the Tugger's farewell news conference: "How do you replace a Tug McGraw? I don't think you can."

Frank Edwin McGraw was an original, a one-of-a-kind showman who was at once an author, humorist, statesman, philosopher, actor, and ballplayer.

He was, as club president Bill Giles pointed out, both left-handed and Irish. "An irrepressible combination," said Giles, a man known to appreciate such things.

Tug McGraw openly savored the perils of his profession. He was at his best in the ninth inning with the tying run edging off third and the fans pressed close to their transistor radios calling for one more scroogie.

That's how we'll remember McGraw, swaying on the tightrope in the `80 World Series, a parasol in one hand, a baseball in the other, winking down at us as if to say, "Isn't this fun, boys and girls?"

We'll remember his 1–2 fastball to Willie Wilson and the leap that followed. "Seeing [the film] again today," Giles said, "brought a tear to my eye. You talk about the thrill of victory."

Most athletes merely understand the theater of sport. A select few, like McGraw, raise it to an art form: the familiar strut from the bullpen, the glove slapping against the thigh, the organist playing an Irish jig. Like him or not, you knew when the Tugger was on his way.

"I can't think of another pitcher who displayed such emotion and enthusiasm," Giles said. "Everything Tug did turned you on.

"There are only two players I ever saw who moved me to say, `Geez, I love that guy.' One was Pete Rose; the other was Tug. They both had that something extra. Color, charisma, whatever you want to call it, they had it."

Giles was one of the executives who pushed hardest for the December 1974 trade that brought McGraw to the Phillies from the New York Mets. Dallas Green, then farm director, was the man most opposed to the deal.

To acquire McGraw, then a thirty-year-old veteran coming off a 6–11 season, the Phils had to part with a young reliever (Mac Scarce), a valuable utility man (Del Unser), and the best catching prospect in the organization (John Stearns).

"I was ticked off," Green recalled yesterday from his snow-bound headquarters in Chicago. "I didn't want to give up Stearns. The Pope [Paul Owens] and Hughie [Alexander] had a helluva time selling me."

According to Owens, they never did.

"Dallas was mad at me for six months after that," the Pope said. "But we felt our club was at a point where we could finally make a move in our division, and we wanted that experienced reliever.

"At the time, we would have been happy to get three or four productive years out of Tug. As it turned out, we got a helluva lot more. Tug gave us ten great years; he set the club record for saves [ninety-five], and he helped us win the division five times.

"More than that," Owens said, "he made us a better team just by being around. When he talks about loving the game and loving this city, it's not a put-on. He had the kind of attitude you wish everyone had—ballplayers, fans, the whole world."

It is ironic that the man who least wanted Tug McGraw in Philadelphia is the same man who later entrusted him with his destiny.

As the Phillies' manager in 1980, Green handed McGraw the ball night after night down the stretch and watched while the thirty-five-year-old pitcher dragged a season off death row.

The `80 Phillies were in third place as August wound down, and it looked as though they were going nowhere. But after September 1, they were 23–10 and a stunning 12–4 in one-run games. More than anyone else, McGraw was the difference.

Mike Schmidt hit the homer to defeat Montreal; Manny Trillo's relay saved the National League playoffs; Unser had the clutch hits in the World Series, but it was the Tugger who was out there every night in the ninth, closing the door.

McGraw appeared in twelve of the last fifteen games that season, including all five in the Houston series and four more against Kansas City. He allowed just three earned runs in fifty-two innings after recovering from tendonitis in his shoulder on July 17.

"We would have never made it without Tug," Green said. "He gave us every inch, every last ounce of strength. He just kept reaching back for that little extra.

"No other relief pitcher has ever had a run like that. Willie Hernandez had a helluva year in Detroit, but you put his record up against Tug's in `80, and it's no contest. Every time we were in a bind, I went to Tug and he came through.

"I knew he was getting tired," Green said, "so we had a code worked out. Every day around four, he'd give me the thumbs up if he was OK to pitch or the thumbs down if he was hurting. I can't remember him giving me the thumbs down once."

"I considered it a few times," McGraw said, smiling. "But I'd see the trainer and get a rubdown, then I'd go out and have a catch and I'd loosen up. I'd figure, `Yeah, I can give it a shot.'

"You get to that point, and adrenaline takes over. Nobody wants to sit down when they're fighting for a pennant. But, yeah, I was running out of gas. If it wasn't for the pills [aspirin and Tylenol], I wouldn't have made it the last month.

"That last game, my arm was dead. That pitch to Wilson was it. I knew if I didn't get him there, I was coming out. [Ron] Reed was warmed up, and Dallas was on the top step.

"I remember looking around before I threw the pitch. I looked at the fans and tried to siphon off some of their energy. I saw the police dogs on the field and thought, `K-9 Corps. . . . Yeah, I need a `K' [strikeout] right here.' Anything to keep me going.

"When I got [Wilson] . . . I don't know how to describe the feeling. I remember waiting for Mike [Schmidt] to run over from third base. It seemed like it took forever. Then came the champagne and after that . . . I remember waking up with an awful headache."

The victory parade down Broad Street followed with McGraw holding up the *Daily News* with its now famous "We Win" cover.

At JFK Stadium, McGraw stepped to the microphone and, with typical bravado, told New York to "take this championship and stick it."

The remark was directed at the New York press, which McGraw felt was anti-Philadelphia during the series. However, the New York fans took it as a personal affront and let McGraw know it when he made his first appearance at Shea Stadium the following year.

McGraw entered the game and, instead of the customary cheers, he heard boos. He waved his arms, urging the fans to boo louder, which, of course, they did. Asked about it later, McGraw laughed.

"Just giving the people their money's worth," he said.

McGraw gave the people their money's worth for seventeen seasons. He appeared in 824 games and threw an estimated 30,000 pitches. He worked 1,302 relief innings, a National League record, and posted 179 saves, sixth on the all-time list.

The numbers are impressive, but they aren't what we'll remember about the Tugger. We'll remember a free spirit who brought joy to a sullen clubhouse, a man who never forgot what it meant to be twelve years old and in love with a bat and ball.

"I know Tug appeared a little zany at times," Paul Owens said, "but deep down, he was one of the most competitive guys I've ever known. He was a winner, in every sense of the word. I'll miss him."

So will we, Pope. So will we.

Epilogue: Tug McGraw was stricken with a brain tumor in March 2003. He lived long enough to attend the closing ceremony for Veterans Stadium, where he reenacted his final strikeout in the 1980 World Series. He died on January 5, 2004.

*Originally published in the *Philadelphia Daily News*, February 15, 1985. Reprinted with permission by Philadelphia Newspapers, LLC.

The End Is Here*

No one would deny Steve Carlton his place in Philadelphia sports history. He is a legend; he will be for as long as they play baseball in this town, but the time has come to say goodbye.

OK, in deference to His Cyness, we won't ask that he say anything. A simple wave will do. One last tip of the cap from the dugout step. Lower the curtain slowly and tearfully if you must; just lower it.

Please.

The Carlton era is over. The only people who aren't willing to admit it are the people who run the Phillies, which helps explain why the team is slipping toward its third consecutive non-winning season.

They keep sifting through the rubble of each defeat, looking for some trace of the great lefthander who once ruled the National League. They grasp for the slimmest and most brittle of straws.

Yesterday, Bill Giles noted Carlton had six strikeouts in Saturday's 8–6 loss to St. Louis. Yes, but two came against Vince Coleman, who is in the worst slump of his career (zero for thirty-six). Three others were against Danny Cox, the opposing pitcher.

"Lefty had pretty good stuff," Giles said, "but he had trouble with his location."

Translated, that means Carlton can no longer throw strikes when he has to.

He has walked sixteen in his last twenty innings, and he is behind in the count to almost every hitter. He comes in with that flickering fastball, and the result is both predictable and sad.

Carlton has thrown fifteen home-run balls this season, an average of one every 5.5 innings. He has allowed thirty-seven hits and twenty-seven runs in his last five starts, an 11.07 earned-run average. Most guys have to pitch grenades to cause that much damage.

At forty-one, Lefty should be a plaque on the Veterans Stadium wall, a retired number hanging in the trophy case, a Hall of Famer in waiting. He should not be shuffling to the mound every fifth day dragging what's left of his dignity and slider behind him.

The Phillies brass plans another meeting today to discuss the plight of the team. The question of what to do about Lefty will be raised again. It has been three weeks since Carlton (4–8) has gone past the fifth inning.

Giles says it's unlikely the Gang of Six will do anything dramatic. The current plan is to keep Carlton in the rotation. Part of the reason is loyalty. Giles wants to give Lefty every chance to work out his problems.

Another reason is the Phillies don't have many better options. Two potential replacements for Carlton, Mike Maddux and Randy Lerch, were roughed up in yesterday's 7–4 loss to the Cardinals. Another, Fred Toliver, isn't ready to come off the disabled list.

"This is an agonizing situation," Giles said. "We have three choices. We can release Steve, we can convince him to retire, or we can keep pitching him.

"Our number-one thought is to do what's best for the team. We don't want to give up on Lefty if he can still get the job done. If he's in a slump, we'll give him a chance to work out of it. If he's through . . . "

Giles's voice trailed off. He never did finish the sentence.

The Phils' president said the team was on the verge of making a move in early May after Carlton lost three straight and saw his ERA climb to 6.89. But Lefty came back with three wins, including a 6–2 decision over San Francisco on May 27.

That night Carlton worked eight innings and allowed seven hits. He had eight strikeouts and no walks. It was just like the old days, but the moment passed almost as quickly as it came.

Since then, Carlton has deteriorated to a point where he is painful to watch. Last Monday, he walked three Cubs in a row (including the eighth and ninth hitters) in a 7–5 loss. He was gone in the fourth inning.

On Saturday, Carlton could not hold a 4–0 lead against a Cardinal lineup that included four starters hitting under .200. He was lifted in the fifth after allowing six hits, six walks, and six runs to the worst offensive team in the league (.227 average).

"I hoped he'd crank up a good one [Saturday]," Giles said. "The fans were pulling for him. When the Cardinals had their big inning, there was a feeling of sadness in the air.

"The guy was so great over the years, the thought keeps rolling around in your mind: Hey, he can do it again. I talked to him Friday. He said he feels fine. He just needs to work out some problems in his delivery.

"What can I say?" Giles said. "I hope he's right."

Carlton has been likened to Robin Roberts and Curt Simmons, two former Whiz Kids who were written off by the Phillies and found new life in other Major League cities.

It should be noted Simmons was thirty-one when the Phillies let him go in 1960. Roberts was thirty-five when he was released one year later. Carlton is forty-one and coming off a rotator-cuff injury. There's a big difference.

Watching Carlton nibble at the corners Saturday was enough to make people who remember the old power pitcher squirm. The man who once buried lefthanders with his plunging slider now struggles to get it near the plate.

Carlton used 112 pitches in five innings against St. Louis. Last Monday, Boston's Roger Clemens threw 105 in a complete-game victory over the Yankees. Clemens was ten years old when Carlton won his first Cy Young Award in 1972. It gives one pause.

"Lack of command, that's hurting Lefty," pitching coach Claude Osteen said. "He's working from behind, and he's wearing himself out. He's throwing a lot of pitches under extreme pressure.

"He's under a microscope every time he goes out there. He's aware of it. Nobody wants to turn this thing around more than he does.

"Physically, I think he's fine," Osteen said. "His problem—and we've discussed this—is his motion is too slow. It's causing him to throw a big, fat breaking ball. He went out [Saturday] with better stuff, though.

"We'll discuss Lefty again [today], but I've said all along we should give him until the All-Star break. I can't defend his last three or four starts, but we don't have anybody else knocking the doors down [in the farm system], so we might as well stick it out."

Giles claims that the decision not to re-sign Pete Rose was his toughest call until now. However, the prospect of releasing the greatest left-handed pitcher in Phillies history clearly pains the baseball fan inside Giles.

"I'd hate to release a player like Steve Carlton," Giles said. "The word `release' should never be attached to a player of his stature. I'd hope we could talk it over. . . . Maybe he would agree to retire if it came to that."

Giles kept staring at the field. "But Steve is such a competitor, I doubt he'd see it that way," he said. "He'd probably want to keep going.

"I remember Robin Roberts going through a similar time in Houston when I was there [in 1966]. He said later the biggest mistake he ever made was pitching that last year. But he couldn't turn those juices off. Lefty is the same way."

The Carlton era is over. The pitcher who won twenty games six times and threw fifty-five shutouts has long since passed. The forlorn figure that remains shares only his uniform, and his silence.

Epilogue: Steve Carlton was released by the Phillies shortly after this column appeared in the *Daily News*. He was claimed by the San Francisco Giants but lasted only six games. He had brief stints with the Chicago White Sox, Cleveland Indians, and Minnesota Twins before retiring in 1988. He was inducted into the Baseball Hall of Fame in 1994.

*Originally published in the *Philadelphia Daily News*, June 23, 1986. Reprinted with permission by Philadelphia Newspapers, LLC.

Lieberthal Receiving Good Reviews*

Mike Lieberthal knew what he wanted by the time he was fourteen years old.

He wanted to play professional baseball. He wanted to be a Major Leaguer. He had made up his mind, simple as that.

He quit football in the eighth grade. He stopped practicing the piano. He wasn't interested in girls. He didn't want his MTV. All he wanted to do was play baseball.

His father built a batting cage in the back yard of their Southern California home. Mike practiced his hitting every afternoon, then played in a game almost every night. He usually did his homework in the back seat of the car on his way home from the field.

"Mike lived, ate, and breathed baseball," said Dennis Lieberthal, Mike's father, a part-time scout for the San Francisco Giants. "He was a field rat. Wherever I went, he went with me. He just loved being around the game.

"There were people who accused me of pushing Mike, but that's not the way it was at all. There were nights when I couldn't stand the thought of seeing another baseball game, but Mike would be standing at the door saying, `C'mon, Dad. Let's go.'

"This career was something Mike really wanted," the elder Lieberthal said. "That's why I think he'll succeed."

Last month, the Phillies selected Lieberthal, an eighteen-year-old catcher from Westlake Village, California, with their first pick in the amateur draft. He signed a contract with a $231,000 bonus and joined the Phils' rookie league team in Martinsville on June 17, two days after his high-school graduation.

So far, the six-foot, 165-pound Lieberthal has struggled at the plate (.163, three home runs, ten runs batted in), but he has impressed everyone, especially Martinsville manager Roly DeArmas, with his defense and his grit.

"Mike is the best catcher I've ever seen come straight out of high school," said DeArmas, now in his fourteenth year in the Phillies' farm system. "He can do some things behind the plate that are incredible. He has great hands, and his arm is outstanding."

"Watch him catch the ball," said Del Unser, director of player development for the Phillies. "He's so smooth, he looks like he's picking cherries back there. He already frames pitches like a veteran. It's hard to believe he's just eighteen."

Lieberthal is, indeed, a very polished receiver. He is good at blocking pitches in the dirt (there are a lot of those in the Appalachian League), and he snaps the long throw to second base with laser-like precision.

The kid calls his own game and does a good job handling the Martinsville pitchers. Lieberthal has worked with Rick Dempsey, the veteran Los Angeles Dodgers catcher, and obviously absorbed a lot of his knowledge. (Dempsey lives near the Lieberthals and uses their batting cage in the off-season.)

Lieberthal plays the old-fashioned way, hustling down the line to back up first base on routine ground balls and directing traffic on infield flies. Unser says the lean, handsome rookie reminds him of a "young Bob Boone," and that's praise of the highest order.

At the moment, no one in the organization seems too concerned about Lieberthal's batting average. Like most kids fresh out of high school, Lieberthal is slow adjusting from the aluminum bat to wood exclusively. Also, the pitching here is several notches above what he faced at Westlake High School.

Lieberthal opened a few eyes Monday in Huntington, West Virginia, when he cracked two home runs in a game against the Cubs' rookie team. It was the first indication that the kid's offense might be coming around. The scouts said it would eventually.

This past season, Lieberthal batted .500 for a Westlake High team that won twenty-eight of thirty games. Officially, he was forty-two for eighty-four, with thirteen homers and forty-two RBIs, so it was quite a shock for him to join Martinsville and go hitless three or four days at a time.

Lieberthal tossed his helmet and bat in disgust after popping out in a game against the Bluefield Orioles last week. It was his first display of temper, but, given the team's performance, it was easy to understand. Martinsville is 11–22 following last night's 2–1 victory in Huntington.

"Mike doesn't say much, but I know he feels he should be doing more," DeArmas said. "I told him, 'Hey, relax. Give it time.' The thing is, Mike is such a hard-nosed kid, he wants to succeed right now."

"The scouts warned me this could happen," Lieberthal said, sitting in the empty bleachers two hours before a recent game. "They said pro ball was different, and they were right. I just have to adjust.

"I talked to my father quite a bit the first month I was here. He told me to keep my head up and swing the bat, everything would fall into place. We've still got half the season left to play, so there's plenty of time to get things straightened out.

"I know a lot of people are watching me because I'm the number-one pick, but I'm not worried about that," Lieberthal said. "I have confidence in my ability, and I know the Phillies are going to give me every opportunity to make it.

"Now it's up to me to show them what I can do."

The Phillies took a lot of heat for selecting Lieberthal with the third overall pick in last month's draft. Most people thought they would take Tim Costo, the All-America shortstop from the University of Iowa.

At twenty-one, Costo figured to be ready for the Major League in two years, three at the most. At six-foot-five and 210 pounds, he had right-handed power reminiscent of another college shortstop the Phillies drafted in 1971, a fellow named Mike Schmidt.

When the Phils bypassed Costo and selected Lieberthal, the local talk shows were flooded with angry calls. Most fans seem to feel general manager Lee Thomas and farm director Jay Hankins blew the pick, the Phillies' highest since 1974.

Their logic was as follows:

- Lieberthal was a high school kid, which meant he was a long-term project.
- He was a catcher, and the Phillies have a history of striking out when they draft a catcher in the first round. (Examples: Lebo Powell, 1980; Trey Mc-Call, 1985).
- He was marginal in size at 165 pounds.

Also, Lieberthal was a catcher for just one year in high school. He was a middle infielder before that. He switched positions as a senior because his father said (correctly) that catching was a quicker route to the pros.

Lee Thomas agreed it was a tough call between Costo and Lieberthal, but he felt Costo would have to play third base in the Majors, and the Phillies already had two good prospects, Charlie Hayes and Dave Hollins, at that position.

They were thin behind the plate, however. "We don't have a catcher in the Minor Leagues who's going to be an impact player, in my opinion," scouting director Jay Hankins said, so the right-handed–hitting Lieberthal was the pick.

Costo wound up being drafted eighth overall by Cleveland.

Lieberthal is well aware of the controversy surrounding his selection. He's heard all about the talk-show critics, but he doesn't seem fazed one way or the other.

"It all comes down to performance," said Lieberthal, a bright young man who seems mature beyond his years. "If I play well enough, those [opinions] will change."

Mike Lieberthal is used to doing things the hard way.

Too young, too small . . . He has heard it all before and overcome it.

Consider:

- He was the first freshman in the history of Westlake High to make the varsity baseball team. (He not only made the team, but he started every game at second base.)
- At fourteen, he was playing weekends in a men's hardball league near Los Angeles. His first at bat was against Ed Farmer, the former White Sox and Phillies pitcher. He hit a double and knocked in two runs.

- At sixteen, he was catching for an elite team (coached by his father) in the Los Angeles winter league that included several high draft picks and future pros. He was handling fastballs and sliders thrown by current Giants Trevor Wilson and John Burkett, among others.

Obviously, we're not talking about a typical eighteen-year-old rookie here.

Lieberthal estimates he has played two hundred fifty baseball games in the past year, combining high school with various leagues in the Los Angeles area. He also toured the Far East with a team of high-school All-Americas, playing the best amateurs from Korea and Japan.

That's a lot of baseball.

Too much, maybe?

Is there a chance the kid could burn himself out?

"No way," Lieberthal said. "I enjoy the game too much.

"I used to hear that [question] in high school. Other kids would be going to parties and dances. I'd say, `I can't make it. I've got a game.' They stopped asking me after a while."

"Did you ever feel like you missed out on anything?" someone asked. "Socially, I mean."

"Not really," he said. "I liked playing ball. I'd rather play ball than go to the beach or go to a party."

It is easy to see why the Phillies love Lieberthal's attitude. It would be nice if it came in a larger package, but they are hoping nature takes care of that.

Unser points out that Steve Lake and Darren Daulton each weighed about 160 pounds when they were Lieberthal's age. Today, Lake is six-foot-one and 200. Daulton is six-foot-two and 190.

The big question, of course, is how long will it be before Lieberthal makes it to the Major League?

Lieberthal says he hopes to arrive in Philadelphia by 1993, but that is probably optimistic. It is a long climb from the Appalachian League to Veterans Stadium, even for a number-one pick. If he is there by `94, he will have done well.

This much is certain: Lieberthal will finish this season in Martinsville, then report to Clearwater for two months of instructional league play. He will be back in Clearwater next March for spring training and assignment to his next Minor League stop.

"Mike came into this with his eyes wide open," said Dennis Lieberthal, who operates a gas station in Ventura, California, when he isn't scouting for the Giants. "He knows what's involved with professional baseball. He has seen the good and the bad.

"He has a lot of good friends who signed pro contracts, played a few years, and got released. He has heard all the horror stories about the lousy food and the bus rides and the pressure of, `Gee, will I make it?' We talked about all that, and he still was determined to sign right out of high school."

Lieberthal, who graduated high school with honors, was recruited by every major baseball school in the nation. He liked Arizona State and would have enrolled if he had not been selected in the first round of the draft.

Once the Phillies called, however, the issue was closed.

"I still remember when the phone rang," Dennis Lieberthal said, recalling the morning of June 4. "Mike answered. He only said two words: `Hello' and `awesome.' It was Jay [Hankins] calling with the good news."

And what did young Mike do to celebrate?

He went into the back yard, turned on the pitching machine, and took batting practice.

Epilogue: This was the first profile done on Mike Lieberthal following his selection in the 1990 draft. I have to admit that my first reaction on meeting him was, "He's so small." Lieberthal filled out to six feet tall and 185 pounds and set the Phillies record for most games by a catcher (1,139).

* Originally published in the *Philadelphia Daily News*, July 25, 1990. Reprinted with permission by Philadelphia Newspapers, LLC.

THE FLYERS

For Hard-Luck Parent, Another Damaging Blow*

A gray-haired nurse slowly wheeled Bernie Parent down the seventh-floor corridor of Pennsylvania Hospital. She wheeled him into his room, helped him into bed, then gently taped a piece of clean white gauze over each eye.

She took Parent's left hand and gave him a brief touch tour of his nightstand. Here, she said; this is your urine bottle. Here, she said; this is your control switch. The button on the left is for music; the button on the right is for the TV; the button in the middle calls for the nurse.

Parent took the instructions quietly, running his fingers across the dials and nodding his head. The nurse told the Flyers goalie to lie still and rest. "If you have to get up," she said in a motherly tone of voice, "call one of us."

When she left, the room was silent for a long time. Parent lay there, trying to figure out how all this happened. Just four hours earlier, he was tending goal against the New York Rangers, protecting a one-goal lead, stopping point-blank shots by Phil Esposito and Pierre Plante. Suddenly, he was left groping and frightened in the dark.

"This is a terrible feeling," Parent said. "I've had injuries before; injuries are part of the game, but this is different. An eye injury isn't like a bruised arm. An eye injury, you never know how it will turn out. The way the doctor was talking, the eye is badly damaged.

"I still don't know how it happened. The last thing I remember, there was a scramble in front of the net. Two guys were fighting next to me, then I got hit with a stick. I don't know who hit me; I don't know how the stick got through my mask. All I know is everything went black, and there was so much pain."

What happened was the most freakish sort of hockey injury. At 13:49 of the first period, Flyers defenseman Jimmy Watson was wrestling with the Rangers' Don Maloney near the goal crease. Watson grabbed Maloney and threw him to the ice, drawing a holding penalty. As Maloney was falling, his stick swung back and struck Parent in the right eye. The goalie threw off his mask and skated to the bench in obvious pain.

Dr. E. David Pollock, the team optometrist, examined Parent in the locker room and found blood in the interior chamber of the eye. He sent the thirty-four-year-old goalie to Wills Eye Hospital, where he was examined by Dr. James Tasman. Tasman said Parent suffered two conjunctivial tears of the eye and admitted him to Pennsylvania Hospital. Parent will remain in the hospital, under observation, for at least one week.

Originally, the doctors said Parent's injury was similar to the one suffered by Rick MacLeish earlier this season in Boston. MacLeish was back in action ten days later, so yesterday afternoon everyone felt Parent would be OK after some rest and medication. It wasn't until last night that the full extent of Parent's injury was determined.

"At first, they told me this was like Ricky's injury," Parent said. "Now they tell me this is worse. I asked them when I might be able to play again. They told me they'd have to wait and see. I don't know what to think. I don't usually worry, but this makes me worry."

Last night, Dr. Edward Viner, the Flyers' physician, said Parent would be sidelined for a minimum of three weeks and probably longer. If complications arise, it is possible Parent could miss the rest of the regular season and perhaps the Stanley Cup playoffs. At this point, Viner admits, a long-range prognosis is almost impossible.

"This is what we call a blunt trauma," Viner said. "The stick does not even have to strike the eye itself. The shock, the bang of the stick striking the mask, can cause this internal bleeding. Bernie has hemorrhaging into the chamber of the eye. We are hoping that blood will reabsorb in time, and Bernie will be fine. We'll keep him in the hospital for a week; we'll keep him on medication to reduce the swelling; and we'll keep him under observation for possible complications.

"We've certainly had an unusual number of eye injuries. There was Barry Ashbee, Ricky, Ross Lonsberry, Jimmy Watson, now Bernie. I don't know what we're doing wrong. I've been after the players for years to wear helmets and [eye] shields, but, of course, Bernie had his mask on when he was injured. If all goes well, Bernie could be back in three weeks. I don't want to be too optimistic, because we were so wrong about him [coming off his neck injury] in 1975."

The injuries have taken their toll on Parent, mentally as well as physically. There was the ankle injury in 1972, the disc problem that cost him most of the 1975 season, and now this, the most frightening injury yet. As Parent lay there in that hospital room last night, his eyes covered by two pieces of gauze, he talked about the game and the high price of hanging on.

"It's a contact game," he said. "You try not to think about injuries; you hope they won't happen to you, but they do. Something like this hits you when you're thirty-four years old, it makes you think a little bit. Before this season, I said I wanted to play another four or five years. Now I don't know. I'll just play it cool, see how the eye comes around, and go from there."

Might Bernie hang it up after this season? After all, he does have a lifetime contract guaranteed by the Flyers. He could retire to his fishing boat, pick up a nice paycheck, and never have to stand in front of another Guy Lafleur slap shot.

"I can't talk about [retirement] now," he said. "I still don't know how this [injury] will turn out. This scares me, though. It scares the hell out of me.

The doctor tells me there is bleeding in the front and back of my eye. I can't even see you now. It makes you appreciate your health, eh? This is what happens to old goalies, I guess. You forget to duck.

"Most of the young goalies are using these new masks with the helmet and the [face] bars. They're probably better. If I was wearing one of those, I don't think this would have happened. I tried those masks in practice, but I didn't like them. I didn't like looking through the bars. I'm used to the [mask] I have now. I shouldn't complain. I've been playing a long time, and this is the first time this ever happened to me."

Parent asked about the game, which the Rangers finally won, 4–2. A visitor told Parent his substitute, Wayne Stephenson, played exceptionally well for almost two full periods. Parent nodded.

"Steff will do a good job," he said. "Tell the boys I'm doing OK. Tell them I'll be back."

He just couldn't say when. Neither, for that matter, could anyone else.

Epilogue: I had no idea when I went to Pennsylvania Hospital that night that I would be writing about the end of Bernie Parent's career. The severity of the injury took all of us by surprise. The lens of Parent's eye was torn. His career was over. In fourteen NHL seasons, he won 271 games and recorded fifty-four shutouts. In 1984, he became the first Philadelphia Flyer inducted into the Hockey Hall of Fame.

*Originally published in the *Philadelphia Bulletin*, February 18, 1979.

"The Officials Killed Us," Snider Sizzles*

Ed Snider was pacing the hallway outside the Flyers locker room, his hands jammed tightly in his back pockets, his eyes scorching the paint off the walls.

Upstairs, the New York Islander fans were tearing through the Nassau Coliseum, whooping and toppling the wooden barricades like Huns pouring through the gates of Rome. They had just won the Stanley Cup with a 5–4 victory over the Flyers, and the spray of warm champagne was everywhere.

Ed Snider was angry. The Flyers' owner felt like a guy walking away from a crap game with his wallet turned inside out and a gnawing feeling that the dice were loaded. His team had lost in sudden death. Ed Snider thought it was a clear case of homicide.

"The officials killed us, the bastards," Snider said. "It was an absolute, total (expletive) disgrace. The most crucial game of the year, the game that's going to decide the championship, and they act like total (expletive)."

Snider walked away a few steps, then doubled back. He resumed talking. As he spoke, his voice rose, and the profanities poured out in a torrent.

"Anybody who is impartial knows we took a screwing today," Snider said. "This was a travesty. Their first two goals should have been disallowed. The one [Denis] Potvin knocked in with a high stick. The other one came on an offside pass. It was obvious to everyone except the linesman.

"Well, I'm damn sick of it. I walk in that locker room and see those guys, knowing how hard they worked all year, only to have this game taken away from them. It's a (expletive) disgrace. Why do we have to beat the other team and the officials, too? Every (expletive) night.

"I believe the [league officials] who come out of Montreal and Toronto don't want the Flyers to win," Snider said. "I believe that right down to the pit of my stomach. They don't want us to win, so they take every opportunity they can to screw us.

"I'll be damned if I'm going to be quiet about this. I don't care how much John Ziegler [the National Hockey League's president] fines me. Let him suspend me as owner, I don't care. I'd just like to watch the film of this game with him. I'll go over it inch by inch with him anytime at his convenience.

"I'd like to have him look me in the eye when it's over and say this was a well-officiated game. I'd like to see if he has the nerve to do that. This was a rough damn hockey game. The Islanders are a rough team, yet we got the worst of every penalty situation. You tell me why.

"Every time [referee Bob] Myers called a penalty on the Islanders, he immediately called one on us to even it up. He let the crowd call one penalty in the first period. He knows he let the crowd call it. The (expletive). I hope he can sleep this summer.

"The problem with this league," Snider said, "is [referee-in-chief] Scotty Morrison. He should be shot."

The Flyers have had trouble with the NHL hierarchy—Morrison, in particular—ever since the old Broad Street Bully days. The league cracked down on them, first with rule changes designed to eliminate the fighting and intimidation tactics the Flyers once used so effectively.

Today, the Flyers claim they have cleaned up their act and the NHL is still persecuting them. They are like the neighborhood thug who tries to go straight, except nobody quite believes him. Every time the candy machine gets robbed, they still point at the guy in the black leather jacket.

"We've been paying the price [for that reputation] as long as I've been here, and that's eight years," winger Bill Barber said. "It'll probably continue that way. Things aren't getting any better.

"To get the calls we got today in this kind of game is very discouraging. We were killing penalties the whole afternoon. I don't know if we skated even strength the whole second period. And the second [Islander] goal, my God, the play was two feet offside."

In an age when it seems that every major sport title is decided by a controversial call, the one rendered by linesman Leon Stickle yesterday stands alone for its glaring inaccuracy. Stickle was standing right there as Clarke Gillies dropped a pass to Butch Goring, who was nearer to Jones Beach than the Islander blue line.

Goring picked up the puck and carried it into the zone, and, incredibly, Stickle did not call the play offside. The Flyers' defense froze for a moment, expecting a whistle. When Stickle did not make the call, Duane Sutter broke free in the slot, and Goring hit him with a pass to set up an easy goal.

Afterward, Stickle was apologetic. "I was in the right position," he said. "The puck came back across [the blue line]. I guess I blew it. Maybe there was a tape on the stick and it confused me. Maybe I was too close to the play. Apparently, the replay showed I missed it."

"He admits he blew it," Snider said. "That does us a lot of good, doesn't it? The players were ready when they went on the ice today. Why weren't the officials ready?"

Stickle's blunder, combined with Myers's allowing Potvin's first goal, had the Flyers in a rage after the opening period. Personnel director Marcel Pelletier argued with Frank Udvari, a supervisor of NHL officials, during the intermission. The two reportedly almost came to blows, but Snider and several other bystanders separated them.

"That was just emotion," Snider said. "Frank was hot because he knew his officials blew two goals in that period. I just wish they would have let the players decide this series, not the guys in the striped shirts. Then maybe we would've had a chance to win.

"It was that (expletive) penalty they called on Jimmy Watson in the overtime of the first game that put us in this damn hole. One of our scouts, Walt Atanas, is an ex-linesman, and he said they were offside on the winning goal today. I didn't see it, but I'm sure as hell going to look at the films.

"This is a recurring thing," Snider said. "I have other [NHL] owners call me—I'm not going to name them, but they are respected men—and they agree with me. Even they can't believe the screwing we take every night.

"What can I do? I'm in a damn no-man's land. Every time I complain, Ziegler sticks it to me one more time. And the rest of the league laughs at me. I want Ziegler to read this. I hope he does fine me. I'll make plenty of noise then. What's he going to say? He knows I'm right."

In this case, being right is very little consolation. Much of the complaining the Flyers do about the officiating during the regular season grates on the nerves. Often, it is downright illogical. The fact is that they are still a very physical team, and they deserve most of the time they spend in the penalty box. They don't want to hear it, but that's the truth.

However, there is no question that poor officiating cost the Flyers at least one goal yesterday, and when that goal leads to an overtime loss and a Stanley Cup clinching by the opposition, it is worth tossing your head back and howling loud enough to be heard in Montreal.

Ed Snider sounded off, and rest assured, he will soon be writing a hefty check to John Ziegler. But the fact remains, Snider is right.

The Flyers put forth a remarkable effort throughout this series. They battled the Islanders until their muscles ached and their legs buckled from exhaustion. Paul Holmgren played on a crippled knee. Jimmy Watson played until he almost collapsed from the pain in his back. Bob Dailey was bone-weary, yet he played valiantly right to the end.

They came back to tie yesterday's game with two goals in the third period, then almost won it early in overtime. The Flyers were never really defeated in this series; they simply ran out of ammunition. They did not deserve to lose because Leon Stickle could not pass an eye test.

Afterward, in the funereal quiet of the locker room, Bill Barber put the season in perspective.

"We never quit, we never let down," Barber said. "We've been that way all year. We've accomplished a lot. I'm disappointed, but I'm proud of each and every guy on this team. We didn't win today, but we're still winners."

Epilogue: This was a case of being in the wrong place at the right time. In the mad rush to get to the locker room after the game, I became separated from the other reporters. I found a stairway that led to a restricted area near the visitors' locker room and, quite by accident, I found myself alone with Ed Snider, who was just waiting for the opportunity to vent. Sometimes getting the story is all about skillful reporting. Other times, it is dumb luck. This was one of those times.

*Originally published in the *Philadelphia Bulletin*, May 24, 1980.

Stickle: It Could Have Been Worse*

At 7:05 p.m., Leon Stickle was sitting nervously in the officials' dressing room at the Spectrum. There was a knock at the door. Stickle opened the door a crack and peeked into the hallway.

He saw Reverend John Casey, the Flyers' team chaplain, standing there in his clerical collar, his hands folded solemnly in front of him. Stickle's knees almost buckled.

"Oh my God," the linesman thought. "They've sent a priest to walk me to the ice."

Leon Stickle returned to the Spectrum last night. Standing in the tunnel, waiting to step onto the rink, Stickle knew just how Gary Gilmore felt as he pondered the bull's-eye; he knew how Caesar felt on the Ides of March.

He knew Philadelphia's hockey fans were out there, teeth bared, fists clenched, waiting for him. They had spent the summer tacking his picture up on the telephone poles all over town. "Wanted for Robbery," the posters read. "Stole the Stanley Cup from the Flyers."

Stickle is the linesman who blew the now famous off-sides call that led to the New York Islanders' second goal in the decisive sixth playoff game. That was six months ago, time enough for the local fans to whip up a nice batch of tar and feathers for Leon's next visit.

When he did not make a Spectrum appearance in the first four weeks of the season, there was speculation that the National Hockey League office, inspired perhaps by Mr. Stickle's life-insurance company, was deliberately steering him away from Philadelphia.

Naturally, the NHL brass denied it. They insisted Stickle would take his "regular turn" at the Spectrum. Sure, folks said, and the Ayatollah Khomeini will be the next commencement speaker at West Point.

Well, Leon Stickle's "regular" Spectrum turn came last night when the Flyers met the Los Angeles Kings. It was a match-up of hockey's hottest teams, but before the game, hardly anyone was thinking about the players. Everyone was too busy piling sandbags around the press box.

"I don't want to say things are tense," one newsman observed, "but they are asking all the fans to walk through a metal detector."

The three officials were dressing before the game when referee Wally Harris looked over at Stickle. Harris has worn a moustache for years. Stickle was wearing his for the first time in Philadelphia.

"You picked a fine time to grow that moustache," Harris told Stickle. "These people are liable to mistake me for you. I'll just tell them to look twice before they open fire."

Leon Stickle took a deep breath and skated onto the ice last night at 8 P.M. He was greeted with a loud chorus of boos that followed him as he lapped the rink. People leaned over the glass and shouted in his ear. Stickle skated past, expressionless.

One man dangled his eyeglasses in front of the thirty-two-year-old linesman. Stickle skated by as if he never saw him. The next time around the ice, the man waved a pair of binoculars in Stickle's face. Stickle calmly adjusted the sleeves on his jersey.

There were posters scattered throughout the arena. They ranged from surly ("Stick It Stickle") to mildly sympathetic ("To Err Is Human, But Don't Let It Happen Again"). One fan carried a sign with a tin can mounted on top. "Help the Handicapped," it read. "The Leon Stickle Foundation for the Blind."

The best sign was hanging from the upper deck. It was a neatly painted handlebar moustache flanked by the message, "We Still Know Who You Are." In one corner was a drawing of an NHL linesman wearing dark glasses, holding aloft a Stanley Cup.

The jeering lasted perhaps three minutes, until the Flyers and Kings came onto the ice. The booing was loud, but it could hardly be described as vicious. Nothing was hurled from the stands, except a few insults. There were no incidents, and a beefed-up security force—led by NHL police chief Frank Torpey—breathed a sigh of relief.

Oh, there were a few derisive cheers when Stickle called his first off-sides against Los Angeles. One fan held up a sign: "Six Months Too Late." Actually, it was all very civilized, a fact that speaks well for both the Flyer fans and Leon Stickle himself.

The fans expressed their displeasure but, thankfully, stopped short of New York's mob violence. Stickle, one of the game's true gentlemen and a fine official, quietly accepted the boos. He refrained from smirking or showing any behavior that might have antagonized the crowd.

As a result, the fans settled back and enjoyed an 8–2 Flyer romp, and Leon Stickle was able to leave the ice the way he likes best, virtually unnoticed.

The crisis had passed. Leon Stickle knows he will never win any popularity contests in Philadelphia, but at least now he can walk into the Spectrum without ducking from doorway to doorway like some two-bit hood on the run.

Someone asked Leon Stickle how it felt to be such a celebrity in the City of Philadelphia.

"If this is what it's like to be a celebrity," Stickle said, "I'm glad I'm not a celebrity in any other cities."

Leon Stickle came out to meet the press ten minutes after the game. He was in his stocking feet, his T-shirt was wet with perspiration, and he was smiling.

"I'm glad I finally got this over with," he said. "I knew I had to come in here eventually; it was only a matter of time. I felt the longer it went, the tougher it would be. That's why I was glad to see this one on my schedule.

"I had worked a Flyers game in Quebec earlier, so I had seen the players. They were super towards me. They didn't say a word about the call. They're pros; they understand how [quickly] things happen out there. No, it was the fans I was worried about.

"I know the Philadelphia fans can be rowdy at times. They really support their club, and, well, they get upset. But this [reception] wasn't bad at all. I thought it would be much worse. Really, it's a credit to these fans," Stickle said. "They just solidified what I always thought about them. They have a lot of class."

Someone asked Stickle if he had heard the things the people were shouting over the glass, if he had seen the signs in the upper deck. He smiled.

"I was aware of them," he replied. "I was told about the signs before we went out. I didn't look for them, but you catch things out of the corner of your eye. When play stops, you glance around.

"The shouts, I expected those. This is something I've carried around for six months. I heard about it when I was home [in Ontario] in the off-season. I'd be fishing, trying to relax, and someone would give me a jab about it. It kept it fresh in my mind.

"It's tough, but I have to face the fact . . . I blew the call. I saw the videotape at Bruce Hood's referee school this summer. It couldn't even qualify as a `controversial' call. I was definitely wrong. The puck was well over the line when [Butch] Goring picked it up.

"It was one of those things. It had been a rough period, and I saw Clark Gillies carry the puck into the zone. I followed him with my eyes because I thought there might be trouble. He dropped the puck [back], but I committed the cardinal sin: I kept my eyes on Gillies.

"By the time I turned around, Goring had the puck on the line. I never saw it leave the zone. It was my mistake, and I'll have to live with it. But I don't think there's ever been an official who didn't have at least one incident like this to test his character.

"I've been a linesman eleven years. This is mine."

When Leon Stickle left the Spectrum last night, he took the sign with the handlebar moustache with him. Stickle liked it so much, he asked the fans if he could keep it.

"He'll probably hang it in his recreation room," said Scotty Morrison, the NHL's *referee-in-chief. "Twenty years from now, he'll probably get a chuckle out of it."*

Epilogue: Leon Stickle spent twenty-seven years as an NHL linesman. In 2003, he was named the league's supervisor of officials.

*Originally published in the *Philadelphia Daily News*, November 7, 1980. Reprinted with permission by Philadelphia Newspapers, LLC.

In Flin Flon, They Knew He'd Be Great*

I never really understood Bobby Clarke until I heard about the underwear. I mean, you don't hear about frozen underwear that often. Not here, anyway.

But long johns freeze in Flin Flon, Manitoba, where Clarke grew up. I never thought about that until Gerry Hart, the former New York Islander defenseman, mentioned it once after a game.

Hart and Clarke played junior hockey together in Flin Flon, then they played against each other in the NHL. They were a lot alike, which is to say they didn't waste much time with finesse. They were all elbows and will.

I asked Hart if there was something about Flin Flon that made kids grow up that way. He talked about the mines and the winters and how fathers told their sons if God meant for them to have it easy, He wouldn't have let them be born in Manitoba. Certain stuff is just handed down.

Then Hart talked about the hockey trips. When the Flin Flon juniors traveled, the equipment rode under the bus. After ten hours at forty degrees below zero, everything would freeze solid. That included the long johns the players wore under their uniforms.

Hart said the players would unpack their long underwear and, as a joke, stand it in the corner of the dressing room. Then they would put it on and play the game. Talk about the Big Chill.

No one thought much about it. The players just skated until they thawed out. The harder they skated, the faster they got warm. It was, everyone agreed, a wonderful motivator.

"You watch the [pros] from Flin Flon," Hart said with a smile. "They still play like their underwear is frozen. Some things you never forget."

Bobby Clarke never forgot. Even after fifteen NHL seasons, three MVP awards, and two Stanley Cups, he remained the Manitoba rink rat, the toothless kid with frost in his britches and fire in his heart.

His career cannot be measured in goals and assists, although his totals are more compelling than he would care to admit. No, Clarke is best remembered for the way he played the game.

Clarke wasn't pretty to watch. He wasn't as fluid as Gilbert Perreault or as prolific as Marcel Dionne, but he knew more about winning than either one of them. He embodied the spirit of the game in a way Wayne Gretzky, for all his greatness, never will.

Hockey is, after all, a grinders' sport. Clever stick handlers have their place, but the game was best defined in the corners by the likes of Eddie Shore and Ted Lindsay, men who would skate through barbed wire for a loose puck.

Clarke brought back those good old days with heroic efforts, like the one this season in Chicago Stadium when, with his left eye sewn together, he flattened a Black Hawk defenseman, stole the puck, and set up the winning goal.

Twelve stitches for two points. Who else but Clarke, the throwback, the last of the Broad Street Bullies, would figure he got the better of the deal?

"The thing I remember about Bobby is he would do anything—I mean, anything—to beat you," said Orest Kindrachuk, who played against Clarke as a junior, then played with him in Philadelphia.

"I was with Saskatoon, and we dreaded the trips to Flin Flon, because we knew what was waiting for us. The Bombers had the toughest, most intense team in the league, and it was all because of Bobby. He was their captain, their leader.

"The best part of joining the Flyers was knowing I wouldn't have to play against him anymore. I never saw a man who worked as hard night after night. It didn't matter if he was sick or hurt; he suited up and played. He expected the same from the people around him.

"Clarkie never had to say much," said Kindrachuk, now an insurance adjuster in South Jersey. "All he had to do was give you that look, and you knew, `Uh oh, I'd better pull up my socks and get going.'

"There's no question our [Stanley] Cup team drew its strength from him."

Bobby Clarke arrived in Philadelphia in 1969, a choirboy in horn-rimmed glasses, quietly fighting a disease (diabetes) that should have ended his NHL career before it ever began.

The scouts weren't sure Clarke could withstand the rigors of the pro game. The Flyers selected him in the second round of the draft and called it a gamble. All the kid did was make hockey a major-league sport in this town.

It didn't happen overnight. The Flyers weren't much of a team back then. Clarke's first line mates were Lew Morrison, a rookie who used his stick as a balancing pole, and Reggie Fleming, a veteran who had more miles on him than Lindbergh's plane. (That's Charles, not Pelle.)

But in Clarke, the franchise had both its foundation and its ethic. Gradually, Keith Allen fit the right pieces around him. In 1974, with Kate Smith's voice rising in the background, the Flyers scuffled to the mountaintop.

The most memorable goal of Clarke's career came in the second game of the first Stanley Cup final against Boston. It was also the most typical goal, coming as it did with the Flyers hanging by their fingernails on the ledge called sudden death.

"We had lost the first game," Kindrachuk recalled, "and this one was in overtime. It was a make-or-break situation. If we didn't score, we'd be down 0–2 to a team with [Phil] Esposito and [Bobby] Orr.

"We got the puck, and somebody—I think Cowboy [Bill Flett]—took a shot. There was a scramble near the crease, and somehow Bobby dug it out. Next thing I knew, the puck was in the net, and Bobby was ten feet in the air."

Two weeks later, Clarke and Bernie Parent were carrying the Stanley Cup around the Spectrum ice. Philadelphia, the City of Losers, had turned the corner. No one seemed to mind that it took a kid from Flin Flon to show us the way.

The following year, the Flyers won again. This time, the final scene was played in Buffalo, 2–0. The clinching goal was scored by Bill Clement on a pass from Kindrachuk, with a minute left.

Kindrachuk was crushed against the boards by defenseman Jerry Korab. He recalls looking up, blinking through the cobwebs, seeing Clarke's jack-o'-lantern smile glowing above him.

"Bobby was saying, `Get up, O, we just won the Cup,'" Kindrachuk said. "You ask for the one [career] moment I remember, that's it."

Bobby Clarke's playing career ended yesterday with his appointment as the Flyers' vice president and general manager. The club referred to it as a transition, and I suppose it's not such a bad thing.

There is no doubt Clarke is qualified for the dual position; nor is there any question he deserves it. The only regret we have is knowing that, after fifteen seasons, he will no longer be a visible part of the action.

Even though his point total declined in recent years, Clarke remained the fiercest competitor on the team. He played the final period of the last Washington playoff game the way he played for two decades, digging down for everything his weary body had to give.

The fact that the cause was lost and the Spectrum was empty did not matter. Anyone who ever saw Clarke play—from Manitoba to Madison Square Garden to Moscow—knew this was a man who operated by a different standard.

Quitting, he once said, was the only real defeat. Maybe now, after watching him this long, we can finally understand.

In Flin Flon, of course, they knew all along.

Epilogue: Bobby Clarke was the Flyers' general manager from 1984 until 1990 and later served the team in other executive capacities. He was inducted into the Hockey Hall of Fame in 1987.

*Originally published in the *Philadelphia Daily News*, May 16, 1984. Reprinted with permission by Philadelphia Newspapers, LLC.

Hextall's Goal Always Was to Be in Goal*

It is the dream of every National Hockey League goaltender, but no one has thought it out as carefully as the Flyers' Ron Hextall.

No one has talked about it with his teammates, no one has flat out predicted it, except this rookie with all of twelve games of NHL experience.

"I'm going to do it; I'm going to score a goal," Hextall said.

Say what?

"I know I can do it," Hextall said. "I can hit the [other] net from our zone. I've done it a hundred times. I've even practiced the bank shot [off the boards]. I'm just waiting for the right situation."

Like what?

"It has to be a two-goal lead," Hextall said. "I wouldn't try it in a one-goal game. I wouldn't want to risk missing [the empty net] and having an icing call. I wouldn't want to lose the puck and give up the tying goal.

"But if we're up two, and the other team pulls its goalie and I have a shot at it," Hextall said, a smile spreading across his face, "yeah, I'm going to take it. I'll hit it, too."

Hextall's plan was passed along to coach Mike Keenan. He never blinked.

"It doesn't surprise me," Keenan said. "The way Ron roams around and handles the puck, I'm sure the idea has occurred to him.

"It's not the kind of thing I'd call for [as a coach], but I trust Ron's judgment. If he feels the situation is right, OK. [Smiling] But he'd better make it."

Just for the record, only two professional net minders ever have scored a goal. Michel Plasse hit an empty net while playing for Kansas City in the Central Hockey League (1970).

In the NHL, the New York Islanders' Billy Smith is the lone goal-scoring goalie. Smith was credited with a goal in a 1979 game against Colorado. Ironically, Plasse was with the Rockies at the time.

"It was a cheap goal, though," said Hextall. He was fifteen in 1979, but he has researched the matter thoroughly.

"It was a delayed penalty. One of their [Colorado] players accidentally knocked the puck into his own net. Smith was the last Islander to touch it, so he got credit for the goal. It isn't like he shot it in or anything."

Hextall figures when he scores, it will be a work of art. A flick of the wrists, a whistling shot through a defenseman's legs, a roar that grows louder as the puck crosses center ice and the blue line. Then . . .

"Flyers' goal scored by number 27, Ron Hextall . . ."

Can you dig it?

"He can do it," captain Dave Poulin said. "In practice, Ron will hit the corners [of the net] from center ice. The first few times he did it, I thought it was an accident. But he kept doing it.

"With his size [six-foot-three, 175 pounds], his mobility, and his stick-handling ability, he's really a new dimension in goal."

The rookie's swashbuckling style helped him win eight of his first ten starts and earn NHL Rookie Player of the Month honors for October.

But it also left Hextall hung out to dry more than once. Several times he was caught out of the net, and a defenseman, usually Brad Marsh, had to dive into the crease to prevent an almost certain goal.

Last Saturday, Hextall was burned when he roamed to the corner to poke the puck past New York's Mike Ridley. Hextall missed, then watched helplessly as Ridley fed Pierre Larouche, who hit the open net for the first goal in a 3–2 Rangers win.

This followed a four-goal third period in a 5–5 tie at New Jersey Thursday and constituted the first mini-slump of Hextall's NHL career. Flyers fans, who had seen other young goalies fade after auspicious starts, grew wary.

Was Hextall the real thing or just another Robbie Moore illusion? Could the Flyers seriously consider dealing a proven veteran, Bob Froese, on the basis of a rookie's hot month?

"We believe in Ron Hextall," general manager Bob Clarke said. "We don't think what he's done thus far is any fluke. He's a terrific young goalie."

So he's number one?

"Without a doubt," Clarke said.

"I have no reservations about Ron Hextall," Keenan said. "He has size and tremendous quickness, an unusual combination. He'll only get better the more he plays."

Hextall's statistics are, indeed, eye-catching. He has a 2.23 goals against average in his twelve starts. He has eight wins, including a 2–1 masterpiece against Edmonton in the opener on October 9.

Hextall's worst moment was the third period in New Jersey when he allowed four goals in 6:14 to blow a 5–1 lead. However, it should be noted the Devils had thirty-nine shots, a dozen at point-blank range, and a lesser goalie would have gone home that night with an "L."

"Our goaltender kept the score down," Keenan said afterward. "He played an outstanding game."

Hextall, naturally, blamed himself. That is a family trait. All the Hextalls are fierce competitors.

Ron's father, Bryan Jr., played nine NHL seasons. His uncle Dennis played thirteen. They left a trail of welts and penalty minutes across the United States and Canada.

Ron's grandfather, Bryan Sr., played twelve seasons with the New York Rangers and led the NHL in scoring in 1941–42. He had twenty-four goals and thirty-two assists for fifty-six points that season.

That doesn't seem like much by today's standards—Wayne Gretzky had 215 points last year—but it was a different game back then. The NHL has become a shooting gallery, and Ron Hextall has chosen to make his living standing in the bull's-eye.

It was a career decision Hextall made when he was eight years old, playing pee-wee hockey in Brandon, Manitoba. His mother, Fay, hasn't had a good night's sleep since.

"I think Ronald wanted to be a goalie the day he was born," his mother said. "That was all he talked about.

"When he was three, he would stand in the goal when the neighborhood kids played street hockey. I'd tell him to come away from there. The minute I'd turn my back, he was in the goal again.

"He wanted to play goal when he signed up for [youth] hockey, but Bryan wouldn't let him. He felt it was better for Ronald to play another position so he could develop his skating. Ronald would watch the goalie get dressed for games. We all knew what he was thinking.

"One day, the goalie didn't show up," Fay Hextall said. "Ronald said, `This is my big chance.' He played and won. He's been a goalie ever since."

That is not to say that his father and mother didn't try to talk some sense into him along the way.

"Ronald loved to handle the puck," his mother said. "He'd skate it out to the blue line sometimes. He gave the other parents heart failure. He's probably doing the same thing in Philadelphia now."

Well, there have been moments . . .

"That's Ronald," Fay Hextall said. "I'd say to him, `Wouldn't you like to take the puck and just keep going?' I thought he might still change to another position. He'd say, `I like playing goal.' That was it."

"I never seriously tried to talk him out of it," Bryan Hextall said. "Once he got in there, it was obvious that's where his interest was.

"He would come to my practices and sit behind the goalies. He'd watch how they moved, how they played the shooters. I played with Eddie Giacomin in Detroit, and Ron watched Eddie come out of the net and handle the puck.

"Dan Bouchard worked with Ron in Atlanta. The kids played after our practices, and Dan would stand behind Ron with his hands on his shoulders. He'd move him side to side; he'd show him how to play the angles. That's why Ron's fundamentals were so good."

Hextall grew up in an NHL environment. When his father was in Pittsburgh, many of the players would come to the house for dinner.

Glen Sather was a frequent visitor. Ron Hextall recalls Sather shooting rubber balls at him in the driveway one night. Sather, of course, was the coach Hextall defeated in his Flyers debut. Small world, the NHL.

"How well did you do shooting against him?" someone asked Sather following the Oilers' 2–1 loss.

"About as well as my players did tonight," Sather said.

"Glen always treated me well," Hextall said. "My father worked as an instructor at Glen's hockey camp, and I'd tag along. Now here I am playing against him. I'm sure I'll face a lot of these situations.

"There are players I saw play against my father. Larry Robinson [of Montreal] is one of them. Now I'll get to play against them. That will feel strange. It will probably feel strange for them, too."

Hextall has established a reputation around the NHL in a short time. After his first loss, 2–1, against the New York Islanders, Bryan Trottier said Hextall played like an All-Star.

"People ask me, `How good can Hextall be?'" said Bernie Parent, the Flyers' goaltending instructor. "I say, `How high is the sky?'"

Bryan Hextall did not allow himself to get carried away with his son's peewee hockey accomplishments. He understood better than anyone what a long road it was to the NHL.

"Ron was good, no question about it," Bryan Hextall said. "But I had seen a lot of good kids who never made it to the pros—goalies, especially.

"The first time I can honestly say I saw that [NHL] potential in Ron was when he was sixteen. He helped the Brandon midgets win the province championship. He was like [Ken] Dryden, a big kid with a quick glove.

"The other thing was he really wanted it [a pro career]. It was his dream to play in the NHL, and he was willing to work to make it come true."

Hextall played for a weak Brandon junior team, which accounts for his bloated goals-against average (5.33 in three seasons), but Flyers scout Jerry Melnyk saw enough of the youngster to recommend him for the 1982 draft.

The Flyers selected Hextall in the sixth round, number 119 overall. He spent two more seasons in Brandon; went to Kalamazoo, Michigan, in 1984–85; and was promoted to the Flyers' American Hockey League (AHL) affiliate in Hershey, Pennsylvania, later that season.

Hextall won thirty games and posted five shutouts last season as he led the Bears to the Calder Cup final. He was named AHL Rookie of the Year.

Next stop, Philadelphia.

"He came along faster than I expected," Parent admitted. "When I first saw him [in 1984], he was a raw talent. You think he leaves the net now? You should have seen him then. He was all over the place.

"I didn't try to change him. You change a goalie's style, you throw him off. All I did was teach Ron our [Flyer] system and fit him into it. I gave him a few basics to remember, then turned him loose.

"His greatest strength is here," Parent said, tapping his head. "He can allow a bad goal or have a bad period and put it out of his mind. He's on an even keel. A goalie has to be like that or he won't last."

You don't have to search far to come up with names of young goalies who fizzled after hot starts: Tom Barrasso, Steve Penney, Brian Hayward, etc.

Sometimes the shooters find holes in the kid's armor. Other times, the goalie becomes a victim of too much success. That was Stanley Cup MVP Patrick Roy's problem earlier this season in Montreal.

None of this figures to bother Ron Hextall.

For one thing, he is a stand-up goalie, not a flip-flopper, which means he won't be giving the snipers any more net to shoot at in March than he is right now.

For another, he is unusually mature for a twenty-two-year-old and he won't let his sudden celebrity status affect the way he approaches the game.

"I'm basically a quiet person," said Hextall, who is married to a former figure skater (Diane) and is the father of a six-month-old daughter (Kristin). "Bright lights and glamour, you can keep all that.

"My idea of a good time is staying home and playing with the baby. I sit for hours, talking to her, making her laugh. To me, that's the most exciting thing in the world."

Hextall smiled. "Does that make sense?" he asked.

Yes, it does.

"Ron is twenty-two going on thirty," his father said.

This maturity is reflected in the way Hextall has handled the sensitive questions about moving out Bob Froese. Hextall says all the right things when asked about last year's All-Star.

He calls Froese a "great goalie," and he is sure to point out that Froese led the NHL in wins (thirty-one) and shutouts (five) last season. Hextall says there is no animosity between himself and the veteran.

"I feel for Bob," Hextall says, "but that's hockey."

Hextall says, without hesitation, he is ready to be a number-one goaltender in the NHL. He admits, however, he would not have been ready if the Flyers had recalled him last year following the death of the Vezina Trophy winner Pelle Lindbergh.

Flyers management chose to leave Hextall in Hershey, where he could play regularly. The call went to Darren Jensen, who saw action in twenty-nine games backing up Froese. The decision to give Hextall a full year in the AHL is paying off now.

"It's the best thing that could have happened to me," Hextall said. "The minor-league life wasn't the greatest. Three games in three nights, traveling by bus. It was rough, I hated it, but I learned a lot.

"I came to camp this summer ready to compete for a job. I didn't worry about the odds; I just went out every day to do my best. The decision was in the coaches' hands, anyway.

"At first, I was a little reluctant to play my [roaming] game. Mike [Keenan] pulled me aside one day and said, `What are you doing? Get aggressive.' That gave me a lift. I realized they believed in me."

Hextall was unbeaten in the pre-season, and Keenan felt he earned the right to start against the Oilers on opening night. Who would have guessed it was a commitment for the season?

"I called it," said Dennis Hextall, Ron's uncle. "Ron's brother [Rod] works with me, and I told him that day Ron would start.

"I said one of two things would happen. Either the Oilers would blow him out, in which case he'd go back to the American League. Or he'd win the game and he'd be number one ahead of the other guy [Froese].

"It was the logical thing to do. There's no sense keeping a rookie goalie around and not letting him play. Put him in there; see what he can do. If he's not NHL material, it's better to find out quick.

"I felt sure Ron could handle it. He's a good goalie, and he's playing for a team where he won't face a lot of second and third shots. The Flyers are one of the best defensive teams around; they have been for years. It's a great situation for Ron."

Dennis Hextall watched the Flyers–Oilers game at a neighbor's house. He taped the broadcast and mailed it to brother Bryan so he could replay it. Ron's parents don't have cable TV in Manitoba.

"Ron played very well that night," Dennis said, "but he was nervous. I could see it. He looked fidgety, especially in the first period. But he made the plays.

"The big one was the save on [Wayne] Gretzky. He had a breakaway, but he came in a little too casual. Ron came out on him. Gretzky wasn't expecting that; he wanted to get in closer. Ron took the shot away from him.

"I think Ron will develop into a great NHL goalie, and I don't say that because he's my nephew. He has all the attributes. He has physical ability; he has great work habits and a positive attitude. You need all that in the game today.

"I played a long time," Dennis Hextall said, "and I saw a lot of rookies come through the league. I could tell after one week which ones would make it and which ones would not. If a kid was a goof-off, it didn't matter how good he was, he wouldn't last.

"With Ron, you can tell exactly where he's going, and that's straight to the top."

"My goal is to be the best," Ron Hextall said. "I don't expect to get there overnight, but that's what I'm striving for eventually.

"The [fan] attention is nice, but it isn't what I'm playing for. As an athlete, you have to keep it all in perspective. I've seen players who let a little success go to their heads. They usually wind up as one-year players.

"I don't want to be a one-year player. I want to stick around a while. I enjoy the game. My father played a long time, and when he retired, I could see how he missed the [hockey] life. I want to last; I want to make my mark.

"What I've done so far is a good start," Hextall said, "but that's all it is, a start. I've still got a long way to go."

Epilogue: On December 8, 1987, Ron Hextall became the first goalie in NHL history to score a goal by actually shooting the puck into the opposing team's net. On April 11, 1989, he became the first goalie to score a goal in a Stanley Cup playoff game.

*Originally published in the *Philadelphia Daily News*, November 13, 1986. Reprinted with permission by Philadelphia Newspapers, LLC.

They're Already Champions*

One more game remains to be played. One more chapter in a novel we can't put down. The icemen will goeth, one way or the other, Sunday night.

But no matter who wins this Stanley Cup final, the Flyers and the Edmonton Oilers have given us a series to remember and cherish. It is so glorious, you are almost willing to forgive them for playing hockey on May 31.

The next time someone tells you this is a third-rate sport, plug in the VCR and replay the final twenty minutes of last night's game at the Spectrum. That one period of hockey had more drama and raw emotion than a whole decade of Super Bowls.

There were no fights, no slashes across the ankles, no sticks and gloves littering the ice. Just the top two teams in the NHL trying to settle the question of who's best. And it was beautiful.

If the NHL is serious about selling its product to the masses, put this game on prime time and let the folks in El Paso and Palm Beach see what real hockey looks like. If this doesn't pull them away from NASCAR and the PGA Senior Tour, nothing will.

"It was exciting just to be a part of it," Flyers defenseman Brad Marsh said. "The intensity was unbelievable. It just seemed to build with every shift. All you could do was keep pushing."

There were the Oilers, with the great Wayne Gretzky, trying to hang on to a 2–1 lead. The Flyers were coming at them, wave after exhausted wave, summoning strength from who knows where.

Meanwhile, the clock bled down to the last seven minutes.

"I looked at the time," Flyers executive vice president Keith Allen said, "and I wondered, 'Geez, can we do it again?' How many times can you come back against a team like Edmonton?

"But there's something about these [Flyers] kids. You know they'll never quit, so you just keep hoping for that one break."

Last night, it came in the form of a Pelle Eklund pass to Brian Propp for a bull's-eye that tied the score, 2–2. Then, one minute and twenty-four seconds later, J. J. Daigneault slapped the puck past Grant Fuhr, and the Flyers had escaped the gallows, again.

This was the second consecutive game in which the Flyers staked the Oilers to a 2–0 lead and survived. They came from three goals down for their other win, 5–3, in game three.

Don't bother quoting them the odds on such a thing. Frankly, they don't want to know. It might break the spell.

"It's like someone is watching over us," winger Scott Mellanby said. "It's like fate or something."

"We've been lucky, no question," defenseman Mark Howe said, "but we've made some of our own luck, too. It's amazing how many things go your way when you keep working."

Daigneault's goal is a perfect example. The young defenseman was turning to come off the ice when Howe waved from the bench for him to stay on. "I was just out there for two minutes," Howe said. "I had to catch my breath."

If Daigneault had not paused to look at the bench, he would have been well inside the Edmonton zone when Jari Kurri threw that blind pass back toward the blue line. Chances are it would have skittered harmlessly into center ice, and we might still be in overtime.

But because Daigneault was a split second late trailing the play, he was in perfect position to read Kurri's pass, line it up, and one-time it past Fuhr for the game winner.

You don't try to explain breaks like that. You just stick them in your pocket and keep skating. Let someone else find the logic in all this. Maybe we will understand after game seven. Then again, maybe we won't.

These Flyers still may not wind up with their names engraved on the Stanley Cup. They could lose Sunday in the Northlands Coliseum, but their legacy in this town is secure. These Flyers will be remembered as champions, and rightly so.

They fought their way through three playoff rounds despite a casualty list that included Dave Poulin, Tim Kerr, and Ron Sutter. They eliminated Montreal, the defending Stanley Cup champion, despite falling behind in four of the six games.

They faced elimination themselves in game five at Edmonton, staring at a two-goal deficit, but they fought back to win, 4–3, and send the Oilers' fans home with the confetti still stuffed in their pockets.

"You can't put your finger on one quality this team has," said general manager Bobby Clarke. "It's a lot of things. Tremendous desire, a ton of guts. I'm just so proud of what these kids have accomplished."

Clarke's eyes swept the dressing room, full of eager young faces, some still a little dazed by it all. "They deserve the credit," Clarke said. "They had all the excuses in the world to quit, and they wouldn't do it. Look at the players we lost [with injuries].

"You take Gretzky and [Mark] Messier away from the Oilers, and how would they have done?"

"This is probably the greatest comeback ever in the NHL," said Chico Resch, backup goalie and historian. "I went back in the record books, and I can't find another team that has had to overcome as much as we have in these playoffs.

"I might go back to Montreal the first year they won it with Ken Dryden [then a rookie] in goal. But the Canadiens had a great team. You look at this series on paper, and the Oilers should be blowing us out, especially when they keep getting the lead."

For all of the thousands of teams that talk about "character," there are precious few that really know what it means.

The original Stanley Cup Flyers knew, and these Flyers have picked it up. Certain things, it seems, are handed down.

"This is the proudest team I've ever played for," said defenseman Doug Crossman. "I think that's where it all starts. . . . [T]he pride that goes with the Flyer tradition.

"I remember watching the Flyers win their first two Cups when I was growing up. They were the toughest, hardest-working team in the league. They set a standard, and those guys are still around. I'm talking about Bob Clarke, Bernie Parent, Bill Barber [both coaches].

"You walk in this [dressing] room, and you can feel it," Crossman said. "That tradition is in the air. It wasn't anything like that when I played in Chicago. I was there three seasons, and I only met one [former] Blackhawk. That was Stan Mikita.

"The only reason I met Stan was he worked as a golf pro. There was no pride there, not like here. When we get down like we did tonight, it's something we draw on. That's the well we dip into.

"It's amazing how deep it is."

Is there one good scoop of adrenaline left in that orange-and-black well? We will find out Sunday.

"How many of these [comebacks] can your heart stand?" someone asked Keith Allen.

"Just one more," he replied.

One more is all it will take.

Epilogue: The Flyers lost game seven in Edmonton, 3–1. Ron Hextall, the Flyers' rookie goalie, played so valiantly that he won the Conn Smythe Trophy as the Most Valuable Player in the series.

*Originally published in the *Philadelphia Daily News*, June 1, 1987. Reprinted with permission by Philadelphia Newspapers, LLC.

THE SIXERS

Moses Makes His Private Life Most Valuable*

Moses Malone was peering out from behind that invisible wall, his eyes narrowed, his heavy bass voice rumbling way back there in the distance.

"Got nothin' to say," Malone said.

The Sixers had just finished practice at St. Joseph's University, and a newsman was trying to arrange a one-on-one interview with the NBA's Most Valuable Player.

Malone, who moments before was laughing with his teammates, had slipped on his public face. It is the face he wears through airports and hotel lobbies to discourage autograph seekers. It is not full of warmth.

"Talk to somebody else," Malone said.

"The story is supposed to be about you," the newsman said.

Malone shook his head. He was dropping his gear into his equipment bag. As far as he was concerned, the conversation was over.

"But the people in Philadelphia don't know much about you," the man said.

"I was in Houston six years," Malone said. "They don't know me there, either. I like it that way."

"Why?"

Malone shrugged. "Just do," he said.

With that, Moses Malone was gone, brushing silently past the students and fans waiting outside the Field House.

A week later, Lee Fentress, Malone's lawyer, asked the All-Star center to do the interview. Malone refused.

"Lee Fentress works for me," Malone said. "I don't work for Lee Fentress."

Billy Cunningham talked to Malone, then club president Harold Katz. Still, no interview.

"Moses," Cunningham said, "is his own man."

Finally, the newsman asked Malone's wife, Alfreda, if she would consent to an interview. She paused before answering.

"I'll have to talk it over with Moses," she said.

The next day, Alfreda conveyed her regrets.

"Moses wants his private life kept private," she said. "I'm sorry."

What is it with Moses Malone, anyway?

At twenty-eight, he earns $2.2 million a year. In Philadelphia, he has found the adulation—and the supporting cast—that was denied him in other cities. He is just three wins away from an NBA championship.

He should be riding this moment as if it were a float in the Rose Bowl parade, waving and blowing kisses, sharing himself with the masses. But that isn't Moses Malone's style. Never was, never will be.

Moses is there, yet he is not there. At the Spectrum, he walks expressionless through his pre-game standing ovation. He waits, head down, for the cheers to subside. Does he hear it? Does he care?

With the Sixers in the NBA finals, Malone finds he must deal with the media horde he waved off most of the season. Even so, Malone makes it clear he is available only on his terms.

He answers questions after games, but he keeps it all within the realm of basketball. The moment someone reaches beyond that, probing for his psyche, Moses frowns and slams the door.

A writer once described Malone as "either painfully shy, painfully rude or both." His coaches and teammates, here and around the league, like the man but admit they don't know him very well.

Malone is the game's premier center—indeed, its dominant player—yet he is back there, behind the moat, behind the wall, leaving us all to wonder just what it is that drives him.

To understand Moses Malone, friends say, you first have to understand where he comes from.

He was born and raised in Petersburg, Virginia. Not in the Old Towne area, with its cobblestone streets and historic landmarks. Not in Walnut Hill, with its shady drives and stately white columns.

Moses Malone grew up on St. Matthews Street in the Heights, two doors from Johnny Byrd's grocery store. Johnny Byrd has been held up and shot at so many times, he now works the cash register with a .38 strapped to his hip. A tough place, the Heights.

Moses's father left when Moses was two years old. Mary Malone put him out, folks say, because he took to drinking too much. That left Mary alone to raise Moses the best she could. Like everything else in her life, it came hard.

Mary Malone worked days as a packer at the local Safeway, and she worked nights as a nurses' aide. She brought home $100 a week. It was enough for food and clothes for Moses, but not much else.

They lived in a tumbledown frame house where quite often the plumbing didn't work and, for a while, there was a big hole in the wall where a window was supposed to be.

The living room was decorated with portraits of the Kennedy brothers, Martin Luther King, and Jesus. The only literature on hand was a Bible passed down from Mary's father. The Malones didn't have much, but what they had said a lot about who they were.

"Mary is a very proud woman with a strong sense of what's right and wrong," said Pro Hayes, the assistant coach at Petersburg High and Moses's longtime father figure.

"She raised Moses as well as a child can be raised in those surroundings. She gave him love, and she gave him the values he needed to survive on the Heights.

"A kid can go either way there, real good or real bad. Moses turned out good. It wasn't because he could play basketball; it was because of what he was. Moses is a good person."

"I've seen a lot of poverty, traveling through Alabama and Mississippi, but Moses's situation was the worst," said Smokey Gaines, the coach at San Diego State, who recruited Moses as a high-school senior.

"I was an assistant under Dick Vitale [of the University of Detroit] then. One night, we went over to Moses's house, and there was a pack of wild dogs around. There must have been twenty-five of them, all jumping up, snapping at the car. Vitale was scared to death.

"It was a tough neighborhood. Guys hanging on the corner, drinking all night. You put a kid there with no father, no brothers or sisters, he's gonna be tested to the max. And Moses was, every day."

Malone wasn't a great natural athlete. A boyhood friend, David Pair, recalls that when Moses first came around the Virginia Avenue schoolyard to play basketball, the older kids used to run him off.

"He had the height and the long arms, but he had bad hands," said Pair, who still lives one block from the school. "You'd pass him the ball, and it would hit him in the chest. Guys would say, `Mo, go sit down.'"

But he kept working at it. He would stay out after dark, shooting baskets by the streetlights. Johnny Byrd recalls locking up his store one night at 2 A.M. and hearing this rhythmic pounding around the corner. It was Moses working on his hook shot.

"Kids in the neighborhood say Moses slept with his basketball," Byrd said. "Could be."

Moses made the Petersburg High varsity as a freshman. In his first game, he scored thirty points in an upset of Midlothian. Another time, he out-scored and out-rebounded the entire Dinwiddie High team.

"Unheard of," coach Carl Peal said.

As a junior and senior, Moses led Petersburg to fifty consecutive wins and two state championships. Suddenly, this quiet kid from the Heights—the one his classmates nicknamed "Jughead"—became the most sought-after prep athlete in the country.

"At first, it was like a game," said David Mitchell, a former classmate, now a disc jockey at WPLZ-FM in Petersburg. "All these big coaches coming around. Norm Sloan. Lefty Driesell. Dick Vitale.

"But then it got out of hand. Every day, there were eight, maybe ten of them at the house. I'd drive Mo home, and he'd recognize their cars. He'd say,

`Take me around the back.' He'd sneak through the rear window, then lay on the floor with the lights off.

"Then the news media got into it. They had camera crews coming to the house at all hours, banging on the door. Mo tried going over to David Pair's house, but they found him there, too. It was hard on Mo and Mary both."

The recruiting of Moses Malone is legendary. One coach lived in a Petersburg motel for a month. Another left a new car parked outside the Malone house. In other words, "This is yours, Mo, if you want it."

Malone visited twenty-four colleges. Many fixed him up with dates while he was there. When he returned home, the girls would call long distance. "They'd pretend to be in love with me," Moses said. "What kinda stuff is that?"

Mary Malone wound up with an ulcer. Oral Roberts, the evangelical faith healer, came along and promised to cure her if her son would play basketball for dear old Oral Roberts U.

Is it any wonder the Malones became cynical?

What few people knew was that Moses had made a promise to himself: He was going to be the first player to go straight from high school to pro basketball. He wrote a note to that effect following his junior year, and he stuck it inside his mother's bible.

Mary Malone didn't like the idea; she wanted her son to go to college. But one night, the American Basketball Association's Utah Stars came in and spread $100 bills across her kitchen table. For the first time, Mary saw her way out of the Heights.

"Maybe you're right," she said.

A few days later, Moses Malone signed a seven-year, $3 million ABA contract, and the American college system cried rape.

Political columnists such as Carl Rowan, who knew nothing about Mary Malone's medical bills and the plumbing that didn't work, passed moral judgment.

"Moses can race up and down that basketball floor for a few years," Rowan wrote, "provided his knees don't give out. . . . But when some new hotshot comes along to replace him, he'll discover he has no other way of making a living.

"How pitiable those once super jocks are, who exploited their brawn and ignored their brains and . . . go blabbering about, hardly capable of putting one meaningful sentence together."

Rowan's reaction was typical. Moses was a big dummy who didn't have the brains to go to college, people said. It was the kid's first taste of criticism. It went down hard.

"Moses is very sensitive," Pro Hayes said, "and the things that were said about him hurt. But I told him, `Moses, you have to follow your heart. Do what you feel is right.'

"The strongest influence, I believe, was his desire to make a better life for Mary. He didn't want her to struggle anymore. He thought, `Why should I wait four [college] years when I can help her now?'

"Tell me," Pro Hayes said, "can you criticize a man for that?"

Malone took his $100,000 bonus and bought his mother a nice rancher in the suburb of Ettrick. He had the Stars guarantee her $500 a month so she would not have to bag groceries anymore.

Then he took a deep breath and headed for Salt Lake City, where they already were posting "Moses Will Lead Us" billboards around town. He was six-foot-eleven with a thirty-nine–inch sleeve, so it was easy to overlook one important detail.

He was only eighteen years old.

You know what it's like to be an eighteen-year-old black millionaire in Salt Lake City? It's many things, almost all of them strange and lonely.

Malone lived in a hotel across the street from the arena. His only friends were his teammates, but they were married and settled in the suburbs.

So Moses stayed in his room, watching TV and listening to his stereo. He always was shy with strangers, but the media blitz that descended on him in the ABA made matters worse.

He spoke softly and rapidly, with syllables clipped Southern-style here and there. In the Heights, Moses got by just fine. But in Utah, it was as if he was speaking a foreign tongue.

A Salt Lake disc jockey nicknamed him "Mumbles." The name stuck. Malone pulled back even further into his shell. He would look out his hotel window at night and wonder, "What am I doing here?"

"It was very hard for Moses, being that young, that far away from home, and under that kind of pressure," said Tom Nissalke, the Utah coach. "He wouldn't even look me in the eye.

"I finally had to demand it. We had a timeout one night, and he was staring at the floor, like always. I said, `Moses, look at me.' That's how withdrawn he was."

The next year, Malone's world began to crumble. He broke his foot, then the Utah franchise folded. He was claimed by the Spirits of St. Louis. Then the ABA went out of business.

His rights were acquired by Portland in the dispersal draft, then traded to Buffalo. He lasted one week with the Braves. Coach Tates Locke decided Moses couldn't play in the NBA.

Nissalke, then with Houston, acquired Malone for a number-one draft choice in 1977. That made five pro teams in three seasons—a lot of turmoil for a kid fresh out of high school.

"I'm sure those years left a scar on Mo," Nissalke said. "He learned early that you're just a piece of luggage in this business. You get shipped here, shipped there."

"Even though Mo settled down and had a great career in Houston, he never forgot how he came up. If he seems a little wary now, he has his reasons."

"The people who call Moses aloof and arrogant don't understand him," Pro Hayes said. "He just wants to be left alone to play ball and listen to his music. He doesn't like a lot of hustle and bustle.

"You've gotta realize what it's been like for him. Ever since high school, he's had people grabbing at him. Do this, do that, sign here. Everybody has an angle. Most of them are just out to take advantage.

"When he was here, I'd talk to him every day," Hayes said. "I'd tell him, `Moses, you can't go through life not trusting people.' He'd listen, then he'd run into a [college] recruiter who'd offer him something under the table, and we'd be right back at square one.

"Moses keeps people at arm's length now, at least until he has time to size them up. If he likes them, they're his friend for life. If he finds he can't trust them, forget it. He'll drop `em like dead flies."

David Pair smiled. "People think Moses is what?" he asked.

"Aloof," he was told.

Pair shook his head.

They are still best friends, Moses and Pair. Even though Moses has two homes and seven automobiles, and Pair remains tied to the Heights, nothing between them has changed.

"When the season is over," said Pair, thirty-two, the four-time Virginia state judo champion, "Moses comes back here. He says, `Let's get something to eat.' So we go to the Fish House.

"That's the same place we went fifteen years ago. All you can eat for $3. Last year, we went and Moses ate twenty-four pieces of fish. Ran the poor waitress half to death.

"After that, we rounded up the old gang—Jimmy Snake and that crowd— and we played ball. Moses was there in the schoolyard, fooling around. Does that sound like a guy who's aloof?"

Malone's loyalty runs deep. When he signed his offer sheet with the Sixers, he phoned Mitchell in the WPLZ studio at 6 A.M. so his old classmate could break the story.

When Pair got married last year, Malone flew in from Houston to serve as best man. He spent the ceremony looking down on the five-foot-seven Pair, saying, "You're short, man. . . . When you gonna grow?"

"Even the minister was laughing," Pair recalled.

Moses recently bought a new home for his mother. This one is tucked away in exclusive Chesterfield County, with a circular drive, an electronic gate, and two acres of trees out back.

She still drives back to St. Matthew Street every so often just to remember what it was like before her son found his way to the offensive boards.

"The thing I admire about Moses is he earned everything he's got," David Pair said. "Nobody gave him nothin'. He came out here and worked every night on his game.

"I used to come over and keep him company. We'd be shooting free throws at midnight, talking. I was a big Wilt Chamberlain fan. I had a poster of him hanging up in my house.

"One time Moses said, `How come you like Wilt so much?' I said, `Because he's the best.' Moses said, `Someday I'm gonna be the best.' I said, `OK, when you're the best, I'll put your poster up.'"

There is now a Moses Malone poster hanging on David Pair's bedroom wall. It is autographed, naturally. Neighborhood kids line up to see it, as if it were a religious shrine.

"Moses don't have to say much around here," David Pair said. "He lets his game talk for him."

Epilogue: Moses Malone led the 76ers to the NBA title in 1983. He was named Most Valuable Player in the regular season and playoffs. In 2001, he was inducted into the Basketball Hall of Fame. He died in 2015 at the age of sixty.

*Originally published in the *Philadelphia Daily News*, May 26, 1983. Reprinted with permission by Philadelphia Newspapers, LLC.

This One's for You, Jack McMahon*

This one's for you, Jack McMahon. This one is for the ten years you've spent with the Sixers and the thousands of lonely miles you've traveled in search of an NBA championship.

This is for the night you spent driving from El Paso to Canyon, Texas, to watch a guard named Maurice Cheeks. This is for the expedition you took through the Louisiana bayous to find a wonder named Andrew Toney.

This is for the night you talked your way into a crowded high-school gym in Orlando, Florida, to see Darryl Dawkins. This is for the snowstorm you drove through to see Franklin Edwards play at Cleveland State.

This is for all the two-lane highways you traveled with a road map in your lap and a college game on the radio. This is for the countless hours of film that you watched and the nights you ate your dinner out of a motel vending machine.

Lord knows, it hasn't been easy. There were too many weekends away from Kay and the children, for one thing. Then there was the heart attack that almost put you away three years ago. And, of course, there are the kids like Monti Davis, who just don't pan out.

But that's OK. On Tuesday night, when Maurice Cheeks slam-dunked that ball with one second left and brought the NBA title to Philadelphia, you knew it was all worthwhile. All the camps, all the hick towns, all the musty little gyms, all of it.

Piece by piece, you helped build this championship team, and so you looked on, smiling, as the champagne sprayed the Forum locker room and wiped clean the memory of "We Owe You One."

You didn't need the CBS-TV spotlight or the public adulation. You had the moment, Jack, and that was enough.

"For me, the satisfaction lies in seeing these kids like Maurice and Andrew become world champions," said McMahon, fifty-three, the Sixers' assistant coach and player personnel director.

"I've seen them from the beginning. I've watched them develop and gain confidence. I've seen them become All-Stars and now champions. In a sense, it's like watching your own children grow up.

"Maurice was a three-time All-Missouri Valley player. The only other guy who did that was Oscar Robertson, who played for me in Cincinnati. I figured anybody who could be in Oscar's class deserved a look.

"So I went to see him in Canyon, Texas. That's where his school, West Texas State, is located. Did you ever try to find Canyon, Texas? It's not easy. You go to El Paso and make a left, then just keep going. I was thinking, `This kid better be worth it.'

"He was impressive," McMahon said. "The coach didn't allow anybody to shoot past fifteen feet, so I couldn't tell what kind of touch he had. But he handled the ball well, played tough defense, and went real hard to the basket.

"We had a tryout camp in Cincinnati before the draft, and we brought Maurice in. Billy [Cunningham] liked him very much. We agreed he was the kind of kid who would get even better when he was surrounded by better players.

"We didn't have a first-round pick that year, so we had to keep our fingers crossed and hope nobody took Maurice ahead of us. No one did, and we got an All-Star guard on the second round.

"With Andrew," McMahon said, "I saw him as a junior [with Southwestern Louisiana University] when he played at Arizona State. I was looking at other players, but he jumped out at me. He didn't have a particularly good game, but he had that great frame.

"I made a note to check back on him. The next year, I went to the Cajun Classic, and he had an easy thirty-one the first game. He was much smoother; he was putting things together. The next day, he had forty-eight. Couldn't miss.

"There were a lot of good prospects in that draft, but Doug [Collins] was having so many physical problems, we felt we needed insurance at guard. We took Andrew, and he has turned out to be a great one.

"It might seem like a lot, all this traveling, but I love it. The travel only seems long when you go someplace and the guy you're scouting turns out to be a stiff. Then you say, `Why did I bother?'

"But if you go somewhere and find an Andrew Toney, that's like finding buried treasure. It's exciting. I can't imagine ever tiring of it."

Jack McMahon has been around pro basketball for thirty years now.

He played five seasons with the St. Louis Hawks, teaming with the great Bob Pettit, Cliff Hagan, and Slater Martin.

The Hawks went to the championship finals twice. In 1957, they took Boston to the limit, losing a seventh game in double overtime.

"I still think about that one," McMahon admits.

The next year, the Hawks beat Boston in six.

McMahon broke into coaching with the Cincinnati Royals, featuring Oscar Robertson and Jack Twyman.

"We won a lot of games," McMahon said, "but we could never win a championship. We didn't have the big guy. Our center was Wayne Embry, and he was only six-foot-seven."

After Cincinnati, McMahon joined the expansion San Diego Rockets as coach and general manager. The owner was a nice fellow but a little short on basketball sense.

"One day, he said, 'It looks like our players can't shoot, rebound, or play defense,'" McMahon recalled. "I said, 'If they could shoot, rebound, or play defense, they wouldn't be in an expansion draft.'"

McMahon's next NBA stop was the Chicago Zephyrs. The owner there was in the insurance business. When the Zephyrs were losing, he had his actuarial staffers work on the problem.

They came up with a computer printout of every Zephyr, with points and minutes played projected over four quarters. The owner told McMahon to follow this printout in the next game.

"He said if I used the players at the designated times, we would score 159 points," McMahon said. "I asked the [general manager], 'Is this guy serious?' He said, 'Yeah, Jack, I'm afraid he is.'

"Next game, I'm there with my printout, and the guy I'm supposed to lift blocks two shots and runs six points. What am I gonna do? I leave him in. I told my assistant, 'I probably just blew my job.'"

McMahon was right. He was fired a few days later. He bounced through the ABA with Pittsburgh and Kansas City before finding his way to the Sixers in 1973 as a scout.

"That was when we were 9–73," McMahon recalled. "Back then, we talked about someday just being competitive. Now here we are, ten years later, and we have one of the all-time great teams.

"I'm as happy as I've ever been. This is a great bunch of guys. No ego problems. They all like each other, and they work hard. They're fun to be around. There's no reason to believe this team can't stay on top for a while.

"I want to stay a part of it. You know, three of the four coaches in the semifinals played for me. Billy played for me here; Pat Riley played for me in San Diego; and Don Nelson played for me in Chicago.

"The only one who didn't play for me was Stan Albeck, and he didn't play [in the NBA]. It makes me feel good, seeing these guys come along."

He watches college kids grow into NBA stars; then he watches them grow into NBA coaches. Doesn't it ever make him feel old?

Jack McMahon laughed. "You don't get older in this business," he said. "Only smarter."

Epilogue: Jack McMahon died on June 11, 1989, at age sixty.

*Originally published in the *Philadelphia Daily News*, June 2, 1983. Reprinted with permission by Philadelphia Newspapers, LLC.

Erving Can't Make Sense of It All*

This isn't the way Julius Erving envisioned his distinguished career winding down, playing with a pickup team known loosely as the Philadelphia 76ers.

Can't you see the Doctor in his farewell address at the Spectrum next spring saying, "I'd like to thank the players who were here in our 1983 championship season. Bobby Jones, Andrew Toney, Moses Malone . . .

"And I'd like to acknowledge the guys I played with this season. Charles Barkley, Maurice Cheeks and . . . uh . . . Give me a minute, folks. I know the other names will come to me."

Erving spent yesterday like the rest of us, trying to make sense of the Sixers' remodeling. They traded Moses Malone, two first-round picks in this draft [including the number one overall], their top pick from last year [Terry Catledge], and a first-round choice in 1988.

For that, they received Roy Hinson, a six-foot-nine swingman; Jeff Ruland, a center who missed ninety-seven games the last two seasons due to injury; and Cliff Robinson, a forward who has been shipped around the league so often his nickname should be Federal Express.

General manager Pat Williams says these deals helped the Sixers "close the gap" on Boston. If you saw the Celtics' general manager, Red Auerbach, on TV yesterday, you saw how concerned he was. Red almost burst out laughing when the deals were mentioned.

"If I were Philadelphia," Auerbach said, "I'd be a little concerned about [team] chemistry."

Of course, Auerbach isn't Philadelphia, so he isn't concerned at all. Erving is Philadelphia—he has been for ten seasons, and he hopes to be for one more—but after yesterday he doesn't know what to think.

He had hoped to play his final season with a healthy Malone and Toney, a re-signed Cheeks, and a blue-chip rookie, Brad Daugherty. The Doctor felt that lineup, along with Barkley, could challenge for another NBA title. It would be a team with talent and something to prove.

But now Erving, thirty-six, is a free agent surrounded by five other veteran free agents (including Cheeks) and a lot of young players he hardly knows. He is a legend but a legend without a contract or any sense of what might come next.

"I'm waiting for the next move," Erving said as the shock of yesterday's events sank in. "One wave has gone by. I have to think another is coming.

"I don't know what it will be. We [the players] aren't consulted. It's all in management's hands. We can only assume they have a master plan. At least, we hope they have a plan."

The Doctor was unable to reach Moses Malone by phone yesterday, but he will keep trying. He wants to thank the big man for helping the Sixers to the title. Too many things go unsaid in the course of a season.

Erving and Malone are different personalities, but they would not have won their championship rings without each other. It is a bond they will always share, and when Moses said he wanted to stick around for Doc's final season, he meant it.

It is ironic that the last time they were together as Sixers was during the NBA Championship Series, when they went on CBS and aired their views on management. It has been theorized that Malone's remarks might have prompted owner Harold Katz to unload him.

"I doubt it," Erving said. "We didn't say anything to alienate the organization. I made a few comments [referring to Sixer `mismanagement'] but nothing inflammatory.

"At this point, I'm a little disappointed with the organization. I don't feel the people in the front office have been totally candid. They put out the party line Moses wasn't being shopped around the league, then they traded him.

"It creates a credibility gap, especially for a guy like me, who's out on a limb. They said repeatedly they intend to re-sign me, but who knows? I made my intentions known [about playing another season] in February, but I don't feel I've been dealt with fairly at all.

"I'm not angry at Harold personally," Erving said, "but it pains me because I feel after all these years I deserve better. I realize my role won't be what it was eight to ten years ago, but I can bring stability and leadership to the team."

It is clear the Sixers' brass fell in love with the team that finished the season. They liked the up-tempo offense, with everyone handling the ball. The half-court game with Malone banging in the low post wasn't coach Matt Guokas's style.

It was a different team after Malone went down with his eye injury on March 28: quicker and more entertaining. But was it a better team?

Put it this way: The new-look Sixers struggled past Washington and were eliminated by Milwaukee in the playoffs. The season before, with Malone, the Sixers took the Bullets and Bucks out easily, seven games to one.

Also consider that Malone ranked first among NBA centers with a 23.8 scoring average last season. He was second among centers to Detroit's Bill Laimbeer in rebounds (11.8). Moses wasn't pretty, but he got the job done.

Ruland, by contrast, played in just thirty games. He suffered three different injuries—shoulder, foot, knee—and was replaced by seven-foot-seven Manute Bol.

"The perception that our team was better and more cohesive without Moses is wrong," Erving said.

"People rallied behind us because we overachieved. But if we had Moses, I feel we would have beaten Milwaukee and offered the only real challenge to Boston.

"This [trade] creates a void. Moses was the cog at the center of the wheel. Take him out and it leaves the spokes hanging. The rest of us will have to distribute the weight."

The revised game plan calls for Barkley, Hinson, and Robinson rotating at forward, with Ruland and Clem Johnson at center.

The Doctor will set up practice full time in the back court, along with Cheeks. The guard role is fine, Erving said.

He has started working out already. He knows this team will live or die by the fast break. Ruland needs swift guards to make his outlet pass effective. Doc will have to sprint this final lap around the NBA.

"That doesn't bother me," Erving said. "Physically, I'll be ready. I'm more concerned with the team. There are so many `ifs.' I hate to speculate, because [management] might not be done making moves.

"If I were to view the trades now, I'd say they are very risky. Cliff and Jeff are good players; Roy is a talent, but Moses has established himself as one of the all-time greats. He has the numbers to prove it.

"Moses gave us stability inside. The only time he was injured was a freak thing [a poke in the eye]. It isn't like he broke down. Jeff is a [physical] question mark. Can he still play an entire season? I hope so.

"And Cliff is a good player, but you have to wonder why he has moved around so much [five NBA teams since 1981]. These are all the things that are going through my mind.

"I didn't expect any of this," Erving said. "I thought we'd keep the number-one pick, select Daugherty, and take a big guard [number 21]. I thought the wheeling and dealing would come later on. Shows what I know.

"I'm surprised, but I'm not stunned. That's the business. Life goes on. I'm just glad I got to play with Moses as long as I did. I look back on that [title] team now, and I realize how great it was.

"It's a shame," the Doctor said, "we can't make those times last."

Epilogue: This will be remembered as the day the Sixers' front office drove the team bus off a cliff. The trades, which looked ridiculous at the time, proved to be even worse than that. The Sixers went from a fifty-eight–win team in 1986–87 to an NBA bottom feeder in just two years.

*Originally published in the *Philadelphia Daily News*, June 18, 1986. Reprinted with permission by Philadelphia Newspapers, LLC.

Barkley Uncomfortable with Life in the Glare of the Spotlight*

Charles Barkley's world came into focus last week as he commuted between NBA playoff sites.

He was a hero when he boarded the plane in Philadelphia. He was a public enemy when he touched down in Milwaukee. Two cities, two passions, same guy.

"Don't make sense to me," Barkley said.

Fame is like that sometimes. That's why the 76ers' star forward doesn't trust it much. Matter of fact, he doesn't trust it at all.

Sure, Barkley will toy with fame now and then; he'll wear it around like a Halloween costume, but he knows better than to live in it. He tried that once, at Auburn, and it taught him a lesson.

Barkley was a big man on campus in every sense of the word. He was an All-America basketball player and cartoon character rolled (literally, some would say) into one.

He was six-foot-six and 280 pounds. The Round Mound of Rebound, Boy Gorge. Auburn's sports publicist had him pose for pictures stuffing down pizza. All those people smiling; Charles thought they meant it.

His junior year, Barkley hurt his back. He tried to play but he couldn't run or jump. Fans grumbled about the "fat boy." Barkley watched the bandwagon empty, and he could hear his mother's voice in the background.

"Just remember," Charcey Glenn told her son when the accolades were pouring in, "the only part of this that's real is you." Charles didn't understand what she meant until now.

Barkley came back to win Player of the Year honors in the Southeast Conference, and folks gave him the old "we-were-with-you-all-the-way" routine. He knew better, of course. He still does.

That's why he is careful to keep his newfound NBA celebrity at arm's length. That's why he will leave the cheering crowd in the Spectrum and drive to his City Line apartment alone. That's why he will occasionally shut himself off from the media.

"That's not a real world I'm living in," Barkley said during a rare break in the Milwaukee series, a seven-game war that he threatened to win single-handedly.

"I'm a success, yeah, but for how long? It could end any day. I could wreck my knee tomorrow, then what? I have one thing I can count on, and that's my family. They'll be there for me, win or lose. The rest of this is all superficial.

"It's like wrapping paper," Barkley said. "It looks pretty on the outside, but you can't see what's underneath. It might be nothing but an empty box."

The Milwaukee series was a bitter experience for Barkley, not merely because the Sixers lost by a point in game seven, but because he was at the center of so much hostility.

The Bucks fans chanted obscenities at Barkley in game one; they threw coins at him in game five. Every time Barkley spoke ("They can kiss me where the sun don't shine"), the fire grew. Finally, Barkley stopped talking.

"The type of player Charles is," Sixers general manager Pat Williams said, "he'll have to learn to deal with that. He stirs people's emotions, pro and con."

"I don't try to rile the fans," Barkley said. "I'm not out there showboating, I'm just playing my game. If they don't like it . . ."

He shrugged.

Barkley remembers what it was like in college. Fans in visiting arenas threw pizza boxes at him during warm-ups. That got old in a hurry. The Milwaukee chorus falls into the same category.

"There are two things I hate," Barkley said. "The first thing is losing. I hate to lose at anything.

"The second thing I hate is people who don't treat us like human beings. They think we're machines or robots; they act like we have no feelings. I have feelings the same as anyone else.

"It bothers me when people shout stuff," Barkley said. "You should hear the things [fans] call me. And if I get mad, the press writes what a bad guy I am. It's like they build you up just so they can cut you down."

The worst thing, Barkley said, is when he is with his girlfriend, Donna Gerard, who is white, and people make racial remarks. His impulse is to "knock 'em out." Only Donna's peacemaking has prevented some nasty incidents.

"That stuff cuts deep," Barkley said, "because I know how it makes her feel.

"There are two sides to being a celebrity. The one side is what everybody sees . . . the money and the TV. The other side is having to deal with ignorant people who think you're public property.

"I might learn to deal with the one side, but I won't never learn to deal with the other."

Pat Williams is a basketball executive with an eye for the unusual.

In years past, Williams has brought to the Spectrum wrestling bears, singing pigs, and clowns. A few were pre-game attractions; the rest were Sixers draft picks.

So it was with considerable delight that on June 19, 1984, Williams introduced Charles Barkley, a Sixers number-one pick who also qualified as a human curiosity.

Williams announced Barkley's selection with a string of one-liners from Joan Rivers's cellulite gag book:

- "When Charles walks down Broad Street, it instantly becomes a one-way street."
- "When Charles goes swimming, we have to worry about him being harpooned."
- "Even his bathtub has stretch marks."
- "Charles came in the office the other day wearing a form-fitting poncho."

No one would have blamed Barkley if he had come back with a line of his own, say, "Take my general manager—please." But he didn't. He politely shrugged it off as "teasing."

Williams didn't have to sell Barkley to the Philadelphia fans, not after they saw the kid play. He had the rim-snapping power of a Darryl Dawkins but a lot more polish.

Barkley was the kind of player who sent a buzz through the crowd just by pulling off his sweats. He moved the 2,240 pound basket support half a foot with one mighty dunk. The last person to do that had been driving a forklift.

Of such feats folk heroes are made.

"How many players," New York coach Hubie Brown asked, "can turn on a crowd and keep it at a steady roar for six or seven minutes? I'm talking home and away. How many players can do that?

"Michael Jordan, Dominique [Wilkins], and this kid. He might be more exciting than any of them because he's so emotional. If you don't enjoy watching Barkley, there's something wrong with you."

This season, Barkley was profiled in *Sports Illustrated* and *Inside Sports*; he was featured at halftime on CBS (he cooked a pizza on camera); and he cut a TV commercial for Nike.

You can now buy a Charles Barkley T-shirt and a Charles Barkley poster, and his attorney, Lance Luchnick, has a dozen promotions on hold, with more offers coming in daily.

If Charles wanted to go all out, he could market himself into a league with Magic Johnson and Air Jordan. Heck, Patrick Ewing has his own line of clothes, and his Knicks had the NBA's worst record.

"Charles could be one of the dominant figures in American sport," Williams said. "In terms of visibility and appeal, he could be right at the top. It's already happening for him, and he's only in his second season.

"Look at what's happened with [the Chicago Bears'] William Perry. He's a phenomenon, and there's no comparison between Perry and Barkley as athletes. It's like the difference in height between City Hall and the Empire State Building.

"Charles might be the most gifted athlete in all of pro sports," Williams said. "Can you think of anyone else with that size, speed, and agility?"

The question is, does Barkley want to become Refrigerator II? Does he really want to appear on the next Bob Hope special and spend his summer signing autographs in car showrooms?

The answer to all the above is a flat no.

Barkley will do a few appearances, but not many. He would rather spend his free time with his family and friends in Leeds, Alabama. He is having the old house refurbished, and his bedroom (now one of five) awaits.

"It's been a long season," Barkley said as the Milwaukee series wound down. "I'm burnt out on basketball. I'm not even going to touch a basketball this summer. I mean it.

"I'm going to ride my bike and play tennis, that's all. I just bought a new racket. If my serve gets any better, I might not come back next season. I might join the tennis tour. McEnroe looks like he's slipping."

Someone asked Barkley when he last played a set of tennis.

"Last night," he said casually.

But the playoffs were still going on. Wasn't Barkley worn to a frazzle by playing forty-plus minutes a game? Wasn't he supposed to rest on his nights off?

"We didn't play hard," he said. "We just hit around. It felt good. Loosened me up. Cleared my head."

Suppose he had twisted an ankle charging the net? Suppose he had disabled himself for the series? Harold Katz might have sought to clear Charles's head with a two-by-four.

"I never think about stuff like that," Barkley said, his eyes wide and innocent. "I think positive."

Charles Barkley is due back in Leeds next week. Diana Seale, the waitress at Old Smokey's Bar-B-Q, knows what that means.

"Two large barbecue sandwiches, a large order of french fries, and a Coke," Seale said.

She has waited on Barkley for three years now; she has the order memorized.

"Not too many folks can handle two barbecues," Seale said.

Barkley can?

"Easy," she replied. "Then he says, `I'd like another . . . but I'm tryin' to cut down.' He has lost weight. I can see that on TV."

"You're a basketball fan?" a visitor asked.

"Not really," Seale said. "I only watch when Charles is on. He's in here every day in the summer, and he's just as nice as he can be.

"He'll sit at that [corner] table for hours and talk to everyone who comes in. He doesn't act like a superstar at all. I tease him, he teases back."

"Success hasn't changed Charles, not as far as I can see," said Billy Copeland, the basketball coach at Leeds High School. "He was always an outgoing kid, easygoing. His personality changed on the court, though."

Barkley returned to Leeds during the NBA All-Star break in February. He had an offer to take part in the slam-dunk competition but declined. He said he'd rather "cool out."

Barkley worked out with the Leeds basketball team one afternoon, then came to the game against rival Shades Valley. Someone asked Copeland if he considered letting Barkley take part in the pre-game warm-up.

Copeland smiled. "Wish I had thought of it," he said. "I would've liked to see their faces when Charles came on the floor. It might have been worth a couple points."

As it was, Leeds lost to Shades Valley by one.

"Leeds is where I feel comfortable," Barkley said. "I don't like big cities. Philadelphia? It's all right. I like it more now than I did last year, but it's still not the same.

"The people in big cities aren't as friendly as the people in Leeds. The [Philadelphia] fans are nice to me because I'm playing well, but that will change if I go bad. It will be like Auburn all over again.

"I'm happiest when I'm home with my family, eating a nice chicken dinner or playing ball with the neighborhood kids in the field across the street."

Last summer, Barkley offered to pay $1 to any kid he could not strike out. He went through all the money in his pocket and finally asked his mother for a loan.

"Stick to basketball, Charles," Glenn said.

Barkley unwinds by watching TV (*The Cosby Show* and *Miami Vice* are his favorites) or by taking in a movie. He enjoys listening to Whitney Houston and Luther Vandross. He favors mellow evenings.

Several writers have portrayed Barkley as a loner. He says that's not the case. It is true he doesn't party every night, but he is hardly a recluse. He has friends in Philadelphia, and they "hang out" from time to time.

Barkley likes to watch baseball. He attends Phillies games whenever he can. He shocked everyone by going to the Brewers game in Milwaukee the night after the Bucks' fans were screaming for his head at the Mecca arena.

Barkley bought a Brewers cap and sat in the upper deck, chatting with the people around him and signing autographs.

"Everyone was real nice," he said. "A few people even apologized for the way the [Bucks] fans were treating me."

"They were probably the same people who were cussing you out at the Mecca," someone said.

"Yeah, probably," he said. "And they'll do it again."

"That's life."

Barkley shook his head. "That's basketball," he said.

Epilogue: Charles Barkley played eight seasons with the Sixers. His number 34 jersey was retired by the club on March 30, 2001. He was inducted into the Basketball Hall of Fame in 2006.

*Originally published in the *Philadelphia Daily News*, May 15, 1986. Reprinted with permission by Philadelphia Newspapers, LLC.

PART TWO

AMERICAN SPORTS AT HOME

AND IN THE WORLD

◆ ◆ ◆

FOOTBALL

Elevating Frankford*

There's a team in Frankford here,
A team that can't be beat.
For them, we surely hold no fear
That they'll ever taste defeat.
—Frankford Yellow Jackets fight song

Once upon a time, the best team in professional football played on a converted horse track in Northeast Philadelphia.

The Frankford Yellow Jackets, that was their name, and in 1926 they defeated every team from the Chicago Bears to the Providence Steam Roller en route to the National Football League championship.

They are virtually forgotten now. Their stadium at Frankford Avenue and Devereaux Street was torn down half a century ago. Today, a car dealership stands where the Yellow Jackets once played. Time has passed; memories have faded.

But one person who remembers fondly is ninety-year-old Bill Hoffman, the last surviving member of the 1926 Yellow Jackets, now retired and living near Allentown, Pennsylvania, with his wife, Dorothy.

"The people in the neighborhood knew who we were," said Hoffman, who played every minute of every game that season at offensive guard and defensive tackle. "We were like celebrities."

Follow the trail through newspaper clippings and record books and you begin to realize that Philadelphia's first pro football franchise was something quite special.

Consider: In their championship year, the Yellow Jackets won fourteen regular-season games. No NFL team equaled that mark until 1972, when the Miami Dolphins went 14–0 in the regular season on their way to the Super Bowl.

The Yellow Jackets shut out eleven opponents in 1926. They blanked Canton, with Jim Thorpe, 17–0. They stopped Duluth, with Ernie Nevers, 10–0. They handed George Halas's Bears their only defeat of the season, 7–6. (Said Halas: "They are quite a team. They tackle like demons.")

The Yellow Jackets lost one game that season, a 7–6 heartbreaker to Providence, but they came back to defeat the Steam Roller in two later meetings, 6–0 and 24–0, to finish with a 14–1–2 record.

It was a colorful team with its own fight song, its own cheerleaders (six young men with megaphones), its own mascot, and a legion of loyal supporters who filled the nine-thousand–seat stadium almost every weekend.

The Yellow Jackets were a neighborhood team, made up largely of area college stars and funded by a group of Frankford businessmen, each of whom kicked in $50 to cover the expenses. There were no millionaire NFL owners in those days and certainly no millionaire players.

It was a simpler time in pro football.

Today, the local NFL franchise plays on a carpet in South Philadelphia. The owner lives in Miami. The quarterback earns about $3 million a year. The team plays exhibition games in London rather than Clifton Heights (as the Yellow Jackets did).

"I never dreamed the game would get this big," Hoffman said. "I watch it on TV; I read the stories in the newspaper, and I think, `This is the same game I played?' We had no agents, no holdouts, no training camp. We just showed up and played. It was a great life.

"I watch the players today, the way the fans boo them and the [media] picks them apart, and I'm glad I played when I did," said Hoffman, a former Lehigh University standout who played both ways as a five-foot-ten, 225 pound interior lineman.

"We didn't get rich in our day, but we had a lot of fun. We had to love what we were doing or else we wouldn't have lasted. Of course, we won, and winning is fun any time."

In 1926, the National Football League was a barnstorming circuit. Schedules were haphazard. Rosters were shuffled at will. Teams sprang up and vanished in a matter of weeks.

How crazy was it? In `26, the league had a team called the Los Angeles Buccaneers, but it never played a game west of Kansas City. (Commissioner Joe Carr just liked the idea of having a team with a Los Angeles label. He thought it added a touch of glamour.)

Back then, Pennsylvania's Blue Laws prohibited organized athletic activity on Sundays, so the Frankford Yellow Jackets were forced to play their home games on Saturdays.

Other NFL teams preferred to play their home games on Sundays, thus avoiding conflicts with the local colleges. As a result, the Yellow Jackets wound up with a lot of back-to-back bookings.

They would play a home game on a Saturday, then catch a train to, say, Chicago, and play the Cardinals the following day. Considering that the Frankford players went into these Sunday games dragging and their hosts usually were rested and healthy, it's amazing the Yellow Jackets won as often as they did.

In their first six NFL seasons, 1924–29, the Yellow Jackets won sixty-four games, lost twenty-six, and tied thirteen. No other team came close to matching Frankford's win total. (Green Bay was a distant second with forty-eight.)

Granted, the Yellow Jackets' record was skewed by the fact that they played more games than other teams because of their quirky schedule, but, really, that's nitpicking. Frankford's winning percentage over those six seasons was a sparkling .685.

"We got very little rest [on the train], but we knew we had to play the next day, regardless," Hoffman said. "It is surprising we didn't have more serious injuries. We only had eighteen players on the roster. It wasn't like today, with [fresh] players shuttling in and out all the time.

"I hurt my knee once, and the trainer made a brace out of two leather straps. He said, `Here, wear this,' so I did. The knee collapsed two or three more times, but I kept on playing. Later, I found out I had torn cartilage. Today, I'd probably have surgery and be out for the season.

"Everything was different back then," Hoffman said. "Our helmets were leather lined with felt. We didn't have pads in our pants; we had pockets that we stuffed with shredded newspaper, papier-mâché, whatever we could find. If we got a charley horse, we taped it and played.

"It was just part of the game."

The average salary for an NFL player in those days was $150 a game. The superstars, such as Thorpe and Nevers, were paid more, usually a percentage of the gate.

But no one, including the owners, was getting rich.

Most of the Frankford players lived together in boarding houses near the stadium. They ate at the local YMCA and played cards on the front porch at night. Hoffman, then a bachelor from upstate Pennsylvania, was one of the boarders.

"The women baked us cakes," Hoffman said. "The men brought us fresh seafood from Maryland on the weekend. We'd sit outside and talk. We'd play ball with the kids. Everyone had a smile and a kind word for us. We were a part of the community.

"I think that's why we were so successful. We [the players] became like a family because we lived together, and the people in Frankford supported us because we were their friends and neighbors. It made for a college-like atmosphere at our games."

"The Yellow Jackets drew the community together. It was a wonderful thing to see," said Howard Barnes, eighty-one, curator of the Historical Society of Frankford. He attended the games as a teenager with his late father, William.

"On Saturdays, we would walk along Frankford Avenue on our way to the field, and every store would have a sign in the window [saying], `We will be back after the football game.'

"There was a solid wave of humanity surging from the [elevated train] station on Bridge Street to the field. The trolleys were full, and people were hanging onto the sides, chanting and singing.

"We all felt a sense of pride in the team because it made Frankford famous," Barnes said. "The [NFL] standings appeared in newspapers from Los Angeles to London. Really, I have old clippings from the *London Times* showing Frankford in first place, ahead of Chicago, New York, Detroit . . .

"The Yellow Jackets gave us an identity apart from Philadelphia. Frankford was number one at something. You didn't have to be a football fan to feel good about that. The spirit was contagious. Literally everyone in the community was caught up in it."

The Yellow Jackets won with the same basic formula that wins in the NFL today: good players, fine coaching, and a little luck.

Frankford had a solid nucleus, with quarterback Harry Homan (Lebanon Valley), center Bill Springsteen (Lehigh), end Les Asplundh (Swarthmore), halfback Ed Weir (Nebraska), and tackle Swede Youngstrum (Dartmouth). The stumpy Hoffman was one of the league's better run blockers.

In 1925, Guy Chamberlin was hired as the player–coach in Frankford. A strapping six-foot-two, 210 pound end, Chamberlin already had led two teams (Canton and Cleveland) to NFL titles.

He was a free spirit who didn't believe in staying in one place for more than a year or two. He liked new challenges, and the rules of the day—contracts were signed but seldom enforced—allowed him to follow his muse wherever he desired.

By all accounts, Chamberlin was a superb coach, ahead of his time in his ability to organize and conduct a practice. He worked his players hard (sometimes three and a half hours a day), but he developed crisp timing and peerless execution.

Said Hoffman: "We only had a dozen plays. A couple of off-tackle runs and sweeps. Four or five passes, including a screen. A reverse and an end-around. That was it, but we practiced those plays over and over until we could run them in our sleep.

"Chamberlin didn't have any assistant coaches, but he didn't need any. He was a taskmaster like [Vince] Lombardi. He kept us on the field for hours, even in the bitter cold. We couldn't complain, though, because he was out there practicing with us [as a two-way end].

"As a player, Chamberlin was outstanding. He had unusually large hands, so he could catch any ball that came near him, and he had a knack for coming up with the big play when we needed it."

Case in point: Frankford's 1926 showdown with visiting Chicago. The Bears came into the game unbeaten and could have eliminated the Yellow Jackets from title contention by saddling them with their second loss of the year.

Chicago scored a fourth-quarter touchdown to take a 6–0 lead. However, Chamberlin blocked Paddy Driscoll's extra-point attempt, and that proved to be the difference, as Frankford scored a late touchdown and added the conversion for a 7–6 victory.

Chamberlin, who compiled a 56–14–5 record as a coach with four different teams, was elected to the Pro Football Hall of Fame in 1965.

He is the only member of the `26 Yellow Jackets formally enshrined at Canton, Ohio. However, Barnes sent a copy of his scrapbook on the Frankford team to the Hall of Fame, and it now is in the hall's library alongside works on the Packers, Lions, Giants, and so on.

"That's my greatest satisfaction," Barnes said, "knowing that all these [Frankford] players are in the Hall of Fame. Even if it's only in writing, at least they're there.

"They certainly belong."

There was no NFL title game as such until 1933. In the `20s, teams simply played out their schedules, and when the smoke cleared, the one with the best record was declared the champion.

But for the `26 Yellow Jackets, their season finale was tantamount to a title game, since they knew a loss would drop them to second place behind Chicago (12–1–3). Their opponent was rugged Pottsville (10–2–1).

An estimated eight thousand spectators turned out on a frigid December afternoon in Frankford. The game ended in a 0–0 tie. As one newspaper reported: "The feet and hands of the players were numbed by gale-force winds and temperatures near zero. The gridiron was frozen solid."

With the tie, the Yellow Jackets clinched their only league championship. That night, Chamberlin and his players were honored with a dinner at the Benjamin Franklin Hotel. Already, rumors were circulating that Chamberlin was leaving the team.

A reporter cornered Chamberlin at the hotel, and the coach would only say: "It is a long time between now and the next football season. I have no idea what I'll be doing by then."

In truth, Chamberlin was looking around for a team that would pay him more than Frankford. A month later, he signed with the Cardinals as a player–coach, but he had two dismal seasons in Chicago and retired in 1928.

The Yellow Jackets didn't last much longer. They ran short of money after the `29 season, and most of their top players signed elsewhere. The team tried to make a go of it with rookies and walk-ons, but it proved unsuccessful.

The Yellow Jackets bowed out of the NFL midway through the 1931 season after their stadium was left in disrepair because of a lack of funds, coupled with several episodes of vandalism. Interest had waned, and the team played out its final days at a field on Erie Avenue. All that remained were the memories of a year that was.

A new team, the Philadelphia Eagles, came along in 1933, and pretty soon it was hard to find anyone who remembered much about the Yellow Jackets.

One by one, those pioneers passed away. Now Hoffman is the lone survivor. He can't remember the last time he visited Frankford. He says it has been ten years at least, maybe more.

Hoffman played just three seasons of pro football, then quit to take a job with Bethlehem Steel. He worked for the company as a plant supervisor until 1966, when he retired. Now he lives quietly with his wife of sixty-one years, watching the NFL on TV.

"You want to see something?" Hoffman asked a visitor.

He reached into his desk and removed a small box wrapped with a rubber band. He slipped off the band, opened the box, and ever so gently removed what appeared to be a velvet pouch.

Inside the pouch was a handsome silver watch. On the back was engraved: "To The Champions of the National Football League, 1926."

"Every so often, I take it out and look at it," Bill Hoffman said, "just to remember."

Epilogue: Bill Hoffman died in 1994 at age ninety-two.

*Originally published in the *Philadelphia Daily News*, August 29, 1991. Reprinted with permission by Philadelphia Newspapers, LLC.

The Black Athlete: Jackie Robinson? He Wasn't the First*

Marion Motley doesn't follow pro football that closely anymore, so he didn't realize the Philadelphia Eagles have a black head coach and not one, but two, black quarterbacks.

"Is that right?" Motley said. "What's the coach's name? Ray Rhodes? How's he doing?"

Told that Rhodes was doing pretty well in his first season, Motley nodded and smiled.

"That's good," the former Cleveland Browns great said. "I wish him well. I know it wasn't easy for him getting there."

Motley knows from experience. He helped pave the way for Ray Rhodes, for Randall Cunningham and Rodney Peete, for all the black players and coaches who now work in the National Football League.

Motley was one of four black players who, in 1946, broke the color line in modern professional sports. They were playing pro football a year before Jackie Robinson integrated baseball by joining the Brooklyn Dodgers. If you asked most people, they'd swear it was the other way around.

"Jackie's signing got a lot more notoriety because baseball was much bigger than pro football in the `40s," said Motley, seventy-five, who attended the recent dedication of the expanded Pro Football Hall of Fame in Canton, Ohio.

"What we did in football helped get Jackie into the Major Leagues. There was a quote from Branch Rickey [the Dodgers' general manager] who said, `If these men can play a contact sport like football, then Jackie Robinson can play baseball.' So we really opened the door in two sports."

This marks the fiftieth season since the race barrier in pro football came down. The men who led the way were Motley and Bill Willis of the Browns in the All-America Football Conference and Kenny Washington and Woody Strode, who signed with the Los Angeles Rams of the rival National Football League.

Washington, who played in the same UCLA backfield with Jackie Robinson, lasted only two seasons in the NFL before a knee injury ended his career. Strode was thirty-one when he signed, so he played only one season. He quit to become an actor. Among his film roles was the gladiator who fights Kirk Douglas in *Spartacus*.

But Motley and Willis had great careers, playing eight seasons for a Browns team that dominated the AAFC, and enjoyed similar success on joining the NFL in 1950. Motley, a fullback and linebacker, was inducted into the Pro Football Hall of Fame in 1968. Willis, a two-way guard, was inducted nine years later.

Motley and Willis still reside in the Cleveland area and remain close friends. They sat together at the dedication ceremony. Afterward, they sat side by side, autographing items for sale in the gift shop. Willis, seventy-four, now walks with a cane. A pleasant but private man, he no longer grants interviews.

Motley and Willis are revered by those who know their story. At the Hall of Fame, the Steelers great Franco Harris greeted Motley with a smile and warm handshake. Said Harris: "It's always an honor to speak with you."

All the hate that Jackie Robinson faced in baseball, Motley and Willis faced first in football. Like Robinson, they knew that if they failed to produce, or if they fought back at those who cursed and spat on them, they would set back the cause of all black players.

The burden was tremendous, but Motley and Willis shouldered it with remarkable skill and courage. Whenever they became angry for something that was said or done on the field, they channeled the emotion into the next play. As Motley said: "We'd knock the hell out of the guy. We hit him hard enough that we didn't have to say anything."

At six-foot-one and 240 pounds, Motley was a frightening runner in an era when the linemen averaged 220. In 1950, his first season in the NFL, Motley led the league with 810 yards rushing and a 5.8 yard average. He ended a streak of three consecutive rushing titles for the Eagles' Steve Van Buren.

The draw play, now part of every team's offense, began with Motley. It happened by accident as Browns quarterback Otto Graham faded to pass, saw the rush coming, and handed off to Motley, who was setting up to block. Motley took the ball up the middle, past the on-rushing linemen, for big yardage. Coach Paul Brown had the play in his book the following week.

Willis was a six-foot-two, 215 pound lineman who dominated blockers with his extraordinary quickness. No one could figure out how Willis got such a great jump. His secret: He watched the center's fingers. The instant he saw them tighten on the ball, he took off.

"When Paul signed us, there were a few [Browns] who weren't too happy," Motley said. "Paul addressed that at the first meeting. He said, `If you can't get along with your teammates, you won't be here.' He didn't have to spell it out. Everyone knew what he meant."

Motley was twenty-six; Willis, one year younger, when Brown signed them. Brown had coached Willis at Ohio State, and he coached Motley during World War II at the Great Lakes Naval Training Center. After the war, when he started his team in the AAFC, Brown signed both men, although he knew it would not be popular with many football people.

There were only thirteen blacks known to have played pro football through the 1920s, including Fritz Pollard, a player–coach with Akron in 1925–26. In 1933, all black players disappeared from the pro ranks, and the game was lily-white for thirteen years until Motley, Willis, Washington, and Strode were signed in 1946.

Today, almost 70 percent of NFL players are black, and the number increases every year. Yet only two head coaches, Rhodes and Minnesota's Dennis Green, and a handful of coordinators are black. It saddens Motley to see the small number of minorities in positions of power in the NFL. It makes him realize that, on some fronts, the battle he fought a half-century ago still is far from being won.

"It bothers me, but I'm tired of squawking," he said. "I saw a piece on TV about this coach, [Tony] Dungy, who does such a great job with the defense in Minnesota. He has been one of the best for years, but he can't get a head-coaching job.

"They said he isn't tough enough; that he doesn't project the image these [NFL] teams want. That's a poor excuse, if you ask me. If the man can coach—and this man obviously can—then he should get a shot."

Motley takes pride in his role as a pioneer, someone who, through his stoic courage, helped change the face of professional sports in America.

"I look at some of the players today and wonder if they could've done what we did," said Motley, now retired after working for the Ohio Department of Youth Services. "Most of them, 99 percent, have no idea who I am."

Asked if that bothered him, Motley shook his head.

"They don't owe me anything," he said. "I've got this Hall of Fame ring, and the people who saw me play know what I did. I don't need any more than that."

Epilogue: Marion Motley died on June 27, 1999. In February 2007, Tony Dungy became the first African American head coach to win an NFL championship when he led the Indianapolis Colts to victory in Super Bowl XLI.

*Originally published in the *Philadelphia Daily News*, October 22, 1995. Reprinted with permission by Philadelphia Newspapers, LLC.

Larry Brown: King of the Hill*

It's not hard to find the Hill district in Pittsburgh. Just follow the trail of abandoned ambitions and transparent dreams leading from the center of town. Keep going until you see the streets begin to crack from neglect. Look for the mountains of trash to rise up on either side, spilling over sidewalks bearing chalk-scrawled names from other generations. The nearer you get to the bottom of the Hill, where Kirkpatrick crosses Fifth Avenue, the chalk is too often replaced by blood.

Lawrence Brown Sr., a crew caller at the Conway railroad yard, and his wife, Rose Lee, lived at 2525 Fifth Avenue, where the thick white smoke from the Jones and Laughlin steel plant mixed dangerously with the combustible fury of a black ghetto.

Lawrence Brown was aware of the Hill's environment of hatred and hopelessness, and he worried about his three sons, especially the oldest, Larry Jr. Lawrence Brown figured if he could keep Larry from stumbling into the neighborhood's dead-end way of life, that would be enough direction for his two brothers, William and John.

Lawrence Brown noticed immediately that Larry had a gift for athletics. It wasn't hard for him to detect because he had much the same skill when he was growing up. There are folks who will tell you that Lawrence Brown Sr. could have been a big-league ballplayer, except that when he was in his twenties, black baseball players were still condemned to a bush-league life. Jackie Robinson didn't come soon enough to free men like Lawrence Brown, who put their gloves and bats away like broken boyhood dreams and scattered to the big city's railroad yards and steel mills.

But the future had now opened for black athletes, and Lawrence Brown looked in his son's eyes and dreamed his dreams all over again. He would take young Larry out to a nearby lot almost every afternoon and hit baseballs to him until dark. Often the grounders would kick crazily off hunks of brick.

"He got into the Little League, and right away he was the best," Lawrence Brown will tell you to this day. "Why, at ten he was stealing bases, even though you weren't allowed to take a lead."

Larry Brown played baseball, and in his spare time he took on odd jobs to help bring additional money into the house. In the summers, he washed cars and cleaned the windows for an elderly lady who lived up the block.

"Washing windows was a good deal," Larry Brown recalls. "In Pittsburgh, with all those factories, the air was so filthy you'd wash a window one day and it would be black the next morning."

In the winters, he prayed for snow so he could shovel the sidewalks in more affluent neighborhoods. He'd go off with his shovel before 8 A.M. on non-schooldays ("You had to get the jump on your competition") and wouldn't return until dinner time. A day like that might be worth as much as $8 or $10.

"Larry was such a good boy," Rose Lee Brown said. "He was the one who wanted to work; no one asked him to. He insisted it was his responsibility to help out since he was the oldest son."

He landed one steady summer job as an orderly at Presbyterian Hospital. The pay wasn't too good, but he supplemented it with more after-hours window and car washing.

Larry Brown was carefully sidestepping the drugs, the crime, and the gang violence that lurked at each corner. Oh, there was an urge to succeed among the young people on the Hill, alright, but the price of success and the means of making it were frightfully high.

"The guys wanted out, but they didn't want to struggle like their parents," Larry Brown said. "They dreamed of being black Al Capones. Who could be the baddest dude? Who could be the richest pimp? The hell with how you make it, just make it. The guys I grew up with thought the only way to make money was to rip off somebody else.

"Some of them were pathetic. One guy walked into a bank alone and robbed the joint. He ran out with the money in a bag and flew into high gear. The cops came, and you know where they found him? Two blocks from the bank. Here's this black dude who just ripped off a bank in an all-white part of town, and he's sitting on a curb two blocks away, holding the money.

"The cops said, `You planned a good robbery, boy, but your getaway wasn't too cool.' He told the cops he started running and had an asthma attack. He said, `It was the money or my life, so I sat down.' I think he's still sitting in a jail somewhere. Most of the guys I grew up with are either in prison or dead or they're hopeless junkies, which is probably the worst of all."

Through it all, Lawrence Brown Sr. clung tenaciously to the belief that Larry would be a big-league ball player. That dream did not even survive Larry's sophomore year at Schenley High School, when he became disgusted with sitting on the bench and quit the baseball team. He went out for football.

His family did not like the idea of Larry switching sports. Football at Schenley had a tragic history. Just a year or so earlier, two neighborhood boys were killed in a gang rumble after a game.

The tense expectation of violence hung over the Pittsburgh City League. Once Schenley was rolling up a big score on the predominantly white Allderdice High School, and the hatred that had festered so long finally erupted. A husky senior from Allderdice ripped a rotting five-foot plank from the bleachers and began swinging it back and forth in a savage arc.

"Come on," he shouted, daring any Schenley players or fans to disarm him. "I'll rip your damn heads off."

The police hustled the Schenley team onto a bus, but it was several blocks later before the rocks, bricks, and bottles finally stopped clattering off the sides and smashing through the windows. Larry Brown remembers hunching under a seat, listening to his young heart pound with fear, his mind bending under the weight of racial sickness.

"It became clear to me," he said, "what the Hill was all about. We're here, and the whites are there, simple as that. It wasn't one country at all. The history books were lying to me."

But instead of enlisting in the endless madness of gang warfare, Larry Brown rededicated himself to sports. He stuck with football because he knew it could help him earn a college scholarship and lift him above the Hill and everything it had come to represent.

First, he went to remote Dodge City Junior College in Kansas for two years ("My first day there, they had a cattle drive through the center of town. Honest.") and then transferred to Kansas State University, where he spent two years blocking for a speedy halfback named Mack Herron. He didn't think any pro scouts would notice a five-foot-eleven, 195 pound back who did nothing but bury his face in the numerals of a linebacker play after punishing play. However, he was wrong. Mike McCormack, an assistant coach with the Washington Redskins, was watching from the spotter's booth one afternoon.

"Larry proved time after time he was a contact player," McCormack said. "That's the kind of back that's made to play pro football."

So the Redskins grabbed Larry Brown in the eighth round of the 1969 draft. When he reported to training camp, he found himself face to face with the famous—and feared—Vince Lombardi. Lombardi was starting his first season with the Redskins after having transformed a dog-meat franchise in Green Bay into a five-time world champion. The Redskins, with a heritage mixing dreary mediocrity with outright futility, represented another massive challenge.

"I was prepared to break my back, but I wasn't too sure about my chances," Brown said. "Here I was, an obscure rookie, working under a coach who always had great backs like [Paul] Hornung and [Jim] Taylor. Besides, he had about thirty-two running backs in camp at one time or another. Every time I turned around, there was a new face next to me in the huddle."

But those new faces kept coming and going. Larry Brown stayed. He earned his place on the team in Lombardi's infamous "nutcracker" drill, the ultimate test of a runner's heart. Lombardi set up two cones four feet apart, and through that narrow chute a runner would have to crash into two linemen and a defensive back positioned five yards apart. There wasn't, Lombardi observed, any place to hide.

The first day was almost barbaric. Rookie linebacker Roger Jarvis suffered a broken arm. Tight end Pat Richter had his nose broken twice and was ordered back into the pit. Other players limped away with assorted cramps and bruises. But Brown was splitting the other side of the nutcracker almost every time. His mouth was open, and he was sucking air in labored gulps, but he never slowed down. He kept scrambling back in line to carry the ball some more.

"On one carry, I blasted by both linemen before they could raise up," Brown said. "Right there, in front of God, Sonny Jurgensen, and everybody else, Coach Lombardi stopped practice and said, 'Nice going.' It was the most extravagant praise anybody heard from Coach Lombardi the whole first month of camp.

"He never let you get your balance. One minute you were in with him; the next he would be whipping you with that baseball cap of his. I remember one night I was packing my bags to leave camp, and my roommate, Harold McLinton, talked me out of it. The next night, he was packing, and I was the one telling him to stay."

Lombardi growled at Brown, but whenever it came cut-down time, he always spared him. It was Lombardi who discovered that Brown was deaf in one ear, so he had a special helmet devised with a hearing aid to help him pick up the quarterback's signals. It was Lombardi who stuck with Brown until he became adept at catching passes, something he'd never done in college. And in the end, it was Lombardi who gave Brown the confidence he needed to survive.

It was Lombardi who made Brown a starter as a rookie and watched him gain 888 yards, including 105 in a game against the New York Giants, the first one-hundred-yard game for a Redskin runner in eight years. But Lombardi died before the 1970 season and was not there to share in the triumph when Brown hammered out his 1,125 yards. The tough, determined kid from Pittsburgh's gloomy Hill exceeded that last season when he rushed for 1,216 yards, scored fourteen touchdowns, and was named the NFL's Most Valuable Player by an overwhelming margin.

Now Larry Brown is a wealthy young man. He has negotiated a new contract that earns him as much as $100,000 a year, not including assorted fringe benefits such as endorsement and appearance money. Yet according to Brown's attorney and adviser, John Perazich, Larry spends more time speaking in ghetto areas and schools for delinquent boys for free than he does traveling the lucrative banquet tour.

"As a criminal lawyer, I've dealt with any number of Larry Browns," Perazich said, "guys with great potential who grew up in a bad end of town and blew their futures. To see this guy make it is an inspiration to me. I was up to here with the legal cycle. Every case seemed alike. A kid started at sixteen, lifting petty crap from a department store. Four years later, the kid is holding up a gas station. Two years after that, he shoots somebody. Before I met Larry, I thought justice was nothing more than a revolving door.

"That's why Larry is so involved with young people. He made it, and he wants to impress on today's kids that they can make it, too. This morning, we were in the worst-looking elementary school you could ever imagine. No windows, just cardboard where the glass should be. Larry sat there and talked to those kids for four hours. When it was over, a little boy said to him, 'I wish I had a father like you, Mr. Brown.'

"You should have seen Larry's face light up. We walked out and he said to me, 'Man, after that, who needs the Super Bowl?'"

Last year, the Redskins played Atlanta in a Monday night game, and Lawrence Brown Sr. watched the telecast at the train yard, crowded into a room with three hundred other workers. That night, Larry Jr. gained his four thousandth career yard, a first for a Redskin. The game was stopped while they presented him with the football and the Washington fans poured out their hearts in an emotional standing ovation. Back at the train yard, three hundred guys lined up to shake the hand of Lawrence Brown, who needed his other hand to brush away the tears.

"At that moment," he said, "no man alive could have been prouder."

And perhaps at that moment, back in Pittsburgh's crumbling Hill district, one more father could see past the frustration and despair outside and find hope for the future of his son. If so, it would be the one record Larry Brown would cherish most of all.

Epilogue: Larry Brown played eight seasons in the NFL, all with Washington. He finished his career with 5,875 yards, second on the Redskins all-time rushing list behind Hall of Famer John Riggins.

---

*Originally published in the *Philadelphia Bulletin*, September 25, 1973.

Just a Truck Drivin' Man*

Back before Madison Avenue discovered professional football, before quarterbacks flew their own Cessna jets and halfbacks spent their off-seasons making movies on the French Riviera, the game belonged to small towns like Canton, Massillon, and Rock Island.

Once a week, the men would emerge from the coal mines and steel mills, strap on their leather helmets, and wage war like an army of ragged knights clinging to their last crusade. People would gather—friends and family, mostly—and they would drop a few pennies in an old cigar box to keep the dream alive.

Back then, there was no glossy mystique to professional football, no plastic grass or silver-domed stadiums, no Super Bowls with June Taylor choreography. Pro football was an unpretentious, craggy-faced game played by men named Bronko, Tuffy, and Fats, men who figured five bucks and a bloody nose was all the glory they could handle. They played, as Johnny (Blood) McNally once said, for the sheer exhilaration of it.

Joe Klecko would have fit right in. Klecko, you see, was meant to play on the same team with Grange and Nagurski, but something went wrong in the time machine and he arrived fifty years too late. Instead of barnstorming on trains with the Decatur Staleys, Klecko, a six-foot-two, 260 pound defensive tackle, wound up flying on charters with the New York Jets.

To say Joe Klecko, better known as Killer Klecko, clashes with the attaché cases and blow dryers in the laid-back New York locker room would be an understatement. A moosehead hanging in the Louvre would seem chic by comparison.

"Joe is a throwback," said Dave Herman, the former Jets lineman who now handles the club's radio broadcasts. "He reminds me of the guys I met when I broke in in the early `60s. He's a competitor; he puts the game ahead of everything else. He doesn't go around with the attitude: `OK, what can football do for me today?' Joe isn't a taker; he's a giver. He'd play this game for nothing, and nowadays that makes him unique."

Joe Klecko is a throwback, all right. He's a tough kid from blue-collar stock who made it to the National Football League the hard way. He started pumping gas at his uncle's garage when he was eleven, and he never even tried out for his high-school football team until his senior year. After graduation, he took a construction job and played semi-pro ball in his spare time.

The team's equipment manager recommended Klecko to a local college coach; the coach offered Klecko a scholarship, and, as they say on television, the rest is history. Five years later, Klecko can sit on the porch of his new home nestled in Pennsylvania's quiet West Chester farm country, watch his wife Debby chase their two-year-old son Mike around the swimming pool, and reflect on the way things turned out.

"What really makes this satisfying," Klecko said, wrapping a meaty hand around a glass of iced tea, "is knowing nobody ever gave me anything. Everything I've got, I earned. Some of these guys have life handed to them on a silver platter. They win all the awards in high school, they get hundreds of scholarship offers, then they become a number-one draft choice and sign for a million dollars. All of that, just because they can play football."

Klecko shook his head. "You know, there were rookies in the Jets camp last year who didn't know how to fill out a W-2 form?" he said. "They had never even seen one before. I thought, 'What planet did these guys come from?'

"I've worked my whole life, and I'm proud of it. I worked as a mechanic and a laborer. I've driven tractor trailers. I could walk away from football tomorrow and still take care of my family. How many second-year [NFL] players you know can say that?"

Klecko, now twenty-five, reflects the strict, working-class ethic he learned growing up in Chester, a racially mixed, row-house community ten miles down Interstate 95 from Philadelphia. His father was a truck driver, and his mother was a hospital dietician, and between them they taught Joe how to scuffle for a dollar.

They encouraged their son to participate in athletics, but only when it didn't conflict with more important things, such as his chores around the house or his job at the gas station. In high school, Klecko worked every Friday and Saturday night, so he didn't have much of a social life. Kids used to laugh at the dirt under his fingernails and say things like: "Hey, Joe, can I double with you to the prom? I never rode in a tow truck before."

"My father was a great semi-pro football player," Klecko said with considerable pride. "He was one of those triple-threat halfbacks—you know, run, pass, and kick. He's sixty-two years old, and he still can dropkick a forty-yard field goal. He wanted to see me play ball, but not to the exclusion of everything else. I was a good catcher in Little League baseball. I wasn't that interested in football, even though I made the all-star team every year. Football coaches always seemed like maniacs to me.

"I didn't even go out for the football team my first three years of high school. I was too busy working at the garage to waste time hitting a tackling dummy. Besides, they had this attitude it was a big deal to be a St. James [High School] football player. I figured, 'Who needs it?' Finally, my senior year, I looked at the guys on the team, and there wasn't one of them whose butt I couldn't kick, so I tried out. I made all-county, all-league, the whole bit."

Several colleges, including Temple and Villanova, expressed interest in Klecko, but he had a real distaste for academics. "All I could think of was four more years of reading *Great Expectations*. No thanks," Klecko said.

He took a job with a construction company instead, and pretty soon he was driving tractor trailers and pulling down $6.22 an hour. There were plenty of ten-hour days, with double time on weekends, enabling him to take home as much as $1,200 a month.

"That was fantastic money for a kid right out of high school," Klecko said. "It was hard work. I was up at five or six every morning hauling heavy stuff around, but I could handle it. I was pretty contented except for one thing: I missed football. I'd sit in front of the TV on Saturday, and I'd think, `I'm that fast. I'm that strong. I'm as good as that guy. How come he's an All-American and I'm driving a truck?' It irked me, it really did."

The following spring, Klecko heard about a semi-pro football team, the Aston Knights, forming just down the road. The team would be composed mostly of former high-school players living in the area and would replace the disbanded Pottstown Firebirds in the Seaboard Professional Football League.

It wasn't exactly the big time, but Klecko figured it was as close as he would ever come to it. He called the owner, Nick (Butch) Verrati, a local paving contractor, and asked for a tryout.

"I'll never forget the first night of practice," Klecko said. "I got all dressed and drove by to pick up Debby. We had been going out for eight months, and she said that's all I ever talked about: how much I wanted to play football again. She asked if she could come to practice. I said OK. It's a good thing for me that I did.

"We pulled up to the field, and I froze. I looked at all those guys warming up, and I panicked. I said, `Aw, the hell with it. Let's go get something to eat.' Debby took the keys and threw them out the window. She said, 'We aren't going anywhere until you finish practice.' No kidding: If it wasn't for her, I would've driven away and never gone back. I'd still be getting up at five in the morning to mix concrete."

Klecko was the youngest of the Knights. Most of the players were like guard Leo Levandowski, married guys in their late twenties who had bounced around the sandlots for years. Levandowski, a veteran of the championship Pottstown teams, gave up ten years of seniority at Scott Paper to try out with the Philadelphia Eagles in 1967. He lasted just three weeks before being cut by coach Joe Kuharich.

The Knights' quarterback was John Waller, a five-foot-seven, 165 pound sixth-grade teacher from Ridley Park. Waller, who once held virtually all of the Temple University passing records, played his football in horn-rimmed glasses. The center was Larry Kozak, a thirty-five-year-old saloon owner who previously had played for the Swedesboro Red Devils, the Gloucester Vikings, the Delaware Clippers, and a dozen other teams whose tattered jerseys now hang behind his bar.

Waller was the highest-paid Knight, earning $50 a game. Three other players made $30 a game. Levandowski, Kozak, Klecko, and the other Knights got nothing. Since Klecko was only nineteen and someday might just decide to play college football, he was advised to play under an assumed name. He became Jim Jones, number 71. On the roster, his college was listed as the University of Poland. The Aston fans, being a rather unsophisticated lot, never suspected a thing.

"Playing in that league was a real education," Klecko said. "Our first game, we played Hagerstown [Maryland], and I was beating the guy across from me to death. This one time, I knocked him flat on his back and he kicked me in the crotch as I jumped over him. My buddy, Jack Mercandante [the other tackle] saw the whole thing. He said, 'Joe, you can't let him get away with that. You gotta even it up on the next play.' Next play, I knocked the guy down and kicked him in the ribs.

"That's the kind of league it was, everybody biting, kicking, and scratching. I was just a kid out of high school; I didn't like getting involved in all that dirty stuff, but Jack and Leo told me I had to do it to survive. Players in the bush leagues pull stuff you wouldn't believe. I saw one guy from Hartford play with a plaster cast on his arm and shatter the damn thing over the head of one of our backs. It was like a war going on out there.

"The social aspect was a trip, too. I was a quiet kid, but hanging around those animals brought me out of my shell. You know what they used to drink before a game? Blackberry brandy. I don't mean they sipped it; they *drank* it. Our second-strong quarterback didn't have a thumb, and he was the hardest drinker of all. Every time he opened his mouth to call a play, it smelled like a distillery blew up. We used to tell Waller, 'Whatever you do, don't get hurt.'

"Our first road trip was to Hartford [Connecticut]. It was a long bus ride, and my mother packed me a lunch: a kielbasa sandwich, a Tastykake, and a bag of pretzel nuggets. I knew if Leo and Jack saw the bag, they'd take it off me, so I kept it out of sight until we got in the Holland Tunnel. Once we got in the tunnel, where it was dark, I opened the bag up real slow so nobody would hear the paper rattling.

"Just as I was about to take a bite of the sandwich, the bus came out of the tunnel, and there were Leo and Jack, turned around in their seats, staring at me. They ripped the lunch out of my hands and devoured it in about five seconds. They left me with four lousy pretzel nuggets. I remember Leo belched and said, 'Hey, kid, tell your mother thanks.'"

Like all sandlot teams, the Knights had their moments, both funny and poignant. They played before small crowds—1,500 was a good night—at Sun Valley High School. They wore old, washed-out uniforms that had been handed down by the Eagles in the 1960s and worn by the Firebirds the year before. They practiced two nights a week or as often as the guys working four-to-midnight shifts could get off.

Still, the Knights won nine games and advanced to the division playoffs. The only team that overpowered them was Hartford, which was understandable, since Hartford was the league's richest franchise, a luxury that allowed it to stock up with NFL veterans such as Marv Hubbard, Donnie Shanklin, and Tom Sherman.

After the season, John DiGregorio, the Knights' equipment manager, took a similar job at Temple University. He told Wayne Hardin, the Temple coach, about Jim Jones—er, Joe Klecko—and Hardin tracked him down. Hardin was in the process of revamping the Temple football program, scheduling major college powers such as Penn State and Syracuse. He didn't care how many aliases a kid had as long as he could play.

"I told Hardin I'd play for him, provided I didn't have to go to prep school for a year," Klecko said. "I didn't want to wind up in some hokey military academy with a fourteen-year-old kid half my size telling me how to stand. Hardin said not to worry, I didn't need prep school, so I said OK.

"I didn't mind quitting work and going to college. After busting my butt doing manual labor for two years, the thought occurred to me: 'Do I really want to spend the rest of my life doing this?' The answer was no. Working a construction job one winter, freezing every day, convinced me I should give the books another try. Besides, after that season with the Knights, I was thinking seriously about playing in the NFL."

A broken hand sidelined Klecko for the first month of his freshman year. In his first game against the University of Delaware, he recorded seven quarterback sacks and twenty unassisted tackles. "Who was that kid?" Delaware coach Tubby Raymond said after the game. "Where did he come from?"

"The next day in the papers, I got written up like Mighty Joe Young," Klecko said. "Some [reporter] checked into my background and found out about my year with the Knights. Tubby said it was disgraceful, Wayne Hardin was recruiting professionals to play at Temple. I knew I hadn't done anything wrong. I never took a penny from the Knights. I thought it was funny, the way everybody got so worked up over nothing."

Klecko matured considerably in his four years at Temple. As a junior, he was considered the finest middle guard in the East, and several scouts had him rated with Lee Roy Selmon as the best in the country. In the off-season, he lifted weights to gain strength. He spent the summer hauling three-ton loads of steel up and down the East Coast in his tractor trailer. That didn't hurt his conditioning, either.

While at Temple, Klecko began working out at Joe Frazier's North Philadelphia gym to improve his footwork. He joined the Temple boxing team and wound up winning the Eastern Intercollegiate Heavyweight Championship. The daily roadwork helped him trim four inches off his waist and lower his time in the forty-yard dash from 5.0 seconds to 4.75.

When it came time for the 1977 NFL draft, Klecko figured he would go early. He sat by the phone in his apartment and waited. And waited. The first day of the draft was completed, and Klecko's phone never rang, except for an occasional call from his parents asking if there was any news. At nine o'clock, Klecko went outside and sat, alone with his thoughts, until midnight. The next morning, the draft resumed with the sixth round. The New York Jets, picking fifth in that round, selected Klecko.

"I was really bugged," he said. "I figured any player drafted the second day is strictly a body, something to take up space at training camp until the veterans report. I knew I was a better ballplayer than they gave me credit for, and I set out to prove it.

"Remember the sequence in *Rocky* where Sylvester Stallone is training for the big fight? Well, that was me the two months before I reported to camp. I went nuts. I lifted weights every day. I was bench pressing four hundred fifty pounds. Every night, I'd run two miles. I went into camp with a great big chip on my shoulder. I looked around at the guys drafted ahead of me, and I wanted to kill.

"We were scrimmaging one day, and this other rookie gave me some lip. I lifted his facemask and dropped him with one punch. I got in three fights the first week. That's when Randy Rasmussen [a veteran guard] started calling me `Killer.' Pretty soon, everybody, including the coaches, was calling me Killer."

Killer had plenty of wrath left over for the rest of the NFL. He led the Jets in quarterback sacks during the pre-season. He had four in one game against the Giants. Head coach Walt Michaels liked the rookie, but he was afraid to start him, fearing the opposition would exploit his inexperience. Michaels used him as a pass-rush specialist until Carl Barzilauskas, the starting left tackle, went down with a knee injury. Klecko took over, and his play in the final two months of the season gave the victory-starved Jets fans something to cheer about.

Klecko sacked Terry Bradshaw twice in a hard-fought 23–20 loss to Pittsburgh. The following week, he sacked Archie Manning in the final minute to nail down a 16–13 win over New Orleans. He was voted defensive player of the game, with three sacks and three pressures against Buffalo. He finished the season with eight sacks and ninety tackles, fifty-eight of them unassisted. He outplayed the all-pro guards Joe DeLamielleure of Buffalo and Gene Upshaw of Oakland and put to rest any doubts the scouts might have raised about his NFL future.

"There were quite a few raps against Joe in the scouting reports," Michaels said, explaining why Klecko was the one-hundred-forty-fourth player drafted. "They said he was short and might get lost in all the traffic inside. They also said he was inconsistent. They couldn't decide if he was a good player who had a few bad days or a bad player who had a few good days.

"I might have passed him up, too, if I hadn't seen him play myself. I was still coaching with the Eagles when Joe was a senior. Temple played Penn State at Veterans Stadium. Our offices were right there, so I stayed to watch. Joe played a helluva game. Penn State tried everything, and they couldn't find a way to block him. I figure if a kid can play that well in a big game, he can play. He turned out to be a helluva pick for us.

"Did you ever see that beer commercial where the bull comes crashing through the door? That's how Joe came into camp last summer. He only had one speed, and that was full. Even in dummy scrimmages, he went all out. If somebody objected, Joe was ready to fight. He had a couple beauties, too. I just moved the practice to the other end of the field and let them go at it. After a few weeks, Joe had the respect of everybody. No one wanted to mess with him.

"Joe wasn't your typical rookie. Those years of knocking around, working for a living, gave him a maturity some other guys will never have."

"Joe will be the Alex Karras of the 1980s," Dave Herman said. "Joe is built along the same lines as Karras. He's not real tall, so he has a low center of gravity. He's stronger than Alex and probably quicker. I've seen Joe come off the ball and be around a blocker before he can set up. With his desire, there is no telling how good Joe can be."

The nice part about all this success is that it hasn't changed Joe Klecko. He is still a tough, purposeful kid from the west end of Chester. When some guys make it in the Big Apple, they spend the off-season endorsing everything from razor blades to foot powder. Klecko figured an athlete's market value lasts only as long as his playing career. He wanted something with a future.

Last year, he went to work for Robbins Motor Freight in Essington, Pennsylvania, an outfit that specializes in jobs other companies can't handle. "Oversize loads, bad roads, stuff like that," Klecko said. He became friendly with the owner, Maurice Robbins, who is now teaching Klecko the business. At the present time, Klecko is a driver and dispatcher, but he hopes to move into the front office by the time he quits football.

"Driving for [Robbins] can be a little hairy, though," Klecko said. "We take some loads that would snap a normal tractor trailer in half. I hauled a propeller for a ship to the Navy Yard in Jacksonville one time. The thing was 130,000 pounds and twenty-eight feet wide. That's wider than most roads. Another time I took a propeller for a nuclear power plant—ten feet wide and 80,000 pounds—to Arizona. Try driving that through rush-hour traffic.

"The only time I was ever scared was when I had to haul a snowplow to Buffalo in the middle of that blizzard. The plow was fifteen feet high, so I wasn't allowed to take the normal roads. Anything over thirteen feet has to be cleared for a special routing. They sent me the long way, through Wilkes-Barre and Scranton, and the roads were almost impassable. The New York Thruway was closed except to emergency vehicles.

"I had the plow on a low-bed trailer, and that thing couldn't have been more than an inch and a half off the ground. It was one hundred fifty miles between Syracuse and Buffalo, and I was plowing snow all the way. I was on the road for twenty-five hours. I kept calling on the CB radio, hoping I could pick up another driver, but I never did. I was all alone. If I had a breakdown, they never would've found me in time. They would've had to chip me out of the front seat.

"I'll never forget driving into Buffalo. The snow was piled up above the exit signs on the highway; it was even piled up above the overpasses. It was like driving through a long, white tunnel. All I could see were these twenty-foot walls of snow on each side and the clouds directly overhead. It was spooky. I remember thinking, `If I ever get out of here, I'll never curse the heat at training camp again.'"

"Have you?" someone asked.

Klecko smiled and took a long sip of iced tea. "Only about twenty times a day," he said.

Epilogue: Joe Klecko played twelve seasons in the NFL. In 2004, the New York Jets retired his number 73 jersey. He was voted into the Pro Football Hall of Fame in 2023.

*Originally published in *Pro Magazine*, 1978.

"America's Team": Cowboys Corral a Nation*

The Dallas Cowboys operate out of a gleaming, high-rise office building along the North Central Expressway. There is a Playboy Club downstairs and a Texas conglomerate upstairs, and the elevator reeks of Halston musk and oil money.

Most pro football teams would seem out of place in this environment. The Pittsburgh Steelers would never make it here; they would have to check their brass knuckles at the door. And could you imagine Vince Lombardi sharing his quarters with a Playboy Club? Why, he would have gone through the place like Carrie Nation.

But the Dallas Cowboys, the football chic, fit in like a Calvin Klein suit. On the surface, the Cowboys look and sound like Texas Instruments, Inc.; Neiman-Marcus; or any other flourishing Dallas enterprise. They are cool and efficient, slick as a mahogany desk, and just about as emotional.

They prepare game plans the way most firms prepare stockholders' reports. They feed the Xs and Os into a computer, then sit back and clean their fingernails while the information is sifted, analyzed, and projected into what the coaches call "tendencies."

They dunk their players in water to determine their body fat. They clock their quarterbacks' passes with a radar gun. They administered written psychological tests to assess their rookies' "character," but an NFL Players Association grievance outlawed that a few years back.

The Dallas Cowboys have taken this whole macho business and put it in an attaché case. There was a time when football coaches were craggy-faced guys perched atop blocking sleds, screaming profanities. In the Dallas system, the coaches wear white smocks and call their plays by slide rule.

The organization has a mystique all its own, dynamic and progressive. If the Cowboys were politicians, we would say they had charisma. They stir intense feelings wherever they go. Some folks swear by them; others swear at them, but no one can ignore them.

This year, the Cowboys—in characteristic modesty—began referring to themselves as "America's Team." The idea, club executives are quick to point out, was proposed by someone outside the Cowboys family—namely, Steve Sabol and Bob Ryan of NFL Films.

It was their contention that the Cowboys, more than any other professional team, transcend geographic loyalties. Whenever they processed film of a Cowboys game, no matter where it was played, they noticed a large number of fans wearing Dallas shirts and waving Dallas pennants, often putting their lives in jeopardy in the process.

Sabol, NFL Films' president, mentioned this phenomenon to Tex Schramm, the Cowboys' general manager, last winter. Sabol wanted to use the "America's Team" theme for the 1978 Dallas highlight film, which Ryan was producing, but he did not want to sound the trumpets without first clearing it with Schramm. After all, the title is a bit grandiose, even for the Cowboys.

Schramm, once a publicist for the Los Angeles Rams, loved it. Within a month, the Cowboys had printed up a hundred thousand calendars with "America's Team" emblazoned across the cover in red, white, and blue. They advertised in the local papers, and the name took off across the Panhandle like a wind-blown brush fire.

Dallas played three pre-season games at home, and before each one, the public address announcer introduced the Cowboys as "America's Team." The players on the other clubs did not receive the announcement particularly well. Neither did the out-of-town press. So the practice was discontinued.

The concept, however, remains valid. The Cowboys are, in a very real sense, America's Team. If you don't believe it, just call them sometime and ask for the figures. Consider the following:

• Twenty-eight percent of all goods sold by NFL Properties (T-shirts, caps, pennants, etc.) are Dallas Cowboy items. The Super Bowl champion Steelers are a distant second, with 10 percent.

• The Cowboys have been involved in three of the four highest-rated sporting events in television history.

• They hold the TV rating record for a Super Bowl, a division playoff game, and a conference championship game.

• They also hold the ratings record for a Sunday afternoon NFL telecast, a Sunday night telecast, a Monday night telecast, a Thanksgiving Day telecast, a Thursday night telecast, a Saturday afternoon telecast, a Saturday night telecast, and even a pre-season telecast.

• This year, the Cowboys will be seen on national television fourteen times, not counting the playoffs. The Steelers are next, with seven national TV appearances.

• The team's newspaper, the *Dallas Cowboy Weekly*, has a circulation of more than one hundred thousand, with a subscription list that touches all fifty states and literally stretches from Antarctica to the Philippines. By 1980, the Cowboys expect the circulation to surpass that of the *Austin American Statesman*, a major Texas daily.

• Within the past year, the Cowboys have distributed more than eight hundred thousand team posters and four hundred fifty thousand decals. A Dallas taco chain came out with an autographed Cowboys glass and sold its entire stock of three hundred twenty-five thousand glasses.

- The Cowboy Cheerleaders made a two-hour special for ABC last year, and it had the second highest rating of any made-for-TV movie ever aired. A sequel—*Cowboys Cheerleaders II*—is currently in the works, and the girls just finished a guest appearance on *The Love Boat*.
- The famous Cheerleader posters have long since passed Farrah Fawcett posters and now are nearing the million mark in sales. This season, by popular demand, the Cheerleaders have published their own yearbook, *A Touch of Class*. It sells for $4.95, and the first printing of two hundred twenty-five thousand is almost gone.

The bottom line is obvious: The Dallas Cowboys sell. There are numerous theories why, starting, naturally, with their win–loss record. This will be the Cowboys' fourteenth consecutive winning season. They have won their division ten times since 1966. They have been to the playoffs twelve of the past thirteen years. They have appeared in five Super Bowls, which is as many as Green Bay and Pittsburgh combined.

They are a dynasty, but dynasties don't always sell a lot of pennants. There are plenty of winning teams that have little or no national appeal. The Oakland Raiders were a merchandising disaster as Super Bowl champions. The Minnesota Vikings have been to the Super Bowl three times, but when was the last time you saw anybody walking down the street in a Vikings T-shirt?

The Cowboys, by contrast, have fan clubs all over the world. NFL Properties reports that Dallas items sell out in Tokyo. A subscriber to *Cowboy Weekly* wrote to inform the editors he had just returned from Scotland, where he found a Glasgow resident jogging in a Cowboys sweatshirt. Why?

"I don't know if there's one reason," Schramm said. "I think it probably started back in the `60s, when we played Green Bay in those two championship games. To most people, we were still an expansion team then. We were like the little kids from up the block who took on the big, bad Packers. We were the underdogs. People identified with us.

"We've always had colorful characters, guys like Don Meredith, Bob Hayes, Bob Lilly, Roger Staubach, and now Tony Dorsett. We were never just another good, faceless team. We had personality. We had players who captured the imagination. When we were on TV, people watched.

"There are other things," he said. "We have great-looking uniforms. We have a very distinctive emblem [the Lone Star]. We have a reputation for doing things first. We were the first team to use a computer in the draft. We were the first team to bring track men [Hayes] and basketball players [Cornell Green, Pete Gent] into the NFL.

"And, of course, we were the first to have the new cheerleaders. They haven't exactly hurt our image the past few years."

There is also something to be said for the fact the Cowboys are based in Dallas. America has an enduring fascination with Texas. It's what enables

Billy Martin to sell ten-gallon hats in Manhattan, what keeps Willie Nelson on juke-boxes in Chicago, what has lifeguards dipping snuff on Laguna Beach.

There is an unmistakable aura about Texas. You hear the word, and you immediately think in twangy superlatives. The purdiest women, the meanest hombres, the fastest guns. Texans are cocky and garish, and so are the Cowboys. Their home field, Texas Stadium, is as humble as, say, the LBJ Ranch.

There is nothing understated about the Cowboys. Every week, they swagger onto the field with their Stetsons pushed back, thumbs hooked in their jeans, and they dare the other team to knock them off. As fans, we either love them for their style or hate them for their arrogance. It is impossible to yawn at the sight of Thomas (Hollywood) Henderson.

None of this happened by accident. Over the past decade, the Cowboys have been packaged and sold like Big Macs and Polaroid cameras. They have been cleverly slipped into our daily lives, almost without our realizing it, in the form of magazine ads (Roger Staubach for air conditioners) and TV exposure (Tony Dorsett for soft drinks), free team photos and bumper stickers.

"Our objective," Schramm said, "is to put the Dallas Cowboy name in front of as many people as possible every day. When people think `pro football,' we want them to think `Dallas Cowboys.'

"We were promotion-conscious from the very beginning. We came in as an expansion team the same year the American Football League started [1960]. There was an AFL franchise in Dallas [the Texans], and we really had to hustle to compete with them, because at that time they were winning and we weren't.

"We weren't drawing that well [fewer than twenty thousand per game], and we had to reach out to the community. We worked to get exposure. We tried things no one had ever tried before, like the computers. We made up our minds that everything we did, we were going to do it first class. We adopted an expression: doing things `Dallas Cowboys style.' That meant doing them better than anyone else."

The Texans won the AFL title in 1963, but they lost the struggle for the Texas market the same year. The Cowboys were outdrawing them, even in the midst of a four-game losing streak. In 1964, the Texans moved to Kansas City and became the Chiefs. The Cowboys settled in and flourished.

It is interesting to note the original Cowboys brain trust—owner Clint Murchison, Schramm, personnel director Gil Brandt, and head coach Tom Landry—has remained unchanged through two decades. Schramm says that accounts for the team's success and, from a public-relations standpoint, its credibility.

"The public gets disgusted with the way most teams play musical chairs in the front office," Schramm said. "We represent stability."

Schramm himself reflects the Cowboy philosophy. A former sportswriter, public-relations man, and CBS network executive, Schramm understands the importance of a good team image, so he goes out of his way to meet the public. He has his own TV show, he does a radio spot three nights a week, and he has a question-and-answer column in *Cowboy Weekly*.

Unlike many football executives, Schramm never attends a practice and never sits in on a film session. In fact, his office and Tom Landry's office are at opposite ends of the floor. This is not a coincidence. "Around here," Schramm said, "we don't have people looking over other people's shoulders." In other words, Landry takes care of the flex defense; Tex tends to the cash register.

"I hate to use the word `image' because it sounds like something contrived," Schramm said, "but we believe it's a very important aspect of our team. It's not an ego trip. We believe things like the newspaper, the stadium, the TV exposure all have a positive effect on what we do on the field.

"We feel our image is most helpful when it comes to signing players, especially free agents. Very often, a kid will have the chance to sign with a half-dozen clubs, and he will pick the Cowboys because he's heard free agents have a good shot of making it here. Cliff Harris and Drew Pearson were both free agents, you know."

The Cowboys make sure college seniors are aware of such things. Brandt barrages potential recruits with literature, stickers, and Super Bowl pens, all designed to educate them on the joys of being a Cowboy. It works. This spring, Dallas signed seventy-five free agents, the most in the NFL.

"Pride is a very strong motivator," Schramm said, "and we feel our image is something our players are proud of. When the New York Yankees were the dominant team in baseball, it was said a player would become better when he put on the pinstripes. We want our players to feel the same way about the Cowboys uniform, and I think they do.

"That's one reason we made the trade for John Dutton. John has not played up to his potential for several years [in Baltimore], but we hope that coming to Dallas, becoming a Cowboy, will bring him back to that All-Pro level."

The Cowboys protect their All-American image as fiercely as if it were a one-point lead in the Super Bowl. Last year, when a local theater showed the film *Debbie Does Dallas*, an X-rated rip-off of the Cowboy Cheerleaders, the club had the place closed down and the owner tossed in jail.

When Gent turned his scathing novel *North Dallas Forty* into a major motion picture, the Cowboys' front office lashed back. In an interview in *Cowboy Weekly*, Schramm denounced the film as a "totally distorted, dishonest portrayal of pro football, so far from the truth, it's ludicrous."

"It's taken twenty years to build what we have now," Schramm said, explaining the club's sensitivity to these matters. "We don't appreciate people taking potshots at us."

For the most part, the players downplay the commercialization of the team. The only Cowboy actively involved in the marketing is halfback Preston

Pearson. He makes his off-season home in Pittsburgh, and he got a little tired of Steelers fans waving their Terrible Towels in his face all last winter.

Pearson decided the Cowboys should have a banner of their own, so he designed a bandana with the Dallas colors and team emblem. He gave the pattern to Sears, which has already sold twenty-thousand of the bandanas in the Dallas area. The bandanas are called the "Dread White and Blue," and you'll see them flapping every time the Cowboys score a touchdown.

"I'm not too crazy about the `America's Team' thing," Pearson said. "I don't think most of our guys are. I think it arouses jealousy among the players around the league. They hear that or read it and they figure we're looking down on them, like they're second-class citizens. They want to knock our blocks off.

"It's tough to be in our position, because every week we walk into a fired-up stadium. We don't sneak up on anybody. Plus, we have to adjust our schedule because we're on national TV so much. We have three games in the next ten days, and that will put even more pressure on us.

"But playing for the Cowboys has its advantages," Pearson said. "I'm not even a starter, yet I'm a nationally known figure. I was actually recognized running through an airport last year. Me, Preston Pearson. I thought that only happened to O. J. Simpson."

Epilogue: The Dallas Cowboys now have their offices in Frisco, a Dallas suburb. It is a new address and a new regime—Jerry Jones, not Tex Schramm, is running things—but the Cowboys still have that "America's Team" swagger.

*Originally published in the *Philadelphia Bulletin*, November 12, 1979.

Montana Magic*

To begin with, you must understand that Notre Dame heroes are not like any other. They are not like Trojan heroes or Buckeye heroes, or even Hollywood heroes. Notre Dame heroes are knights in leather helmets; archangels in high-top cleats. Notre Dame heroes are saints who walk forever along the misty banks of the Wabash.

Knute Rockne was a Notre Dame hero. Rockne, the coach with the nose of a broken-down pug and the tongue of a Shakespearean actor. Rockne, the immigrant Swede who came to the little Catholic college to study chemistry and stayed to build a football legend.

George Gipp was a Notre Dame hero. The Gipper, the cavalier halfback who spent more time in Hullie and Mike's Pool Hall than he did in chapel. The Gipper, the All-America whose dying request was that someday, when the boys are up against it, that they go in there and win one for him.

The Four Horsemen were Notre Dame heroes. Crowley, Miller, Layden, and Stuhldreher, outlined against the blue-gray October sky, galloping through the 1924 Army defense like Cossacks set loose on the steppes. Grantland Rice saw them once and was moved to the now classic literary analogy.

Johnny Lujack was a Notre Dame hero; so was Paul Hornung. Lord knows, Rocky Bleier was a Notre Dame hero. He scored two touchdowns against Purdue on a busted leg. Ask any parish priest, ask any cloistered nun with a transistor radio. They'll tell you all about it.

Joe Montana is part of the Notre Dame legacy. He was the miracle quarterback, the kid with the icy swagger and the pocketful of four-leaf clovers. Drama was his stock in trade. He entered every game like Superman crashing through the kidnappers' skylight.

He would show up just when the South Bend faithful were down to their last few rosary beads. Two touchdowns behind, a minute to go? Don't worry, that's Joe Montana over there, reaching for his helmet. Don't ask where he's been, Father, just be thankful he is here now. Everything will be all right.

Joe Montana was the savior of the fourth quarter, the patron saint of the two-minute offense. He took seconds and multiplied them into hours. He raised his arms and parted defenses. He inspired his followers like few Notre Dame quarterbacks before or since.

"Charisma is a grossly overused word," said Ken MacAfee, Notre Dame's All-America tight end, "but it's the only word that does Joe Montana justice. When he's in a game, you always feel like you've got a shot. It doesn't matter how many points you're down or how little time is left. You look in Joe's eyes, and you know he's not giving up, so you don't give up, either."

Legend.

Joe Montana rolls the word around in his head for a moment or two, a whimsical smile on his face. He had heard this before, of course, and it never ceases to amuse him.

"Me, a Notre Dame legend?" Montana says. "I can't picture my name up there with Rockne, Leahy, Gipp, guys like that. Heck, they practically built Notre Dame.

"I can't believe legends do the things I do. Every afternoon, I go to the barn [he has two Arabian horses] and shovel it out. Do legends do that? I go to the store, buy milk, and forget the bread. I try to hammer a nail and hit my thumb. Do legends do that?"

Looking at Joe Montana, sitting there in his T-shirt and blue jeans, struggling to keep the sliced tomato from escaping his roast beef sandwich, you figure he has a point. He doesn't look at all like a legend.

He is tall, but not as tall as you imagined. He is slim, almost skinny. His six-foot-two, 200 pound listing in the San Francisco 49ers program seems generous. He is blond and dimpled in a choirboy way. His voice is soft; his manner, gracious and understated. A nice package, but not what you expected from Joe Montana.

From Joe Montana, you expected a Clint Eastwood type. Raspy voice, gunslinger eyes, the kind of guy who walks into a saloon and the music stops and everyone gets real quiet. Great image, but it just doesn't fit.

Montana is sitting at his kitchen table with Bosley and Broadway, his miniature dachshunds, curled up at his feet. He is drinking a root beer, talking about trimming the hedge on the side of the house. He looks and sounds like any other suburban husband on his day off. Even his 49er teammates admit to having some difficulty reconciling the man and the myth.

"The first time I saw Joe, we were at the 49ers rookie camp [in 1979]," wide receiver Dwight Clark said. "I thought, 'Gee, he's not too big. I wonder what position he plays.' Somebody said he was a quarterback, and I was surprised. Then I learned who he was, and I was *really* surprised. I thought, 'That can't be Joe Montana.'

"We played Notre Dame when I was at Clemson. We had them beat in the fourth quarter, and Joe brought them back. They scored two touchdowns right at the end of the game, just about broke our hearts. I couldn't believe this was the same guy. Then I got in the huddle with him and that quick, I knew. The man commands your attention."

Montana does not dwell on his college heroics. He does not point out there was once a "Ballad of Joe Montana" written and sung in South Bend. He does not bring up the time he entered the Purdue game, and the Notre Dame publicist, Roger Valdiserri, turned to his Purdue counterpart and said, "You're in trouble now."

To raise such issues would only fuel the notion that Montana is already numbered among the game's immortals, and when you are twenty-five years old and still working fourteen hours a day to beat the New Orleans Saints, immortality is not a practical concern.

"The things that happened to me at Notre Dame, they could've happened to anybody," Montana says. "It's not that I had any mystical power. I just happened to be in that place at that time.

"Some of the games were unusual, I admit. But I never stepped back and said, 'Wow, this is Gipper material.' I was just out there, trying to win. And I was fortunate enough to be surrounded by other players who hated losing every bit as much as I did.'

When you get right down to it, Montana's college career was one long series of ups and downs. It wasn't all as grand as the Irish balladeers would have you believe. He had those spectacular relief appearances as a sophomore, then he sat out an entire year with a shoulder separation. When he came back the following spring, he was third string behind Rusty Lisch and Gary Forystek. No one ever told him why.

"I was surprised and hurt," Montana admits.

The Irish started sluggishly that year. They won their opener at Pitt, but only because the Panthers quarterback, Matt Cavanaugh, was knocked out in the first half. They lost to Ole Miss, and they were getting pushed around by Purdue in week three when coach Dan Devine finally changed quarterbacks. He benched Lisch and inserted Forystek, who went down with a broken collarbone in his first series.

There was a minute left in the third quarter, and Purdue led 24–14, but when Montana shook off his parka, the Notre Dame fans went bananas. They knew what was coming, and so did the players.

"We were jumping up and down, clapping," center David Huffman recalls. "We must've looked like idiots. Here we were, getting our butts kicked, acting like we were three touchdowns ahead. But seeing Joe was like, 'OK, here we go.'"

Montana brought Notre Dame back to win that day, 31–24. He started the rest of the year and ran off eight consecutive victories, including a memorable Cotton Bowl rout of previously unbeaten Texas. The Irish were crowned national champions.

His senior year was a bit of a downer. The Irish were upset by Michigan, then the University of Southern California. They never were a factor in the final polls, but the 1979 Cotton Bowl—ah, that made it all worthwhile. That was the definitive Joe Montana comeback.

"The weather was nice all week," Montana says. "But the night before the game, a cold front came in. There was a big ice storm. Closed highways, knocked-down power lines. The day of the game, it was sleeting. The temperature was in the twenties. The winds were forty miles an hour. I was never so cold in my life. Every time I came off the field, I ran straight for the sideline heaters.

"We were playing Houston, and they couldn't do anything wrong. They were ahead 24–6 in the first half. We were fumbling, falling down. People started leaving in the second quarter. They figured the game was over. I got the shakes in the locker room at halftime. The doctor checked me, and my body temperature had dropped to below normal. It was ninety-four, I think. He said he'd never seen that before.

"They stretched me out on the locker-room floor, covered me with blankets, and kept feeding me hot soup. The team went back for the third quarter; I stayed. I kept hearing the Houston band playing. I'd think, `Oh no, not another touchdown.'

"Finally, I went back in the fourth quarter, and Houston was winning, 34–12. I told the guys, `Look, let's just take it one drive at a time.' We scored on our first possession, and that got our confidence going. Then we scored again. And again."

The game ended with Montana throwing a touchdown pass to Kris Haines with no time left on the clock, to pull the Irish within a point, 34–33. Montana then hit Haines for the two-point conversion and a 35–34 triumph that warmed every Irish heart from Dallas to County Mayo.

The victory was so stirring, the university's president, Father Theodore Hesburgh—scholar, statesman, and adviser to six U.S. presidents—bolted from his warm, glass-enclosed booth and personally led the band in its post-game rendition of the Notre Dame Victory March.

"Yeah, it was a nice way to go out," Montana says. Nice—and typical.

As the 1981 National Football League season entered its stretch drive, the San Francisco 49ers were leading the NFC West with a 10–3 record. Heady stuff for a team that was 2–14 just two years ago.

Along the way, the 49ers handed the Dallas Cowboys their most humiliating loss in over a decade, 45–14. They defeated the Los Angeles Rams in San Francisco for the first time since 1966, 20–17. They beat the Steelers for the first time since 1968, 17–14, becoming the first NFC team to win in Pittsburgh since 1971. They upended Atlanta, 17–14.

The 49ers were once again selling out Candlestick Park. They were being talked about proudly on Nob Hill. Indeed, they had wrested the attention of Bay Area football fans away from the Super Bowl champions in Oakland.

In the midst of all this euphoria, naturally, was Joe Montana. Through thirteen games, he led the NFC with a 62.9 percent completion rate. He passed for 3,068 yards and fourteen touchdowns.

"I can't say enough about the way Joe has come through for us," coach Bill Walsh says. "He's playing so well, it's hard to believe he's only in his third [pro] season. He has the poise of a ten-year veteran."

Even Montana admits to being a little surprised by his rapid ascent in the treacherous waters of pro football. After all, many gifted young quarterbacks have been ruined in their first three seasons.

"I have to give most of the credit to Coach Walsh," Montana says. "He is a great teacher of the passing game, probably the best in the league. He's taught me so much in just three seasons. Plus, he's brought me along one step at a time.

"When I joined the team [in 1979], I was the backup to Steve DeBerg. I spent that first year studying the offense, watching from the sideline, basically learning the pro game. It was totally different from what I experienced in college.

"In college, I didn't read a defense until my junior year. I just reared back and threw the ball. Our offense didn't vary that much from week to week. We had our few things that we did well, and we just kept doing them. We didn't care who we were playing.

"In the pros, it's like a chess game. The defense does this; we do that. The defense shows this; we shift to that. The mental preparation is tremendous. It took me one whole year just to digest our playbook."

DeBerg started the first six games of the 1980 season. The 49ers opened with three consecutive victories, then lost the next three games by a combined score of 127–57. With the team's confidence sagging, Walsh switched quarterbacks. He went to Montana for two games, and the 49ers lost to the Rams and Tampa Bay. He switched back to DeBerg, and the team lost to the Lions, Packers, and Dolphins. Then he switched back to Montana and, suddenly, there was the spark.

Montana led the 49ers to a 12–0 victory over the Giants. Then he threw three touchdown passes in a 21–17 upset of the Patriots. "That gave me the confidence that I needed," Montana says.

The following week, Montana pulled out his old South Bend shillelagh and used it on the New Orleans Saints. The Saints were leading 35–7 at halftime. In other words, old Backstretch Joe had them right where he wanted them. In the second half, Montana ran for one touchdown and passed for two more, and the 49ers won 38–35 in overtime. It is documented as the greatest comeback in modern NFL history—and it was only his fifth start.

Walsh traded DeBerg to Denver in the off-season. In doing so, he took the 49ers franchise and placed it squarely on Montana's slender shoulders. Some people called it a gamble. They couldn't imagine Walsh putting that much faith in a young quarterback who had appeared in only a handful of regular-season games.

Walsh's argument: Montana wasn't just another young quarterback. He was special. He was ready for the big time.

Walsh believed in Montana. He believed in him from the first time they met in the spring of 1979. Walsh had gone to Los Angeles to watch James Owens, the UCLA halfback, work out prior to the draft. Walsh asked Owens to bring someone with him, someone who could throw the ball. Montana happened to be working out in the Los Angeles area at the time, so Owens got in touch with him. Joe went along as the designated passer.

"I'll admit, I went hoping to impress Coach Walsh, too," Montana says. "I knew the 49ers were looking for a quarterback. I figured Coach Walsh probably would draft Steve Dils, who played for him at Stanford. But I thought if I had a good day, it couldn't hurt. I did throw the ball well, and we talked. As he was leaving, he said, 'Keep in shape, Joe. You might be hearing from us.'"

On draft day, Walsh made Owens and Montana his first two selections.

"I liked everything about Joe," Walsh says. "I liked his quickness. I liked his attitude. I particularly liked his willingness to learn. I knew he was a young man who would improve every week. Some scouts had questioned his consistency, but I felt that was more the fault of the [Notre Dame] system than anything else. Joe is a tremendously fluid athlete with excellent snap in his arm and an instinct, an on-the-field awareness that you just can't coach.

"And there was that intangible factor: Joe was a winner all through college. If you're around him any length of time, you can feel it. He's a born leader, a champion."

"Confidence is a very fragile thing," Montana says. "Just because you have it in college doesn't mean you'll have it in the pros. A lot of young quarterbacks get eaten up in the NFL because their confidence is shattered. Coach Walsh really helped me in that area. I remember the first time I played against the Rams, I looked across the line and I thought, 'Wow, there's Hacksaw Reynolds, there's Jack Youngblood.' Coach Walsh said, 'Forget that. You belong here, too.'"

Montana gazed around his family room, at the photograph of the Golden Gate Bridge hanging over the sofa, at the stuffed teddy bear in the 49ers number 16 jersey leaning against the stereo.

"I have the feeling I'm in the right place at the right time," he says. "I came to a young, progressive team with a head coach who specializes in the passing offense."

The truth is, Montana is a football workaholic. He has great rapport with his receivers because he stays after practice and works with them. He has a precocious grasp of NFL defenses because he studies film until dawn. Montana is no fluke. He has made a quantum leap to pro football stardom, but he has paid full fare. His coaches and teammates respect that.

"I roomed with Joe last year before he got married," Clark said, "and he didn't go out much. Every night he was either looking at film or studying the game plan. It was like living with a guy who had exams every day for five months. But it paid off on Sunday. Bill sends in all the plays, but Joe is free to change them depending on what he sees in the defense. Joe audibles a lot, and he's right almost all the time. You never see him throw the ball into coverage."

It is Tuesday, the 49ers' off day, and Joe Montana is relaxing at his new home in Woodside, California. Later, he will drive into town for an appearance at the 49ers' Booster Club. From there, he will drop by the club offices and pick up his game plan for Sunday's opponent. Then it will be practice and study the rest of the week.

But for the moment at least, Joe Montana is free of all that. He is in his yard exercising his two Arabian horses, El Makata ("We call him `Mac'") and Ghafad Asim ("He's `Simmy'"). Cass is watching from the fence.

It is a glorious October day, the sun shining, a warm breeze sweeping through the hills. The Pacific Ocean is sparkling off in the distance. Look down the canyon and there is San Francisco, so close you feel like you can reach out and touch it.

This is quite a change in lifestyle for a kid who grew up in Monongahela, Pennsylvania; who went to college in Indiana, where the winter snows have been known to cover the sycamores. Here he is, living high in California pumpkin country, raising Arabian horses and listening to coyotes howl in the night.

"After four years at Notre Dame, I had it with cold weather," Montana says. "I made a vow. I was never gonna live anywhere where I had to scrape snow off my windshield again.

"I remember one time I had just moved into an apartment off campus. I didn't have a TV, a phone, or anything. A blizzard hit South Bend. Snowed me in for five days. My car was buried. I couldn't see it, much less get it out of the parking lot. I was going nuts, locked in that room with nothing to do.

"Finally, I went next door and used the phone. I called a city councilman I knew and asked if he could use any pull to have a snowplow sent over to get my car out. He said he'd see what he could do. Four o'clock the next morning, there's a knock on my door. It's my neighbor. He says, `Hey, man, there's a tank out here, and the driver is asking for you.'

"The councilman had called the National Guard, and they sent a tank over to get my car. The driver was a sergeant, so he made this other poor guy burrow down into the snow and hook the cable to the axle of my car. I thought he was gonna suffocate. I guess that's when it hit me, standing there at 4 A.M., freezing, watching a tank pull my car out of a snowdrift, that there had to be a better way to live. So here I am."

Joe Montana and El Makata are walking behind the house. They walk to the edge of the canyon, looking out toward the Pacific. Joe is smiling. He is among the top-rated quarterbacks in the NFC; his team is in first place; he is the master of all he surveys.

Standing there, framed by the ocean, his blond hair tousled gently by the wind, he looks, well, like a legend.

Epilogue: I was assigned to write this profile in October 1981. Montana was playing well, but he was not yet a superstar. He was twenty-five and very laid back. He laughed at the idea of being a celebrity. Within three months, he had led the 49ers to their first Super Bowl, and his life changed forever. He played fifteen seasons in the NFL and won four Super Bowls. He was inducted into the Pro Football Hall of Fame in 2000.

*Originally published in *Pro Magazine*, 1981.

Passing of the Chief Marks the End of an Era*

$\mathbf{A}$rt Rooney Sr. died in a Pittsburgh hospital yesterday at the age of eighty-seven. An era in pro football died with him.

The Steelers' founder was the last flesh-and-blood link between today's glitzy NFL and the tramp game that ran one step ahead of the bill collectors fifty years ago.

Rooney was there in 1933 with George Halas, Bert Bell, George Preston Marshall, and Curly Lambeau. They were the stubborn pioneers who shared a vision of pro football growing up and becoming big league some day.

The NFL was their dream; the Norman Bramans and Jack Kent Cookes of the world simply hitched a ride when it became fashionable.

The new owners never had to carry the game on their backs. The Halases and Rooneys did. Therein lies the difference.

"I didn't like losing games, and I didn't like losing money," Rooney once said in an interview, "but I'll tell you something, and this is from the bottom of my heart: Whatever I lost in money, I was lucky to be able to lose it. I'd pay to lose it just to stay in this game. I love it that much."

The Chief, as he was known, had a wonderful perspective, warm and genuine, full of caring for the sport and its people. Now he is gone, and the NFL won't be quite the same.

Super Bowl parties won't be as much fun without old Art holding court amid the ice sculptures. He would wave his cigar in the air and tell stories about Johnny Blood and Bobby Layne, two Hall of Famers who did their best broken-field running after curfew.

There was always a crowd around the Chief. He made people feel good.

"Art Rooney is the greatest man who ever walked," Steelers quarterback Terry Bradshaw said. "When we won those Super Bowls, we won them for him. We loved the man."

The feeling was mutual. Rooney was a sucker for his players, too. They were like part of the family.

Rooney kept Rocky Bleier around for two years after he was wounded in Vietnam. The coaches wanted to dump Bleier, but Rooney insisted they give the halfback time to recover and compete for a job. The Rock went on to become the fifth-leading rusher in Steelers history and a key contributor to their four championship teams. One of the most touching scenes after the Steelers' Super Bowl win in 1975 was a tearful Bleier embracing Rooney in the locker room.

"Thank you for giving me the chance to play," Bleier said.

Rooney held up the game ball.

"Thank you for this," he said.

Art Rooney bought the Pittsburgh franchise for $2,500. He spent another $100 to buy iodine and tape on his way to the first game. Pro football owners were expected to do things like that in the 1930s.

Rooney sold tickets, swept floors, and hustled space in the newspapers. He didn't mind working hard. He was raised that way, the oldest of eight children born to an Irish saloonkeeper on Pittsburgh's North Side.

As a youth, Rooney boxed and played semi-pro baseball. He turned down Knute Rockne's offer of a football scholarship to Notre Dame. Instead, he formed his own team and played exhibitions for money. He once lost to Jim Thorpe and the Canton Bulldogs, 6–0.

"I missed a field goal, and Thorpe ran it back all the way," Rooney recalled.

At twenty-three, Rooney visited his first racetrack and got hooked on the horses. One weekend, Rooney hit it big at Saratoga. That was the money he used to buy the Steelers.

The team was a loser from the beginning, both on the field and at the box office. Over the years, Rooney had dozens of offers to sell the club or move it to Atlanta, New Orleans, Phoenix, places like that. He turned them all down.

"My heart is here," he said. "I could never leave."

The Chief was rooted in Pittsburgh, all right. He and his late wife, Kathleen, lived in the same house for fifty years. It is a three-story Victorian just up the hill from Three Rivers Stadium. Rooney walked to and from the ballpark every day. That should tell you all you need to know about the man. In this era of jet-set owners, with their limousines and helicopters, the Chief preferred to hoof it.

What about bad weather?

"I walk faster," he said.

Rooney didn't watch the game from a luxury suite, either. He usually stood in the back of the press box with his cronies and ate the same cold hot dogs as the sportswriters. He had a handshake and a kind word for everyone, win or lose.

Incredibly, Rooney did not see the most memorable play in Steelers history: Franco Harris's Immaculate Reception in a 1972 AFC playoff game against the Oakland Raiders. He was on the stadium elevator at the time, mourning.

There was less than a minute left, and the Steelers were trailing, 7–6. The Chief was on his way to the locker room to offer his condolences to the coaches and players. After forty years of losing, Rooney knew the routine by heart.

Suddenly, a cheer shook the stadium.

There was no radio in the elevator, so Rooney had no idea what had happened. It seemed like an eternity before the doors opened, and he asked a security guard what was going on.

"You won't believe this," he said, "but we just scored a touchdown."

Rooney watched the replay on the guard's portable TV.

"A ball finally bounced our way," the Chief said. "Maybe our luck is changing."

Four Super Bowl wins followed.

The Steelers had just eight winning seasons in their first four decades, so it was nice to see Bradshaw, Harris, Mean Joe Greene, and that bunch put the Chief on top for a while in the `70s.

Rooney never cared for his image as the NFL's lovable loser. The truth was, he hated losing as much as the next guy, but he kept the frustration bottled up. Just because he didn't carry on like George Steinbrenner didn't mean there were no scars on the Chief's insides. There were plenty of them.

Rooney wanted to bring an NFL championship to Pittsburgh more than anything in the world. When the Steelers finally climbed the mountain in 1975, Art figured the mission was complete, and he turned over the club presidency to his son, Dan.

The Chief kept his office at Three Rivers Stadium, and he still hung out there. He answered his own phone and visited with any old player or coach who happened by. And they did, every day.

Now that Art Rooney is gone, there will be hundreds of stories going around. Believe them all. He was a remarkable man, a member of the Pro Football Hall of Fame and the most beloved owner in professional sports.

Two stories bear repeating.

The first concerns a testimonial dinner the City of Pittsburgh gave in Rooney's honor a while back. The sponsors wanted to present Rooney with a car, a boat, something nice like that. The Chief said no way. He insisted all the money go to the Crippled Children's Fund. So it did.

Another time, Rooney was in New York City, and he shared a cab with a missionary. The priest explained he was on a fund-raising drive and mentioned the names of several prominent businessmen he hoped to visit in Manhattan.

Rooney knew one of the men and told the priest, "Put him at the top of the list."

Then he stuffed a thick wad of bills in the missionary's hand.

"When you talk to him," the Chief said, "tell him Art Rooney started you off with ten grand."

True story.

That was Art Rooney.

*Originally published in the *Philadelphia Daily News*, August 25, 1988. Reprinted with permission by Philadelphia Newspapers, LLC.

The day I'll never forget
—August 1, 1998. My
boyhood idol, former
Eagles receiver Tommy
McDonald, asked me to
be his presenter when he
was inducted into the Pro
Football Hall of Fame in
Canton, Ohio.

It was always a challenge
trying to get a decent
quote out of John Unitas,
the Baltimore Colts Hall
of Fame quarterback.
Years later when I pro-
duced an HBO special on
Unitas, I asked him about
it. "I'd rather be known
as a bad interview and a
good player than the other
way around," Unitas said.

The Phillies clubhouse was a hostile place in the late '70s with players and reporters at odds most of the time. The one player who was always willing to talk was Pete Rose, whose drive to win helped the Phillies finally capture their first World Series in 1980.

Eagles general manager Pete Retzlaff (left) and owner Leonard Tose (center) are presenting me the winners trophy for the "Paper Bowl," a touch football game played between the *Philadelphia Bulletin* and the *Inquirer* at Franklin Field in 1970. Also taking part in the ceremony is my *Bulletin* co-captain Nick Nagurny.

Checking out the action from the Cotton Bowl press box on New Year's Day, 1978. This was my first in-person look at Joe Montana, who led Notre Dame to an upset victory over #1-ranked Texas and Earl Campbell.

My first taste of broadcasting was calling Temple football and basketball games on WRTI, the campus radio station. I handled the color while Charles Liebman (right) did the play-by-play.

I was the covering the Eagles for the Bulletin when Dick Vermeil took over the team in 1976. When I joined NFL Films, I worked on an ESPN documentary about Vermeil: "A Coach for All Seasons." Dick and his wife Carol came to the premiere with NFL Films President Steve Sabol (center) and my co-producer Chris Barlow (far right).

It was an exhausting summer covering the 1984 Olympics in
Los Angeles. I was the last one out of the press center almost every
night. That is *Daily News* columnist Rich Hofmann working
behind me.

The media "extras" gather on the set of the *Invincible* in July, 2005. Disney asked real-life reporters to appear in the film based on the life of Eagles special teamer Vince Papale, I'm in the middle with Mark Wahlberg, who played Vince. The other writers are (left to right) Bob Glauber (*Newsday*), Vic Carucci (NFL.com), Don Banks (*Sports Illustrated*) and Sam Farmer (*Los Angeles Times*).

Comcast SportsNet took the *Post-Game Live* show to Super Bowl XXXIX. The usual *Post-Game* crew was on hand. (Left to right) Vaughn Hebron, myself, Governor Rendell and Michael Barkann.

The Shulas Always Have Felt at Home near the Gridiron*

Don Shula was relaxing on the sofa. His son, Mike, was petting the family cat. The TV was tuned to—what else?—a football game.

It was New Year's Day; Auburn was playing Texas A&M in the Cotton Bowl. Don liked Auburn. Mike, naturally, picked the Aggies. The Shulas will find a way to compete at anything.

"Look at the defense," Don was saying. "They're coming with the blitz."

"Bet they're not," Mike said.

The ball was snapped. The Auburn linebackers dropped off, and the Aggies completed a pass for a first down. Mike smiled as he watched the replay.

"They didn't blitz, Dad," he said.

"Well, they should have," Don grumbled.

Dorothy Shula was listening from the kitchen. She agreed this sounded familiar. Don and Dorothy have been married twenty-seven years. Make that twenty-seven seasons.

"I can't imagine our lives without football," she said. "I can't remember a time when we weren't watching a game, going to a game, or talking about a game.

"It's a great life," she said, "especially when you win. And we've been lucky. We've won a lot."

The Shulas are, indeed, the First Family of Football. Consider:
- Don, the fifty-six-year-old patriarch, is the NFL's second all-time–winningest coach. His total of 255 career victories (including playoffs) trails only the legendary George Halas (326).

Shula has won sixteen division titles and led his Miami Dolphins to the AFC championship game three of the past four years. His six Super Bowl appearances are the most by any coach or player.

"If he's not the best coach ever, I don't know who is," said Bob Griese, who quarterbacked the Dolphins for fourteen years (1967–80).
- David Shula, twenty-six, is an assistant coach working with the Miami quarterbacks and receivers.

The former Dartmouth receiving star is a strong candidate to take over as the Eagles' next head coach. He would become the youngest non-playing head coach in NFL history.

"They said I was too young when I was named head coach in Baltimore [at thirty-three]," Don Shula said, "but if you can do the job, age doesn't matter.

"Based on what I've seen—and I'm speaking strictly as a head coach, not as a father—David can handle it. He's bright, and he works well with people. He made a real contribution here."

• Mike Shula, twenty, is a junior at Alabama. A left-handed quarterback, Shula led the thirteenth-ranked Crimson Tide (9–2–1) to a 24–3 rout of Southern Cal in the Aloha Bowl.

Mike threw sixteen touchdown passes this season, a school record. His father was shocked when he heard the news on TV.

"I thought, 'Didn't [Joe] Namath and [Ken] Stabler go to Alabama?'" Don Shula said. "'Didn't Bart Starr go there, too? You mean Mike broke their records?' That's quite an accomplishment.

"I'm proud of Mike, the way he handled himself when he was hurt and benched [1984]. He was down in the dumps for a while, but he battled back. He's a competitor. Guess it runs in the family."

The Shulas' three daughters—Donna (married), Sharon (at law school), and Annie (a college student)—felt slighted at times, Dorothy admits, but they never complained. They went to the games and cheered faithfully for the home team.

Sharon, in fact, became a sideline photographer. Her father got her a field pass, and she shot every Dolphins home game for three seasons. She sold several photos to the NFL magazine, *Pro*.

"It wasn't easy for any of them, boys or girls, to carry that name around," Don Shula said. "They were under a microscope. Kids would say [unkind] things, even some adults.

"But I'm proud of the way they handled themselves. They won their own respect. They never wanted something for nothing. In that sense, they were a lot like me. They wanted to earn everything and they did.

"Football was part of the equation, a big part, but not the whole thing."

There have been other great coaches whose sons showed an interest in football, but very few found their way to the sidelines.

George Halas Jr. was an executive with the Chicago Bears. Mike and Pete Brown (sons of Paul) have served in the Cincinnati Bengals' front office since the team's inception.

Vince Lombardi Jr. and Bruce Allen (son of George) became general managers in the USFL. They were all in the family business, but they pushed ballpoints, not blocking sleds.

Aside from Shula, Bum Phillips was the only NFL coach with a son in the trenches. Wade Phillips was an assistant on his father's staff in New Orleans. When Bum resigned recently, Wade served as interim head coach.

But who would have expected to see father and son as rival head coaches in the NFL? That will be the case next season if Norman Braman hires David Shula. (The Eagles meet the Dolphins in the '86 pre-season.)

And consider this scenario for 1987: Mike Shula is drafted into the NFL. That would mean Don would be coaching in Miami, David coaching in Philadelphia, and Mike playing quarterback somewhere.

"I hadn't thought about it until recently," Don Shula said, "but you're right: It would be interesting."

What would it be like when they face each other, jut-jaw to jut-jaw?

"The same as when we compete in tennis or anything else, it would be intense," Don said. "We'd give it our best shot, then shake hands afterwards. Business is business.

"I know who Dorothy would be rooting for, though. She'd root for the young ones to beat me."

"Don's right, I would," Dorothy said. "A mother's instincts are always the strongest."

Don and David competed against each other in 1981, David's one and only season as an NFL player. Their first meeting was billed as the Shula Bowl.

Don was on the Miami bench. Mike, then sixteen, was at his side, charting plays. David was returning punts for the Baltimore Colts. Sharon was on the field taking pictures.

And Dorothy?

"I was in the press box, covering my eyes," she said. "I told people I was rooting for the Dolphins, but that was a lie. I was rooting for David."

Don Shula remembers walking into the locker room at halftime, upset with his team's listless performance, and seeing his wife being interviewed on the TV monitor.

"Turn that off," Shula hollered. "We've got a ballgame to concentrate on."

The Dolphins won the game, but it was a struggle (31–28). David never did handle the ball that day. All four Miami punts went out of bounds.

Later, someone asked Don Shula how he would have reacted if his son had broken away on a long punt return.

"I would have chewed out my coverage team," Shula said. "It could have cost us the game."

Like the man said, business is business.

"People see David and Mike [in football], and they assume I pushed them," Don Shula said, "and that's not true. I exposed them to the game; they worked around the team when they were kids, but I never told 'em they had to play or coach.

"The fact David and Mike are where they are is a reflection of, number one, a choice they made, and number two, their ability. They were both good players; they would have won college scholarships no matter what their last name was.

"What did I give them? The fundamentals. Discipline. They learned a lot watching Griese and [Nick] Buoniconti, players like that. They learned the importance of a winning attitude."

"My father never pressured me to do anything," David Shula said. "He never said, 'These are my shoes. . . . Fill 'em.'

"What he would say was, 'If you want to do something, give it your all, and don't come out a quitter. You can't always come out a winner, but you can always give it your best.'

"That's the philosophy he's lived by," David said, "and it's served him well. I applied it to everything I did; so did Mike. As it turns out, we're both in football, and I know our father couldn't be more pleased."

The photograph ran in the *Miami News* on December 11, 1982. It showed Don Shula embracing Mike after he had led Columbus High School to a 31–24 overtime win against Vero Beach in the state semifinals.

The elder Shula looked more elated in this photo than he did after the Dolphins defeated Washington in Super Bowl VII to complete their 17–0 season. His eyes were closed; his smile was unlike anything the Miami fans had seen before.

"I was a nervous wreck when that [Columbus] game ended," said Shula, who has survived thirty NFL post-season games, including the longest game ever played (Miami's 27–24 win over Kansas City in double overtime in 1971).

"When I watch Mike, I'm strictly a parent. I'm not used to that helpless feeling. At least when I'm coaching, I'm in the game; I have some control. At Mike's games, I see everything, but I can't do anything.

"I usually find a row [in the bleachers] where I can be alone so I can pace and concentrate. Am I vocal? You might say that."

"One game," Dorothy Shula said, "Don was alone in the back and he shouted, 'Timeout.' You could hear him all over the stadium.

"He's not much better now. We were watching Alabama–Auburn on TV. It was Don, myself, and our daughters. Don was carrying on so badly we all left the room. It was just Don and the cat here in the fourth quarter.

"I can understand," Dorothy Shula said. "Watching your son play is agony and ecstasy. I'm more nervous watching Mike than I was watching David. The quarterback has so much pressure. And some of those hits . . ."

Part of her uneasiness stems from the crippling neck injury suffered this season by Marc Buoniconti, Nick's son, a linebacker at the Citadel. Marc and Mike were high-school teammates, so the news hit the Shulas hard.

"I sat with Nick and his wife, Terri, at the [Columbus] games," Dorothy said, "and we would hold our breath any time a player was down. When I heard what happened to Marc, I began to see the game differently.

"I worry more than I used to. But I'd never ask Mike to quit; it's too important to him. So I'll keep going to the games and lending whatever support I can. I'll just pray harder the night before."

It was never easy, wearing the Shula name in Dade County. As much as Don Shula is revered here—a state highway was named after him in 1983—his sons were easy targets for every losing high-school coach and frustrated parent in the area.

The week before Columbus opened its 1982 season, an anonymous caller to the Dolphins' office reported there was a bounty on Mike Shula's head. "He won't finish the game," the voice said.

"I didn't know what to think," Dorothy said. "I had heard [fans] shout things like, `Get Shula. . . . Break his leg.' I hated it, it made me angry, but it didn't frighten me. This [call] frightened me."

Mike never blinked. "You just go out and play," he said. "I've taken a few cheap shots, but that's part of the game."

The youngest Shula threw three touchdown passes that night en route to a brilliant year. The six-foot-two, 185 pounder was voted first-team All-Dade County quarterback by the *Miami News.*

"I still remember the day Michael was born," Don Shula said. "The doctor came out and said, `Coach, you didn't get that fullback you wanted.'

"I was disappointed. I really wanted another boy. I said, `Aww . . .' Then he said, `But you got one helluva quarterback.'

"Pretty good scouting report," Shula said, "for a doctor."

If Don Shula has any regrets about his twenty-eight years of coaching, it is that he built his 255–99–6 record at the expense of a normal home life.

Shula is a man who cherishes family and friends. After the Dolphins' win in Super Bowl VIII, Shula passed up owner Joe Robbie's formal victory party to celebrate with a dozen old friends from his hometown, Painesville, Ohio.

In many ways, Don Shula has never changed. He still attends mass every morning. He refuses to drink hard liquor. He says his greatest source of pleasure is playing with his grandson, Danny, David's feisty two year old.

Dorothy recalls a recent visit when Don shook his finger in Danny's face and said, "Don't you do that." Danny replied by putting his tiny finger under Don's nose and saying, "Don't you do that."

There isn't a 280 pound defensive tackle in the world who would have dared to do that, but Danny did, and Don couldn't stop laughing for an hour. See, ol' Shoes isn't so tough, after all.

"Football has its rewards," Shula said, "but it also has its price. The loss of a family life was the one part of this job I always hated. Still do.

"We made the most of our time together. We'd take trips in June before camp. One year we took my parents to Hungary so they could visit our relatives. Another year we took a cruise to Alaska. Had a great time.

"But we didn't have the daily routine. We didn't sit around the dinner table together. I was either away or working late. The boys were usually at practice. Dorothy did a wonderful job keeping everyone in line.

"I did what I could," Shula said, "but I never felt it was enough."

"We understood what our father did for a living; it was never a problem," David Shula said.

"Actually, he was around a lot. It seemed like every time I was in a [music] recital, spelling bee, or class play, he was there. He made time. I do the same thing now with Danny.

"Times when we were together, we never discussed football. We knew what the Dolphins were doing; it was my father who had to catch up. He'd ask Annie about her horse show [she rides], or he'd ask Donna about school. He was interested in what we were doing."

Was he a strict parent?

David laughed. "What do you think?" he said. "When he told us to clean our rooms, we cleaned our rooms. And we knew better than to bring home a bad report card.

"But he was a great parent for the same reason he is a great coach; there's no ambivalence in the man. You know where he's coming from all the time. He tells you what he expects, and he makes it clear he means business."

Did he bring the rare Dolphin losses home with him?

"He'd brood," Mike said. "He hates to lose. Mom would tell us, `Better leave Daddy alone. He had a tough day.'"

For Don Shula, the one good thing about the 1982 NFL players' strike was that it allowed him to share in Mike's senior year at Columbus High.

Shula spent the two strike months working with Mike, studying films and discussing strategy.

Don minimizes his influence, but the fact is Mike had a dazzling season. He passed for 1,683 yards and eighteen touchdowns. Most folks figure Daddy was signaling the plays from the bleachers.

"Mike had a good coach [Dennis Lavelle]; it wasn't my place to interfere," Don Shula said. "I'd sit with Mike while he watched film of his next opponent. I might point out something in a particular defense but I didn't say, `Run this and this.'"

"My father saw things I might overlook," Mike said, "and he worked on my footwork, my release. Basically, he took what I was doing and refined it.

"I learned a lot just working [charting plays] at Dolphins games. I saw him make [strategy] adjustments as the game went along. As a quarterback, you couldn't ask for better experience."

Mike Shula's football IQ was so high, Lavelle allowed him to call his own plays at Columbus. How many quarterbacks, at any level, can make that claim today?

"Shulas are different," Lavelle said.

We noticed.

Epilogue: Don Shula holds the NFL record for most career victories by a coach (328). He was inducted into the Pro Football Hall of Fame in 1997. David Shula became a head coach with Cincinnati, and, in 1994, Don and David became the first father and son to coach against each other in the NFL. Mike Shula was head football coach at the University of Alabama from 2003 through 2006. Dorothy Shula died of breast cancer in 1991.

*Originally published in the *Philadelphia Daily News,* January 14, 1986. Reprinted with permission by Philadelphia Newspapers, LLC.

BASEBALL

◆ ◆ ◆

The 500 Club*

We stand in awe of the Slugger. He is part man, part myth, and All-American.

He is the heavyweight champion of our national pastime, Paul Bunyan with a thirty-six—ounce switch. He swings hard, he hits hard and even when he fails, he fails hard. It is all part of the mystique.

The Mighty Casey, now there was a Slugger. He struck out, and they still wrote a poem about him. Roy Hobbs, "the Natural," was another one.

Did you ever notice there aren't any literary classics devoted to singles hitters or middle relievers? It is always the man who carries the big stick. That is because the Slugger is a special breed.

We can all close our eyes and make a lucky catch. Given enough chances, we can all throw a strike. But we can't all hit a baseball over the roof at Yankee Stadium. We can only dream it, and, of course, we do.

The Slugger does it for real—usually in the bottom of the ninth, with a 3–2 count—and we are days trying to catch our breath.

"How does he do it?" we wonder.

There is no mystery in a seven-foot-four Ralph Sampson dropping a basketball through a hoop. Or, for that matter, a 240 pound Larry Csonka running over a 170 pound tackler.

But what is it that enables a man no bigger than your next-door neighbor to drive a baseball 540 feet into the centerfield bleachers? Not just once, mind you, but over and over again.

Say, thirty-five times a year for fifteen years. Say, five hundred times, total.

What is it that allows a Mike Schmidt to become one of just fourteen Major Leaguers to reach that milestone? What is it that sets the 500 Home Run Clubber apart from every other Class A prospect who ever wrapped his dreams around a Louisville Slugger?

That is the fascination of the home-run fraternity. That is why we chase after these men with our notepads and tape measures. That is why we cast them in bronze and give them nicknames—the Babe, the Hammer, the Beast, the Killer—suitable for a legend.

"When you think about it, the home run is the ultimate analogy," said Reggie Jackson, the former Cheltenham High School star and the leading active home-run hitter in the majors with 548. His total ranks sixth of all time.

"When people want to describe a great feeling," Jackson said, "they don't say, `It was like serving an ace at Wimbledon.' They don't say, `It was like making a hole in one at the Masters.' They don't say, `It was like winning the Indy 500.' They say, `It was like hitting a homer in the World Series.'

"Why? Because baseball is a game we can all relate to. It's the American game. And the power . . . Who doesn't dream about power? I know that's what I love about hitting. It's a show of strength.

"It's two against one at the plate: the pitcher and the catcher versus you. When I'm up there, I'm thinking, `Try everything you want. Rub up the ball. Move the fielders around. I'm still gonna hit that ball.' God, do I love to hit that ball outta the park and hear `em say, `Wow.'

"That," Jackson said, "is what it's all about, that moment. Really, there are no words to describe it. But I'll tell you this: You could do it five hundred times—or five thousand times—and it would never get old."

Indeed, there is no athletic feat so neatly defined, no moment of triumph quite so focused as the home run.

All eyes follow the majestic flight of the ball, then return to The Slugger as he circles the bases. The stage is his alone. The game has stopped. Nothing more can happen until he allows it to happen.

With a single stroke, the Slugger has electrified an entire stadium, not to mention a vast TV and radio audience. He has put his stamp on the contest. And there were no downfield blocks, no assists, no helping hands of any kind.

Just the Slugger and his bat. That is the beauty of it, and it has not changed in almost a century.

That is what we pay to see, and that is what we talk about the next day at work. "You should've seen it. . . . You should've heard it. . . . That ball must have gone five hundred feet, at least." OK, so maybe it went four hundred. Who's counting?

"Do you think about hitting them far?" a newsman once asked Babe Ruth, the man who established the home run as a staple of American culture.

"Well, kid," the Babe replied. "I don't think about hitting `em short."

That is what made the Babe the Babe, the Hammer the Hammer and Schmitty, well, Schmitty. And we wouldn't have it any other way.

It is baseball's select circle, the 500 Home Run Club. It is the prestige address in Cooperstown, New York, an executive suite within the Hall of Fame.

Consider the men who don't belong: Lou Gehrig (493), Stan Musial and Willie Stargell (475), Carl Yastrzemski (452), and Duke Snider (407). Joltin' Joe DiMaggio didn't even come close (361).

Great players, every one, but they still could not get past the doorman at Club 500. That, folks, is what you call an exclusive membership.

Michael Jack Schmidt was formally welcomed Saturday. He joins Mel Ott (511), Ernie Banks and Eddie Mathews (512), Ted Williams and Willie McCovey (521), Jimmie Foxx (534), Mickey Mantle (536), Jackson (548), Harmon Killebrew (573), and Frank Robinson (586).

Willie Mays is a notch above at 660. Ruth had the record they said would never be broken: 714 home runs. Then there is Hank Aaron, the Hammer, who surpassed the Babe and now stands alone at 755.

That is fourteen men in more than one hundred years of baseball.

"I don't think you'll see fourteen more," said California Angels manager Gene Mauch. "You might not see four more. How many guys come along with that combination of power, consistency, and longevity? You're talking about guys who play at another level."

Agreed, but what was it that made these men tick? Do they have something in common aside from keen eyes and quick hands? Did I say keen eyes? Scratch that. Reggie Jackson wears glasses. His eyes are as bad as Ted Williams's eyes are good.

OK, so what is it?

Physically, there are similarities. Ten of the fourteen are within an inch of six feet tall. Most weighed around 190 pounds. Killebrew, Jackson, Foxx, and Mantle are listed at six feet and 195 pounds, although Foxx (he was the Beast) was probably a little heftier.

Ott was the smallest at five-foot-nine, 170 pounds. McCovey, better known as "Stretch," was the tallest at six-foot-four. It should come as no surprise to learn Ruth was the heaviest. The Hall of Fame records list the Babe at six-foot-two, 215, but that was probably his weight as a Boston Red Sox rookie.

During his glory years with the Yankees, the Babe was lugging around at least 230 pounds, and that's not counting the blonde on each arm. His appetite, in every area, was legendary.

As you might expect, all fourteen men were superb all-around athletes. The eleven modern-era sluggers starred in football as well as baseball in high school. It was football, in fact, that led to the knee problems that haunted Mantle and Schmidt throughout their Major League careers.

Killebrew was one of the nation's top high-school quarterbacks as a senior in Payette, Idaho. Jackson was a halfback with 9.6 speed who went to Arizona State on a football scholarship. Mathews passed up a football scholarship to Georgia to sign a $6,000 contract with the Boston Braves in 1949.

"I signed at my senior prom, one minute after midnight," recalled Mathews, now a Minor League hitting instructor with the Braves. "I was tired of school, and my dad was sick [tuberculosis]. Six thousand was a lot of money back then."

Ernie Banks was an end in football and a high jumper (five feet, eleven inches) in track. McCovey set a school record with eleven varsity letters in Mobile, Alabama. And to this day, Willie Mays insists football, not baseball, was his best sport in high school.

"I was a quarterback," Mays said recently. "I could run the ball, throw the ball. Whatever you want, I could do. Football was my game, but the [bonus] money was in baseball, so that's where I went. Can't say I regret it now."

They weren't huge men even among their Major League peers. There were other players with wider shoulders and bigger biceps—guys like Ted Kluszewski, Frank Howard, and Boog Powell—but they didn't come close to the five-hundred class. They had the power but not the consistency.

Make no mistake: Strength is a necessary part of the equation. We think of Banks as a wispy six-foot-one, 175 pound shortstop, but he had the wrists and forearms of a blacksmith. "You grab a hold of him," former Cubs manager Bob Scheffing said, "and it's like grabbing steel."

Aaron was rather average in appearance at six feet, 180 pounds, yet he hit the ball harder more often than anyone who ever played the game. He never lifted a weight, but he hit forty or more home runs eight times in his Major League career.

Aaron's secret, if you could call it that, was his wrists. You could make the same statement about most of the 500 Clubbers. Even a big stud such as McCovey relied more on timing and quick hands than muscle to drive balls through the wind at Candlestick Park.

"Willie's hands travel with lightning speed for about a foot and a half," former Giants manager Bill Rigney said. "He packs the power of a good boxer's right hand. It is sudden and explosive. . . . Boom."

"People got fooled by Hank Aaron's follow-through and his distance," Mauch said. "They assumed he took a big cut. He didn't. His swing was really from here to here [roughly the length of home plate].

"He didn't get that nickname 'Hammer' for nothing. He hammered that ball; he chopped down on it. That's what you call power hitting. The players today have these big, long swings. All that's doing is making them slow [with the bat]."

Former Pittsburgh pitcher Bob Friend agrees. "Those wrist hitters don't have the weaknesses other hitters have," Friend said. "It's fantastic how long Henry can look at a pitch. It's like giving him an extra strike.

"The best thing you can do is keep the ball where he'll only hit singles."

Aaron's power figures are stunning. He is the all-time Major League leader in total bases (6,856), extra base hits (1,477), and runs batted in (2,297), as well as home runs.

But what often is overlooked is Aaron's .305 career batting average. He won two National League batting titles in the '50s. He was a tougher out then because he hit the ball to all fields. When the Braves moved to Atlanta in 1966, Aaron went for power and tried to pull everything.

Early in his career, Aaron's teammates marveled at how he never seemed to crack a bat. He went through a half-season using the same thirty-three–ounce Louisville Slugger. No one could understand it.

One day, Warren Spahn examined the bat and found all the dents—the places where Aaron had hit the ball—were in the same "sweet" part. In other words, Aaron never got jammed or fooled by a pitch. His concentration and bat control were virtually flawless.

"The amazing thing about Henry was he made [hitting] look so easy," said Mathews, who combined with Aaron to hit 863 homers for the Braves, surpassing Ruth and Gehrig as the most potent one–two punch in baseball history.

"Henry would look so loose and relaxed at the plate. You almost never saw him grinding the bat handle. Then the pitch would come in, and he'd just uncoil. We had a friendly rivalry about who would hit more [homers], and Henry usually got the better of me.

"But it was just a pleasure to watch that man handle a bat. He looked like an orchestra conductor with his baton, you know, just that smooth."

Babe Ruth was not a wrist hitter. He believed in taking a lusty whack at the ball, putting all his weight into it. Sometimes the Babe fell down after a swinging strike. No problem. He would simply adjust his cap and take a similar cut at the next pitch.

Mel Ott was famous for his exaggerated stride. A left-handed hitter, Ott would raise his right leg to knee height as the pitcher was in his windup, then Ott would step down just before impact. It looked funny, but it worked just fine. Ott won the National League home-run title six times.

Of the recent 500 Clubbers, Jackson is the closest thing to an old-school slugger. He swings savagely and often in futility. Going into this season, Jackson held the Major League record for career strikeouts (2,500).

If that sounds like a lot, it is. That is almost as many strikeouts as Ruth and Banks combined (2,566). Put another way: Reggie has more strikeouts than the Yankees' Don Mattingly has at bats. The straw that stirs the drink also stirs a lot of air.

The 500 Club accounts for seven of the top fourteen all-time strikeout victims. Schmidt is fifth, with 1,744. Aaron's strikeout ratio was a modest one for every 8.9 at bats.

Among the great power hitters, only Ted Williams was tougher to fan. The Splendid Splinter struck out once for every 10.8 at bats. Even more remarkable, Williams retired with almost three times as many walks (2,019, number two behind Ruth) as strikeouts. That is unheard of.

Williams put his baseball philosophy in a 1960 book entitled, *The Science of Hitting*. It still is considered the definitive thesis on the subject. Williams stresses the need for the batter to be selective, "to get a good ball to hit."

"A good hitter can hit a pitch that is over the plate three times better than a great hitter with a questionable ball in a tough spot," Williams wrote. "Pitchers still make enough mistakes to give you some in your `happy zone.' But the greatest hitter living can't hit bad balls good."

You might want to circle that last sentence and leave it in Juan Samuel's locker.

"When you start fishing for the pitch that's an inch off the plate," Williams wrote, "the pitcher—if he's smart—will put the next one two inches off. Then three. And before you know it, you're making fifty outs a year on pitches you never should have swung at."

Williams was the Morris the Cat of 500 Clubbers: He was finicky about his pitches. That is why he retired after nineteen seasons with a .344 average, sixth best of all time and just one point behind the ultimate Punch-and-Judy hitter, Wee Willie Keeler.

"Takes all kinds, you know?" Willie Mays said. "Ted Williams wrote a book about hitting, and I couldn't write a page. Hitting was just something I did naturally.

"I couldn't teach you how to hit home runs anymore than I could teach you how to jump off the roof and fly. Certain folks, God just made to hit. Williams was born to hit, but he spent a whole lot of time thinking about it. I never did.

"People say I hit a lot of bad balls for home runs," Mays said, giggling. "I say, `Well, they were bad until I hit them. Then they got good.'"

If there is a common thread in the 500 Home Run Club, it is that the members arrived at the Major League with a fair amount of dirt under their fingernails.

None of them had a butler to pitch them batting practice when they were kids, in other words. Schmidt grew up in a middle-class family in Dayton, Ohio. The other thirteen players, particularly the blacks, saw their share of hard times.

Aaron and McCovey grew up in Mobile, Alabama, although they hardly knew each other back then. Aaron's father earned $75 a week as a boilermaker's helper. McCovey's dad worked on the railroad.

Banks lived in Dallas, where his father was a warehouse porter. Ernie's first baseball glove cost $2.98. Mays went to an industrial school in Westfield, Alabama, where he was trained as a laundry presser. He decided to sign with the Birmingham Black Barons of the Negro League instead.

"My father told me to stay away from the factory as long as I could," Mays recalled. "He said, `Son, you take one of those jobs, and you're a goner.' He was right, too."

Jackson lived with his divorced father, a tailor in Wyncote, Pennsylvania. Foxx worked on a farm in Sudlersville, Maryland. Williams was raised by his mother, a clarinet player in the Salvation Army band near San Diego. Mantle earned $35 a week as a teenager digging in the zinc mine near his Oklahoma home.

Tough roads, all of them. The one thing that brought these fourteen very different men together was their gift for hitting a baseball. It was that skill that brought them fame and wealth, but learning how to deal with that wasn't easy.

A few, such as Ruth and Jackson, had personalities that seemed to flourish with the attention. Others, such as Schmidt, Killebrew, Mays, McCovey, and Banks, grew into the role after some initial discomfort.

Mathews never did like the spotlight. He was that way as a Boston Braves rookie in 1952, and he didn't change in seventeen seasons as a player. He had to open up a little when he served as the Braves' manager (1972–74), but it didn't get any easier.

"I was from the old school. . . . I'd tell them, 'You saw it, you write it,'" Mathews said.

"[Newsmen] were always asking, 'How did this feel?' and 'How did that feel?' I didn't know what to say. If we won, I felt good. If we lost, I felt horse-bleep. End of story. But I guess they wanted more.

"They paid me to play this game, not analyze it. I got off to a good start [seventy-two homers his first two seasons] and got a lot of attention. I was just twenty-two, shy as hell. I didn't like talking about myself, but it came out like I was a bad guy.

"That's the trouble with being at that level," Mathews said. "Everything you do becomes magnified. I steered clear of that pretty much, but I saw it eat other guys alive."

After a while, the daily pressure of living in a fishbowl got to most of the great sluggers. Even Jackson, a man who sucks up adulation the way a thirsty lawn sucks up water, is known to snap when the five hundredth autograph book of the day is shoved through his car window.

Mickey Mantle came to New York a quiet, wide-eyed kid of twenty-one, fresh from the zinc mine. It didn't take long for him to develop a hard edge in dealing with the public. The first one to write about the Mick's dark side was teammate Jim Bouton in his tell-all book *Ball Four*.

"There were . . . times when [Mantle] would push little kids aside when they wanted his autograph," Bouton wrote, "and times when he was snotty to reporters, just about making them crawl and beg for a minute of his time. I've seen him close a bus window on kids trying to get his autograph.

"And I don't like the Mantle that refused to sign baseballs in the clubhouse before games. Everybody else had to sign, but Little Pete [the clubhouse man] forged Mantle's signature. So there are thousands of baseballs around the country that have been signed not by Mickey Mantle but by Pete Previte."

Mantle might have been tough to deal with at times, but he was an absolute prince compared with Ted Williams. It wasn't unusual for Williams to spit at an unruly fan or answer a loud boo with an obscene gesture. His own general manager, Joe Cronin, referred to the rookie Williams as "that busher."

Wrote Harry Ober in the *New York Mirror*: "The public image of Williams has been that of an acid-tongue, frequently obscene, sputtering and often vulgar man. In a word, unlovable."

What could be more unlovable than a man who hits a poor old lady in the head with a baseball bat? That is what Williams did in 1958 when he hurled his bat in disgust after popping up in the ninth inning.

Williams's bat flew seventy-five feet and struck Gladys Heffernan, sixty-nine, the housekeeper for Cronin. She was OK, but she asked Cronin to get her tickets in the upper deck after that.

Even Williams was remorseful over that display of temper. He never again threw his bat into the stands. He held on to it and smashed the water cooler instead.

"Ted was, at times, a victim of his own intensity," said Frank Malzone, a former Boston teammate, now a Red Sox Minor League instructor. "He worked so hard at his game and took such pride in his performance that he couldn't just shrug off an 0 for 4 the way most guys do.

"I didn't join the team until later [1955], when Ted's career was winding down. He had mellowed by then. He was still feuding with the writers in Boston, but he wasn't the [terror] he was in his early years. Basically, Ted just didn't want to be bothered.

"That's where the problems start for all these [superstars]. They are decent enough guy,s but they are under that pressure all the time—not just pressure to perform on the field, but to do interviews, sign autographs, the whole bit.

"Most people I know don't have the patience for it," Malzone said. "Ted didn't. He just wanted to work on his hitting and fish. He didn't have that much to say unless you were talking about those two things."

Williams, now sixty-eight, is more easygoing these days. He spends spring training with the Bosox in Winter Haven, Florida, working with the Minor League hitters and chatting with the fans. He even talks to the writers, a sure sign the old Thumper is at peace with the world.

To a man, the retired 500 Home Run Clubbers reflect a kind of blissful serenity. Their place in baseball history is secure; they know that.

Five hundred home runs is not an achievement that will be diluted in time. We're not talking about a one-shot deal, like the four-minute mile or the one-thousand–yard season in football. Any athlete can have one great day or season, but five hundred home runs requires two great decades.

That is the stuff of legends, and the eleven living 500 Clubbers, counting Schmidt, fully appreciate that fact. They might not say it, but they know they always will be considered baseball royalty. It is a nice, warm feeling to carry into middle age.

"I never thought much about what I was doing while I was doing it," the fifty-five-year-old Mays said this spring. He was at the Giants' camp in Scottsdale, Arizona, along with McCovey, as a "special assistant" to club president Al Rosen.

"I didn't worry about my one hundredth home run, my two hundredth home run, and junk like that," Mays said. "The only one I paid much attention to was number 512. That broke Mel Ott's [National League] record at the time. But even then I predicted Aaron would pass me before he was done.

"I passed some great hitters on my way up the ladder. Gehrig, Musial, Kiner, people like that. But I didn't take the time to appreciate it because there was always another game the next day. I had enough confidence in my own ability; I knew if I just played the game, the numbers would be there.

"The satisfaction comes now, when I see how people react to what I did. I've seen [former manager] Leo Durocher quoted as saying I was the best player he ever saw. Frank Robinson, a man I respect to the utmost, said something similar. That means more to me than a lot of trophies and clippings."

"It bothers me when a rookie has a good year and they refer to him as a 'superstar,'" Willie McCovey said. "That cheapens the meaning of the word. One year is just that, one year. A superstar is a player who stands the test of time.

"I don't know how many center fielders I've seen compared to Willie Mays. We've had six right here [with the Giants]. You'd think people would learn after a while. There will never be another Willie Mays. There will never be another Aaron."

"Will there ever be another McCovey?" a visitor asked.

A smile spread slowly across McCovey's face.

"Well, I've never been the kind of man who boasts," he said. He paused and stared across the empty clubhouse. The Giants players were on the field loosening up for the morning intra-squad game. Old number 44 would be along directly.

"Let me put it this way," McCovey said. "I always felt I belonged with the best. I played alongside Mays; I played against Musial, Snider, Mantle, Robinson. I didn't feel I had to take a back seat to anybody. I just didn't brag like some.

"I knew how the other players felt about me. I had guys tell me, 'Man, you're too good for this league. You're in a league all your own.' Banks told me if I played in Wrigley Field, I'd hit eighty home runs a year. I said, 'Yeah, you're probably right.'

"I never said too much to anyone—sportswriters, other players, anybody— because it wasn't my nature. I also liked to keep a little air of mystery about myself. Pitchers weren't quite sure how I'd react if they came inside on me, so they left me alone.

"Mays, he fraternized all the time. He'd spend an hour joking [with the other team] around the batting cage. Then he'd get knocked down three times during the game. I got a little edge by keeping my distance."

Reggie Jackson had a different kind of mystique during his five seasons in New York. He fraternized with the opposing team largely because he could not fraternize with his own. He was, in the words of former teammate Elrod Hendricks, "an outcast" in Yankeeland.

"I'd describe Reggie as a combination of Muhammad Ali and Frank Robinson," said Hendricks, now the bullpen coach in Baltimore. "He was a great self-promoter, which rubbed a lot of players the wrong way. But he was also a great competitor like Robby. He knew how to win.

"I was with that [1977 Yankee] team, so I know how Reggie was received. There was a very strong veteran nucleus, and those guys just never accepted Reggie. He didn't help matters with a few of his statements [most notably, the famous "I am the straw that stirs the drink" line] but he produced."

"What made Reggie so great was he never let anything get in his way," said Oakland coach Joe Rudi, Jackson's former A's teammate. "He never had a wife or family [he was divorced early]. His whole life was baseball, and he put everything he had into it.

"He was a showman, that's true, but he seemed to thrive on the controversy. The hotter things got, the better he performed. It would be interesting to see how many of his home runs came in the eighth and ninth innings. I'll bet it was a bunch."

"That's confidence," Jackson said. "I've been in that situation so many times, I know how to handle it. The pitcher knows that, and maybe he's a little more nervous than he would be ordinarily.

"If you can win that battle of the minds, chances are you'll win that battle at the plate, too."

Mike Schmidt brings with him to the 500 Club an impressive collection of ten Gold Gloves. He is a complete player, which pleases his new fraternity brothers no end.

They would not be terribly thrilled to see a one-dimensional figure such as Dave Kingman waddle into their midst. Call them old-fashioned, but the five-hundred gang takes pride in the fact it could play the game . . .

The whole game.

OK, Reggie Jackson was no gazelle in the outfield, and granted, Ted Williams's mind seemed to wander when he didn't have a bat in his hands. It is true Harmon Killebrew stole just nineteen bases in twenty-two Major League seasons but, really, that's nitpicking.

The fact is, Jackson and Williams never were less than adequate defensively, and Killebrew, although slow of foot, played first base, third, and the outfield for Minnesota. In his *Baseball Abstract*, Bill James ranked Killebrew as the second most valuable multi-position player of all time, behind Pete Rose.

Willie McCovey is often thought of as a gangly first baseman who was employed strictly for his bat, but the fact is McCovey made himself into a solid Major League glove man. Stretch also played the outfield and once saved a Juan Marichal no hitter with a diving catch that robbed Houston's Carl Warwick of extra bases.

"We all get stuck with labels; mine was the big brute," McCovey said. "But I wasn't like [Dick] Stuart and [Steve] Bilko or Kingman today. I could do a lot of things on a ball field. I would have done more if I didn't have so many [knee] injuries.

"But I look at Aaron, Mays, and Robinson; they deserved all the credit they got. Mays was the best ever, in my opinion, and I saw him every day for thirteen years. People would ask me, `What's the one play [by Mays] that stands out in your mind?' Who could pick out one play by Willie Mays?"

Folks who followed the Giants in 1954—that's five years before McCovey came aboard—would have no trouble picking out one play. It was Mays's breathtaking, over-the-shoulder catch against Cleveland's Vic Wertz in the `54 World Series.

It might be the most talked about defensive play in baseball history, and it was made by a man who also hit 660 homers, stole 338 bases, and batted .302 for his career. Players don't come more "complete" than that.

"I did a lot of things well because I enjoyed them all the same," Mays said. "I got as much of a thrill out of making a good play in the outfield as I did hitting a home run. I never broke the game down and said, `OK, this is more important than this.' I did what I had to do to win the game, that's all.

"That's where I think young players today go wrong. They concentrate on doing this or doing that. I tell them, `Hey, play the game. You've got to hit, run, and throw.' You've got guys twenty-two or twenty-three talking about being a [designated hitter]. What kind of stuff is that?"

Ernie Banks played his first nine Major League seasons at shortstop, the only 500 Clubber to make more than a token appearance in the middle infield. He spent his last ten years at first base, a traditional power position, so younger fans might not realize what a remarkable all-around player Banks was.

The fact is, Banks won back-to-back National League MVP awards (1958 and `59) while playing shortstop for a losing team. (No player on a losing team ever had won the MVP award, much less two years in a row.) Banks also won a Gold Glove and set a league record with a .985 fielding percentage.

Mel Ott said Banks could have played shortstop on any team in any era. "How many shortstops could bat fourth in a lineup?" Ott asked. "I can think of Arky Vaughan, Glenn Wright, and maybe Travis Jackson. But this fellow [Banks] can do more things than any of them."

Mathews was regarded as the best third baseman of all time before Schmidt came along. Even now, Mathews ranks as the number-one home run hitter at the position (481 to Schmidt's 463), although that will almost surely change in the weeks ahead.

Mathews wasn't much of a fielder when he signed with the Braves, but he learned fast under the direction of Billy Jurges, a former Major League shortstop. Jurges taught Mathews to bend his knees, not bend from the waist, when reaching for a ground ball.

"You'd be amazed how many guys do it wrong," Mathews said. "You've got to see the ball before you can catch it. [Jurges] must have hit me five hundred ground balls a day. It was a pain in the rear end, but it paid off."

Mathews became a solid defensive player. In fact, he brought down the curtain on the Braves' lone World Series championship (1957) with a brilliant backhanded stop on the Yankees' Gil McDougald in game seven.

Mathews also could run with the league's fastest players. As a rookie, he was timed from home to first in 3.5 seconds. Mathews could have stolen more bases, but the way he was swinging the bat, his manager, Charlie Grimm, didn't want to risk an injury.

Mathews got off to the fastest start of anyone in the five-hundred circle. He hit twenty-five homers as a rookie, then led the National League with forty-seven his second year. The next two seasons Mathews hit forty and forty-one.

That is 153 homers after just four years. Aaron, by comparison, had 110 home runs after his fourth season. Schmidt had 131. Babe Ruth still was a pitcher. Mathews seemed destined to break all the records.

Wrote the *Saturday Evening Post*: "This apple-cheeked third baseman has smashed epic clouts in every National League park. He stops traffic all over Milwaukee where the fans insist he will break the Babe's record."

Those expectations probably hurt Mathews in the long run, as injuries and the daily grind of playing third base slowed him down. The fact that Aaron, a teammate, passed Mathews on his way to Ruth's record leaves, in Bill James's words, the feeling that Mathews was "a mild disappointment."

"I never looked at it that way," Mathews said, sipping a beer in the Braves' West Palm Beach, Florida, clubhouse. "The numbers never meant a damn thing to me. Other people set those goals. I just played hard every day, and what happened, happened.

"Yeah, I remember [the press] talking about me breaking Ruth's record. Even then I knew it was crazy. I had four seasons under my belt; I wasn't one third of the way there. I'm happy as hell I made it to five hundred. How many guys have done it? I'd say I'm in pretty good company.

"I never thought of myself as a superstar," Mathews said. "I felt challenged every time I went on the field. Every series, I'd look at the other third baseman and think, 'I'm going to outplay you, you SOB.' We're talking about guys like Ken Boyer, Richie Allen, Jim Ray Hart. It wasn't easy.

"But I might have been a better competitor than I was a player. I loved the competition. It was a different game back then. They call Pete Rose 'Charlie Hustle.' Hell, we all played that way in the '50s and '60s. If you didn't play that way, they shipped you back to the Sally League."

Mathews was a fierce competitor; so was Frank Robinson. It was inevitable that in the ten years they played against each other, their wills would collide in the vicinity of third base, and shock waves would be felt across the National League. It happened in 1961 at Cincinnati.

Willie Mays wasn't there, but he knows the details well enough by now to provide a blow-by-blow description.

"Frank slid into Eddie real hard, the way he always did," Mays said. "Eddie told him not to do it again. Couple innings later, here comes Frank into third base even harder. Eddie got up swinging.

"Eddie gave it to Frank pretty good. Closed up one eye; left the other one like this [a slit]. The next day, Frank was back in the lineup with both eyes swollen shut, and he hit two home runs. Fred Haney [the Milwaukee Braves' manager] gave Mathews hell for riling Frank up."

"A true story?" a visitor asked Mathews.

He took a slow drag on his cigarette. "Yeah, basically," he said.

Robinson's toughness is legend among players of that era. He had many great seasons—including a Triple Crown with Baltimore in 1966—but his Oriole teammates were more awed by the season he kept playing despite double vision (1968). Robinson was struck in the head by a throw while breaking up a double play.

Fearless? Robinson stood with his toes almost touching home plate. His head and elbows dangled in the strike zone. National League pitchers drilled him 118 times in ten seasons.

Don Drysdale knocked Robinson down four times in one game. Robinson got up and beat Drysdale with a grand slam in the final at bat.

"I had a standing rule: Any of my pitchers who knocked Robinson down got a fine," Gene Mauch said. "He was dangerous at any time, but he was deadly when he was ticked off."

"Frank was the finest leader I've ever seen in this game," Elrod Hendricks said. "Rarely did he lead with words. It was usually by example.

"One night in Boston, Frank jammed his shoulder crashing into the fence on a ball hit by Reggie Smith. He had to bat the next inning, but he couldn't take a full cut. So he dropped a bunt and brought in the tying run anyway.

"George Scott was playing third base. You should have seen his face. He couldn't believe it: Frank Robinson bunting with a man on third. But we needed to get the run in, and Frank did it the only way he could."

There is no telling how good Mantle could have been if he didn't have so many physical problems. Without question, the Mick's ratio of winces per homer is tops among 500 Clubbers.

A look at Mantle's medical file shows two operations on his right knee, one operation on his left knee, surgery on his right hip and shoulder, a broken foot, four broken fingers, six pulled hamstrings, and more groin and thigh tears than the Yankee trainers could possibly count.

He played his last ten seasons with both legs wrapped in elastic bandages. It is said the constant pain and the fear of further injury were what soured Mantle's disposition. In that context, his surliness is more understandable.

"Mantle was not brittle, not really," said Dr. Sidney Gaynor, the team physician. "It was the demands he placed on himself: the stopping, the starting, the turning.

"It's truly remarkable that he could play eighteen years on his legs. It took a remarkable amount of determination for him to do it. He never complained about the pain unless he was trying to help you make a diagnosis. He'd say, `It hurts here,' and that would be it.

"The best description I'd give Mantle is he's the kind of guy you'd like to have in your outfit in a war."

Mantle was forced to retire at thirty-seven after eighteen Major League seasons. He went out with 536 homers, but folks kept saying, "What if . . . ?" The Mick passed the 400 mark at thirty-one and looked like a cinch for 600. Even the Babe's record wasn't out of the question.

"It wasn't meant to be," Mantle said. The passage of time has left him more philosophical than bitter.

"It wasn't a tough decision [to quit]. It was obvious I couldn't do the job anymore. I didn't hit worth a damn my last year [.237], and our team wasn't very good. I was walked an average of once every four at bats.

"It was more frustrating than anything else. People ask if I feel cheated. I really don't. I had a lot of great years, I loved being a Yankee. I had an eighteen-year career. I never figured I'd last that long."

The best player of all time? Bill James votes for Babe Ruth, and it is hard to argue.

It is common knowledge that Ruth began his Major League career as a pitcher, but he wasn't just any pitcher. He was 23–12 in 1916, with nine shutouts (league high) and a 1.75 earned-run average. He was 24–13 the following year, with thirty-five complete games (also a league high).

The Babe threw twenty-four consecutive shutout World Series innings, a record that stood for almost a half-century before the Yanks' Whitey Ford finally broke it in 1961.

So switching Ruth to the outfield was a move not unlike, say, the Red Sox putting Roger Clemens at third base.

Ruth was known for his power—he won a dozen American League home-run titles—but he also hit for a .342 career average.

The Babe batted .356 in 1927, the year he hit sixty home runs. Roger Maris hit .269 the year he broke Ruth's record, 1961.

Ruth was not the blubbery lummox that revisionist authors made him out to be. He was a fine defensive outfielder who had twenty or more assists in two different seasons. (Last year, Glenn Wilson and Toronto's Jesse Barfield tied for the Major League lead with twenty outfield assists.)

Bill James rated Ruth with Frankie Frisch as the most aggressive base runners of the '20s. Yes, the Babe could run. In 1921, Ruth had forty-four doubles and sixteen triples to go along with his fifty-nine homers. (Last year, Juan Samuel had thirty-six doubles and twelve triples.)

Simply put: The Babe could hit for power and average, throw strikes from right field and the pitcher's mound, handle a glove, and run the bases as well as anyone in his era.

He wasn't the most disciplined athlete around, but as the Babe himself pointed out: "We ain't playing in no Sunday school league." He seldom let his carousing interfere with his career, however. He loved the game too much for that.

The best pure hitter ever probably was Ted Williams. James agrees on that. So does Mauch, who was a utility infielder with Boston in 1957, the year Williams won his fifth American League batting title.

"Ted was the perfect hitting machine," Mauch said. "Great eyes, quick hands, strength, and intelligence. He knew every inch of the strike zone.

"You give him the two thousand at bats Uncle Sam took away [Williams missed parts of five seasons due to military service] and you'd see numbers that might be unmatched by anybody. He would have had six hundred homers for sure, maybe seven hundred.

"Ted was so confident in his ability that if he faced a pitcher for the first time, he'd usually take two strikes just to see what the guy had. He'd say, `OK, that's his fastball. . . . That's his curve. . . . Fine, now I've got him.' One swing was all Ted needed."

Confidence describes Williams as well as anything. When he joined the Sox in 1938, teammate Bobby Doerr told him: "Wait until you see this [Jimmie] Foxx hit."

Williams shot back, "Wait until Foxx sees me hit."

Doerr, the Sox captain, walked away shaking his head. It took a while before the other players got used to Williams. A few never got used to him at all.

Williams liked to bring his bat back to the hotel after games and study his stance in the mirror. Once Williams was taking his cuts when he accidentally hit the bedpost and knocked the whole thing to pieces.

His roommate, Charley Wagner, heard the crash and came running out of the bathroom to find the mattress and box spring on the floor. Williams viewed the wreckage with typical detachment.

"Geez," Williams said. "What power."

Maybe that is how Williams got his nickname, the Splendid Splinter. The history books are unclear on that. But they are specific on the matter of Williams's eyesight: It was extraordinary and no doubt contributed to his ability to put his bat on a pitched ball.

When Williams went into the Marines, the doctors determined his eyesight was so keen, it might be found once in one hundred thousand men. At flight school, Williams broke the student gunnery record one week, then broke his own record the next.

As a hitter, he had no equal. He hit .406 in 1941, and no one has come close to touching that mark since. George Brett, Rod Carew, and Wade Boggs have flirted with it in recent years, but it is not likely to be done again in this era of the short reliever and the split-finger fastball.

It is interesting to note how the 500 Home Run Clubbers influenced each other and created their own little chain.

Williams, for example, had Babe Ruth's picture hanging in his bedroom. The Babe was Williams's idol. Mathews grew up copying the left-handed stance of Williams. And Schmidt chased after Mathews for an autograph when he was going to games at Crosley Field in Cincinnati.

Around and around it goes.

Who knows? Maybe a future member of the 500 Club is waiting outside the Vet for Schmidt's autograph tonight. That is the cycle of baseball. And that is what keeps the game alive, for all of us.

Epilogue: The 500 Home Run Club has expanded considerably since this story was written in 1987. Now there are twenty-eight members, and obviously the line describing them as "no bigger than your next door neighbor" no longer applies. The dark cloud of steroids now hangs over the game and makes it hard to distinguish what is authentic and what is not. Reading this story may make you long for a return to a simpler time.

*Originally published in the *Philadelphia Daily News*, April 20, 1987. Reprinted with permission by Philadelphia Newspapers, LLC.

Munson: A Man of No Frills*

Four hundred mourners jammed the Memorial Auditorium in Canton, Ohio, yesterday to honor Thurman Munson. Men wept. Women sobbed into their handkerchiefs. Teammates, past and present, rose to eulogize him. God, how Thurman would have hated it.

Thurman Munson hated sentiment the way he hated a knuckleball at twilight. "Hearts and flowers," he called it. Munson never had much time for romantic musing. He didn't cry unless the American League pennant was at stake. Ten years of squatting in the dirt can do that to a man.

Thurman was a throwback to the old baseball players. He was at home in the back of a team bus, spitting tobacco juice and playing penny-a-point gin rummy on a suitcase. He was a millionaire, but if you ever saw him walk through the Yankee clubhouse in his soiled T-shirt, cussing at newsmen who stood too near his locker, you would have sworn he was some yokel just up from the Carolina League.

Munson was crude and brusque, testy yet truthful. There was no polish to the guy, but there was no deceit, either, and in a world of phonies and con men, he stood alone. He came right at you, high and hard, like a Nolan Ryan fastball. Unlike Reggie Jackson, Thurman never tried to be a poet or a philosopher. Just playing ball was enough for him.

Thurman resented it when the Yankees became more famous for their sub-plots than for their wins and losses. On June 19, when George Steinbrenner rehired Billy Martin as manager, Munson stood in his corner of the club-house, sneering at newsmen who debated and moralized the issue as if it were an Edward Albee play.

"I swear to God," Munson said, "you writers are more melodramatic than my wife."

Thurman Munson was a man of fascinating contrasts. He was sullen and short-tempered around the press, yet people in New York and Canton talk about the hours he spent working with kids and raising money for charity. "Thurman was one of the most kind-hearted men I've ever met," Yankees publicist Larry Wahl said, "but he just never wanted any of that stuff in the newspaper."

Munson was a dumpy little guy, jowly and never quite clean-shaven. He had a catcher's body, all right: potbelly; short, thick legs; rear end that looked like the door to a two-car garage. The other Yankees laughed at his waddle. They called him "the Pillsbury Doughboy" and worse. Yet anyone close to the Yankees would tell you Munson was the guts of the team.

While Reggie preened for the October spotlight, while Ron Guidry rested between starts, Munson carried the Yankees with his heart and his bat. In 1977, he became the first American Leaguer since Al Rosen (1954) to hit over .300 and drive in over one hundred runs three straight years. Overall, he batted .339 in fourteen American League playoff games and .373 in three splendid World Series. No hitter was more feared in the clutch.

Thurman played in pain most of the time, but nobody knew it. Last year, he had two sore knees and a bad right shoulder that required surgery in the off-season, but he still caught 127 games. He was tough, and he kept bouncing back. Maybe that's why everyone finds it so hard to believe he died in that plane crash here last Thursday.

Yesterday, on a typical Middle American morning in this typical Middle American town, Thurman Munson was buried. The people of Canton began lining up at 8 A.M., gathering quietly behind police barricades, waiting to pay their last respects to their native son.

The service was due to start at 9:30 A.M., but the Yankees' plane was late arriving. By the time the three team buses pulled in, it was almost 10. The doors opened, and the players filed quickly into the auditorium. Most of the players were accompanied by their wives. Billy Martin led the way, wiping away tears with every step.

Baseball Commissioner Bowie Kuhn, Ohio Governor James Rhodes, and Cleveland Mayor Dennis Kucinich were there. Many ex–Yankees showed up, including Mickey Rivers, Bobby Bonds, Paul Blair, Doc Medich, and Jay Johnstone. The altar was covered with over two hundred floral pieces. The organist played songs written by Neil Diamond, the only man Munson openly idolized.

The service opened with outfielder Lou Piniella, the Munsons' closest friend, addressing the gathering.

"Thurman was the best competitor I've ever played with or against," Piniella said. "He played rough and tough, but he played fair. He was our captain, and he led us with his example, not with idle chatter in the clubhouse.

"As gruff as he might have seemed, we [his teammates] found Thurman to be a kind, affectionate man. He was a good family man, so much so that he took up flying so he could spend more time with his family during the baseball season.

"We don't know why God took Thurman Munson," Piniella said, "but we know as long as we wear Yankee uniforms, Thurman will never be too far from us. God bless you, Thurman, wherever you are."

Bobby Murcer followed Piniella. Murcer came up through the Yankee farm system with Munson in the late '60s. They were inseparable, acquiring the nickname "the M & M boys." Murcer returned to the Yankees this year after spending four seasons in the National League. He and Thurman were enjoying a wonderful reunion this summer. No one dreamed it would end this suddenly, this way.

"Thurman lived, he led, he loved," Murcer said. "He lived blessed with his lovely wife, Diane, and their three wonderful children. He led his team to three American League pennants and two world championships. And most of all, he loved. He loved his family, he loved his friends, and he loved the game of baseball. He will be missed, but he'll not be forgotten.

"As Lou Gehrig once led the Yankees as captain, so, too, did Thurman Munson. Someday someone else will earn the right to lead this team. That's the way Thurman—Tugboat, as I called him—would have wanted it.

"Five years, ten years, however long it takes, no greater honor could be bestowed on a man than to be the successor to Thurman Munson. Thurman wore the pinstripes with number 15 on the field. He will be number 15 in the record books. But as a living, loving legend, history will . . ."

At that point, Murcer began sobbing. He struggled to get out the final few words. "History will record this man as number 1."

"Thurman Munson was a very real person who knew what he wanted and worked hard to achieve success," Reverend J. Robert Coleman, pastor of St. Paul's Catholic church of Canton, said in his eulogy. "He was hard to get to know, but he made real friends. You knew where you stood with Thurman, and some people can't take reality. One of his favorite songs was `I Did It My Way,' and that describes his way of life.

"Thurman, the lovable grump, wanted to protect his family from the circus that often invades the private life of a public person. As a young man, he was a tower of strength for his teenage buddies. In his first Little League game, as a late-inning sub, he saved the game by reaching over the fence to catch what would have been the game-winning home run.

"The media and Thurman didn't always get along," Father Coleman said. "How many times can you answer the same question? How many times can you give up precious family time for the sake of a cheap headline? Jim Bouton of *Ball Four* fame seemed to have difficulty communicating with Thurman. This weekend, he said he only wished he had gotten to know him better. Don't we all?"

*Originally published in the *Philadelphia Bulletin*, August 5, 1979.

"Fernando Has Been Touched by God"*

He is only twenty, the youngest player in the Major Leagues. He cannot drive a car and, until recently, he lived alone in a *cuarto pequeno* (tiny hotel room) in downtown Los Angeles.

He cannot speak English, and he amuses himself by watching cartoons on television. He eats at diners and taco stands; he walks the streets in his T-shirt and jeans. He still gets lost once in a while.

He is just a kid, they say. Pleasant, but shy. He is the youngest of twelve children born to a family of Mexican farm workers. He learned to play ball on a dusty field with chickens and pigs in the outfield.

Three years ago, he was playing for Guanajuato, a semi-pro team, earning 4,000 pesos ($180) a month. Today, he is the winningest pitcher in baseball, the hottest rookie property to come along since Mark (the Bird) Fidrych.

He is Fernando Valenzuela, and already he is being compared to Babe Ruth and Sandy Koufax. He has started six games for the Los Angeles Dodgers and won them all. Four were shutouts. He allowed one run in each of the others.

"Fernando has been touched by God," his agent, Antonio DeMarco, said. At this point, no one is about to argue.

Fernando has sold out the last three stadiums in which he has pitched. A near-capacity crowd (fifty thousand-plus) is predicted for his next start, Friday night at Shea Stadium against the New York Mets.

A song has been written in his honor. A lady is mass-producing T-shirts bearing his picture. A Señor Cero (Mr. Zero) fan club has formed in the Spanish-speaking Los Angeles community.

He has been profiled in national magazines. He has network TV chasing his every step. Authors are lining up to write his life story. Surely, the movie cannot be far behind. What's Fernando's reaction to all this?

"*Muy bueno*," he says. Translation: "Very nice."

"Fernando does not get excited by outside things," DeMarco said. "The interviews, the applause, the [money] offers. . . . That is OK, but it is secondary.

"What excites Fernando is playing baseball. He is still very much a boy. He could be back in Etchohuaquila [his hometown] playing ball with his brothers and be as happy.

"To the American people, he is a phenomenon. To the Mexican people, he is a hero. But in his own eyes, he is still just Fernando."

Fernando Valenzuela came to town with the Dodgers yesterday and, even though he will not pitch in this series, he was taken to a separate Veterans Stadium locker room for a press conference.

This will be standard procedure for the Dodgers on the road now, setting up one mass interview in each city, informing newsmen this will be their only chance to talk with Valenzuela. One-on-one sessions simply won't work anymore.

"The demand was too great," DeMarco said yesterday from his Los Angeles office. "There were dozens of requests every day, and everyone wanted an exclusive.

"I saw the problem growing during the last home stand. I saw Fernando before a game, surrounded by reporters and cameramen. For the first time, I saw pain in his eyes. He looked worried.

"I took him aside; I asked him what was wrong. He said, `Batting practice is very close, and these people still want to talk. What can I do?' I said, `Tell them you have to go. Be polite, but tell them.' Fernando was afraid he would insult them.

"He has handled the attention very well," DeMarco said. "A boy his age could get dizzy answering the same questions over and over again. Fernando knows it is his responsibility to cooperate, so he does.

"But the fame . . . the fame means very little to him. He sees his picture on magazine covers and laughs."

Yesterday, Fernando Valenzuela stepped onto the interview platform and smiled weakly to the roomful of newsmen. His large brown eyes flashed in the TV lights, then dropped quickly to his chest.

The five-foot-ten, 190 pound pitcher had the look of a lamb climbing atop the sacrificial altar. Clearly, he feels more comfortable when he has the world at a safe distance—say, sixty feet, six inches.

"What does Fernando think of all this?" was the first question.

"I feel very happy," he replied through interpreter Jaime Jarrin, an announcer on the Dodgers' Spanish network, "but I feel a little nervous in front of all these people.

"When I'm pitching, I don't feel as nervous as I feel now."

Fernando loosened up as the interview went along and actually seemed to enjoy the give and take about his generous paunch ("I can't ever remember being skinny") and his age ("If people don't believe it, that's up to them").

He talked about dropping out of school at fourteen and dreaming of playing professional baseball.

"But I never thought I would pitch in the Major League," he said. "I thought I would pitch in the Mexican League."

He said he has no personal goals in mind. He is not thinking about winning twenty games, making the All-Star team, or becoming the third Dodger pitcher in a row to be named the National League's Rookie of the Year.

"My only goal," Fernando said, "is to stay in the Major League as long as possible."

He shrugged off the notion he might now want to renegotiate his one-year contract, which pays him a reported $45,000. The way he's drawing, someone suggested, maybe he could ask for a percentage of the gate.

"I will honor this contract," he said, "then I will negotiate a new one for next year."

Fernando indicated his modest lifestyle—a big night consists of some beans and rice, followed by an old John Wayne movie on TV—keeps his expenses to a minimum. He is in no particular hurry to strike it rich.

"I want to make enough to buy a nice home for my family in Mexico," Valenzuela said. "That's all I'm thinking about [in terms of money] now."

Someone asked if he was surprised by his sudden success. After all, no pitcher—not Koufax, not Seaver, not Carlton—had ever started this fast, this brilliantly.

"I'm not surprised," Valenzuela said. "I make good pitches."

"Is he aware of what's happening around him . . . the interest, the excitement?" a reporter asked Jarrin. The interpreter relayed the question.

Fernando smiled, then nodded. Yes, he understood.

The temptation, of course, is to write Fernando off as a fluke, one of those Haley's Comet types that flash brightly across the sky for a moment, then drop from sight.

Remember Karl Spooner, who pitched shutouts in his first two starts with the Dodgers in 1954? He was out of baseball within two years. Remember Von McDaniel, the St. Louis sensation in 1957? He was gone in '58.

And remember Mark Fidrych, the last kid pitcher to trigger this sort of adulation? The Bird is now back in the low minors, a sore-armed junk-baller struggling to hang on.

Is that what will happen to Fernando? Will he be just another funny name in a trivia test three years from now?

"No, this kid is for real," said Dodger manager Tom Lasorda. "I've never seen anything like him. He's amazing, unbelievable. Now I know how Walter Alston felt when he had Koufax.

"He's got everything. He's got great stuff, great control, great command out on the mound. He knows what he's doing out there. He has unbelievable poise. Put him in any situation and he's cool.

"I don't like to compare players," Lasorda said, "but Fernando reminds me of Juan Marichal. He has that same high leg kick, the same assortment of pitches, and he can throw them all for strikes.

"What makes Fernando unique is he throws a screwball. When did you ever see a twenty-year-old kid who could throw a screwball? I call him `Carlos Hubbellito,' after Carl Hubbell, the great screwballer."

Carl Hubbell walked away from baseball with the palm of his left hand facing forward, the result of throwing too many scroogies. It is the most crippling pitching motion imaginable, the hand snapping over, placing all the stress on the elbow.

It is a pitch that shortens, and frequently ends, careers. The risk does not concern either the manager or the pitcher.

"He has a good arm with a nice, loose delivery," Lasorda said. "It won't hurt him."

"It feels natural for me to throw the screwball," Valenzuela said.

Besides, the screwball is only one weapon in Fernando's arsenal. He was the top prospect in Mexico long before Dodger teammate Robert Castillo taught him the pitch. Back then, he was getting the job done very efficiently with his fastball, curve, and slider.

There are those who will tell you Valenzuela does not have an "out" pitch, as such. He relies on mixing up his pitches, changing speeds, and nipping the corners. He gets hitters looking for one thing, then gives them something else.

"Freddie doesn't have blazing speed," said catcher Mike Scioscia, "but, at times, he can be overpowering. He has magnificent control. He can put the ball where he wants it better than anybody I've ever seen."

"It took Sandy [Koufax] years to become a great pitcher," said coach Ron Perranoski. "I'd say that right now, Valenzuela is where Koufax was when he was twenty-eight or twenty-nine."

If that all sounds preposterous, just check the statistics. Valenzuela currently leads the National League in six categories: wins (six), shutouts (four), complete games (five), innings (fifty-four), strikeouts (fifty), and earned-run average (.33).

Add to this the seventeen shutout innings he pitched for the Dodgers following his recall last September, and it drives his ERA down to a breathtaking .19.

We won't even go into his .368 batting average and the fact that he has twice driven in the game-winning run. The implications of such feats are too far-reaching, too eerie to deal with here.

And for those who figure the hitters will tee off on Fernando once he goes around the league a few times, well, think again. He shut out the Western Division champion Houston Astros twice in two weeks.

"He shut out the Giants the first time he faced them," Lasorda said, "but the second time, they really roughed him up. They scored one run."

Mike Brito, the Dodgers' Mexican scout, discovered Fernando Valenzuela in 1978. He discovered him by accident, really.

Brito had gone to Silao to scout a shortstop named Lazaro Usganga. It just so happened that the game he saw, Valenzuela was pitching for the other team. It was like digging for water and striking oil.

"By the fifth inning," Brito recalled, "I forgot all about the shortstop and moved behind home plate to see what kind of movement this kid had on his fastball. He had plenty.

"He struck out twelve batters that day. I knew right away he had the stuff to be a winner in the big leagues. He was very poised, too. It was hard to believe he was only seventeen.

"I turned in a real strong [scouting] report on him, and I followed him for a while. Word got out among other scouts. They started asking, `Who's this Valenzuela?' The Yankees, the Cubs, and the Mets all began coming around.

"They wanted to sign him but the owner of the [Puebla] club said he would only make a deal with the Dodgers because we saw Fernando first. The competition jacked the price up, though. We had to pay $120,000 for him."

Fernando rose rapidly through the Dodger farm system. He spent one season in Lodi (Class A) where he posted a 1.13 ERA. Last year, he started in San Antonio and was leading the league in strikeouts (162 in 174 innings) when the Dodgers called him up in September.

He was not scored on in ten relief appearances with the Dodgers in the heat of a pennant race, and Lasorda suspected right then the kid was something special. This season has borne that out.

Brito, meanwhile, has taken over as Valenzuela's big brother and guardian. It is a responsibility he assumed the day he signed Fernando to his contract there in the Valenzuela family's four-room adobe hut with the thatched roof.

"I remember his mother, Maria Hermenegilda, told me, `Mike, I want you to take care of Fernando when he goes to Los Angeles. He is my youngest. Look out for him.' I've tried to do that.

"Earlier this year, he was living alone in that hotel. I didn't like that. I was afraid if anything happened to him, no one would know. No one could help him. So I told him to come and stay with my family.

"We live in East Los Angeles, just five minutes from Dodger Stadium. We have this small house out behind the swimming pool, and Fernando lives there. It has two TVs, an air conditioner, a refrigerator. This way, he has a family and he has privacy, too.

"I drive him to the stadium, then bring him home. I look out for him. I make sure people don't take advantage of him. I tell him not to sign anything without consulting his agent [DeMarco] first.

"But he's a bright kid," Brito said. "He knows what's going on."

What's going on is a lot of people want to make Fernando Valenzuela a wealthy young man. Antonio DeMarco, an actor turned theatrical agent, gets no fewer than twenty calls a day from advertisers who want Fernando to shill their products.

No small-time outfits, either. We're talking 7-Up, Datsun, Mexicana Airlines, Ortega frozen foods. Studios are calling about screen tests. DeMarco is putting all this on hold, at least for now.

"Fernando and I have discussed this," DeMarco said, "and we both agree his full attention must be kept on baseball. If we begin doing other things, it will only distract him and take away from his pitching.

"There is time enough to capitalize on his success. The offers will not go away. If Fernando has the career I think he will have, the offers will only get bigger and better. He is twenty years old; we can wait.

"Fernando is very aware of his image, the esteem in which he is held by his [Mexican] people. He wants only to do the right thing. He wants to prove himself as an athlete. He doesn't want to be seen as someone who's just out to make a quick buck.

"Fernando is a typical Mexican—proud, independent, with high hopes and higher standards. He will not settle for anything less than his best effort."

There has been only one real disappointment in Fernando's career thus far. It happened during his last start at Dodger Stadium, when a teenage girl darted onto the field and kissed Fernando while he stood on the pitcher's mound.

What was so disappointing, you ask?

"Fernando said he never saw the girl coming," DeMarco recalled. "He said it happened so fast, he didn't have time to enjoy it.

"Next time, he says he'll be ready."

Epilogue: Fernando Valenzuela won Rookie of the Year honors and the Cy Young Award in 1981, the first pitcher in baseball history to accomplish that dual feat. He pitched a total of seventeen seasons in the Major League and finished with 173 career victories.

*Originally published in the *Philadelphia Daily News*, May 6, 1981. Reprinted with permission by Philadelphia Newspapers, LLC.

Aaron's Numbers Speak for Him*

Travis Jackson spoke for twelve minutes. The former New York Giants shortstop reminisced about playing baseball in the 1920s, holding his pants up with a rope instead of a belt.

"Things was differ'nt back then," Jackson, seventy-eight, said in his Waldo, Arkansas, drawl.

Albert B. "Happy" Chandler spoke for twenty-eight minutes. The former commissioner rambled on about the politics of Major League Baseball. At one point, Chandler, eighty-four, brought up the unlikely name of Richard M. Nixon.

"One of our better presidents," Chandler said foolishly.

There was an awkward silence, followed by scattered boos. Chandler tried, but he never could win back the audience. Happy's Daze wound down to lukewarm applause.

Frank Robinson followed by gently chiding the former commissioner for talking so long.

The San Francisco manager said the way Happy was going, he was afraid he might miss the Giants' game in Atlanta tonight. The crowd laughed and cheered.

"I only have a few things to say," Robinson announced.

Then the former Cincinnati and Baltimore great proceeded to talk for thirty-six minutes, or eight minutes longer than Happy Chandler.

"What is this?" someone whispered, "Frank Robinson in concert?"

Henry Aaron was the last man to speak at yesterday's forty-third Induction Ceremonies at the Baseball Hall of Fame. Aaron addressed the masses for six minutes. That's all. Just six minutes.

He had his acceptance speech written out on index cards. He didn't ad lib much, if at all. He didn't quote Shakespeare or Salinger. He didn't strive for dramatic effect. Lord knows, that was never his style.

On this, the day of his enshrinement, Henry Aaron was typically brief and to the point. He thanked his parents, his wife, and his children for their support. He thanked his teammates for twenty-three years of golden memories.

Most of all, he thanked God for giving him "the body and the talent" to hit 755 home runs, more than any other man who ever pulled on a Major League uniform.

"The way to fame, like the way to heaven, is fraught with tribulation," Aaron said. "It's been a long and winding road . . . but to be here today, among all these great players, is a wonderful feeling. Thank you."

That quickly, Henry Aaron was through.

This was the man the thousands of baseball pilgrims had come to see, yet he gave them little more than a fleeting glimpse. There were no jokes, no public tears.

Whatever emotions Aaron felt, he kept them locked deep inside. The moment most ballplayers rush to embrace, the Hammer held rigidly at arm's length. He was cool and unflappable.

For anyone else, it would have seemed strange, but for Henry Aaron, it was perfectly in character. That was the way Aaron played the game, and fittingly, that's the way he'll now be remembered.

"Hank never got his due as a ballplayer," Frank Robinson said. "He wasn't flashy; he wasn't a showman, so for years people overlooked him.

"But day after day, year after year, no one could stack up to him. Check the record books. The numbers don't lie."

In Hank Aaron's case, the numbers speak eloquently, indeed. The home-run record is just one of nineteen Major League marks he leaves behind.

What is most striking about Aaron's career is its consistency. The man hit twenty or more homers in twenty consecutive seasons. He scored one hundred or more runs in thirteen consecutive seasons. He batted more than .300 in ten of his first eleven seasons.

"We [his teammates] could appreciate Hank more than most people, because we saw him all the time," Eddie Mathews, another Hall of Famer, said yesterday.

"He never seemed to go into a slump. Even if he was 0 for 4, he usually hit one or two balls hard. He had those great wrists. He'd snap `em around, and the ball would jump off his bat."

"It was a privilege to play with the man," pitcher Warren Spahn said. "He's the greatest hitter of all time. Number one. How many number ones do any of us know? In anything?"

Henry Aaron, now forty-eight, says he never set out to carve his name in the halls of Cooperstown. As a kid growing up poor in Mobile, Alabama, he sought only "to be the best player I could possibly be.

"If someone had told me I'd wind up in the Hall of Fame one day, I would've said he was crazy," Aaron said during a brief press conference.

"I couldn't put myself in a class with men like Ty Cobb and Babe Ruth— not back then, anyway. But I realized God gave me some ability, and it was up to me to make the most of it. And I did; I worked hard.

"I remember when I first signed with Jacksonville in the Sally League [in 1953], I was so green. I stole three bases in one game. Each time the second baseman tricked me into taking my foot off the bag, then he tagged me out.

"One time, he told me he had to straighten the bag. The next time, he told me he had to kick off some dirt. The third time . . . I forget what he said. My manager, Ben Garrett, told me I had to get a little tougher.

"I could always hit, but I started out hitting cross-handed. My left hand was on top, my right hand on the bottom. I hit .467 like that one season in the Negro League. Don't ask me how."

Two decades later, on a warm April night in Atlanta Stadium, Henry Aaron became an American legend. He ripped an Al Downing fastball over the left-field fence for the 715th home run of his career.

That lifted Aaron past Babe Ruth and made him the game's all-time home-run king. It also freed him from what had become a painful, sideshow existence.

"I lived in a fishbowl the two years leading up to that," Aaron said. "It should have been an enjoyable time, but it wasn't. It was more like an ordeal.

"It was strange because, on the one hand, I had no privacy, yet, on the other, I was very lonely. There were crowds everywhere, so I couldn't go out of my room on road trips. I had to have all my meals sent up room service.

"I had to register under an assumed name. The Braves would have a room with my name, but they left it empty. After every game, I'd have to leave the stadium through the back door. It just wasn't much fun.

"When I hit the [715th] home run, my reaction was more relief than anything else. I was glad it was all over."

Someone asked Aaron if he could pick out the highlight of his career. What gave him the most satisfaction?

"That's easy," he said. "The 1957 season. We [the Milwaukee Braves] won the world championship, and I was named the National League's Most Valuable Player.

"That's what it's all about . . . winning the World Series. Individual accomplishments are nice, but they don't compare to winning a championship.

"I wish we could have put together a contender in Atlanta my last few years [as a player] there. That would've been fun, to be in the hunt one more time.

"We're leading the league now, but I'm in the front office [as vice president of player personnel]. I'm removed from it."

"Do you think anyone will ever come along and break your home-run record?" someone asked.

"I'm sure someone will," Aaron said. "There are some great young hitters out there now. We have two in Atlanta—Dale Murphy and Bob Horner. They might do it, who knows?

"The one thing that might hold them back is the travel. Teams fly from the East Coast to the West Coast and play that night. That's hard. It wears you down. Maybe that will take a toll.

"But I know if I can break Babe Ruth's record, someone can surely break mine. Whoever it is, I wish him luck."

*Originally published in the *Philadelphia Daily News*, August 2, 1982. Reprinted with permission by Philadelphia Newspapers, LLC.

OLYMPICS

Thorpe Nets Golden Debt*

Today, the International Olympic Committee (IOC) will present replicas of two gold medals to the children of Jim Thorpe.

The replicas are meant to take the place of the medals Thorpe won in the 1912 Olympics, medals the IOC took away when it learned that Thorpe had played semi-pro baseball for two summers while attending Carlisle College.

The fact that Thorpe earned just $2 a game, not to mention that, in his naivete, he was unaware he was breaking any rules, didn't matter to the IOC bureaucrats.

They made their decision and stuck to it, stubbornly, for seventy years. Their ruling cast a shadow over Jim Thorpe, a shadow that followed the great Indian athlete to his death in a California house trailer in 1953 and lingers even now.

Today's ceremony is the culmination of a long fight by the Thorpe family and the Jim Thorpe Foundation to rectify this terrible injustice. Still, it is doubtful the scars ever will heal.

Jim Thorpe was arguably the greatest athlete who ever lived. He set Olympic decathlon records that stood for four decades. He outdistanced Red Grange and Bronko Nagurski in the voting for top football player of the half-century (1900–50).

Thorpe was all of that, yet his life was filled with pain. Three marriages, poverty, drink. He was at once a triumphant and tragic figure.

James Francis Thorpe was born May 28, 1888, in Prague, Oklahoma, in a one-room cottonwood-and-hickory cabin long since washed away by the floods.

His father was Hiram P. Thorpe, the son of Hiram G., an Irish immigrant fur trapper, and No-ten-o-quah, the granddaughter of Black Hawk, the legendary chief of the Sac and Fox Nation.

His mother was Charlotte View, a woman of French and Indian (Pottawattomi) descent. She gave her first-born son the name Wa-tho-huck, which meant Bright Path. It proved to be prophetic.

The boy grew up fast and strong. At eight, he bagged his first deer. At ten, he was hiking thirty miles through the woods with his father. At fifteen, he could rope and break a wild stallion faster than any man on the reservation.

Young Jim happily would have stayed in Oklahoma and worked the land, but his father had other ideas. Hiram Thorpe had heard of this Indian school in faraway Carlisle, Pennsylvania, and he was intrigued.

The school was founded by a U.S. Cavalry officer, Lieutenant Richard Pratt, to educate young Indians in the ways of the white man's world. In 1904, Hiram Thorpe enrolled his son at Carlisle.

"You are an Indian," the elder Thorpe said. "I want you to show other races what an Indian can do."

At the time, there were one thousand students at Carlisle, ranging in age from ten to twenty-five. They spent half the day in the classroom learning to read and write; the other half in the shop learning a trade.

Thorpe started in tailoring, then, like many students, he was sent out to live and work with white families in the area. He spent two years on a farm in Robbinsville, New Jersey, tending to the livestock and earning $8 a month.

Thorpe returned to Carlisle in 1907. He did not sign up for varsity sports— he didn't understand the rules and techniques—but he was curious. So he hung around and watched.

One day, the track team was practicing the high jump. Thorpe came by in his overalls and work shoes. An older boy, jokingly, asked Thorpe if he'd like to try. He cleared the bar on his first jump. No warm-up, no nothing.

The next day, Thorpe was summoned by Glenn "Pop" Warner, the track and football coach. Warner informed Thorpe he had high-jumped five feet, nine inches, breaking the school record.

"I told Pop I didn't think that was very high," Thorpe wrote later. "Pop told me to go to the clubhouse and exchange my overalls for a track outfit. I was on the track team."

One month later, Thorpe entered five events in the Pennsylvania Intercollegiate Meet and placed first in all five: the high and low hurdles, the high and broad jumps, and the hammer throw.

He won six gold medals in the Penn Relays and the Middle Atlantic Association championships. He had no formal training, his form was crude, yet he won easily.

"There was nothing he could not do," Warner said.

Well, almost nothing. Thorpe wanted to play football, but Warner wouldn't allow it. He considered Thorpe too valuable as a trackman to risk losing him to a football injury.

Thorpe kept after Warner until the coach agreed to take him on as a kicking specialist. Thorpe could punt a ball seventy yards and dropkick a fifty-yard field goal, so it wasn't as if Pop was doing him any favors.

Still, that wasn't enough. Every day at practice, Thorpe asked the coach to let him run with the ball. This went on for two weeks until, finally, Warner's patience was at an end.

"All right," the coach said. "Let's give the varsity some tackling practice."

Warner handed Thorpe the ball, and he ripped through Carlisle's first-team defense. Fifty yards. Touchdown.

"Let's see you do it again," Warner said.

So Thorpe did it again. As the historian Henry Clune recalls, "Tacklers began to hit him, but it was no use. They bounced off and shriveled up behind him, like bacon on a hot griddle."

Admittedly, it sounds like a scene Hollywood might have written for Burt Lancaster, but it's true. That's how Jim Thorpe became Carlisle's starting halfback, and that's how the legend began.

For four seasons, Thorpe and the Carlisle Indians were unstoppable. They won forty-three games, lost five, and tied two. The first seven games in 1912, Thorpe's final year, Carlisle outscored its opponents, 272–15.

The Indians didn't have a cupcake schedule, either. They played the best: Army, Penn, Harvard, Syracuse, Pitt, Minnesota, Nebraska. And they played them on the road, because they didn't have a suitable stadium at Carlisle.

Each week, the Indians were outweighed and outmanned—there were only twelve players on the 1911 squad—but that didn't matter to Thorpe, Jesse Young Deer, Little Boy, and the rest.

"Carlisle had no traditions," Pop Warner once said, "but what the Indians did have was a real race pride and a fierce determination to show the palefaces what they could do when the odds were even.

"It was not that they felt any bitterness against the whites or against the government for years of unfair treatment, but, rather, they believed the armed contests between red man and white had never been waged on equal terms.

"On the athletic field, where the struggle was man to man, they felt the Indian had his first even break, and the record proves they took full advantage of it."

Jim Thorpe ran up numbers that even now, seventy years later, boggle the mind. In his final season, he led the nation with 198 points. He scored twenty-five touchdowns and averaged nine yards every time he touched the ball.

Thorpe was six feet tall, 195 pounds, with 9.8 speed in the one hundred and the strength of a world-class shot-putter. He had the physical gifts to be a great running back in any era.

Thorpe was bigger than Tony Dorsett, faster than Earl Campbell, stronger than Walter Payton. He was a 1980s All-America turned loose in the 1910s.

"I've seen a lot of great runners," Hall of Famer George Trafton tells the author Robert Wheeler in *Pathway to Glory*, the definitive Thorpe biography.

"I've seen George McAfee and Gale Sayers, and I've played with George Gipp and Bronko Nagurski, but the greatest of them all was Jim Thorpe. The Indian just had something better than all of them."

It would be redundant to list all of Thorpe's great games, but two stand out.

The first was the 18–15 win over Harvard in 1911, a game in which Thorpe, playing on a bad ankle, drop-kicked four field goals, including two from forty-eight yards out, to win it.

Afterward, Harvard Coach Perry Haughton said, "I realized that here was the theoretical super-player in flesh and blood."

The following year, Thorpe ran wild in a 27–6 upset of Army. "There is no one like him in the world," said an awed Cadet halfback named Dwight D. Eisenhower.

Said Pop Warner: "No college football player I ever saw had the natural aptitude possessed by Jim Thorpe. I never knew a player who could penetrate a line as Thorpe could, nor did I know a player who could see holes as well.

"As for speed, none ever carried a pigskin down the field with the dazzling speed of Thorpe. He could knock off a tackler, stop short and turn past another, ward off still another, and escape the entire pack."

It was Pop Warner who signed Jim Thorpe up for the 1912 U.S. Olympic team. Thorpe had never heard of the Olympic Games until Warner told him about them.

Warner told Thorpe this was his chance to compete against the best athletes in the world. Thorpe said that sounded like fun. Pop took care of the paperwork.

The 1912 games were held in Stockholm. Thorpe was entered in the pentathlon and decathlon. The favorites were Ferdinand Bie of Norway and Hugo Wieslander of Sweden. The Americans, it was said, would be lucky to take a bronze.

The Europeans had no idea what this burly Indian could do, but they soon found out.

Thorpe finished first in four of five pentathlon events. He won the broad jump (twenty-three feet, three inches); the two hundred meters (22.9); the discus (168 feet, four inches), and the 1,500 meters (4:40). He finished second in the javelin.

When the scores were tabulated, Thorpe had tripled the score of the runner-up, Bie.

It was the same thing in the decathlon. Thorpe finished first in four events (shot put, high jump, 110 meter hurdles, 1,500 meters), second in four others (broad jump, 100 meters, 400 meters, discus), and third in the last two (pole vault and javelin). Thorpe scored 8,413 points out of a possible 10,000, an Olympic record that stood for twenty years. He finished seven hundred points ahead of the silver medalist, Wieslander.

Recalled Warner: "The wonder and admiration of the onlooking athletes found expression in what came to be a stock phrase, `Isn't he a horse?'"

After the pentathlon, Thorpe went to the awards platform, where Sweden's King Gustav placed a laurel wreath on his head, then presented him with his gold medal and a life-size bronze bust of the king.

After the decathlon, Thorpe returned to the platform. Once again, the king bestowed the laurel wreath and gold medal on him; then the king presented Thorpe with a silver chalice lined with gold, made in the shape of a Viking ship.

What happened next is the most enduring memory of all: Gustav clasped Thorpe's hand and, totally blowing his royal cool, said, "Sir, you are the greatest athlete in the world."

"Thanks, King," Thorpe replied.

Thorpe's answer was lacking in formality, perhaps, but not in feeling. A king had called him "sir." It was a moment the young Indian would cherish forever.

Thorpe returned home to a hero's welcome. He was hailed by the president. Parades were held in his honor. Fifteen thousand people came to Carlisle's Biddle Field to salute him when he arrived in his open carriage.

Some say the post–Olympic scene was what messed up Thorpe's life. A classic case of too much too soon. Poor Indian boy, in over his head. That's not entirely true.

Thorpe, twenty-four, already had tasted national acclaim as a football player. He wasn't really comfortable in the spotlight, but he wasn't bowled over by it, either.

No, what turned Jim Thorpe's world upside down was a series of personal tragedies, the first being the loss of his two gold medals. How Thorpe was found out is a book unto itself.

It seems a Worcester, Massachusetts, newspaperman was interviewing Charley Clancy, the manager of the Rocky Mount, North Carolina, baseball team, in January 1913. Quite innocently, the reporter noticed a framed photograph of Clancy and several players returning from a hunting trip.

He immediately recognized one of the players as Jim Thorpe. He asked what Thorpe was doing with the team. Clancy couldn't lie. He told the reporter Thorpe had played two summers in Rocky Mount. Thorpe was paid $5 a month, a piddling sum that barely covered his room and board, but it made him a professional athlete. Since only amateurs were allowed to compete in the Olympics at that time, it was argued that Thorpe never should have been permitted to take part in the 1912 games.

The story made national headlines. Thorpe wrote a letter of apology to the American Olympic Committee (AOC), explaining he was "not wise in the ways of the [athletic] world."

It was no use. Despite an outcry from journalists and sportsmen around the world, the AOC stripped Thorpe of his medals and wiped his name from the Olympic record books.

Thorpe took the news in his customary stoic fashion, but he was deeply hurt. Years later, he awoke his New York Giants roommate, the Indian catcher, Chief Meyers, tears rolling down his cheeks.

"The King of Sweden gave me those trophies," Thorpe told Meyers, "but they took them away. They're mine, Chief. I won them fair and square."

"It broke his heart," Chief Meyers said in Lawrence Ritter's book *The Glory of Their Times*. "He never really recovered."

Thorpe's other personal tragedy came in 1917, when his first child, Jim Jr., died of infantile paralysis at three.

The boy was Thorpe's pride and joy. The two were inseparable. Thorpe seldom displayed emotion in public, but he was openly affectionate and loving with Jim Jr.

"I remember spring training, 1917," former Giant Al Schacht told Wheeler. "After practice, they'd be on the lawn in front of the hotel. The kid would climb up one of Jim's arms and down the other, and he'd grin that big, wide grin, just like his old man. The two of them would laugh.

"After his death, Jim was never the same."

It wasn't long after that Iva Miller Thorpe, Jim's wife and Carlisle sweetheart, divorced him. He was more alone, more unhappy than ever.

Jim Thorpe signed with the New York Giants after leaving Carlisle in 1913, mostly because there wasn't much else to do.

He had offers from vaudeville agents: $1,000 a week to perform feats of strength on the stage. And he had a few calls from California. Something about "moving pictures," whatever they are.

But Thorpe knew he belonged on the playing field, not the stage. Baseball wasn't his best sport, but it was the only one that paid a living wage back then, so he signed. Three years, $6,000 a year.

Thorpe would have been better off with another team. The Giants were the National League champions. They didn't need a rookie outfielder, but Thorpe wasn't just any rookie outfielder.

"If he can only hit in batting practice, the fans that will pay to see him will more than make up for his salary," Manager John McGraw said.

In other words, Thorpe was a drawing card, strictly an ornament. He went to bat thirty-five times that year. He managed five hits, a .143 average.

Thorpe grew restless. He hated riding the bench. He feuded openly with McGraw, better known as "Little Napoleon."

One day, Thorpe missed a sign while running the bases. McGraw called him "a dumb Indian." Thorpe chased McGraw through the dugout. It took half the team to restrain him. Thorpe was sold to Cincinnati the next day.

Thorpe played regularly in Cincinnati and proved he belonged in the Major League. By 1919, he had raised his average to .327, but he was looking for other mountains to climb.

A professional football league was forming in the Midwest, and Thorpe became involved. Football always was his first love, of course.

Thorpe signed with the Canton Bulldogs for $250 a game. He was well worth the investment. He gave the new league credibility. It would be like Herschel Walker signing with the USFL today.

Without Thorpe, the Bulldogs were drawing 1,200 fans a game. With Thorpe, they filled the 8,000 seat stadium in Massillon.

Thorpe still was in fine form and led Canton to several unbeaten seasons. With his name on the marquee, professional football took a firm hold on the American scene.

Thorpe remarried, and with his second wife, Freeda, he had four children.

But then, as Thorpe got older, the grind got tougher. He left the Bulldogs and bounced around. Nine teams in seven years. Rock Island, St. Petersburg, Portsmouth . . .

For a while, he barnstormed with some former Carlisle players. The team was called "Jim Thorpe's Oorang Indians." They were sponsored by the Oorang Airedale Kennels in LaRue, Ohio.

Thorpe finally hung up his cleats in 1929 at forty-one. He tried to find another line of work, but it wasn't easy.

For a while, he was master of ceremonies at Charlie Pyle's "Bunion Derby," a cross-country marathon race, but the show went bankrupt. Thorpe finally had to sue Pyle for his $50 paycheck.

He worked as a painter, then a construction worker at fifty cents an hour. He picked up a few bucks as a stunt man at MGM. His life was falling apart again. He was drinking, and money was scarce.

In 1932, the Olympic Games were held in Los Angeles, and Thorpe couldn't afford a ticket. Word got out, and Vice President Charles Curtis, an American Indian, decreed that the former champion would sit in his private box while he opened the games.

The Coliseum crowd of 105,000 gave Thorpe a standing ovation. It was very nice and very touching, but, like everything else, it passed quickly. Soon, Thorpe was back in the real world, fighting to survive.

In 1941, Freeda sued Jim for divorce, claiming he was gone for weeks at a time. Jim explained that was the nature of Indian men. Perhaps, but he wasn't living on the reservation anymore. Freeda got her divorce.

When World War II broke out, Thorpe tried to enlist in the Marines, but at fifty-three, he was turned down. He signed on with the Merchant Marine and sailed to India aboard the *U.S.S. Southwest Victory*.

When he returned, Thorpe married for the third time, this time to Patricia Askew, a hard-nosed businesswoman who took over his affairs. She actually turned Jim Thorpe into a moneymaking enterprise, although she stepped on a few toes along the way.

She began charging $500 plus expenses for her husband's personal appearances. Prior to that, Thorpe had done his appearances for nothing. He even paid his own way back and forth.

Pat changed all that. She lined up a lecture tour that covered 67,000 miles in one year. It was exhausting, but profitable. She later added Indian dancers and singers to the act.

In 1951, Warner Brothers released the film *Jim Thorpe—All-American*, with Burt Lancaster in the title role.

The movie was a box-office smash, but Thorpe saw none of the profits. It seems he had unwittingly signed away the screen rights to his own life story twenty years earlier. The price: $1,500.

"That was a mistake," Thorpe admitted.

On March 28, 1953, Jim Thorpe suffered a fatal heart attack while eating dinner with his wife in their house trailer in Lomita, California. He was sixty-four.

Years later, Wilbur J. Gobrecht wrote: "Jim Thorpe's was not a happy or successful life. Maybe he used up his quota of happiness and success as an athlete and had nothing left afterward. It would seem so."

Epilogue: This story was one installment of a four-part series on Jim Thorpe. In studying Thorpe's life, I developed a deeper appreciation for his greatness and also for the pain he endured. I once was asked: "If you could go back in time and interview one person, who would it be?" The answer was easy. It would be Jim Thorpe. To me, he is one of the most intriguing figures in all of American history. In 2022, the International Olympic Committee announced it would reinstate Jim Thorpe as the sole winner of the 1912 Olympic decathlon and pentathlon.

*Originally published in the *Philadelphia Daily News*, January 18, 1983. Reprinted with permission by Philadelphia Newspapers, LLC.

Decker Runs Armed with a Killer Instinct*

*I am more comfortable on the track. I have more confidence there than in any-
thing else in my life.*
— Mary Decker

It was on the final straightaway in Helsinki, Finland, that Mary Theresa
Decker became one with her destiny.

It was there in the 1983 World Track Championships, with Zamira Zaitseva
at her elbow and America's hopes draped across her shoulders, that Decker
finally embraced her promise and carried it home.

All the years of pain, the broken bones, the broken hearts, the broken marriage, none of it mattered anymore. This was Mary Decker, all grown up,
doing the one thing in her life that made sense from the beginning.

She was running . . . running against the Soviets' best. She was ten meters
from the tape, eyes closed, teeth clenched, driving to the finish with a stride
that was more purpose than poetry.

This time, dammit, Mary was going to win.

No boycott, no crutches, no "Sorry, honey, you're too young." No tears, no
excuses, no Harlequin novel endings. Just Mary Decker and her will pitted
against the rest of the world. We all know that's no contest.

Carl Lewis walked away from the long jump to watch. Dave Laut
dropped his shot put. The Finnish crowd was on its feet cheering. Track is a
sport known for its moments of theater, but seldom are they this eloquent or
universal.

"People talk about the Super Bowl," Lewis said later. "Man, Super Bowl is
nothing compared to this."

Zaitseva had done all she could to unnerve Decker throughout the 1,500
meters. She bumped Decker and stepped on her toes early, then she cut her
off on the final turn.

As a teenager, Decker had thrown her baton at a Soviet runner who used
similar tactics. This time, Mary kept her cool.

"I was angry," she said, "but I decided the best way—the only way—to get
even was to beat her."

Decker closed the gap on Zaitseva, overtaking her in the stretch. Desperate,
the Soviet champion threw herself at the line. Zaitseva fell short and sprawled
across the track.

Decker coasted to a stop and finally, almost reluctantly, opened her eyes.

She did not know she had won until she saw the replay on the stadium scoreboard. It was her second gold medal of the championships—she had won the 3,000 meters four days earlier—and it left us all to shake our heads in wonder.

"Until now," said Bob Hersch of *Track and Field News*, "we never knew how good Mary Decker was." (Hersch had predicted Decker would not even make the U.S. team for Helsinki.)

Those last ten meters made Mary Decker famous in a way her seven world records (six indoors) and nine American records never could.

She didn't beat a stopwatch; she beat a Russian. Better yet, she beat a Russian who played dirty. She said, "In your faceski, sister," and it was like Lake Placid all over again.

Months later, Decker's coach at Athletics West, Dick Brown, told *Sports Illustrated*: "I continue to be amazed at the number of people, not necessarily track fans, who come up to say, `I get goose bumps or I get tears in my eyes when I think about it.'"

Recently, several top female gymnasts were discussing the athletes they most admire. Olga Korbut and Nadia Comaneci were numbers one and two, naturally. But Julianne McNamara never hesitated.

"Mary Decker," the two-time U.S. Olympian said. "I can still see her finish in Helsinki. The determination on her face. What intensity, what a killer.

"Imagine if we were all like that," McNamara said, smiling. "Wow."

Mary Decker, now twenty-six, was sitting in the weight room at the University of Oregon track. She was wearing blue slacks and a gray sweater, and she looked nothing like a killer.

She looked slender and lovely and, yes, even vulnerable. Of course, the glowering presence of her boyfriend–bodyguard, the British discus thrower Richard Slaney (six-foot-seven, 290 pounds) more than made up for that.

Decker can't explain what it is that makes her run the way she does. She has heard all the theories—she runs to win because she had a tough childhood, because she needs love, etc.—but she thinks we are reaching for something that's not really there.

Maybe Decker runs to win because that's the only thing she knows. Maybe she runs to win because it beats the hell out of finishing fifth.

"I'm a competitive person," Decker said.

She glanced over at Slaney, who was listening while he wrestled with Decker's rottweiler pup, Samantha. Slaney rolled his eyes.

"OK," Decker said, getting the message. "Make that very competitive.

"I get myself into that frame of mind when I race. You can be best friends with someone off the track, but in the race, only one person can win. That's how I approach it.

"From the time I started running, I won. I got used to it. To me, that was the only place to finish. I wasn't like some kids who would finish second and say, `I ran a good time.' Good time, heck. I want to win. I'll do anything I have to to win.

"People say the other runners fear me," Decker said. "I don't know if that's true. I can't read their minds. All I know is I'm out there to beat them. But afraid? You can't be afraid to win. If you are, then why bother running?'"

"Mary has what Vince Lombardi called `singleness of purpose,'" said Brown, who has coached her for the past four years. "She has mental toughness to fight through anything. And I mean literally anything.

"Look back over her career, count up all the injuries [dozens] and operations [six]. Consider all she had to go through to come back. It would have been so easy for her to say, `This is crazy. Let's try something else.' But she didn't. She won't quit, ever."

"Maybe [the British miler] Steve Ovett is as competitive as Mary," Slaney said. "I can't think of too many others."

That's what attracted everyone to Mary Decker in the first place.

Here was this attractive woman (who else wore gold earrings and make-up to work out?) who loved junk food, stuffed animals, and Rod Stewart, who was so typically *Cosmo* but who carried a stiletto on the track.

Rick Reilly, a writer for the *Los Angeles Times*, described Decker as "farmtown fresh, yet with a certain Manhattan in her smile, as though she could drink Dom Perignon with a straw and make it look elegant." Yeah, Mary Decker was all of that, urbane and charming. But deep down, she was something more.

"Mary," the miler Steve Scott once said in admiration, "is an animal. Don't get in her way or you'll pay."

Case in point: the Great Baton Toss in Moscow. That was 1974 and little Mary, then sixteen, was disqualified for hurling her baton at the Russian who elbowed her off the track in a 4 by 400 relay.

Decker expressed only one regret. "I missed," she said. "Twice."

We liked that, even though we might not have cared to admit it. It was poor sportsmanship and worse politics, but it was undeniably spunky. And Americans are suckers for spunky kids in braces and pigtails. "Mary showed `em," we said. It was as if our daughter had punched out the school bully. We couldn't tell the teacher we approved, but we really did.

Over the years there were other incidents, like the time Decker shoved a lapped runner aside at the Millrose Games in New York. And the way she never bothered to learn her opponents' names. Critics wondered just where was the line between being competitive and being cruel?

"What you've got to understand about Mary," Tracy Sundlun, one of Decker's former coaches, told *Newsweek*, "is that she judges her worth as a person solely by what she accomplishes on the track.

"It's scary to contemplate, but the competitive nature that we so admire in this woman is actually a huge personality flaw."

Bill Bowerman would agree. Bowerman is the retired Oregon track coach who was hired by Dick Brown a while back to supervise Decker's training. He lasted two weeks.

"It was not a pleasure," Bowerman told Reilly. "I couldn't adjust to her. She had quite a temperament. I just couldn't put up with the tantrums. I'm not a very patient person.

"But Dick is exactly right for her. If they hadn't come together, she never would have survived."

Brown is a quiet, unassuming man with a manner best described as soothing. He knows track, and he knows sports medicine, and in short, he knows what's best for Mary Decker, who self-destructs more often than the Democratic Party.

Brown's calm, low-key approach is just what Decker needs, particularly in an Olympic year, when the newsmen, the advertisers, and the promoters are lining up at the door. Brown's temper is as long as Decker's is short, and between them, they make things work. Usually.

There still are occasional problems, like the time Brown told *Philadelphia Daily News* photographer Prentice Cole he could shoot a workout, and Decker decided she didn't want her picture taken that day. She ran off the track and up the bleachers, screaming at the photographer to get out.

"Some days, I just want to be left alone," Decker explained. "Everyone feels that way from time to time, and we say it's natural. I feel that way, and people say I'm a prima donna. I can't win.

"I'm sensitive to it, but probably not as sensitive as I should be. The older I get, the more things there are. It's everything—appearances, interviews, commercial exploitation. Yet you don't want to snub the people who are genuine.

"It's just hard to sort it all out," she said with a shrug. "It's a tough balance. They say you owe the public something, but don't you owe yourself something, too? This [fame] is the worst part of being Mary Decker."

Brown agrees that Decker can be difficult. The same qualities that made her hard to beat in the 1,500 meters at Helsinki also make her hard to deal with on a regular basis. Sometimes tenacity and stubbornness are one and the same.

"To understand Mary, you have to understand what she has gone through to get here," Brown said. "If she were any less competitive than she is, she wouldn't even be running, much less preparing for the Olympics.

"I spend half my day telling people why Mary can't do things . . . TV shows, fashion shows, commercials. They say, `Can't she fly to [Los Angeles] for the afternoon? This will only take three hours.' They don't have any idea what's involved in her training.

"I say, 'No, she can't,' and they feel we're being unreasonable. They say, 'Who does she think she is?' It's not a question of who Mary thinks she is but what she wants to be, and that's an Olympic champion. Like it or not, that takes a special commitment.

"Mary has worked her whole life for this," Dick Brown said. "This is her moment, and she's going to call the shots. She used to try to please everybody, but that didn't work. Maybe this will."

Mary Decker was born in Bunnvale, New Jersey, the daughter of a tool and die maker. The family moved to California in 1967 and settled in Garden Grove, a quiet Los Angeles suburb.

At eleven, Mary was looking for things to do. She saw a notice for a cross-country race sponsored by the local parks department. She liked to run. She figured, "Why not?"

With no training, running in a T-shirt and sneakers, Mary won the race with ease. Don DeNoon, coach of the Long Beach Track Club, was at the finish line asking for her name and address. That's how it all started.

Within a year, Mary was running for the Long Beach club. And running. And running . . .

In one week, she ran five races: the 440, the 880, the mile, two mile, and marathon. The next day, she had an emergency appendectomy that the doctors blamed on "extreme stress."

Everyone blamed DeNoon and Jackie Decker, Mary's mother, but the truth is no one pushed Mary like Mary.

The day after her release from the hospital, she came to practice and jogged with her teammates. She held the surgical stitches together with the palm of her hand.

By the time she was a junior at Orange High School, Decker had shin splints, and her ankles ached when she walked. She was taking twelve aspirin a day to numb the pain, but she never missed a workout.

All along, Mary Decker knew what she wanted.

"I wanted to run," Decker says now, looking back. "I liked it even before I knew I was good at it. Then once I started having success, that only made me like it more.

"People were saying I should have been home playing with Barbie dolls. Hey, I was enjoying myself. My parents never pushed me to train. If I missed my ride to practice, I threw a tantrum.

"A lot of girls would hide in the bushes during workouts, then jump out so they'd finish with the team. Or they'd take off for the restroom and miss five or six intervals. Those girls didn't like to train. I did."

It's not so hard to understand. Track was very good to Mary Decker. She was "Little Mary," so cute and lovable that even crusty old sportswriters would pat her on the head after an interview.

When she was fourteen, she upset Niele Sabaite, the Olympic silver medalist, in a U.S.–Soviet dual meet in Minsk. (She appeared on *To Tell the Truth* the next week. At five feet tall and 86 pounds, she stumped the panel.)

When Decker was fifteen, she broke three world indoor records and toured Africa with the U.S. national team. The premier of Senegal presented her with a bronze statue of a soldier on a horse. (She still has it in her Eugene, Oregon, living room.)

The trouble was, things weren't going well at home—her father had left, and her mom was working as a cocktail waitress to support the three kids— and Mary began using her coaches as a substitute for family.

Track was the one thing she could hold on to as the rest of her world was falling apart. She trusted the sport and its cast the way she would trust mom and dad, and it just didn't work. She was eager to please, and people were quick to take advantage.

Where a father would have seen the pain in her stride and told her to ease up, the coaches sought to keep her running. And where most teenagers can retreat to their rooms and close the door, Little Mary always seemed to be center stage.

"Mary never had a chance to be a kid," Nancy Gregorio, an old friend, said. "She had to be a star from the beginning. She was always around older people, flying around the world.

"Her need to be loved stems from her dad leaving her as a kid. She needs to know someone is there who cares for her."

Decker has heard the story a million times, and she still isn't sure she accepts it. She cringes at the old Frank Shorter quote about her being "exploited." It all sounds so, well, melodramatic.

"Most of my problems stem from injuries," Decker said, "and who's to say what causes injuries? People say I trained too hard, but I've always been like that. To trace it all back to an unhappy childhood is a little much."

Whatever the reason, Decker's career slowed, then came to a crippling halt, at sixteen.

She developed a condition called compartment syndrome, which meant her calf muscles had outgrown her legs. When she ran, the muscles would press against surrounding tissue and cause cramping and severe pain.

For three years, she traveled from doctor to doctor. She had X-rays, cortisone, dye injections, acupressure, and acupuncture. She had her legs in casts for months at a time. Nothing worked. The '76 Olympics came and went without Little Mary.

She probably should have given up at this point, but she did not. She went to Boulder, Colorado, enrolled at the university, and took a part-time job at Shorter's running shop. Anything to stay close to the action.

In 1977, Dick Quax, the 1976 Olympic silver medalist in the 5,000 meters, came to train. Quax had had compartment syndrome in 1973, but he overcame it through corrective surgery. The doctors cut open the tissue sheaths surrounding the muscle and allowed it to expand. Simple as that.

"You ought to try it," Quax said.

"What do I have to lose?" Decker said.

She was in the hospital five days, and two weeks later, she jogged a half-mile. Pretty soon, she was up to a mile. The pain was gone. There was no stopping her.

Quax became her coach, then her boyfriend. That got complicated. "We had what you'd call a personality conflict," Decker said. In '79, Quax ran one way; Mary, the other.

There were two more operations on her legs, not to mention three automobile accidents that set her back. Once she was at a Jackson Browne concert on her crutches and she accidentally was knocked to the floor in the crowd.

"Things seem to happen to me," Decker said. "My mother said I'm my own worst enemy, and maybe I am. The thing is I never stay down long. If I'm good at anything, it's coming back."

In 1980, Decker was at her peak. In January, she broke the world outdoor mile record (4:21.7). Two weeks later, she set the world indoor 1,500 meter record at the Millrose Games (4:00.8). One week later, she ran a 4:17.55 mile in the Astrodome, then she became the first woman to run the 880 indoors in less than two minutes (1:59.7).

She was primed for her first Olympics, then President Jimmy Carter interceded. Disheartened, Decker went on a grueling European tour that wound up with her blowing out her Achilles tendon in Brussels—more surgery, followed by sixteen months of rehabilitation.

In 1982, Decker launched yet another comeback, this time with the paternal Brown providing the direction. She had daily applications of DMSO (an anti-inflammatory drug), and four times a week she had massages to loosen the muscles before she ran.

"If we keep you healthy," Brown said, "no one can beat you."

He was right. Decker broke seven world records that year, three in six weeks. She was the fastest U.S. woman in all six distances from 800 to 10,000 meters. She set a record in the 10,000 meters (31:35.3) at an "all-comers" meet in Eugene. She did it after flying sixteen hours from Oslo, Norway.

She wasn't even wearing track shoes that day. She was wearing flats because Brown didn't want her overdoing it. So she went out and set a world record.

"I didn't know," Decker said later. "It felt easy."

As if Little Mary ever knew what easy was. She was married at the time to the marathoner Ron Tabb. That lasted twenty-two months. Heaviest laundry line in Eugene. She claimed her husband couldn't handle her success. He claimed Mary was too wrapped up in her career.

"There were times when I wanted to do things, I wanted her to be a part of it," Tabb told the *Denver Post*. "Mary felt it would interrupt her career too much. I had a little resentfulness.

"What was good for me wasn't necessarily good for her. I didn't think that was quite fair. She's very selfish with her running. . . . I guess we have to be a little more selfish with our careers if we're going to accomplish what we want to."

Both parties escaped with careers intact. Ron ran second in the `83 Boston Marathon and announced: "Maybe now I'll be known again as Ron Tabb instead of Ron Decker."

Mary went on to Helsinki, where she enjoyed her finest moment, defeating two-time Olympic champion Tatyana Kazankina in the 3,000 meters, then out-gutting Zaitseva in the 1,500 meters.

"Very few people thought I could win at Helsinki," Decker said, smiling at Slaney. "The people close to me knew I could, but the so-called experts didn't think so.

"They said, `Oh, Mary does real well running against other Americans. She doesn't have much competition here. But the Russians and the East Germans . . . that's another story.' Of course, all that did was help motivate me.

"You know how I trained for that meet? I ran with the cross-country team from the college. I knew there were no women around who could push me, and I needed the work. I said, `OK, guys. Get physical. Bump me around. Don't hold anything back.'"

Decker did not finish the story. The first day, four men showed up to run, and three dropped out, exhausted by Decker's pace. One crawled off the track and threw up in the grass.

"I proved a point in Helsinki," Decker said. "I'm sure when the Russians passed me on that final lap, they thought that was it, that I'd break. But I didn't. If I've learned one thing in this life, it's that you can't quit.

"So many people call that meet the turning point of my career. I don't see it that way. I feel like my whole life is like a ladder that I'm climbing, and Helsinki was the next rung leading to the Olympics.

"I don't think I'll be satisfied until I have that [Olympic] medal," she said. "It's something I've always wanted to do, always felt capable of doing; it's just the circumstances kept me from competing. I was too young in `72; I was hurt in `76; and [in] `80, well, let's not get into that.

"But it's worked out so that I'll be competing in Los Angeles, where I grew up. Maybe that's the way it was meant to be all along. I know it's going to be crazy there. It's already crazy. That's why I'm here [in Oregon]. All that Olympic stuff, day and night. I couldn't take it."

But even in Eugene, Oregon, the pressure is building. Surely, Mary Decker knows there are millions of people out there counting on her to win not one but two gold medals in Los Angeles?

Her visibility never has been greater. She is in magazine ads for Nike and Timex. She is also the official Kodak Camera Girl of the Summer Games. (The Kodak press release describes her as "slim, trim, prim, full of vim, and smiling from rim to rim.")

"It's all part of the package," Decker said, smiling weakly. "Like I said, having cameras and microphones shoved in my face is my least favorite part of the day. When I walk away from all this, that's the one thing I won't miss.

"But I've put up with it for ten years, a few more weeks won't make much difference. Dick [Brown] does a good job screening requests. And, of course, Richard [Slaney] can be very helpful discouraging trespassers."

(Reilly's profile suggested that Slaney "eats photographers for between-meals snacks and practices scowling in the mirror at night." Could be. We weren't asking.)

"But that's all secondary," Mary Decker said. "What counts is what happens out there [pointing toward the track]. And out there is where I'm at my best."

Epilogue: Mary Decker's world collapsed in the 3,000 meter final at the Los Angeles Olympics. She collided with Zola Budd of South Africa and fell to the track, injuring her hip. She competed for another ten years and won races all over the world, but she never won the one thing she wanted most, an Olympic medal.

*Originally published in the *Philadelphia Daily News,* June 21, 1984. Reprinted with permission by Philadelphia Newspapers, LLC.

Teti Always Seems to Stand Out on Rowing Team*

Mike Teti was an alternate on the U.S. Olympic rowing team in 1984, which means he never left the dock in Los Angeles.

But that's not to say he didn't make a splash at the last Summer Games.

Take, for example, the opening ceremonies, when Teti marched into the Coliseum with the other U.S. athletes and unfurled a pillowcase with the handwritten message: "Hi, Mom. I'm here."

The shot made network TV and *Sports Illustrated*.

"I was the center spread in the magazine," the Upper Darby native said. "Pages twenty-six and twenty-seven."

Then there was the night Teti went to Dodger Stadium for a ballgame.

Between innings, the Diamond Vision camera was panning the crowd and stopped on Teti's row. The six-foot-two, 185 pound rower did what most folks do when they see themselves on a stadium scoreboard.

"I pointed, I waved, I looked stupid," Teti said.

Slowly, the camera zoomed in for a close-up. It kept pulling tighter and tighter until it focused on Teti's shirt, with its U.S. rowing team crest.

The crowd, still full of the Olympic spirit, began chanting, "U–S–A, U–S–A."

"I got a standing ovation," Teti said. "I had to take a bow, sign autographs, and everything. I didn't have the heart to tell anybody, `Look, I didn't really row at the Games.'"

Teti enjoyed himself so much in Los Angeles that he could not bear to leave when the games ended. He stayed in the Olympic village for an entire week after the rest of the U.S. athletes had cleared out.

"I had the dorm to myself," Teti said. "I had six SWAT teams guarding me. Stuff was arriving every day from different sponsors—sweat suits, running shoes, gym bags—and I was handing it out to the cops. They loved me. We were having a blast.

"Finally, Anita DeFrantz [of the U.S. Olympic Committee] came to me and said, `Mike, do you have any idea how much this is costing? Could you please go home so we can close up the village?'"

Teti, thirty-one, arrived in Philadelphia just in time to be honored by Mayor Wilson Goode along with the city's other Olympians: Meldrick Taylor and Tyrell Biggs (boxing), Gwen Cheeseman (field hockey), and John Marzano (baseball).

"There was a parade and speeches," Teti said. "It was great. Then I walked back to my car and found a meter maid writing me a ticket.

"I said, `Hey, I was just with the mayor. I was honored by the city.' I pointed to my [Olympic] jacket. She said, `Yeah, you guys were great. I watched you on TV every night. You really made me proud.'

"She shook my hand, then she handed me the ticket," Teti said. "That's when I knew I was back in the real world."

For Teti, the real world consisted of his nine-to-five job as a financial planner with Karr and Barth Associates downtown and his part-time duties as crew coach at Temple University.

He had an Olympic ring and an Olympic watch, plus dozens of stories from his summer in Los Angeles. But he didn't have the one thing he wanted most, and that was the satisfaction of competing in the Olympics and winning a gold medal.

Next month in Seoul, South Korea, Teti finally will get his shot.

He was selected to row in the men's Olympic heavyweight eight in trials that concluded last week in Princeton, New Jersey. Teti is joined by another Vesper Club oarsman, John Pescatore, who also made the elite eight.

Most people probably consider Teti's selection a given, since he was part of the U.S. eight that won the world championship last summer in Copenhagen. Also, Teti was named Male Athlete of the Year by the U.S. Rowing Association.

But the truth is, Teti's spot on the Olympic team wasn't a sure thing.

He was the oldest rower in the trials by six years. He also was one of the smallest oarsmen in the U.S. camp. The trend is toward rowers who resemble NFL tight ends or NBA power forwards.

There is an irony here: Teti was big enough to make the varsity basketball team at St. Joseph's University in 1978, but he wasn't sure he was big enough to make an Olympic rowing team ten years later.

"The sport is evolving," Teti said. "Most of the guys coming into it are six-foot-four or six-foot-five, 220 pounds. I stand in the middle of these animals and I look like the coxswain.

"But you still can be small and explosive. That's the kind of [crew] we had when we won the gold medal at the Worlds last summer. We probably were the smallest crew in the finals, but we could really turn it on."

The final selections for this year's Olympic crew were made by coach Kris Korzeniowski, the Polish native who has rebuilt the U.S. rowing program since taking over in 1984.

The year before Korzeniowski came aboard, no U.S. boat had even made the finals at the world championship.

At the 1984 Olympics, every U.S. boat entered won a medal. That's single and double sculls, fours and eights, as well as pairs, without coxswain. What a difference a year with Korzeniowski made.

"Kris is a master," Teti said. "I learned more about rowing in ten days with him than I learned in the previous ten years combined."

It was Korzeniowski's arrival that brought Teti back to the sport. The Monsignor Bonner High School graduate had ruptured a disc in his back in 1982 and sat out an entire year. He was thinking about retiring from serious competition.

"But when Korzeniowski came, it was like a chance for a fresh start," Teti said. "I knew I'd have to start at the bottom, but I had worked my way up before."

Teti was part of the U.S. eight that toured Europe before the 1984 Summer Olympics. He appeared a cinch for the Los Angeles games, but his boat lost in a major upset at the U.S. trials.

Teti went to the Olympics, all right, but as a backup.

"It was a mixed emotion," Teti said. "It was fun to be part of the scene. Living in the Olympic village was great. The cafeteria was open twenty-four hours. I got my hair cut by Vidal Sassoon himself, for free. It was like fantasy land.

"But it hurt the day the eight shoved off [to race] and I had to watch. That's when it hit me what `alternate' means. It hurt me, and I'm sure it hurt my relatives who made the trip to LA, hoping I'd get a shot."

Teti is one of ten children, so when he talks about his relatives traveling to the West Coast, he is talking about a serious migration.

But how did an alternate get that many tickets to the rowing competition?

"We put my little brother, Paul, outside the gate," Teti said. "We painted him red, white, and blue and gave him a sign that said, `I need tickets to see my brother row for the USA.'

"We got eight tickets in less than an hour. All my relatives got in."

The only problem was, Mike Teti didn't get to row for the USA that day, but he will next month in Seoul.

It is a moment Teti has worked for over the past fourteen years, ever since he took up rowing to stay in shape between football seasons at Bonner.

"I'm getting all the credit, but, really, this has been a team effort," Teti said. "I'm talking about my family. I haven't sacrificed that much. I row because I love it. It's the other people who have sacrificed for me.

"I still live with my parents. I'll toss this [sweat suit] down the basement when I get home, and it will be washed and hanging in my closet tonight. If I go to run or lift weights, dinner will be waiting when I come back. That's stuff nobody reads about.

"My relatives go to mass and light candles for me. My mother attends charismatic services and prays for me. I come home from a lousy workout, and somebody's always there to say, `Mike, this is gonna be your year.' It keeps me going.

"People who don't know anything about rowing think it's a blue-blood sport," Teti said. "The fact that John and Jack Kelly rowed for Vesper makes it seem like we're all rich boys living on trust funds. That's not even close.

"Look around. This is a working man's club."

It's true, the Vesper Boat Club (not to be confused with the Vesper Club downtown) is hardly plush. There is no carpeting in the locker room. The training room is nothing more than a few benches and free weights on a hardwood floor.

The Vesper mystique has nothing to do with ambiance; it has everything to do with tradition.

Vesper crews have been winning major titles for a half-century. In fact, a Vesper eight won the gold medal at the 1964 Olympics in Tokyo. Their picture still hangs proudly in the boathouse.

"We have a real cross-section," Teti said. "Construction workers, painters, teachers, laborers. Most of the guys are like me; they come from blue-collar backgrounds. Their families are their backbone.

"We might be the last real amateurs left in the world. Some guys are living hand to mouth just for the chance to compete in the Olympics. You try to explain that to people, and they look at you like you're nuts.

"But I know how I felt when I won the world championship last summer. It was worth everything. I had answered everybody's prayers, including my own."

Epilogue: Mike Teti won a bronze medal in the eight-man crew at the 1988 Olympics. He was named head coach of the U.S. men's team following the 2000 Summer Games. In the 2004 Olympics, Teti led the U.S. men's eight to a world record in the qualifying heat and a gold medal in the final.

*Originally published in the *Philadelphia Daily News*, August 5, 1988. Reprinted with permission by Philadelphia Newspapers, LLC.

Huber Junks Old Diet for Taste of Gold*

Vicki Huber was talking about something close to her heart. Something she thinks about, dreams about, fantasizes every day.

Not an Olympic gold medal, although that would be nice.

Not a world record in the women's 3,000 meters, although that would be OK, too.

"Doritos," Huber sighed.

Say what?

"Really, I could cry when I think about Doritos," Huber said. "I used to eat a whole bag of them at night while watching TV. I loved them. Now . . ."

Long pause.

"I eat carrots," she said, making a face.

Blame it on "Uncle Marty" Stern, the Villanova women's track coach. He is the Grinch who stole Vicki's Doritos—to say nothing of her Twinkies, fudge bars, lemon pies, and late-night pizzas.

What a meanie, you say.

But consider the flip side: The Stern approach also helped make the twenty-one-year-old Huber the brightest—and hungriest—star among Philadelphia-area athletes headed for the Summer Games next month in Seoul, South Korea.

Uncle Marty took away Vicki's junk food and gave her a new, sleek figure and a shot at Olympic gold. You have to admit, that's a pretty good tradeoff.

There will be a number of locals competing for the United States in Seoul—including swimmer David Wharton, of Warminster; modern pentathlete Mike Gostigan, of Newtown Square; fencer Dave Littell, of Philadelphia; and rower Mike Teti, of Upper Darby—but Huber will occupy center stage, and rightly so.

She is coming off a spectacular junior season at Villanova in which she:

- Won the 1,500 meter and 3,000 meter titles on the same night at the NCAA indoor championships.
- Anchored the school's distance medley relay team to a world's best time (10:48.38) at the Penn Relays.
- Lowered the women's collegiate 3,000 meter mark (8:47.35) at the NCAA outdoor championships.
- Won the women's 1,500 meters at TAC (The Athletics Congress) outdoor championships. Her time of 4:07.40 was a personal best.

• Chased Mary Slaney to the wire in the 3,000 meter final at the Olympic trials. Huber finished second and thus became the first Villanova woman ever to make a U.S. Olympic team.

Stern jumped from the bleachers to embrace Huber after her remarkable performance in the oppressive heat (114 degrees) and wilting pressure. The little coach lifted Huber off her feet and carried her down the track, beaming with joy.

All the hard work and sacrifice had paid off.

Chalk up another one for Uncle Marty and the carrot growers of America.

"Vicki surprised me," Stern said. "I never thought she would be this far along in her third [college] year. But what can I say? She's just a very special athlete, one in a million.

"People like that are full of surprises."

Let's go back to the beginning, back to the days when Vicki still knew the sinful pleasures of cherry Cokes and three-scoop ice cream cones . . .

When Stern recruited Huber from Concord High School in Wilmington, she was five-foot-six and weighed 135 pounds. She was all-state in two sports, track and field hockey. Almost everyone, including Vicki's parents, thought she looked fine.

Uncle Marty disagreed.

"The way he looked at these [thighs]," Huber said, "I had a feeling I was in trouble."

Stern put Huber on a strict diet and forced her to run cross-country at Villanova. She lost twenty pounds her sophomore year. Her father, fearful that Vicki's training was turning into anorexia, considered pulling his daughter out of school.

"Every time I went home, my father put me on the scale," Huber said. "He would say, `You've lost another five pounds. You look terrible.' Then my mother would come in with a piece of chocolate cake and say, `Here, eat this.'

"I'd say, `I'm OK. Look at my times; I'm running faster than I ever have. The coach knows what he's doing.'

"Of course, I still didn't like it. I would have loved to pig out, but I knew it would just set me back. So I basically starved."

And what about cross-country?

"I hated it," Huber said, "but it gave me a good base for the track season, so I went along with the program.

"With Marty," she said, "you always go along with the program."

Huber had a promising freshman year, winning the Big East Conference 1,500 meter title both indoors and outdoors. She gained national prominence as a sophomore, capturing the 3,000 meters at the NCAA outdoor championships. Her time was 8:54.41, a meet record.

The next logical step would have been for Huber to qualify for the 1987 World Championships in Rome. She was healthy and her times, competitive.

But Stern convinced Huber to take the summer off and freshen up for the Olympic year.

Looking back, it is clear Uncle Marty knew best.

Huber spent a low-key summer, working as a waitress at the Brandywine Country Club and running just enough to stay fit. When she returned to school in the fall, she was like a thoroughbred fidgeting in the starting gate.

"I knew this was going to be a big season," Huber said. "I was anxious to prove what I did last year was no fluke. And I wanted to see where I stood in relation to the top [world-class] competition."

Huber did not have to wait long to find out.

In February, she entered the mile at Millrose Games with a field that included world indoor record holder Doina Melinte and Olympic gold medalist Maricica Puica, both of Romania, and Kirsty Wade of Great Britain.

That's what you call fast company.

"I was more nervous before that race than any race in my life," Huber said. "I wasn't sure I had the speed for the mile. I looked at the competition and thought, 'Wow, this is a different ballgame.'"

Huber surprised everyone, including herself, by chasing Melinte and Wade to the finish line. Huber finished third in a time of 4:28.31, the fastest indoor mile ever run by a collegian and the second fastest ever by an American, behind Slaney's 4:20.5.

It was a tremendous boost to Huber's confidence, and she has been building on it ever since.

Her showcase, of course, was the Olympic trials, where she lined up against Slaney for the first time and nipped at the legend's heels in the 3,000 meter final. Huber actually had Slaney glancing over her shoulder with one lap to go.

When was the last time a U.S. collegian did that?

Indeed, when was the last time any American runner had Slaney looking in the rear-view mirror?

But Slaney heard Vicki Huber coming on little Wildcat feet last month.

It made an impression.

"It felt good to be pushed for a change," Slaney said. "I had heard a lot about Vicki, and what I heard was right. She's tough."

Said Huber: "I remember watching [Slaney] on TV and wondering how anyone could run that fast. What an incredible feeling it was to run that [victory] lap with her. . . . It was beyond my dreams."

Huber was more relieved than overjoyed about making the Olympic team. The worst of the pressure was over. All those friends and admirers who kept asking the same question—"Are you gonna make the Olympics?"—finally had their answer.

Given her youth, whatever Huber does in Seoul will be a bonus. She does not figure to peak until the 1992 games. She could be the gold-medal favorite by then if she continues to develop.

But for now, just making the U.S. team was the thing. Huber did that, and did it in style.

(Over the years, thirty-nine Villanova men have made Olympic track teams. Huber is the first woman. Somewhere, Jumbo Elliott is smiling.)

"I got so sick of people asking me about the Olympics," Huber said. "It just kept building up. I almost burst into tears a few times.

"My family and my boyfriend were great because they kept it in perspective. Gary [Bagin, her boyfriend] would say things like, `I don't know what you're worried about. You aren't gonna make it anyway. You stink.' He would make light of it, and that's what I needed.

"My parents were cool about it, too. They never asked how [track] was going. They figured I'd bring it up if I felt like it. Sometimes they would tell me not to train. They'd say, `It's raining' or `It's too hot.' They never let the sport dominate our lives, and I'm grateful for that."

Huber is a most unassuming star. A psychology and pre-med major with a 3.5 grade-point average, she is bright and refreshingly genuine. She is so genuine she finds it impossible to conceal her embarrassment when reporters push past her teammates to interview her after a race.

The other Villanova runners have learned to accept it by now. It is to Huber's credit that she has not.

She credits her teammates for much of her success. She cannot afford to let down in practice, she says, because "Kathy [Franey] and Celeste [Halliday] will kick my butt." She wishes more people, particularly those carrying notepads and microphones, would understand.

"It's very awkward," Huber said, "especially after we set a record like we did in the distance-medley relay. Four girls ran the race, four girls set the record, but I'm the one who is interviewed on TV.

"It's just not right."

"If Vicki weren't the kind of person she is, there probably would be a lot of resentment [among other runners]," Stern said. "But you can't resent Vicki. There's no way. She might be the most selfless athlete on the team, and it's no act.

"I'll give you an example. One day after practice I noticed Vicki running up the stadium steps. I thought, `What's this, a new workout?' Then I saw her put her arm around one of our freshmen who just had a really awful day. The kid was upset; Vicki saw her and wanted to lift her spirits.

"There were no reporters or cameramen around. She didn't do this to impress anybody. I'm sure she didn't realize I was watching. But here was this superstar going out of her way to help a freshman.

"That's Vicki Huber."

She is famous now, although she doesn't like to admit it. She still looks slightly baffled when people ask for her autograph. She was seated next to Flyers goalie Ron Hextall at a recent banquet and wound up asking for his autograph.

"For my boyfriend," she explained. "He loves hockey."

Huber can't get over the amount of fan mail that pours into the Villanova track office addressed to her. It comes from all over the United States. There are even a few from Europe.

"Coach [Stern] screens them," Huber said. "Most of them are kids asking for photos or autographs. They're fun. I enjoy reading those.

"Some letters are from guys who want to meet me. I usually write back and say I have a boyfriend on the soccer team here, but thanks anyway. I try to be nice about it.

"Then there was the letter I got from Attica . . ."

Attica? That Attica?

"Yeah," Huber said. "One of the prisoners saw my picture in *Sports Illustrated* and wanted to become my pen pal."

That's fame, all right.

"There's a part of me," Huber said, "that says this is all a dream and I'm going to wake up any minute.

"Like I picked up a copy of *Runner's World* magazine because it had a story on six Olympic hopefuls. The title was 'The Young Lions.' I opened the magazine, and there was a full-page picture of me. I was the lead of the article. I couldn't believe it.

"I read the first few paragraphs and I got the chills," Huber said. "This was several months ago [in March], and the Olympics seemed so far away, yet there I was in this article.

"It made me think back to when I was in high school. My coach told me I had the potential to make the Olympics. I didn't believe him. I thought, 'Yeah, right . . . Vicki Huber from Wilmington in the Olympics.' But he said if I picked the right college, I could do it.

"He was the one who sold me on Villanova. I had offers from Virginia and North Carolina, too, but he said Coach Stern would bring out the best in me, and he was right."

Yesterday, Huber left for Europe, where she will compete in two open meets and join the U.S. track team for a week of training in Switzerland beginning on August 10.

You can bet Uncle Marty packed her lunch.

Epilogue: Vicki Huber finished second to Mary Decker in the 1988 Olympic trials and earned a spot on the U.S. team. She placed sixth in the 3,000 meters at the Seoul games. She finished her Villanova career with nine NCAA titles, including one for cross-country.

---

*Originally published in the *Philadelphia Daily News*, August 1, 1988. Reprinted with permission by Philadelphia Newspapers, LLC.

1980—THE YEAR THAT WAS

◆ ◆ ◆

1980 U.S. Hockey Team: A Cure for America's Blues*

They piled off the bus like a street-corner gang arriving at summer camp, laughing and playfully shoving each other down the steps. They hadn't slept much—their eyes reflected that—but that was OK. These kids had dreams enough to last a lifetime.

They were wearing their blue sweat suits and white cowboy hats. Most of them had small American flags tucked in their hat bands. A few carried cameras. They all wore their Olympic gold medals, and every so often, Mike Eruzione would glance down at his chest as if to make sure that, yes, this was really happening.

The U.S. Olympic hockey team came to the White House yesterday, and these college kids lit up the old South Lawn like no Christmas tree ever could. They filed up the steps to shake hands with President Carter, and for a while we all forgot about Abscam and filled our aching lungs with the sweet scent of Lake Placid.

Jim Craig walked along the driveway, shaking hands with the politicians and White House staffers who were massed behind the ropes. Crusty old congressmen turned into shrieking teenyboppers, all reaching out to touch this twenty-two-year-old goalie who was unknown outside his native New England a month ago.

The Marine Corps Band was off to Craig's left, playing "Stars and Stripes Forever." Women he had never seen before were bursting past security guards to kiss him. Ed King, the governor of Massachusetts, was pleading with him to come over and pose for a few pictures.

"This is incredible," Craig said. "I feel like I walked on the moon or something."

Jim Craig and the rest of the U.S. hockey players were like an Alka-Seltzer for America. They came along at a time when our flag was burning in the streets of Teheran and our inflation rate was crashing the ceiling. They dragged our national pride from the soot heap, dusted it off, and flaunted it in the face of the world for two glorious weeks.

When they clinched the gold medal on Sunday, America turned a Fourth of July cartwheel. In Minnesota, people danced and sang in the icy streets. Students at the University of Texas, most of whom had never seen a hockey game before, held a spontaneous pep rally. In Memphis, people stormed a TV station that dared to preempt the telecast.

We all admired the breathtaking feats of Eric Heiden, but it was this scruffy little hockey team that stole our hearts. It was the sight of all those kids clamoring off the bench at the end of the Russian game that will glow in our memory forever. They looked like fraternity brothers on their first panty raid, and in their clumsy, crazy way, they were beautiful.

There was the sight of Craig, skating around after the gold medal game, clutching an American flag and searching for his father. There was Eruzione, the team captain, a refugee from the minor leagues, waving for his teammates to join him on the winners' platform at the conclusion of the awards ceremony.

"My father works in a sewage-disposal plant during the day and tends bar at night," Eruzione said yesterday. "He says this is the greatest thing that ever happened to him. You know how that makes me feel? All my life, he was my inspiration because he never quit; he kept plugging away for his family. Now I feel like I've given him something.

"There are no words to describe the feeling I had during that [medal] ceremony. We were twenty guys who would not be denied. Every game, we'd fall behind, and we'd just dig a little deeper. We'd go out on the ice and hear those people chanting `U–S–A, U–S–A.' There is nothing like playing for your country, nothing."

"It seems like a twenty-year cycle," Craig said, reflecting on the last U.S. hockey gold medal in 1960, "so somebody up there must be looking out for us. What this team did was a miracle. Let's face it: The Russians are better than we are. They beat the Swedes so easily in that last game [9–2 for the silver medal], it was ridiculous.

"We might play them twelve more times and never beat them again, but we won the one that counted. When I look back on that game twenty years from now, all I'll remember is the guts and determination we showed that day. That's what we won with, guts and determination, and I believe that's what this country is all about. That's why so many people got excited."

Craig lifted the medal from his chest, examined it closely for a moment, then kissed it softly, the way a nun might kiss her rosary beads. "You think Bo Derek is a ten?" Craig said. He held up his gold medal. "This," he said, "is a ten."

"I don't know if I'll ever take this medal off," Craig said. "I might even wear it on the beach this summer. I'm liable to get a stiff neck from wearing it, but so what? Not too many people have these.

"I don't know if I'll ever be able to absorb all of this," he said, looking around at the White House. "I could live to be a hundred and never absorb this. I must've received two thousand telegrams, a lot of them from total strangers. They kept saying how we made them proud to be Americans. Wow, I guess America really needed something like this, something to cling to."

Craig is not much on politics. Ask him what he thinks of the Russians and he'll tell you they have a great power play. He probably thinks SALT (the Strategic Arms Limitation Talks) took place in somebody's kitchen. But thanks to two weeks at Lake Placid, he finds himself climbing the White House steps and talking to the president. What did Mr. Carter say, anyway?

"He said, `I see you shaved,'" Craig said. "Then he said, `You made me a hockey fan.' I said, `I think we did that to a lot of people.'"

A Secret Service man edged behind Craig. A reception was about to begin in the East Room, and all 140 Olympians were expected inside. The Secret Service guy wanted to pull Craig away from the interviewers, but he wanted to do it as gently as possible.

"Anytime you want to go," the man said, tapping Craig on the shoulder.

"Go?" Craig said. "Man, I'm having the time of my life."

The only trouble was, the time was running out. Following their luncheon with the president, the U.S. hockey team split up for good. They had come together back in the August tryout camp. They were strangers then, nervous and resentful of each other, but at some point during the grueling sixty-two–game exhibition schedule, they became a family.

"Blood brothers," Jack O'Callahan, the defenseman from Boston College, called them.

They stunned the world, and yesterday they climbed to the White House balcony and stared across the nation they had pulled together as tightly as the laces on their skates. As they filed out and scattered for the airports and train stations, they leaned on each other's shoulders and wept.

"It's hard to believe it's all over," Craig said. "This time next week, I'll be in Atlanta [playing for the NHL Flames]. Mark Johnson will be in Pittsburgh [with the Penguins]. We have two or three guys going to Minnesota [to join the North Stars]. Next time I see these guys, they'll be shooting pucks at me instead of hugging me.

"We were talking about it last night when we packed up our equipment for the last time. It was a really emotional moment. It's like we were born in August and died Sunday night."

Craig glanced down at his medal one more time. "Nah, that's not right," he said. "This team will never die."

Epilogue: Thirteen of the twenty U.S. Olympians played in the National Hockey League. Goaltender Jim Craig played for three teams (Atlanta, Boston, and Minnesota) but never recaptured the magic of Lake Placid. Team captain Mike Eruzione turned down offers to play in the NHL and became a motivational speaker.

*Originally published in the *Philadelphia Bulletin*, February 26, 1980.

Is Rosie a Real Winner?*

Jock Semple is the crotchety old Scotsman who has looked after the Boston Marathon for the past fifty-one years. Jock has become the event's coordinator and unofficial guardian, the man entrusted with preserving the dignity of this annual tribute to American masochism.

Jock's task has grown increasingly difficult in recent years. The number of entries has grown from a few hundred hearty New England blue bloods to almost anyone who can afford a headband and a pair of Nikes. Yesterday, seven thousand joggers set off on the eighty-fourth Boston Marathon, 449 of them women.

Jock never did approve of women running in the marathon. In fact, until recently women were not allowed to compete here. In 1967, Kathy Switzer tried to crash the race, and Jock chased her down the road, ripping the number off her shirt. The photo made all the papers and caused Jock great embarrassment.

"My expression," Jock recalls, "you'd think I was going to rape her."

Late yesterday, Jock Semple, now seventy-six, was stomping through the garage of the Prudential Building, the final stop in the twenty-six–mile, 385 yard ordeal. He did not even notice the hundreds of runners who were scattered around the concrete floor, groaning and calling for a medic. Jock, like an old combat officer, had seen it all before.

What had Jock upset was the rumor circulating that Rosie Ruiz, the women's champion, was not the women's champion at all. In fact, Jock was announcing to one and all that Rosie was a phony.

"She's as phony as a three-dollar bill," he said. "The TV crew riding in the truck never saw her. An official along the route watching for the top women never saw her. None of the New York officials can vouch for her. She's a fraud."

"It's disgusting," he said, his voice echoing through the garage like bagpipes. "The way things are going, maybe we ought to just forget the whole thing. It's getting out of hand. This woman is Oscar Miranda in skirts."

Oscar Miranda is the gentleman who appeared to have won the masters (senior) division of the marathon last year. Miranda finished in the top twenty with a remarkable time, but on investigation it was discovered he had not run the entire course. He had simply jumped into the crowd of runners somewhere near the finish.

Semple believes Rosie Ruiz pulled the same trick yesterday, and he was hanging around the awards platform, waiting for her to step up and receive her gold medal. As it turned out, Ruiz, a twenty-nine-year-old New Yorker, accepted her medal at the finish line, did her press conference, and split. Semple was, to say the least, annoyed.

Will Cloney, the marathon's chairman, agreed he had "grave doubts" about Ruiz's victory, but for the time being, he will let the finish stand.

Cloney said his aides had watched film of Monday's marathon, and "she doesn't appear in any of it, except crossing the finish line." Cloney, however, conceded: "We've had people call and swear they saw her at different miles. But, really, how credible is that?"

The marathon official will review all of the evidence this week, then disclose his findings.

Marathon folks take these matters very seriously. Last year, Miranda was subjected to a lie-detector test, among other things. At the moment, all the officials have against Ruiz is a pile of circumstantial evidence, but by the time they're through investigating, Rosie will feel like one of the Nuremberg criminals.

"I don't believe she could have done it," said Patti Lyons, who was officially placed third behind Ruiz and Jacqueline Gareau. "I never saw her on the course. I never saw her until I walked in here and saw her with that [winner's] wreath on her head.

"She claims she only ran in one other marathon, and that was New York last October. She said she ran a 2:56:23 [two hours, fifty-six minutes, twenty-three seconds], finished twenty-third. Today, she supposedly ran a 2:31:56. Is it possible for a woman to improve that much in such a short time? I'd say it's possible if a person has an extensive running background, but this girl doesn't."

"I think she's a phony," said Fred Lebow, head of the New York Runners Association. "She doesn't even compete in our [regular] New York events. You mean to tell me she can come up here and win the Boston Marathon and break the women's record? I find that hard to believe.

"Her answers [at the press conference] struck me as doubtful. I asked her what her splits [individual miles] were. She didn't even know what a split was. I asked her for her best time ever in the mile. She said 5:30. Well, she would have had to run twenty-six 5:30 miles to have the time she claims to have had today."

This casts doubt on what was a lovely, up-from-the-sidewalk tale. When Rosie walked onto the interview platform after finishing, no one knew who she was. Not even Bill Rodgers, the four-time men's champion, who was already midway through his press conference.

When Ruiz flopped down in the chair next to Rodgers, he looked at her rather oddly. "Who are you?" he asked.

"I'm Rosie Ruiz," she replied. "I won the women's division."

Rosie then told the fascinating story of her life: how she was born in Havana, then sent to the United States as a youngster because her parents were worried about Castro. She went to high school in Florida and college in Nebraska and began jogging five years ago as therapy after knee surgery.

"How did you injure your knee?" someone asked.

"Playing touch football," she replied.

She became a U.S. citizen in 1972, moved to Manhattan, and got a job with an outfit called Metal Trades Inc. Unlike most big-time joggers, Rosie never joined a fancy running club. Instead, she trained herself, running in Central Park on her lunch hour, then running on the West Side Highway at night.

"I never dreamed I could win this race," she said, blinking into the cameras. "This is all like a dream."

When someone confronted her with her opponent's allegations, Ruiz seemed stunned.

"Well, they can say what they want," she said. "I was the first [woman] to cross the finish line, that's all I know."

"We have to do something about this," Lebow said. "We have to come up with some electronic means to check the competitors. Our biggest races are turning into a joke."

What all this indicates is that the Boston Marathon, once a nice social event for people who were into blisters and chapped lips, has gotten entirely out of control. It has grown into the most chaotic sporting event in America, a combination Woodstock and Super Bowl where the patter of rubber soles has been replaced by the wails of outraged losers and the jingle of a cash register.

The Walter Mitty jogger, once the lifeblood of the event, is no longer encouraged to take part. Runners now must qualify—run a certified marathon in less than three hours—to draw an official number. Oh, you can still tag along if you wish, but the guards glare at you, and you have to run way in the back, where you're likely to choke on the dust of the five thousand superstars.

The event is now a logistical nightmare requiring ten moving vans to haul the seven thousand sweat suits from the starting point in Hopkintown to the finish line. The runners require nine water stations equipped with five hundred-gallon drums and nine barrels of Gookinaid athletic drink with nine canoe paddles to stir it, not to mention two thousand sponges and one hundred thousand paper cups to cool off the survivors.

The whole sport of marathon racing has come under the cloud of commercialism with recently published reports that top-name runners have accepted under-the-table payments for entering races. This has been going on for years, of course, but the matter had never been aired before. It tainted the amateur ideal old-timers like Jock Semple cling to so fiercely.

It's not even as much fun for the non-runners anymore. Traditionally, the finish line outside the Prudential Building was a gathering place for every college student, office worker, and townie on marathon day. The race is always held on Patriot's Day, a New England holiday, so everyone is off.

Folks meet at the Prudential early in the morning, eat a picnic lunch and wait for the runners to stagger down Boylston Street. In the past, the finish line was open so the fans could engulf the winner and carry him off to receive his gold medal. No more. The police have erected barricades to keep everyone back. The fans would get treated with more courtesy if they went to see a warehouse fire.

However, the people keep coming back, drawn by the eternal challenge. Some, like Bill Rodgers, come to set records and promote their line of running shoes. Others, like Steve Marek, a thirty-three-year-old insurance adjuster from Yorktown, New York, come to test themselves against the inevitable agony of Heartbreak Hill, the long, steep grade at the twenty-mile point that weeds out the timid.

Marek bills himself as the "Running Superman." He runs in a Superman costume, complete with a red cape and American flag trunks. He is a bandit, one of the three thousand non-qualifiers at the rear of the pack. He has only finished one marathon (New York), and it took him almost seven hours. He tried Boston last year and quit after fourteen miles. Yesterday, he returned.

"I just want to see if I can do it," he said. "I used to weigh 260 pounds; now I weigh 210. I just want to see if a desk-bound junk-food addict can put himself through the same torture as a guy like Bill Rodgers. This is like a dream world for me.

"Most guys dream of playing baseball with Reggie Jackson, but it'll never happen. Here I can say I ran in the same race as Bill Rodgers. Even if I finish last, I'm still a winner."

Epilogue: Race officials determined that Ruiz cheated and did not complete the 26.2 mile course. They declared Jacqueline Gareau of Canada the women's champion. Ruiz was banned for life from competing in the Boston Marathon.

*Originally published in the *Philadelphia Bulletin*, April 22, 1980.

Jack Nicklaus: Fans' Roar Tells Jack He's Back*

J ack Nicklaus marched up the eighteenth fairway at the Baltusrol Golf Club yesterday, the gallery pouring in behind him like a polyester sea; the cheers rumbling through the humid valley like summer thunder.

Surely, this is how it looked when Caesar returned from his triumph in Gaul, or when MacArthur sloshed onto the beach in the Philippines. The Great One had returned to power, and the people lined his path, giving thanks.

Nicklaus walked slowly up the hill to the green. He was savoring the moment, gently pressing it between the pages of his memory. The fans in the bleachers rose to applaud, and Nicklaus smiled. It was the smile of a weary traveler finally catching a glimpse of home.

Behind him, the scoreboard flashed the message "Jack Is Back," but of course, America already knew that. Jack was just one putt away from his fourth U.S. Open championship. More important, the Golden Bear had proved he wasn't ready for the taxidermist's window after all.

Nicklaus had not won a golf tournament since July 1978, when he won the IVB Classic at Whitemarsh Valley. Since then, his game had plummeted faster than Chrysler stock. Last year, Jack finished seventy-first on the PGA money list. In the previous seventeen years, he had never finished lower than fourth.

He turned forty on January 21, and when he fell apart in the Crosby Pro-Am, then sputtered through the Masters, the golfing community sighed and said, well, the big guy just doesn't have it anymore. When he missed the cut the week before last in Atlanta, they did everything but hang a funeral wreath on his locker.

But yesterday, Nicklaus returned to his throne, shooting a two under par 68 on a day when everyone else took turns sliding clumsily down the leader board. Fittingly, Nicklaus closed out his victory by rolling in birdie putts on the seventeenth and eighteenth holes, shattering the record for lowest Open score with 272 in the process.

An hour later, Nicklaus sat in the interview tent, listening to the rain lash against the canvas roof, sorting out the emotions that had built up during the week. Tom Watson had suggested Jack might retire if he won this tournament, and Nicklaus said the remark was not as brash as it might have seemed.

"I have no idea why Tom mentioned that," Nicklaus said, "other than it's a fairly logical thing to assume. If I looked at things sensibly, I would probably walk in here and say, 'That's it, fellas, goodbye.' That would be the most dramatic way to go out, but I don't have that much sense.

"I happen to enjoy playing golf, and I feel this old body has a few more wins in it, hopefully, this year. I think I'll be like Muhammad Ali. I'll keep going until they make me retire."

Nicklaus paused and let his mind roll over the disappointments of the past two years, the iron shots that strayed like wayward children, the putts that hung on the lip and taunted him. He thought about the times newsmen had asked the inevitable, though carefully phrased, question of whether his skills had, indeed, slipped away.

Nicklaus long ago assured himself a place in golf history. His total of major golf championships, which now stands at seventeen, is a record that may never be challenged. His career earnings, now in excess of $3 million, speak volumes. Yet Jack did not like being packed off to the wax museum before it was time.

"The most satisfying thing about this victory," Nicklaus said, "is that after scoring so badly, after not getting anything done in so long, I was able to play nine of the best holes of my life [in the final nine yesterday], just when I needed them most. I played with a confidence I hadn't felt in, whew, I don't know how long.

"The hardest part of the past year was going week to week, answering the same questions. After a while, you guys [press] had me believing it. That's why when you asked me about my self-doubts after Saturday's round, I didn't want to talk about it. I didn't want to clutter up my mind with negative thoughts. Eighteen holes to go, this was the time to be positive.

"Sure, there were times in the last year when I wondered if I should continue playing this silly game," Nicklaus said. "You ask yourself why you continue to put yourself through it; why you put your family through it. You begin to think maybe you're being stubborn. Maybe everybody else is right, and you're wrong.

"One of the hardest things for any athlete to do is to know when to retire. We've all seen great athletes, winners in their sports, play on past their primes. You wonder why they do it. You talk about how sad it is. I certainly didn't want to fall into that category. I didn't think I was in that category."

Nicklaus did not mention Arnold Palmer by name, but surely everyone in the room thought of him. Palmer has not won a tournament since 1973; he has not made the list of the top sixty money winners since 1975, yet he continues to plod along. Yesterday, Palmer shot seventy-eight to finish this Open at 301, the highest seventy-two–hole score in the tournament.

"I made a promise to myself," Nicklaus said. "I promised I would quit playing when I felt I could no longer compete. By compete, I mean win. Even in the last year, I still thought I could win. Physically, I felt great. I was lifting weights, running. I knew it was a matter of getting myself back into the proper mental state.

"I think I kidded myself the last three years. I told myself I was working hard on my game when I really wasn't. I wasn't working as hard as I should have, given the troubles I was having. This year I said, `OK, that's enough fooling around. I'm really going to work and get my game back to where it should be.' If I did that and still played poorly, then I'd have to reevaluate my future."

It never came to that, of course. Nicklaus spent the winter working with his longtime guru Jack Grout at their course in Muirfield Village, Ohio. Grout firmed up Jack's grip, squared up his stance, and restored his confidence in his swing. And even while Nicklaus was missing the cut in Atlanta, he felt he was making progress.

"I didn't do many things right in Atlanta," he said, "but I did putt well. I shot seventy-eight the first day and knocked myself right out of the tournament, but the second day, I started putting. When I came here this week, my putting stroke got progressively better. After Wednesday's practice round, I didn't say anything [to the press], but I was very optimistic.

"Obviously, the putting was the key to my great Thursday round [an Open record-tying sixty-three], and it stayed pretty solid all week. I didn't do anything spectacular on the greens today, but I didn't let it get away from me, either."

"What was the feeling," someone asked, "walking up the eighteenth fairway to that reception?"

"It was very moving," Nicklaus said. "I remember a few other ovations that touched me like that. I remember coming over the hill on the eleventh at Muirfield one year and getting an ovation like that. I remembered a similar feeling coming up the eighteenth at Augusta in 1975. Then there was St. Andrews in 1978.

"But the ovation today was very special," he said. "It almost moved me to tears. It was a long time coming."

Just then, a radio man brushed past the desk where Nicklaus was sitting. He caught a wire in his leg, and a microphone began to slide off the table. Nicklaus reached out, grabbed it, and pulled it back to his lips.

"Come back here," he said. "I'm not through yet."

The Golden Bear might not be through for some time to come.

Epilogue: Jack Nicklaus added one more major championship—the 1986 Masters—giving him a grand total of eighteen. Nicklaus retired from competitive golf after the 2005 British Open.

*Originally published in the *Philadelphia Bulletin,* June 16, 1980.

Duran Calls It Quits*

With sixteen seconds left in round eight, Roberto Duran held up his Hands of Stone and said he'd had enough.

He handed the World Boxing Council welterweight championship back to Sugar Ray Leonard and slipped off meekly into the Panamanian sunset.

While Sugar Ray was cartwheeling across the New Orleans Superdome ring, Duran was backstage announcing his retirement from boxing at age twenty-nine.

He said he was suddenly "tired" of the sport. He said he quit last night's fight due to "cramps," but he could not explain what brought them on.

Meanwhile, a tight-lipped Louisiana Boxing Commission announced it was withholding Duran's $8.5 million purse until he could be examined by a physician today.

High-rollers who paid $1,000 for ringside seats were jamming the aisles, screaming about a rip-off. People were descending on the Superdome office to demand refunds.

The whole scene played like something out of a third-rate screenplay. It was angry and puzzling, full of whispers and sinister overtones.

Guys who had been around the fight game for years were saying they had never seen anything like it. "Bizarre" was the word you kept hearing over and over again.

It was a stunning finish, not so much because Leonard won, but because of the way Duran lost. Duran (72–2) had never before lost a championship fight; he had never been stopped in thirteen years as a professional.

In a jungle business, Duran was considered the ultimate predator. The sight of him quitting, simply walking back to his corner, left the live crowd of twenty-six thousand, including three thousand horrified Panamanians, in shock.

Duran was trailing on the cards of all three officials, but not by any insurmountable margin. Judges Mike Jacobs and Jean Deswert had Leonard ahead, 68–66, at the time of the knockout. Jim Brimmell favored Leonard but by just one point, 67–66.

Leonard (28–1) had landed some solid punches, particularly in the first three rounds, but he did not appear to have hurt Duran. So what happened?

Why did Duran, the man who gloried in his macho image, suddenly pull out the white flag?

"I think I beat him more mentally than physically," Leonard said, savoring this moment, his vindication of the fifteen-round decision Duran took from him five months ago in Montreal.

"I think I confused him. I totally changed my tactics since the last fight. That was the key right there. . . . I changed, but Roberto Duran could not.

"This time," Leonard said, "the name of the game was boxing. What you saw tonight was scientific technique. Last time, it was just a slugfest. I didn't utilize all my skills. Tonight, I did.

"He couldn't catch up with me. Even with his brute strength, he couldn't dominate me. I could tell he was surprised."

"Duran said he quit because he got cramps," a newsman shouted.

Leonard smiled. "If someone hit you in the body the way I was hitting Duran, you'd have cramps, too," he said.

Many people, including some in Duran's camp, believe Leonard summed up the situation accurately when he suggested sheer frustration had as much to do with the champion's quitting as did any physical discomfort.

Whereas the fight in Montreal was waged along the ropes and in the trenches where Duran is at his best, this one was carried on in the center of the ring, with Leonard using his three-inch reach advantage to score with snapping left jabs.

Duran chased Leonard around, his head down, snorting angrily, like a bull that kept charging but got nothing but cape. Sugar Ray fought a clever, long-range fight, the kind most experts expected him to fight in Montreal.

The former Olympic champion established the pattern in the very first round and piled up points with his jab. In the third, he caught Duran coming in and landed a crisp combination that brought a wince, then a sneer, to the Panamanian's face.

"I knew I hurt him," Leonard said. "That's the way he reacts when he's hurt. He gives you that smile. At that point, I felt good. Things were going according to plan. I was fighting my fight, not his."

In the fourth and fifth rounds, Leonard did not move as much, and Duran was able to press him against the ropes. However, Leonard neutralized Duran's power, smothering his body punches and slipping out of trouble.

The seventh round was, in Leonard's mind, the turning point of the fight. Sugar Ray felt so confident, so totally in command, he actually began taunting Duran.

Normally, this would be as unthinkable as, say, yanking on a lion's whiskers, but Leonard knew he had Duran bewildered, and he couldn't resist rubbing his nose in it.

Sugar Ray dropped his hands to his sides, stuck out his chin, and pointed at it. Duran threw a right hand. Sugar Ray pulled back and watched the punch sail harmlessly into the night.

Then Leonard began cranking up his right hand, bringing it around twice, then three times. Duran pressed forward warily, looking for the bolo punch. Suddenly, Sugar Ray flicked a left jab and caught Duran flush on the nose.

It was not a lethal punch; it did not send Roberto Duran's eyes rolling back into his head, but it hurt him in the worst possible way. It made him look foolish, almost comically inept.

The fans did not cheer the punch; they laughed. Duran is not used to being laughed at. Leonard could not have shamed Duran more thoroughly if he had reached over and pulled down his trunks.

Duran went back to his corner, looking like he had just caught a whipped-cream pie in the face. Leonard, by contrast, returned to his corner, winking to his family at ringside.

When things did not improve in the next round, Duran, the legendary street fighter, simply said the hell with it and reached for his coat.

"At first, I wasn't sure what he was doing," Leonard said. "I saw him drop his hands and walk away. Then I saw the expression on his face; that's when I knew it was over."

"You mean he looked dazed?" someone said.

"No," Leonard replied. "He looked beaten."

Duran left the Superdome with characteristic grace, hurling some eleventh-hour mud at his victor.

Asked if he respected Ray Leonard more now, Duran snapped: "Because he beat me this way does not mean I have to respect him."

"You still think you are a better man?" someone asked.

"Yes, one thousand times a better man," Duran said.

Naturally, this remark was passed along to Leonard during his news conference. Leonard slipped it as neatly as he had slipped everything else Roberto Duran threw his way last night.

"That's his nature," Leonard said. "I don't care. I still respect the man. I walked over to him after the fight tonight, and he showed me respect.

"Hey, whatever his reasons [for quitting], I'm sure they were serious, because he's a great fighter. I hope the people in Panama give him the respect he deserves, because he's still one of the greatest fighters, pound for pound, in the world.

"Don't start knocking him down," Leonard told the assembled media. "And don't try to put [unkind] words in my mouth. As far as I'm concerned, the man is a champion."

Leonard was unusually testy during his press conference. He did not like the tone of the questions. People seemed to be suggesting the curious circumstances surrounding the finish somehow tainted his triumph.

Roberto Duran's heart seemed more an issue than Sugar Ray's tactical brilliance. The re-crowned champion thought he deserved better.

"No, I don't think the way it ended takes anything at all away from the victory," Leonard said. "I'm the champion now; that's all there is to it. That was my goal coming into this fight, and I've achieved it.

"I know I surprised a lot of people. I know what everyone was saying. Even the people back in my hometown were saying I wasn't ready for Duran, I was gonna get knocked out. Well, now I'm getting the last laugh.

"I know it's hard for people to accept the fact that I beat a legend," Leonard said, his voice dripping with sarcasm. "It's hard for people to believe that I beat Roberto Duran, the Hands of Stone.

"Now that it's over with, there are gonna be excuses. They're gonna talk about his heart, his back. I don't want to hear that. I trained hard for this fight; I beat the man fair and square."

Someone asked Sugar Ray Leonard, who earned $7.5 million for his efforts, how he planned to celebrate this, the greatest triumph of his twenty-four very productive years.

"Well, I know all you people bet on Duran," Leonard said, "so I'm going back to the hotel and just watch you drown your sorrows."

Epilogue: No one ever explained what happened that night, but most experts believe Duran was embarrassed by the way Ray Leonard was dominating him and quit out of frustration. Duran and Leonard fought for a third time in December 1989, and Leonard won a unanimous decision.

*Originally published in the *Philadelphia Daily News*, November 26, 1980. Reprinted with permission by Philadelphia Newspapers, LLC.

Jim Plunkett's Journey Ends in Triumph*

I know this might be hard to accept, what with Super Bowl XV sticking in your throat like a bad oyster, but we all owe Jim Plunkett a debt of gratitude.

I mean, there was something about his triumph here in New Orleans that transcends team loyalty, even the game of football itself. Jim Plunkett did not merely win one for the Oakland Raiders yesterday; he won one for every guy who ever came down life's staircase on the seat of his pants.

The next time you find a pink slip in your pay envelope, the next time you're broke and staring out the window at the bill collector, just remember the sight of Jim Plunkett running off the Superdome turf, giving the "We're Number One" sign to the gods that once cursed him.

The next time you reach in your pocket and find nothing but chewing-gum wrappers, the next time you look in the mirror and wonder why you even bother going to the office, just take a deep breath and clutch this thought to your chest: Jim Plunkett won a Super Bowl.

It's true, Jim Plunkett leveled Philadelphia's dream factory yesterday. He defeated the Eagles, 27–10, and quietly pulled a silver-and-black sheet over the City of Champions. But in so doing, Plunkett built onto a larger dream and enriched us all.

Jim Plunkett taught us an eloquent lesson in the human spirit, a lesson that often courage and stubbornness are one and the same. Plunkett is a champion today because he refused to quit last summer when quitting would have been the easy, even logical, thing to do.

We should all take comfort in the fact that, although Jim Plunkett beat the Eagles yesterday, he also beat the system. You know, the system, the management structure that casually tosses you into the unemployment line when you're no longer useful?

Well, Jim Plunkett beat the hell out of the system all year, and that's something even the guys in Kensington can relate to. He came back from hard times. You don't have to be from Oakland to admire that. Adversity is a suburb of everywhere.

"Is there a lesson to be learned from what happened to me?" Plunkett said, after accepting his award as the game's Most Valuable Player. "Oh, perseverance and patience, I guess.

"There were a lot of times when I came close to throwing in the towel, to quitting football altogether, but I never did. I thought, `Well, maybe if I give it one more try, things will work out.'

"For the most part, I had faith in my ability. There was a time, right after I was released by the 49ers, when I wondered if they [the coaches] were right, I couldn't do the job anymore. That was the low point, without a doubt.

"But I have some good friends, people I trust, and they stayed with me. They said, `Look, you can still play. You've just been stuck in some circumstances which weren't the best. It's just a matter of being in the right place at the right time.'

"For me," Plunkett said, gazing around at his joyous Oakland teammates, "this is definitely the right place and the right time. I'm as happy as I can be. I'm not real emotional; I don't jump up and down, but believe me, I'm happy."

Jim Plunkett was the last of the Raiders to arrive at the interview room. He had already showered and dressed, although he had not bothered to tuck his shirttail inside his corduroy trousers. He looked like he had just pulled on a pair of slacks to answer the doorbell.

When he walked into the interview area, he was led to a small platform, which was surrounded by over a hundred newsmen. As Plunkett stepped onto the platform, he caught his foot on a TV cable and stumbled. A newsman reached out and grabbed him.

"Seems appropriate," Plunkett said, smiling.

After all the misadventures that had befallen the thirty-two-year-old quarterback along the way, it was almost fitting that he arrive at his destiny in such an inglorious fashion. A theatrical bow was fine for Broadway Joe, but not for Hard Luck Jim.

Plunkett picked his way through the hour-long interview every bit as neatly as he picked apart the Eagle secondary. He traced his career from the highs ("The Rose Bowl was the biggest, before this") to the lows ("The week before Oakland called me").

He talked about his feelings of exultation ("My rookie year in New England, realizing I could win in this league") and his moments of despair ("I went through our `79 training camp wondering, `Why am I here? I'm never gonna play ahead of Stabler'").

He only appeared annoyed once, when a newsman asked if there were now any plans to turn his life story into a movie. The guy said it would be a natural, opening with the Heisman Trophy at Stanford, then going to the bad days in New England, now Super Bowl XV for a final act. . . .

"I doubt that anybody would want to make a movie of my life," Plunkett said. "I think that's a pretty silly question. I guess this all gets back to that `Cinderella story' you guys have all been writing about.

"You write the stories; I only read them. I can see where the circumstances might dictate a `storybook' angle on this whole thing. I really appreciate the fact that you people feel that way about me. It's very nice.

"But the truth is, with just a few brief exceptions, I never really lost confidence in myself. If I had gotten this chance earlier [in Oakland], maybe I would have done this earlier, who knows?

"People ask me if I feel 'vindicated.' No, not really. I'm just happy to be playing and playing well. Vindication indicates a certain bitterness, and I don't feel any bitterness toward anyone."

"What would you have said," a newsman asked, "if someone had told you back in September that you would be in this position today?"

"I don't know," Plunkett said. "I probably wouldn't have believed them because I wasn't even the starter until the sixth game [after Dan Pastorini went out with a broken leg].

"But once I got in there and I saw the way the club was gelling, I felt we could go all the way. As for me being the MVP in the Super Bowl. . . . No, I wouldn't have believed that. It would've seemed too far-fetched.

"Look," Plunkett said, gazing into the rows of bobbing ballpoint pens. "I'm not trying to be humble or anything, but I've just had one of those years where everything goes right.

"The [AFC] championship game was an example. I threw a terrible pass that was tipped to Raymond Chester—he took it all the way. I misread a coverage today, threw a ball way short. It should have been an interception, but Cliff Branch turned it into a touchdown.

"Sure, I've played well, but I've been lucky, too. I feel lucky every time I look up and see [tackle Art] Shell and [guard Gene] Upshaw standing in front of me."

When Plunkett faced the Eagles back in November, he didn't see much of Shell and Upshaw. Mostly, he saw waves of green shirts swarming all around. The Eagles sacked Plunkett eight times that day en route to a 10–7 victory.

Yesterday, they sacked him only once, for a modest one-yard loss. Most of the time, Plunkett was free to stand in the pocket and read the coverage as leisurely as if it were a highway billboard. He completed thirteen of twenty-one passes, for 261 yards and three touchdowns.

"Yeah, I felt confident coming into this game," Plunkett said. "We should have beaten the Eagles when we played them the last time. I had [Bob] Chandler open on a hook-and-go and over-threw him. I had Branch open another time and under-threw him.

"The whole key was our offensive line. If I had time to set up and throw, I knew we would win. And my blockers did a super job. I was able to pick up second and third receivers all day long. Kenny King broke his pattern [on an eighty-yard touchdown], and I still had time to find him."

"Plunkett gave us the credit, huh?" Art Shell said. "Hey, he's the man. If it wasn't for Jim Plunkett, we would've been home watching this game on TV.

"He came in at a time when we had no leader and gave us leadership. He had hardly played at all for two years, and he took over like he had never been away. Nobody deserves to be a champion more than Jim Plunkett."

As the interviews wound down, someone asked Jim Plunkett what he could possibly do now to top this remarkable season. Plunkett never hesitated.

"Come back next year," he replied, "and do it all over again."

Epilogue: Jim Plunkett added another chapter to his Cinderella story. In 1983, he led the Raiders back to the Super Bowl and upset the favored Washington Redskins, 38–9.

*Originally published in the *Philadelphia Daily News,* January 26, 1981. Reprinted with permission by Philadelphia Newspapers, LLC.

PART THREE

FACTS AND OPINION

◆ ◆ ◆

PROFILES

Water Boy Reaches the Hall of Fame*

If only the old gang from 36th and Sansom could have seen Reds Bagnell yesterday. He was relaxing in his twelfth-floor suite at New York's Waldorf Astoria, sipping a gin and tonic and watching the Christmas shoppers jostle along Park Avenue.

Reds was all decked out in a new tuxedo, and he kept shuffling through the pockets to find dinner tickets for late-arriving friends. Let's see: Chuck Bednarik was in the lobby; Alan Ameche and Tom Brookshier were coming on the Metroliner; and, oh yeah, Billy Cunningham was flying in by helicopter after the 76ers' practice.

Imagine, all those high rollers turning out to see Reds Bagnell inducted into the National Football Foundation Hall of Fame last night. Even Reds couldn't believe it when he heard that Lou Fischer, the chairman of Gino's Inc., was jetting in from Israel for the occasion.

"I haven't had this much fun since we beat Dartmouth," Bagnell said, calling room service to check on the two buckets of ice he had ordered an hour earlier.

There was a large photo of Bagnell on the fireplace. It was a posed photo of Reds, then a Penn senior, throwing a jump pass in a deserted Franklin Field. ("Hey, Reds," a friend said. "You look like Peter Pan.") There was a stack of congratulatory telegrams, most from ex–West Catholic teammates, on the desk near the phone.

"This whole thing overwhelms me," said Bagnell, forty-nine, now an investment banker with Fahnestock and Company in Philadelphia. "I grew up in West Philly, just a couple blocks from the campus. When I was a kid, my dream was to play football for Penn. After school, I'd ride my bike over to River Field to watch them practice.

"[Coach] George Munger asked if I wanted to be the team water boy. He even gave me a Penn jacket. I thought that was the greatest thing in the world. When I finally did play for Penn, I thought that was the ultimate. I made All-American and won the Maxwell Award [in 1950], and I felt all my aspirations were satisfied. I never even thought about making the Hall of Fame.

"To me," said Bagnell, now president of the Maxwell Football Club, "Hall of Fame players were immortals, guys who lived in a different atmosphere. Guys like Red Grange, Doak Walker, and Gale Sayers [Sayers was one of ten players inducted with Bagnell last night] who had unique talents.

"I never put myself in that class. I was a plugger, a hang-in-there kind of player. I didn't have great natural ability. If I had one outstanding quality, it was my competitiveness."

"Reds and I were the same type of players; we were both hotheads," said Bednarik, who was Penn's senior center when Bagnell was the sophomore tailback. "I remember my last game, we were losing to Cornell, and Reds threw a long pass that was incomplete. I didn't know it, but Reds got the hell knocked out of him just as he released the ball.

"I was ticked off about the incompletion, so I asked Reds, 'What happened?' Oh man, did he tear into me. He said, 'Whaddya mean what happened? (Expletive) you.' Well, I was twenty-two years old, I had flown thirty [bomber] missions in the war, I wasn't about to take a lot of (expletive) from some eighteen-year-old kid. I said, 'Don't talk to me like that, you little red-headed so-and-so.'

"Believe it or not, Reds and I didn't speak for eight years after that," Bednarik said, smiling at the memory. "We finally patched things up at a Maxwell Club dinner in the late `50s."

"Reds was stubborn like that," said Bill Talarico, an assistant coach at Penn under Munger, "but that's what made him such a good player. He refused to back down. I remember we were having a staff meeting, and one coach said, 'I'd like to use this play, but Reds isn't fast enough to run it.' We didn't realize it, but Reds was right outside the door. He came charging in the room and said, 'I'm fast enough. Gimme the play; I'll make it go.'

"He was a natural leader, a holler guy. When we played California in 1950, Reds kept us in the game. Cal had a great team with Les Richter and Johnny Olszewski. They had been to the Rose Bowl three straight years. I thought they'd beat us by thirty points. They kicked the hell out of us physically, but Reds kept rallying our guys in the second half. We lost [14–7], but Reds put on the gutsiest exhibition of football I ever saw."

"I can't say I knew he'd be a great player when I made him our water boy," Munger said, nursing a drink in the corner of Bagnell's suite. "I did realize, 'Here's a kid who's willing to pay the price.' In that respect, he never changed.

"One spring he tore up his shoulder playing baseball, so I got him a summer job at Camp Tecumseh. Every morning, he pushed a seven hundred-fifty–pound roller back and forth across six tennis courts. He never complained, and his arm came back better than ever.

"We used to kid him about his [lack of] speed, and he didn't like it. One day he returned a punt for a touchdown against Navy, and he came over to me, still puffing, and said 'No speed, huh?' This will tell you what kind of competitor he was. In his senior year, we scored every time we crossed the twenty-yard line, except once."

While at Penn, Bagnell set NCAA records for most yards passing in a season (1,603) and career (2,013) and most yards total offense in one game (490 against Dartmouth) and career (3,251). He also set national marks by completing fourteen consecutive passes (against Dartmouth) and attempting eighty-eight passes without an interception. All of those records have since been broken, but that doesn't bother Reds anymore.

"I only want to be remembered as a guy who tried hard," Bagnell said, "and maybe made a few friends along the way."

Epilogue: Reds Bagnell died in July 1995, at age sixty-seven. The Maxwell Football Club created a Reds Bagnell Award presented annually to someone who has made a lasting contribution to the game of football. I was honored to receive the award in 2022.

*Originally published in the *Philadelphia Bulletin*, December 7, 1977.

Hard Man to Please, Tough Man to Beat*

Yeah, that's Scotty Bowman, all right, his nose pointed toward the rafters, his chin jutting out defiantly. He always looks like he should be wearing a plume and reviewing the palace guard.

He is standing at center ice, a dozen pucks at his feet, and he is flipping them, one by one, into the corner. He watches as his defensemen go back and retrieve them, then pass them along the board to start the rush up-ice.

His attention is total; his manner as chilly as the arena air. The Buffalo Sabres skate through the drill, heads down, shoulders tense, like tardy school-boys scurrying past the headmaster, expecting any second to feel the yardstick across their backs.

There is no laughing, none of the raunchy chatter heard at most hockey practices. Even veterans like Jim Schoenfeld and Bill Hajt are concentrating on every move. Clearly, no one wants to be the first to mess up.

Larry Playfair, a gawky young defenseman, goes behind the net and struggles to dig the puck out of the corner. As he attempts to make his pass, the puck flips onto its edge and rolls weakly off his stick.

Playfair tries to recover, but, of course, it's too late. He cringes. He knows what's coming.

"Pass the puck, dammit," Bowman snaps.

His voice cracks like a bullwhip in the deserted building. Playfair folds in half and turns slowly to the boards. Twenty other players breathe a quiet sigh, thankful it wasn't them.

"Scotty is a tough man to play for," said defenseman John Van Boxmeer, who played for Bowman in Montreal, as well. "I've been with him a while now, and he still makes me nervous behind the bench.

"He demands perfection, and everyone on the team is aware of that. They know if they make a mistake, Scotty is gonna give them hell. I'll say this for Scotty: He doesn't play favorites. Anybody who screws up gets hell. He's fair that way."

"You play for Scotty long enough," said Jim Roberts, who played for Bowman for ten years and now serves as his assistant coach in Buffalo, "and you wind up cursing him, calling him a nut. It isn't until you play for somebody else that you realize how great the man really is.

"You might gripe the whole time you play under Scotty," Roberts said, "but when you look back over your career, you'll find your most productive years were the years he coached you. He drives you hard, but he drives you in the right direction. He squeezes every ounce of hockey out of you."

"When my players complain about my coaching," Bowman said, "I ask them one question: `Do you want to win?' If they say yes, then I tell them to get back to work."

"What if they say no?" someone asked.

"No one has said no yet," Bowman replied.

In thirteen seasons, Scotty Bowman's teams have won 576 regular-season games, lost 210, and tied 166. Only one coach in National Hockey League history, the late Dick Irvin, had more career victories, and he was behind the Chicago, Toronto, and Montreal benches for a quarter of a century (1930–55).

No one even approaches Bowman's .700 career winning percentage, and his record in the Stanley Cup playoffs is unsurpassed. Before the Sabres' current semifinal series with the New York Islanders, Bowman had 103 playoff victories—an NHL record—and a winning percentage of .661.

In four years as coach and general manager of the St. Louis Blues, Bowman led the expansion team to the Stanley Cup finals three times. In eight years as coach in Montreal, Bowman won five cups, including the last four in a row, equaling yet another league record.

The fact is, Scotty Bowman is a brilliant coach, arguably the best in the world. While Fred Shero gives scholarly lectures on his "system," while Don Cherry talks about his pet bull terrier, Bowman just keeps on winning. The city, the players, the past, it hardly seems to matter.

The Sabres were in a hockey recession prior to Bowman's arrival. The talented young team that went to the Stanley Cup finals against the Flyers in 1975 was sinking steadily into the quicksand of mediocrity.

Three straight years, the Sabres were eliminated in the Stanley Cup quarterfinals, losing twelve of thirteen games at one point. Last year, they finished with a disappointing 36–28–16 regular-season record, then lost to Pittsburgh in the best-of-three preliminary playoff round.

This season, under Bowman, the Sabres improved their record to 47–17–16. They jumped from seventh to second in the overall standings, finishing just six points behind the Flyers. The same team that finished twenty-seven points behind Montreal last year finished three points ahead of the Canadiens this season.

Why?

"Scotty," Schoenfeld said simply.

"Jimmy [Roberts] used the right word: direction," said Sabres captain Danny Gare, whose goal total jumped from twenty-seven last season to fifty-six this year. "Scotty gave us direction, and that's what this organization needed very badly.

"The last few years, we were drifting along, watching clubs like the Bruins and Rangers pass us by. We still had the talent, and contrary to what some people said, we were trying. It just seemed like there was no leadership in the front office.

"Scotty changed all that. He came in and restored our confidence. Scotty's theory is that every player has the capacity to play better; he just has to be made aware of it. And Scotty makes you very aware."

Scotty Bowman, forty-six, is sitting behind his desk in the Sabres' office, sipping a diet soda and discussing, at length, his coaching philosophy. He is not a humble man—but, then, he has no reason to be.

He worked his way up from scouting for the Canadiens to the top of the coaching profession. Bowman turned to coaching at an early age after a fractured skull suffered in a junior game in 1952 ended his promising playing career.

Bowman, a winger, had scored a game-winning goal, and a rival defenseman, Jean-Guy Talbot, in a fit of rage, broke his stick over Bowman's head. Bowman still has a plate in his skull from the operation. Fourteen years later, Bowman signed Talbot to play for him in St. Louis.

"There's no place for bitterness in this game," Bowman said. "Jean-Guy feels as badly about what happened as I do."

Hockey is the only life Scotty Bowman has known since he was a youngster growing up on a farm outside Montreal. He always dreamed of winning a Stanley Cup with the Canadiens, and he has realized that dream five times over. Today, Scotty says he is ready to sit back and enjoy life.

Bowman has already announced this is his final year of coaching. Next season, he will become the Sabres' full-time general manager, and his top aide, Roger Neilson, will take over behind the bench. This season, Neilson has watched the games from the press box, relaying information to Bowman via wireless headset.

Scotty wanted very much to take this Buffalo team to the NHL championship, then retire with two distinctions—first coach to win five consecutive Stanley Cups and first coach to win back-to-back cups with two different teams. The Sabres are currently trailing, 3–0, in their series with the Islanders, so Bowman probably will be denied this last clutch of glory.

"When I took over in St. Louis [in 1966]," Bowman said, referring to his first NHL coaching job, "I had no idea how long I wanted to stay in it. I was fairly young at the time [thirty-three], and I was single. Coaching was my life and my family.

"Then I got married [in 1969], and we started having children [four, including four-year-old twins], and my life changed. Coaching became a drain on my health, my family life. I came to the conclusion I didn't want to spend the rest of my life behind the bench. I wanted to stay in hockey but in some other capacity."

For a while, Bowman talked about quitting the NHL altogether and taking a job as hockey coach at an American university. He has always been fascinated with Notre Dame. He now says such a move would be impractical. "I'm too old to go back to school," he said.

The move Bowman really wanted to make was jumping into the Montreal general manager's chair the moment wily Sam Pollock retired. Bowman had worked alongside Pollock with the Hull-Ottawa Canadiens in the Eastern League in the early `60s, and he thought they had almost a father–son relationship.

Last year, however, Pollock sandbagged Bowman. He stepped down as general manager and appointed Irving Grundman as his successor. Grundman had virtually no hockey background. His only qualification for the job was being an associate of Peter and Edward Bronfman, the Molson Brewery heirs, who purchased the Canadiens for $20 million in 1978.

By placing their cohort in such an exalted position, Pollock put himself in the Bronfman's good graces for life. Bowman, meanwhile, was left behind the Montreal bench with a freshly signed two-year coaching contract and no prospects of ever moving up.

"I'll never understand why they treated me that way," Bowman said. "I served the Canadiens well for a long time. I thought I deserved better. I can't knock Sam for looking out for himself, but I can't understand how a hockey man would turn the team he helped build over to an amateur [Grundman]."

After the season, the Bronfmans tried to coax Bowman to stay on. They offered him more money. They even promised to move him into the front office by 1981. They said he would be the head of a five-man "hockey operations committee." Bowman laughed at the proposal.

"Can you imagine Sam Pollock taking the job under those terms?" he asked. "A five-man committee? I think I know what it takes to win in the National Hockey League. If I want to do something, I don't want to have to put it to a vote. The whole idea was ridiculous. I had to get out; it was as simple as that."

Perhaps the only one who advised Bowman against leaving Montreal was his ten-year-old daughter, Alicia. She told him, "Daddy, if we move, you can't take Guy Lafleur and Larry Robinson with you. You won't win another Stanley Cup."

As you might expect, Bowman had plenty of NHL offers, but he chose Buffalo. Friends advised against it, pointing out that the Sabres had gone through three head coaches since 1977, but Bowman, typically, was stimulated by the challenge.

"It was the best deal in a financial and hockey sense," he said. "Buffalo is a good franchise with good ownership. I didn't have to worry about them selling or moving the year after I came here. I knew I'd be building on a solid foundation.

"It's right in the middle of the hockey activity. Toronto is right up the road. I can go there to scout games. It's only a short distance to the Ontario [junior] leagues. There are four or five NHL games on TV every week. I felt I could keep up on things better here than a place like Atlanta.

"Besides, I thought this team had very good personnel. I had people tell me the Sabres' best days were behind them, but I didn't believe it. [Gilbert] Perreault, [Richard] Martin, Schoenfelt, these guys aren't even thirty yet. I coached most of them [in the Canada Cup], and I knew what kind of people they were. They want to win."

The veterans have produced for Bowman, and he has rapidly rebuilt the Buffalo farm system, which became a wasteland under his predecessor, Punch Imlach. Scotty had a very good draft, including the U.S. Olympians Mike Ramsey and Rob McClanahan, and now the Sabres have one of the finest young teams in the NHL. Six players on their roster are twenty-two or younger. The team's average age is 24.4.

"I feel good about our future," Bowman said. "Next season, I'll be able to devote my full time to scouting, developing our minor-league operation, just stoking the fire. Roger will run the bench. I won't be looking over his shoulder."

But don't be surprised if sometime next year, when Larry Playfair lets a puck roll off his stick in practice, a familiar voice is heard echoing down from the top of Buffalo's Memorial Auditorium.

"Scotty will still be there," Danny Gare said, "if only in our minds."

Epilogue: Scotty Bowman coached for another twenty-two years and retired following the 2001–2002 season after leading the Detroit Red Wings to the Stanley Cup. He won a total of nine cups with three different teams: Montreal (five), Pittsburgh (one), and Detroit (three).

*Originally published in the *Philadelphia Bulletin*, May 5, 1980.

Sugar Ray Pulls People Together*

By noon, the basement of the Sheraton Lanham Hotel was jammed. Prosperous businessmen on their lunch hour mingled with T-shirted youths bused in from a Washington, D.C., community center.

Teenage girls in cutoff jeans and elderly women in polka-dot dresses crowded the stage. There were college students and high-school dropouts, country-club ladies and grubby kids in worn-out sneakers gathered in this stuffy little corner of a suburban shopping center in Landover, Maryland.

Camera crews from two TV stations set up lights around the room. A photographer from a national magazine was there to shoot this week's cover. A dozen reporters were sprinkled through the audience, dutifully taking notes. Clearly, something big was about to take place.

Just then, a small, almost boyish figure came bobbing through the doorway, his wide, smiling eyes peeking out from beneath a white towel. The people cheered and Instamatic cameras flashed and Sugar Ray Leonard glided through the crowd, a surfer riding on an ocean of love.

For two hours, the people watched the World Boxing Council welterweight champion train for the biggest test of his life, Friday's showdown with Roberto Duran in Montreal. This was not a typical, cigar-chewing fight crowd. Several fans asked if Sugar Ray was actually sparring with Duran on this muggy June afternoon.

Leonard, you see, has his sparring partners wear T-shirts with "Duran" stenciled across the chest. "I have a tendency to ease up when I spar," he explained, "but I see that name, and I want to tear the other guy's head off."

What the audience lacked in expertise, it made up in enthusiasm. All through the workout, people shouted encouragement to Leonard. He responded with a wink and an occasional wave. When he landed a solid combination, which was often, the kids whooped and slapped hands.

The mood in the room was that of a high-school pep rally or an old-fashioned revival show. It was a fascinating cross-section of society pressed tightly around that ring. Different people brought together, at least for a while, by their affection for a twenty-four-year-old millionaire prizefighter.

When the workout was completed, Sugar Ray did his TV interviews, posed for the photographer, then, still perspiring, took a seat behind a long table. His publicist, Charlie Brotman, divided the crowd into two lines: fans seeking autographs to the right; reporters desiring interviews to the left.

"Don't worry," Brotman said. "No one will be slighted."

Indeed, no one was slighted. For thirty minutes, the fans filed by in a giddy procession. Most requested personal autographs ("Sign mine, `With Love'"), and Leonard graciously obliged. The reporters took turns jumping into the seat next to Leonard, slipping in questions as best they could.

"I can only give you ten minutes each," Brotman told the interviewers. "I'm sorry, but Ray has to have a little time to himself."

Janks Morton was seated on a folding chair across the room. He smiled as he watched the people hover and fuss around Leonard. Morton, an insurance broker from Silver Spring, Maryland, first met Sugar Ray when he was just a skinny thirteen year old learning to throw a jab at the Palmer Park recreation center.

Along with Dave Jacobs, Morton taught Leonard the fundamentals and guided him through an illustrious amateur career that included two AAU championships, three national Golden Gloves titles, a gold medal in the 1975 Pan-American Games, and, finally, international stardom in the Montreal Olympics.

It was Morton who persuaded Leonard to turn professional in 1977, and it was Morton who predicted the kid with the swift hands and the electric smile would become boxing's hottest attraction. Today, Morton sits back smugly and watches the money gush skyward like oil from a freshly struck well.

For this fight with Duran, the former world lightweight champion, it is estimated that Leonard will earn $8.5 million. His take could swell to as much as $10 million, depending on the closed-circuit–TV revenue. Regardless, it will mark the richest payday ever for a boxer, topping the $6.5 million Muhammad Ali earned for his third bout with Ken Norton.

It is astounding that Leonard, a pro just three years, could eclipse the legendary Ali and command the biggest purse in boxing history. There were those who believed no fighter outside the heavyweight division would ever break into the million-dollar class. This time next week, Ray Leonard's career earnings will have gone over $13 million.

Why? Granted, Sugar Ray can fight. His 27–0 record (eighteen knockouts) is proof of that. But what is it about this young man that has the promoters talking about a near sellout of the seventy-eight-thousand–seat Olympic Stadium? What is it that has people who don't even like boxing rushing out to buy $20 closed-circuit–TV tickets?

"Personality," Morton said. "Sugar Ray is a beautiful person and it comes across. People see him fight once on TV, and they like him. They say, `He seems like a nice guy.' He's articulate, but not smart-alecky. He's charismatic, but not controversial.

"Sugar Ray appeals to everybody. Look at this crowd. Young people, old people. Rich kids, poor kids. Blacks, whites. People don't look at Ray and see color; they see good."

"I knew he was something special the first time I saw him on TV," said Angelo Dundee, his manager. "The kid lit up the screen. It was like instant sell. I hadn't seen anything like it since Ali. This kid was even more likeable than Ali because he didn't have that braggadocio. Ray was mom and apple pie.

"With Ali, you were fascinated; you wanted to see him fight. With Ray, you wanted to hug him, you wanted to bring him home for dinner, you wanted to call him up and say, `Let's go to a movie.' He had those big eyes and that great smile, and you just had to love him.

"That's why this fight is so big. The casting is perfect," Dundee said. "You have Sugar Ray, the kid next door, the guy in the white hat, against Duran, the killer, the guy with the gunfighter eyes. It's the kind of fight where you can't be neutral.

"It's going to be a classic, but Ray will win. Why? Because behind that great big smile is the best fighter in the world."

Ray Leonard was sitting pensively at the autograph table. All of the fans had gone, and only two reporters remained. As he talked, Leonard doodled a mis-shapen, bug-eyed little man ("Duran, after the fight," he said) on the table-cloth.

He seemed weary and drained of emotion. He said it was just the train-ing-camp blahs, a natural leveling off that takes place a week or so before every fight. "You store up all that adrenaline," he said, "then you climb into the ring, open the valve, and, whoosh, it's there."

Leonard was talking about the way his life has changed over the past five years, how he has gone from the poverty of Palmer Park to top billing on *The Tonight Show*. "Johnny Carson asked me how it feels to be a superstar. Johnny Carson asked *me*," Leonard said. "Imagine that."

Growing up, Leonard never figured to make a name for himself in athletics. In fact, sports bored him. He spent most of his free time in his room, reading comic books. His older brother, Roger, started boxing at the local recreation center, and he literally dragged Ray into the program.

At the center, Ray was discovered by Morton and Jacobs. Jacobs drove a delivery truck for a Virginia pharmacy all day and worked with the kids at night. He had boxed as an amateur, and he knew talent when he saw it. Ray had talent, and with prodding, he displayed an immense capacity for training.

"Ray was like a diamond in the rough," Jacobs said. "He needed some chipping around the edges, some polish, but the stone itself was priceless. The thing I remember was how quiet he was. He never said a word to anybody, but, Lord, how he could work.

"Tell him to spar five rounds, he'd spar ten. Tell him to run three miles, he'd run six. I think it was a case of a kid who had never really been good at any-thing finding his niche. All of a sudden, people were telling him, `Hey, baby, you're gooooood.' It turned him on."

Leonard rose swiftly through the amateur ranks, winning the Golden Gloves, the national juniors, and the international juniors as a 132 pounder in 1972. Four year later, he won the Olympic gold medal with a stylish performance that exhausted Howard Cosell's thesaurus of superlatives and captured the imagination of America.

When he left Montreal, he had managers and promoters lined up, pleading with him to turn professional. He turned down every offer, insisting he would enroll at the University of Maryland in the fall, study business administration, and prepare for a career in public service. Ultimately, he said, he wanted to work with kids.

"If you want to know the truth," Leonard said, "I was sick of fighting. I had six fights in less than two weeks [at the Olympics]; the pressure was incredible, and when it was over, I just wanted to get away. The thought of starting all over [as a pro] did not appeal to me at all."

But then things began falling apart in Leonard's life. His father, Cicero, a supermarket manager, was stricken with meningitis. His mother, Gertha, a nurse, suffered two heart attacks. His girlfriend, Juanita, whose picture he wore taped to his socks in Montreal, sued him for support of their two-year-old son.

Suddenly, Leonard needed money. He knew he could make a quick dollar in boxing, but he did not want to go that route. He agonized over the decision for days, finally going to Morton for advice.

"I told Ray he would be a success at whatever he tried, and I believe that," Morton said. "I had no doubt if he went to college, he would be an excellent student. But I had to be honest with him. I thought he should start boxing again, if only for his family's sake.

"I told him, 'Ray, you can always go to college, but you won't always have this opportunity to break into the fight game. Your fame will be gone before you know it. If you want to take advantage of it, do it now. Six months from now might be too late.'"

To prove his point, Morton took Leonard with him when he made his rounds in Washington. He brought Leonard along and introduced him to his clients, most of whom did not remember him. A few vaguely recalled him from the Olympics but weren't quite sure of his event. ("Yeah, you ran track, right?")

"This was just six weeks after I won the gold medal, too," Leonard said. "It was a pretty jarring experience. I never realized fame could vanish so quickly. Take the 'Sugar' away, and Ray Leonard was just another guy on the street. Janks opened my eyes to that."

So Sugar Ray turned pro. Mike Trainer, a lawyer friend of Morton's, was hired to negotiate the contracts and keep the books. Brotman, another friend of the family, was recruited as the public-relations specialist. He was responsible for keeping Leonard's social calendar in order and warding off any flakes who might try to attach themselves to the bandwagon.

"Ray has one weakness: He can't say no to anybody," Brotman said. "I can."

The key addition to the brain trust was Dundee, the streetwise manager from South Philly who has been around the fight game longer than the Marquis of Queensberry. Dundee was brought in to plot Leonard's course to the title. Morton and Jacobs both felt Dundee's longtime association with Ali would be invaluable in developing Sugar Ray, a boxer with Ali-like skills.

"When you have a car you think can win at Indianapolis, you don't get some guy off the street to drive it," Morton said. "You hire the best. We felt Angelo was the best, and we were right."

Lucrative offers poured in from big-name promoters, but they were all for multi-fight contracts that gave the promoters a percentage of Leonard. Trainer rejected the deals, insisting that "Sugar Ray Leonard will not be owned, and he will not be cut into pieces. He is not an animal."

That same philosophy exists today. Everyone in the Leonard camp is paid on a straight salary. No one owns a percentage of Sugar Ray. Said Morton: "I told him, `Ray, don't ever sell your body, because once you do, it means you've got nothing left.'"

Leonard made his pro debut on February 5, 1977, decisioning Luis (the Bull) Vega at the Baltimore Civic Center. The bout was televised by CBS, and Leonard took home $40,000, an unheard of sum for a kid fighting his first six-rounder. Luis Vega was terrible, but no one seemed to mind. The good guy won, and the TV ratings were through the roof.

Sugar Ray spent two years skipping through a field of lackluster opponents— Willie (Fireball) Rodriguez, Hector (Chinto) Diaz, Floyd Mayweather—and making big money in the process. Some boxing people grumbled that Leonard was being carried up the welterweight rankings on a satin pillow. They said Sugar Ray was strictly a TV creation, that he was no more a contender than Mork from Ork.

Last summer, Leonard silenced his critics with three straight knockouts over opponents of known quality: Tony Chiaverini, Pete Ranzany, and Andy Price. He stopped Price in just 2:52, finishing him with a flurry of punches that put Andy to sleep for five minutes. Leonard's performance was so spectacular that it overshadowed the rest of the TV card, which included Larry Holmes and Duran.

Last November 30, Leonard stopped Wilfred Benitez, who had not lost in thirty-eight pro fights, at 2:54 of the fifteenth round to claim the WBC welterweight title. It was a savage fight between two brilliant technicians, and for the first time in his life, Leonard was pushed to the limit.

"I remember sitting on my stool between rounds, thinking, `This guy is really good,'" Leonard said. "`He's making me look bad. He's beating me.' I had to suck it up and come back. I had to call on strength I didn't know I had.

"When it was over, I could hardly move. They had a victory celebration at the hotel, but I couldn't go. I sat in the bathtub all night. The next day, my face was all swollen and bumpy. I couldn't stand to look in the mirror. Janks was there; he remembers.

"I said, `How do I look, Janks?' He said, `You look like the champion of the world.' That snapped me out of it. Yeah, champion of the world. The swelling was gonna go down, but the title was still gonna be there."

Leonard was putting the finishing touches on his tablecloth sketch of Roberto Duran. He was adding a few more circles around the swollen eyes. He was drawing a single hair growing straight up on the top of his head. For some reason, he added a necktie, a detail that seemed to amuse him.

"Does the magnitude of all that's happened stun you?" someone asked. "Fighting for $8 million? Breaking Ali's record?"

"It doesn't stun me," Leonard said, "because I worked hard for it. We all worked hard for it. This didn't happen overnight, and no matter how you boil it down, it didn't come easy. We took our lumps. We've got our scars.

"We started in the basement and worked our way up to the penthouse. If anybody thinks it's so easy, how come more people aren't doing it? I don't think I'm at the top yet. Far from it. My best years are still ahead of me. I'll probably break this [purse] record before I'm through. That's my intention, anyway.

"I'm a perfectionist. My record might be perfect, but I'm not. I can look back on every fight and tell you things I could have done better. That's the way I am. I don't want to be just another fighter. I want to be something special. Years from now, I want people to say `. . . and then there was Sugar Ray Leonard.'

"I don't want to be lumped in with everyone else," Leonard said, peeling some loose tape off his hands. "I don't want to be compared to anybody else. Not even Ali, as great as he is. I didn't come all this way to stand in somebody's shadow."

"Did you ever stop to think," someone asked, "what you'd be doing now if you had enrolled at Maryland, the way you planned?'

"Yeah, I'd be under pressure, only a different kind," he said. "I'd be a senior, getting ready to take my final exams, wondering what I was gonna do after graduation. I'd be plain old Ray Leonard again. I wouldn't have to worry about looking in Roberto Duran's ugly face this week.

"And," he noted, "I'd be a whole lot poorer."

Epilogue: Sugar Ray Leonard lost that fight to Roberto Duran in a majority decision, but he avenged it by defeating Duran in two rematches.

*Originally published in the *Philadelphia Bulletin,* June 16, 1980.

Jim Tyrer Story Ultimate Tragedy*

On September 15, 1980, Jim Tyrer paid his last visit to Arrowhead Stadium. The Kansas City Chiefs were playing the Seattle Seahawks, and Tyrer was there with his ten-year-old son, Jason, taking in the game.

For Big Jim, nothing could have been more in character. Those were the two great loves of his life: football and family. He devoted himself to both in a way that made even close friends envious.

"I always felt Jim epitomized what a pro football player should be," said Fred Arbanas, the former tight end who roomed with Tyrer for twelve seasons in Kansas City.

"He was intelligent, dedicated, someone who had a real good handle on life. He was a great family man and the best offensive tackle I ever saw. Any league, any time."

Jim Tyrer played fifteen years with the Chiefs and helped them to two Super Bowls. He was the player rep, the offensive captain. A leader. He was the AFL's Lineman of the Year in 1969, an All-Pro choice nine times. A gamer.

He was named to the American Football League's Team of the Decade. He was inducted into the Chiefs' Hall of Fame. His bust is on display in a trophy case at Arrowhead Stadium.

"No Chief was more honored, not even [quarterback] Lenny Dawson," said Reverend Ted Nissen, the Tyrer family's pastor.

Jim Tyrer left football following the 1975 season, but he stayed close to the Chiefs. He was a season-ticket holder. He dropped by the club offices now and then to pick up pennants and photographs for friends.

There was talk around town that Tyrer wasn't doing well financially. He had a tire business that had failed several months earlier. He was quietly calling ex-teammates, asking if they knew of any "good jobs."

But if he was suffering, he did not let on. People would pass him on the street, ask him how he was doing. He'd smile and say, "Fine." Always in control, that was Jim Tyrer's trademark.

Yet on this particular Sunday, the former Ohio State All-America seemed preoccupied. One friend noted that Tyrer was "staring at the game" rather than watching it the way he usually did. He didn't cheer much, but folks figured that was due to the outcome. The Chiefs lost, 17–16.

Afterward, Tyrer hung around the stadium for a long time. He walked the deserted corridors, then stood alone in the mezzanine, looking out over the field where he had performed so splendidly for so many years.

He returned to his charming, ranch-style home and, shortly before dawn, took a .38 caliber pistol; shot his wife, Martha, to death; then put the gun in his mouth and pulled the trigger. He was forty-one.

George Daney's phone rang at about 6 A.M. It was a member of the Chiefs' front office. The police had just notified him of a murder–suicide on the west side of town.

"He said a former [Kansas City] player was involved," Daney recalled. "He said he thought it was Jim Tyrer, but the name was spelled wrong, and the address was wrong.

"I knew Jim was the only ex-player who lived in that area, so I feared the worst. I called Jim's house. I got a busy signal. I knew I shouldn't be getting a busy signal at 6 A.M.

"Then I called Fred [Arbanas], and we drove over there," Daney said. "It's a morning I'll never forget."

Of all the friendships that developed among the old Chiefs, the one that sprang up between George Daney and Jim Tyrer was perhaps the least likely. They seemed to have little, if anything, in common.

Daney was a back-up guard, a player of marginal skills. Tyrer was an All-Pro tackle, a Hall of Famer. Daney was a free spirit; he gave the impression he didn't care about anything. Tyrer was just the opposite: intense, no-nonsense.

They weren't all that close when they played, but they had become tight in recent years. Daney settled in the Kansas City area, opened his own business, and he and Tyrer began seeing a lot of each other. They talked about football, finance, and life.

"A year ago," Daney said, "if you had asked me to list all the people I know in two columns—those who are most likely to commit suicide and those who are least likely—Jim would have been at the top of my `least likely' list.

"He exuded strength. He was a huge man [six-foot-seven, 275 pounds] who never said much, always seemed very composed, very much in command. He had a name; he had his degree. He seemed like he could handle anything.

"But near the end, things started to get to him. The Wednesday before he died, he called me. He said he wanted to talk. I said, `What about?' He said, `Just talk. I have to talk to somebody.'

"He drove over to my office. He wasn't the same guy. He was depressed. He didn't have a job, and the bills were piling up. He said he couldn't sleep, he couldn't eat. All he did was sit up nights and worry.

"He kept asking me, `How do I look? Do I look bad?' He had lost about forty pounds. I told him, no, he looked OK. Jim was so big, he could lose forty pounds easy. He just shook his head. He was really troubled.

"Then we talked about business," Daney said. "He asked how my company was going. I said fine. He started talking about all the businesses he had tried.

He said his problem was he jumped from one to another too fast. He said he never gave himself a chance to get established.

"I could tell he was in desperate shape, so I said, `Look, Jim, if you need money, I've got a few extra bucks.' I asked how much he needed. The figure he gave was way out of my league. I told him I'd like to help; I just didn't have that kind of money."

Jim Tyrer said he understood. The two talked a while longer, then Tyrer left. That was the last time George Daney saw his friend alive.

"I talked to people at the [NFL] Players Association shortly after Jim's death," Daney said. "They said they weren't really surprised something like this had happened.

"They said they had calls from others [ex-players] who were close to [suicide]. That's when they told me about this psychological-counseling service they provide. I think it should be mandatory.

"For every year a man plays in the NFL, the league ought to give a year of psychiatric help. And any player who doesn't think he needs it should get two years."

What happened to Jim Tyrer? What caused a sensitive, well-educated man to kill his wife, then take his own life?

Fred Arbanas knew Tyrer better than anyone. They were adversaries in college: Tyrer playing for Ohio State; Arbanas, for Michigan State. They met in the 1962 College All-Star camp, became roommates, and stayed roommates through a dozen pro seasons.

They partied together, hunted ducks together, won a Super Bowl together. Their families were inseparable. Arbanas drove Martha Tyrer to the hospital the night Jim's oldest son, Brad, was born. They were more like brothers than friends.

The walls of Arbanas's suburban office are covered with photographs of Fred and Jim together—meeting owner Lamar Hunt as rookies, celebrating the 1962 AFL title, sitting on the dais the night Jim was inducted into the Chiefs' Hall of Fame.

"We shared a lot," Arbanas says now, staring at the photographs.

"I knew Jim was feeling down," said Arbanas, now a successful advertising executive. "He was worried about his financial situation. But I never suspected he was in such dire shape.

"More than anything, Jim was a victim of circumstance. He worked hard to make a go of it in business . . . damn hard. He just never got a break.

"He tried a lot of sales-type ventures over the years, but he never found one he wanted to stay with. Then he opened a tire store [in 1978], and it clicked. Business was good, and he was as happy as I've ever seen him.

"He was working twelve hours a day, laughing the whole time. He'd come over my house in that half-ton pickup, his overalls covered with grease. It was funny because Jim was such an immaculate guy. Even when he played ball, he hated to get dirty. But in the shop, he seemed to enjoy it.

"He felt good about himself. He felt he was finally in something that would last."

But then Kansas City had its mildest winter on record. There was no snow. No one bought snow tires; no one needed their old tires changed. Tyrer's business slowed, then stopped altogether.

He didn't have the money to hang on. He was forced to sell and swallow his losses. He was offered a few jobs around town, but none of them paid enough. Someone told him the Chiefs were looking for a scout. The salary was $25,000.

"I can't start there," Tyrer said.

Tyrer had become trapped in an All-Pro's lifestyle. For the last ten years of his playing career, he made good money. He bought a big house, enrolled his four children in private schools. He lived well. Too well, according to some.

When he left football, when his income dropped, he would not change his ways. To cut back would be to admit defeat, and his enormous pride—the pride he cultivated as an athlete, a champion—would not let him do it.

So he kept trying different businesses—hardware, insurance, marketing, tires—always in the hope he would strike it rich. When he did not, he became frustrated and despondent.

"After the tire thing, Jim seemed to give up on himself," Arbanas said. "I thought I had a job lined up for him, selling national accounts for the Yellow Pages. I found out later, he never showed up to take the test.

"I asked him why not. He said he had taken a lot of those tests, and he had always done poorly. He said, 'Look, I've been out of school for twenty years. I'm taking these tests against kids who are just graduating college. What chance do I have?'"

Arbanas insists that football had nothing to do with Jim Tyrer's ultimate collapse. Arbanas claims it was failure in the job market that pushed Tyrer over the edge.

"It happens to stockbrokers and bankers all the time," Arbanas said, "and nobody makes a big deal out of it. But it happens to Jim Tyrer, and right away they say it's because he was a football player.

"I don't buy it. That's just sensationalism. The economy's what got Jim. That and bad luck."

Others close to the tragedy disagree.

They say Fred Arbanas is merely protecting the memory of his old friend; that he is bitter about the lurid publicity surrounding the case, and he wants only to draw a curtain over the episode to spare Tyrer's four children, now living with Martha Tyrer's parents.

Perhaps he feels the best way to do that is to absolve pro football of blame. It is a noble thought, but unrealistic.

"It would be wrong to say football played no part in this," said Jim Lynch, the former Notre Dame captain and Chiefs linebacker.

"Football was a part of Jim Tyrer; it was a part of his being. It was the standard by which he measured success. Of course it played a part in what happened.

"Look at the whole process of big-time sports in this country," Lynch said. "Look at what it does to people. Not just football, but baseball, basketball, tennis.

"You take a kid when he's thirteen years old and you start kissing his butt, telling him he's the greatest thing since popcorn. You do that for ten, maybe twenty years. Sooner or later, he [the athlete] starts to believe it.

"Then he gets to be thirty-three, and all of a sudden, instead of kissing his butt, you kick him. Where you used to tell him, `You sure can play,' now you tell him, `You can't play at all. We've got kids here who can play better than you.' It's a crusher.

"Then the guy goes out to get a job. Chances are he doesn't have any prospects. He never does latch on to anything substantial. He becomes disillusioned. His name winds up haunting him."

Lynch paused and took a sip of beer.

"But Jim Tyrer," he said. "He just doesn't figure. He was no football bum.

"It would be one thing if we were talking about some semiliterate tramp who was eighty hours short of his degree, who played four years of pro ball, got out, went broke, and blew his brains out. You'd say, `Well, that's sad, but I understand.'

"Jim Tyrer wasn't anything like that. He graduated college on time. He was settled, had a nice family. He had a great reputation in Kansas City. The people loved him. When he walked down the street, everybody said, `Hi.'

"Yet with all that, he wound up killing himself. That's the really frightening part. If it could happen to Jim Tyrer, it could happen to anybody."

There are many similarities between Jim Tyrer and Jim Lynch. Both were raised in small, football-crazed Ohio towns; both played on great college teams, then won a Super Bowl and put down their roots in Kansas City.

Both actively sought success in the business community. The difference is Lynch succeeded, and Tyrer did not. Today, Lynch is a partner in D. Thomas and Associates, the Midwest's fastest-growing food brokerage.

So why did he make it and his teammate didn't?

"I got involved in a good, sound business when I was still playing," Lynch said. "I started with a stock firm, then joined Thomas.

"Jim . . . Well, he tried hard, but he always seemed to be in quickie, do-it-yourself things. He wanted to be an entrepreneur, but he didn't have the capital for it.

"He would've been better off if he had gone with a good company, even if it was just as a trainee, and worked his way up. But Jim wanted to do it his way.

"The big thing is, you have to come to grips with the system," Lynch said. "You have to realize your football career is only as good as your left knee—or your left toe, for that matter.

"It's OK to think you're gonna play forever when you're fifteen. But by the time you get to college, you'd better realize you're backing a real short horse, and you'd better start lining up alternatives.

"But too many pro football players fall into the old `one-more-year' syndrome. They say, `Oh, I'll play one more year, then I'll get my act together.' They keep saying that until, finally, they run out of years.

"I don't know if Jim fell into that category or not," Lynch said. "All I know is he fell off the top of a helluva big mountain, and it didn't have to happen."

Jim Lynch will never forget the funeral. It was a reunion of the old Chiefs, without fanfare, without marching bands. Hank Stram flew in from New Orleans; Mike Garrett, from Los Angeles; Tom Flores, from Oakland.

They stood together outside the church, these men who crushed the Minnesota Vikings in Super Bowl IV, who once found it so easy to share a laugh, and they wept in silence.

"We all knew why we were there," Lynch said, "yet we were all thinking, `This didn't really happen, did it?' We all shared a sense of guilt . . . like if we had known, we could have prevented it somehow.

"If we left there with any one feeling, it was, `Let's not ever let this happen again.' Here was a bunch of guys who had been through hell together, who had reached incredible heights together, yet through our own indifference we let a teammate destroy himself.

"This reminded us how much we still owe each other," Lynch said. "It was a valuable lesson, but what a helluva price to pay."

*Originally published in the *Philadelphia Daily News*, July 21, 1981. Reprinted with permission by Philadelphia Newspapers, LLC.

Their Hearts Belong to Daddy Mass*

Trying to fit Rollie Massimino into a neatly defined coaching category is like trying to fit him into a pair of Mick Jagger's designer jeans.

It is impossible, and what's more, it is pointless. Yet people persist.

"Who is Rollie Massimino?" they ask.

Is he a drill sergeant in the Prussian mold of Bobby Knight?

Well, Rollie believes in discipline, and his voice has been known to rattle the windows in Villanova's antiquated field house now and again. But, no, he's not a tough guy.

"I'm a puss at heart," Massimino admits.

Is he a chess master, a tactician chiseled in the icy likeness of John Wooden?

Hardly. Rollie is a fine Xs and Os man, and he prepares his team for a game as well as any coach in the East, better than any coach in this city. But he's not the classic, cerebral type.

"People tell me I look like a whacko sometimes," Massimino says, "and they're probably right."

Is he a high-fashion model, like Notre Dame's Digger Phelps?

Aw, c'mon. We've all seen Rollie on the sidelines, his tie at half-mast, his shirttail billowing. After a close game, his wardrobe usually resembles an unmade bed.

A radio announcer once likened Massimino to the Danny DeVito character Louie on the TV series *Taxi*. Rollie wasn't pleased, but he had to admit the guy had a point.

"I buy the top clothes," Massimino once said. "They just aren't made to fit me."

Rollie Massimino is not an evangelist like Louisiana State University's Dale Brown. He is not a stand-up comic like North Carolina State's Jim Valvano. He is not a mannequin like the University of Virginia's Terry Holland. He is not a self-styled legend like the University of North Carolina's Dean Smith.

Rollie Massimino is, well . . .

"Rollie is Rollie, and I mean that as a compliment," said Don Casey, who coached against Massimino for nine years at Temple before joining the NBA's Chicago Bulls this season.

"There's nothing phony about the guy. There's no pretense. He's warm and sincere, and, most of all, he's committed to his job and his kids. He's more like a patriarch than a coach. That's why we call him Daddy Mass."

"I've really gotten to know Rollie the last few years. We've done clinics together; we went to China together last summer. Daddy is one of a kind. To know the man is to love him."

"There are no masks with Coach Mass," senior center John Pinone said. "He's not the kind of man who'll put on one face when he's recruiting you, then put on another face once he gets you. And he doesn't put on one face when you're going good and another face when you're going bad.

"He's honest and he's loyal. When he recruits you, he tells you about his family. That's what he calls the team . . . his family. Coming from another coach, you'd say, `Yeah, sure.' But with Coach Mass, you know it's coming from the heart.

"In four years, he's improved me 100 percent as a basketball player and 200 percent as a person. People say he's prepared me for the NBA. Heck, he's prepared me for life. That's more important."

Roland V. Massimino, forty-eight, is in his tenth year as head coach at Villanova, a decade that has seen him not only rebuild a proud basketball tradition but raise it to new heights.

This year, the Wildcats went over twenty wins for the fourth consecutive season; they knocked off defending national champion North Carolina in Chapel Hill; they climbed as high as fourth in the Associated Press poll; and they won their first outright Big Five title since 1968.

This week, they travel to Madison Square Garden to compete in the Big East tournament, where, as conference co-champion, they are seeded second behind Boston College. After that lies an almost certain bid to the National Collegiate Athletic Association (NCAA) tournament; the Cats have made the Final Eight twice in the last five years.

What makes all this remarkable is not so much the amount of success, but the manner in which it was achieved. Rollie Massimino runs his basketball program with a style that is part godfather, part parish priest, and part dictator. If that seems an incongruous blend, so be it.

"This is the way I've coached for twenty-six years," Massimino said. "It's the only way I know. I'm not saying it's right for everybody, but it's right for me."

The Family, as Massimino calls it, is the real thing. It's no facade; it's not a catch phrase Massimino mouths but doesn't apply. Those hugs you see exchanged on the Villanova bench are authentic. So are the angry words you hear when a game plan, or a transcript, breaks down.

Rollie Massimino cares about his players in a way that is unique in this era of quick-fix college athletics. Whoever heard of a Top Ten school at which the coach's wife not only cooks pasta for the whole squad, but also knits their socks and adjusts their ties on Friday night?

And whoever heard of a big-time basketball coach who spends his Christmas on the telephone, calling all his former players and their families, wishing them a happy holiday? Whoever heard of a coach putting his arm around his star player after a big win and asking, "How's the term paper coming along?"

But that's the Daddy Mass approach, and beneath the cigar smoke, the marinara sauce, and the needles ("Don't worry, Pinone: I'll find a pro team in Italy where you can play"), there is a commitment that sets Villanova apart from the mainstream. It is a distinction that Massimino draws with considerable pride.

"I've always said a kid has to be a bit of a maverick to get along here," Massimino said. "A lot of kids today, they don't want to buy the family thing. They say, 'Hey, I'm goin' to college to get away from the family. I don't want a coach looking over my shoulder, telling me when to do my homework.'

"If that's the way they feel, fine. Let 'em go somewhere else. They don't belong at Villanova. The kid we want here is the kid who's willing to accept the challenge of (1) coping with a tough academic institution; (2) coping with a tough basketball program; and (3) [smiling] coping with me. That's a lot to ask.

"That's why I say our kids have to be a little special, and we recruit with that in mind. If a kid's not the family type, we don't want him. You can't build a program with half good people and half bad people. You've gotta have either all good ones or all bad ones, and I'd rather have all good ones."

If you check the Massimino decade at Villanova, you'll find a succession of prototypical "good kids," starting with the Joey Rogers and John Olive class and extending through the current seniors—Pinone, Stewart Granger, and Mike Mulquin.

Massimino has had only one blue-chip recruit quit his squad in ten years, and that was Roxborough's Chubby Cox, who transferred to the University of San Francisco in 1975.

"It just didn't work out for Chubby here," Massimino said. "Those things happen. There are no hard feelings on either side."

All twenty-seven seniors in the Massimino era received their degrees from Villanova. Only one—Rory Sparrow—is active in the NBA. The rest are either in graduate school—Olive and Bruce Anders are in law school—or working. There are no hard-luck stories, no former All-Americas sweeping floors or taking remedial reading courses.

This year will be the same. Pinone, a two-time Academic All-America, carries a 3.2 average in economics. Last semester, the varsity's combined cumulative average was 2.87. That's actually higher than the campus average. While that reflects credit on Villanova's "good kids," it also reflects nicely on Daddy Mass himself.

"Coach Mass is the program," said Joe Rogers, Massimino's first point guard (1973–77) and now an assistant coach at Drexel. "It all stems from his honesty, his sincerity, his concern for making sure everything is done right.

"He was like a second father to me. We had some tough times that first year [7–19]. We lost a lot of close games, and he'd always find me on the bus ride home. He'd say, `Come see me in the office tomorrow. We'll have a cup of coffee.' He never let you stay down too long.

"His door was always open. It didn't matter what your problem was, you could talk to Coach Mass. If you needed twenty minutes, you got twenty minutes. If you needed four hours, you got four hours. I could go back there today, and it would be the same way. He's loyal to his people.

"That's one reason why he never has any trouble with his players," Rogers said. "They don't want to let him down."

The other reason?

"You know the consequences," Rogers said. "Coach Mass makes it very clear: If you break the [conduct] rules, if you mess up in class, you're done, you're history. All coaches say it. The difference is, Coach Mass means it."

If Rollie Massimino comes off Old World, that's because he is. His father was an Italian immigrant, a shoemaker who came to this country at sixteen and settled in northern New Jersey.

Rollie lost two brothers—one to a gas explosion, the other in an auto accident—ten years apart. It was in those traumatic times that he learned the meaning of family.

Perhaps nothing touches as close to the essence of Rollie Massimino as the story of Jay Underman. Underman was a pretty fair Elyria, Ohio, high-school player Massimino recruited but lost to Bowling Green in 1974.

Underman's father died suddenly in his sophomore year, and the boy was badly shaken. His mother recalled Massimino's recruiting visits and his long talks about the Villanova Family. She asked Rollie if he would take her son and look after him.

Massimino never had taken a transfer before; he turned down potential starters because he didn't feel it was fair to the kids he had recruited. But he made an exception in this case. He put Jay Underman on scholarship, even though the kid never rose above ninth man on a fourteen-man Wildcat squad.

Underman attended Villanova for two years and graduated in June 1978. Two years ago, he was killed in an auto accident during the Christmas holidays. Massimino skipped a recruiting visit with Ed Pinckney and drove four hours through the snow to attend the funeral.

Today, Jay Underman's picture occupies a prominent place on Massimino's office wall, alongside the Pinones, Sparrows, and Herrons. It serves as a reminder that, even in the Big East, winning isn't always everything.

"I was raised to believe the greatest quality a person can possess is compassion," Massimino said. "If you don't have concern for other people, you aren't worth very much.

"My concern has always been for the welfare of young people. When I was coaching in high school, my goal was to see that every one of my players got into college. Now that I'm in college, my goal is to see that every one of my players gets his degree.

"This is something I believe in very strongly," Massimino said. "If I wasn't a coach, I'd want to be a guidance counselor. I'd want to be in some position where I was helping direct these kids. I'm in basketball, so that's my avenue."

There was never much doubt that Rollie Massimino would wind up coaching basketball for a living. He played three years at the University of Vermont ("I was a playmaking guard. . . . In other words, I couldn't shoot"), then began coaching at the high-school level in New Jersey in 1956.

He made his reputation at Lexington High in Massachusetts in the mid-1960s, compiling a 90–36 record. One kid who played for him there was Paul Cormier. Cormier, thirty-one, is now his assistant at Villanova. "That's how you know you're getting old," Rollie said.

Massimino broke into college coaching at Stony Brook, New York, in 1969. He was there for two years and led the Pirates to their best record ever (19–6) before Chuck Daly asked him to join his Penn staff in 1971.

Massimino succeeded Jack Kraft as head coach at Villanova in March 1973, and in just two years he turned the faltering program around. Today, working on a fourth consecutive NCAA appearance and with an 8,500 seat field house on the drawing board, Villanova stands solidly with the nation's basketball elite.

"The sign of a good coach," Don Casey said, "is, number one, his team improves every year; and number two, he gets a few top recruits every year. That means the kids in the program are saying good things about him.

"Rollie scores high in both areas. His team keeps getting better, and he keeps getting good kids. I'll admit, I used to be skeptical of the guy. . . . All that talk about `family.' But I got to know him, and I saw that's the way he is. It must be that Italian blood."

"I may or may not be a good coach," Rollie Massimino said. "That's for other people to decide. But I can read people. That's my number-one asset. I can tell who's on the level and who's playing make-believe.

"That's one thing I tell these kids. Don't play make-believe with me. Don't lie; don't give me a lot of bull. Be straight with me, and I'll be straight with you. If my program is based on one thing, it's honesty.

"I get into it with my players," Massimino said. "I'm tough. I set high standards. I've had Ed Pinckney in my office thirty times in two years. Great kid. Quiet, sensitive. I ask him, `Eddie, why do you stay here? Are you crazy? Do you like being yelled at?'

"I tell other kids, `Get out the directory. I'll find another school for you.' They know when I'm kidding, and they know when I'm serious. Some people say you teach kids with kindness. Other people say you teach with discipline. I think you need both.

"That's the way I run this program. It's no picnic here, but the kids know I'll back 'em to the hilt if need be."

If there is one criticism of Massimino, it's that he sometimes backs his kids too loudly and too harshly. His courtside demeanor long has been a topic of conversation among fans and officials. A bad call brings him off the bench like a flamenco dancer.

Two years ago, he told Syracuse Coach Jim Boeheim to "shut up" during a heated Palestra game. Afterward, Big East Commissioner Dave Gavitt told Rollie he'd better tone down his act.

"Dave was thinking of my health," Massimino said, "and he was right. I was killing myself. I've worked to control my temper since then. But you get in these close games, and the adrenaline starts pumping. . . . The thing is, I don't do it to be a showboat. It just comes out."

Sometimes Rollie lashes out at the media. A post-game question about strategy often will bring a sharp response and glare from Massimino ("I don't like to be second guessed"). And if you rip one of his players, you'd better wear a chest protector and facemask to the next press conference.

Massimino was upset when it was reported that Roman Catholic High School's Dallas Comegys chose DePaul over Villanova because he was turned off by what he considered "negative recruiting" by the Wildcats. Massimino called all over town for two weeks, swearing he'd "get to the bottom of this."

"We don't negative recruit," Rollie announced in a voice that shook the tri-state area.

Last week, he spent an afternoon battling with a TV network over a piece of videotape. The tape showed Dwayne McClain running off the Villanova bench at the end of the last St. John's game and knocking over an official.

The TV folks were planning to have the announcer say something like, "Was this an accident or was it intentional? Only Dwayne McClain knows for sure." McClain had fouled out earlier, so, the implication was, he was getting even.

In truth, McClain was running onto the court to grab the ball, which had rolled loose in the confusion following Pinone's last-second field goal. He shoved several people aside along the way, and the official happened to be one of them.

"I told this guy if he airs that tape, he'd better have a good lawyer," Massimino fumed. "He said he's gonna check with his boss and get back to me. Can you believe they'd do something like that? I'll be damned if I'm gonna sit back and let it happen. If they do it, I'll be all over them."

Five minutes later, the TV station called back. They were scrapping the whole idea. "Wise move," Massimino said.

"That's vintage Rollie," Paul Cormier said. "People see that side of him, and they say he's a wild man, always flying off the handle. But he's not. He's just defending an innocent kid.

"If you're on the outside, you might get the wrong impression. But you work with him every day, you see what he puts into this program. If he didn't care so much, he wouldn't react that way. But if he didn't care so much, he wouldn't be Rollie."

Epilogue: Rollie Massimino led the Villanova Wildcats to an improbable NCAA championship in 1985, when they upset number-one–ranked Georgetown in the title game.

*Originally published in the *Philadelphia Daily News*, March 8, 1983. Reprinted with permission by Philadelphia Newspapers, LLC.

Alcorn's Battle Over*

Mark Alcorn died Sunday afternoon. The wire-service story said he died "peacefully." Obviously, the man who wrote the obituary never met Mark Alcorn.

Mark died quietly, perhaps. He died in his sleep in his St. Louis home, his father and his best friend at his bedside. But peacefully? No, that description will never do.

It suggests giving in, letting go. Mark Alcorn never did that, not once in his whole life. He surely didn't do it in his final hours when the fate he had defied for fourteen months closed in on him at last.

The former Louisiana State University (LSU) guard went down fighting, damn it. If this was a basketball game, he would have kicked open the locker-room door. He would have rolled up his sweaty jersey and splattered it against the wall. Mark Alcorn was many things, but a quitter was not one of them.

He was a competitor, a battler, a kid who never believed a cause was lost until the stands were empty and the gym lights were turned off. Ten points down with a minute to go? Mark would figure things were just getting interesting. That's the way he was.

The doctors found the cancer in his lymph nodes in December 1980. They said he had ninety days to live. When he survived the ninety days, they gave him six months. Alcorn laughed and said he'd prove them wrong again. He did, though to this day no one knows how.

The will to live, like the will to win, ran deep in Mark Alcorn. It kept him going through a year of constant pain. It kept him sane through four operations and months of chemotherapy. It gave him strength when nothing else could.

He had to quit school when the disease was discovered, but he stayed close to the LSU basketball program. Last year, when the Tigers defeated Wichita State in the finals of the NCAA Midwest Regional, Alcorn was fidgeting at the end of the bench, chewing on his fingernails, just as always.

When the game ended, they brought a ladder onto the floor of the New Orleans Superdome. The LSU players and fans gathered around the basket and cheered while Mark Alcorn, resplendent in a blue three-piece suit, snipped away the nets.

He handed the prize to assistant coach Ron Abernathy. Abernathy handed it back. Then freshman guard Johnny Jones took the net and draped it royally around Alcorn's neck.

"The guys want you to keep it," Jones said.

An hour later, standing outside the Superdome, shaking hands, Alcorn still was wearing the net over his open-neck shirt. There were tears in his eyes.

"This is the happiest day of my life," he said. "People keep asking me how I feel. Geez, I never felt better."

The Tigers came to the Spectrum for the Final Four, and Mark came with them. It wasn't easy. First, he had to talk his doctor into postponing surgery to remove tumors behind his spleen and breastbone. No one thought the kid could pull it off, but he did.

"I just kept bugging him until he gave in," Alcorn explained. Persistence, that was his trademark.

LSU lost to Indiana in the semifinals, then lost to Virginia in the consolation game. Afterward, Alcorn sat in the locker room, forcing a smile.

"Wait 'til next year," he said. "We'll be back."

Eleven months later, Mark Alcorn was gone, dead at age twenty-three.

Darren Sneed and Mark Alcorn grew up together in St. Louis. They met when they were teenagers, and they fell in love with the same dame—namely, basketball.

Darren was fourteen, a freshman at Oakville High. Mark was fifteen, a sophomore at DeSmet High, the local Catholic school. They were hotshots on their respective teams when, one day, Darren dropped by Mark's house to get acquainted.

"We only lived a mile apart," Sneed recalled yesterday, "so I thought, 'Why not get together?' I introduced myself. We went around back where he had his basket set up, and we started playing.

"We didn't stop for five years. In the summer, we'd play all day long. In the winter, we'd play until it was dark. We went after each other like you wouldn't believe.

"I pushed Mark; he pushed me. I don't know if either of us were super-talented, but we made each other better. His dad [Harold] worked with us quite a bit. He was a big star at St. Louis University in the '50s. Great teacher of fundamentals.

"I had a pretty good high-school career," Sneed said, "and I owe it all to Mark and his father. I scored thirty points once as a senior, and I was only six feet, 160 pounds. I didn't overpower anybody. I just kept digging. That was Mark's game."

Mark Alcorn was the playmaking six-foot-one guard on a DeSmet team that had Steve Stipanovich and Mark Dressler, two University of Missouri stars, in the frontcourt. Alcorn was quick and smart, and he handled the ball, Sneed said, "like a yo-yo."

He made All-State and accepted a scholarship to St. Louis University. After one year, he transferred to LSU, partly to escape the inevitable comparisons to his father, partly to follow in the sneaker prints of his idol, Pete Maravich.

"That was Mark's dream . . . to play at LSU," Sneed said. "The Pistol was his man. When we played one on one, he'd drive past me, throw in a wild, off-balance shot, and he'd say, 'Pistol Pete strikes again.'

"Mark went to Maravich's summer camp one year. He came back with this photograph of him with the Pistol. He had it hanging in his room. He talked about playing at LSU a lot."

Mark Alcorn did not have a great career at LSU. In fact, he hardly had a career at all. He sat out the year after his transfer, played in only ten games as a sophomore, then became ill early last season.

"I'm sure Mark would have worked his way into the program if he had stayed healthy," said Sneed, who played two seasons at the University of Wyoming.

"He could run an offense as well as any guard around. He'd give you a fake, then take off for the basket, make a play. An unselfish player, a born leader.

"We talked a couple times a week, and last fall he started telling me about these stomach pains he was having. They'd wake him up in the middle of the night. They'd hit him during practice and make him double over.

"He thought he was getting an ulcer. He said he was taking some pills, and they were helping. The next thing I knew, I heard he got real sick when the team was up in Alaska, and they sent him home.

"I went to see him," Sneed said, "and his father took me aside. He told me what the doctors had found [tumors]. I felt numb. I couldn't believe it.

"Mark was such a vital guy. Always in great shape. Never smoked, never drank, never did drugs. It didn't seem possible. But he took it in stride. He said, 'I'm gonna beat this thing.' He had that attitude right to the end."

In June, it appeared Mark Alcorn had, indeed, beaten the odds. The tumors had shrunk significantly, and the doctors felt his cancer was in remission.

There was a brief celebration, followed by a crushing reversal. The cancer flared up again, but this time it spread more swiftly, more savagely. Alcorn was rushed to a special clinic in Houston for treatment.

His condition deteriorated steadily. He lost his hair. His weight dropped from 185 pounds to 110. The pain grew more intense. Still, he refused to complain; he refused to give up.

"They brought Mark home around Christmastime," Sneed said, "and I would sit with him every afternoon. We'd play backgammon and chess. We'd play video games and talk basketball. Anything to pass the time.

"I could see how much he was suffering. . . . I could see it in his eyes. But he never once said a word about it. He never once said, 'Why me?' You know the one thing he kept talking about? Going back to LSU. That was his goal."

Mark Alcorn went back to campus in the fall for the LSU–Alabama football game. Then, several weeks ago, he flew to College Station, Texas, to visit the Tiger basketball team when it played Texas A&M.

"I couldn't believe it when I saw him," said guard Joe Costello, Alcorn's old dorm roommate. "He didn't look like the same person. He seemed so weak, so frail. . . .

"Then I called him on his birthday, January 28. I had a few of the guys here in the room waiting to talk to him. We had trouble hearing him, his voice was so faint.

"But as sick as he was, he was still really into the team," Costello said. "He knew our record; he knew who we had just beaten and by how much. He was asking me about our freshmen and our next game.

"He had just received a postcard from Willie Sims [an old LSU teammate]. Willie's playing pro ball in Israel now. And Rudy Macklin [now with the Atlanta Hawks] had called. We talked about that."

During the weekend, Mark Alcorn's condition worsened. His left lung was riddled with cancer. His right lung was functioning at only 50 percent. He literally struggled for every breath.

At 1 P.M., he took one last, shallow gasp, and he was gone. Harold Alcorn and Darren Sneed were there.

That night, Joe Costello received the news at the dorm. He sat up `til dawn, staring at the bunk where Mark Alcorn used to stretch out, play cards, and listen to his Bruce Springsteen albums.

He recalled the winter day he had to help Alcorn pack his belongings in a cardboard box for the drive back to Missouri. He recalled sitting on the curb, crying, for an hour after the Alcorn family pulled away.

The LSU basketball team practiced yesterday. Joe Costello said it was their worst workout of the year. No one was concentrating; no one was talking.

The Auburn game is coming up tomorrow night. It just doesn't seem that important somehow.

*Originally published in the *Philadelphia Daily News*, February 16, 1982. Reprinted with permission by Philadelphia Newspapers, LLC.

The Mild Side of Broadway*

Dave Herman recalls the summer of 1968 when the New York Jets and Green Bay Packers met in an exhibition game. The teams stayed at the same hotel, and before the game, the lobby was jammed with autograph seekers.

"Most of them were girls, all dolled up like they were waiting for a Hollywood producer," said Herman, a guard on that Jets team. "When Joe Namath stepped off the elevator, it was like a stampede. People went crazy, screaming, climbing over each other just to touch him.

"Five minutes later, Bart Starr walked through the same lobby, and nobody looked twice. That's when I realized what the word `charisma' means. Bart was a great quarterback, but Namath was that and more. Joe was a true superstar, maybe the greatest ever."

Joe Namath. Broadway Joe.

In the tumultuous America of the late 1960s, the Jets' swaggering young quarterback was the cover boy of professional football. He was talented, he was brash, he was glamorous. Whether he was passing for 496 yards in a game (which he did) or throwing six interceptions (he did that, too), he had fans lined up at the stage door.

He guaranteed a victory over Baltimore in Super Bowl III, and he delivered with a Most Valuable Player performance as the Jets shocked the Colts 16–7. It was the first meaningful win for the upstart American Football League against the established National Football League, and it validated the merger between the two, which was agreed on in 1966 and finally enacted in 1970.

Today, when people talk about the Super Bowl, they often bypass the Green Bay Packers, who won the first two games of the series, and start with Namath and the Jets. More than any other man, Broadway Joe married the game and the spectacle.

In October 1969, *Esquire* magazine wrote: "Once in a generation, more or less, a chosen figure detaches himself from the social matrix and swims into mythology, hovering somewhere near the center of the universe, organizing in himself our attention, monopolizing our hopes and fears, compelling our hearts to beat as his.

"Such a figure is Joe Namath."

Twenty-five years have passed since Super Bowl III, and Namath has long since left center stage. Now fifty, he lives in the quiet community of Tequesta, Florida, eighty miles north of the Orange Bowl, site of his epic win over the Colts. He owns a rambling, twelve-room house on the Loxahatchee River, and on a warm, sunny day he likes nothing better than sitting on his private dock, fishing for snook and flounder.

He has been married to his wife, Tatiana, for eight years. They have two daughters—Jessica, seven, and Olivia, three. He laughs about his former image as the swinging bachelor with the lavish Manhattan apartment. He reads old stories about his white llama rug and the chorus-girls-in-waiting and he feels as if he is reading about someone else.

"I'm a Gemini, so there are a couple of me's around," Namath said, relaxing for a moment in his spacious den. "There is a mischievous side to me, and I guess being young and in New York brought that out. But my greatest pleasure now is kicking back and spending time with my family."

The knees that plagued Namath throughout his thirteen-year pro career have been replaced by plastic. He underwent the replacement surgery in April 1992, after several incidents in which his knees, ravaged by surgery and too many games played on painkillers and bravado, collapsed beneath him.

His greatest fear, he said, was that it would happen again one day while he was carrying his daughters, and that they might be injured in the fall.

"I feel better than I have in twenty years," Namath said. "I haven't taken any pain medication in over a year. I can walk; I can exercise on the ski machine, and I feel fine."

"Kids from the neighborhood come to the door and ask if Joe can come out and play," Tatiana said.

"I say, OK," Namath said, "but on one condition: Nobody hits the quarterback."

It has been sixteen years since he retired as a player, yet Joe Willie Namath remains one of football's biggest names. There were a lot of Super Bowl heroes, but there was only one brazen enough to call his shot in advance. There was only one who owned a mink coat and wore pantyhose in a TV commercial. There was only one who romanced Ann-Margret on the silver screen. Surely, you remember the 1970 biker movie *C. C. and Company*.

There was only one Broadway Joe.

There still is.

"As a viewer, Joe was somebody I could relate to," said O. J. Simpson, who was winning the Heisman Trophy at the University of Southern California while Namath led the Jets to the AFC title in 1968. The two men were inducted into the Pro Football Hall of Fame together in 1985.

"Joe came across as a real person. From his time on, fans saw football players as people. They didn't all train on milk and apple pie. I can remember Joe saying he liked his women blonde and his Johnny Walker Red. It probably made some people mad, but I liked it.

"What Joe was saying was, 'Hey, if you don't hurt anybody, it's OK to be yourself.' He wore his hair long and spoke his mind, but that's what the '60s were all about. Joe was the superstar athlete who really reflected what the younger generation was thinking."

Namath was more than just a player; he was the show that sold the American Football League. He gave the new league credibility by signing with the Jets as the top pick out of Alabama in 1965. The AFL had other good quarterbacks, such as Len Dawson in Kansas City, George Blanda in Houston, and Jack Kemp in Buffalo, but they all were recycled NFL backups.

What the new league needed was a star it could claim as its own. Namath was the perfect player, and New York, with its bright lights and media muscle, was the ideal setting.

David (Sonny) Werblin was the Jets' owner, and he had a background in show business. He marketed Namath the way he would a Broadway star, signing him to a $427,000 contract that made him the highest-paid player in the league.

Heads turned, jaws dropped, people took notice.

That was the whole idea.

"I believe in the star system," Werblin said. "That's what sells tickets. Namath has that special stuff. Namath is DiMaggio. He's Clark Gable, Sinatra, Babe Ruth."

"Namath captured the imagination of New York, and that meant the AFL captured the imagination of New York," said Art Modell, who owned the Cleveland Browns. "It was a huge step forward. All of a sudden, here was this guy who people wanted to see, and he was in the 'other' league.

"Of course, all the publicity in the world wouldn't have mattered if Namath couldn't play. But he was the real thing; you could see that from the start."

"Namath was the best pure passer I ever saw, and he had the quickest release," said John Madden, the former Oakland head coach. "We'd put in blitzes and say, 'There is no way he can beat this,' and he would. He took some hellacious shots, but the ball was already on its way, usually for six points.

"The thing that sticks out most in my mind about Namath is his toughness. He was one of the toughest guys who ever played the game. You read all the stories about Broadway Joe and you'd think he was a pretty boy. But he didn't play like a pretty boy. He was one tough SOB.

"The only time I ever went to the other team's locker room to shake a player's hand, it was Namath," Madden said. "We played the Jets in a wild game in Oakland, both teams slugging it out like a couple of heavyweights. We kept hitting Namath, he kept getting up and throwing touchdown passes.

"We won the game, and on my way out, I went to the Jets locker room and shook Joe's hand. I'd never done that before. It was totally spontaneous. All I remember saying is, 'Hey, you're a helluva man,' and I meant it."

On the eve of Super Bowl III, Norm Van Brocklin was asked for his assessment of Joe Namath. A Hall of Fame quarterback himself, Van Brocklin was head coach in Atlanta and a firm believer in NFL superiority.

"I'll tell you what I think about Namath on Sunday night, after he's played his first pro game," Van Brocklin said.

That was the prevailing sentiment, not only within the NFL fraternity, but around the nation.

The Colts were nineteen-point favorites, a spread that reflected their 13–1 regular season and their 34–0 rout of Cleveland in the NFL championship game. Coached by Don Shula and boasting the game's top-ranked defense, the Colts were considered one of the great teams of all time.

The Jets were viewed as just another AFL team, which is to say, one step above the sandlots. Kansas City and Oakland self-destructed in the first two Super Bowls, losing to Green Bay by scores of 35–10 and 33–14. Lombardi said the AFL representatives "did not compare" to the top teams in the NFL. And if Lombardi said it, it was gospel.

The Jets were a classic AFL team, freewheeling and wide open. In the 1968 AFL championship game, Namath and Oakland's Daryle Lamonica combined to throw ninety-six passes. Old-school coaches such as Lombardi and Van Brocklin called it "Mickey Mouse football."

Even the AFL's founder, Kansas City owner Lamar Hunt, had little faith in the Jets. He felt they were the weakest of the three AFL teams to appear in a Super Bowl. At 11–3, the Jets had the third-best record in the league that season. Kansas City and Oakland tied with 12–2 marks in the Western Division.

"My nose was still out of joint because we [the Chiefs] weren't there," Hunt said, referring to Super Bowl III. "We lost to Oakland in a playoff, then Oakland lost to the Jets in the title game. But I thought our team and the Raiders both were better than the Jets.

"Having seen what the Colts did to Cleveland in their championship game, I really thought the Colts would beat the Jets easily."

The Jets saw the match-up differently.

Yes, the Baltimore defense was formidable, but it was aging. Namath saw the right side as vulnerable, with end Ordell Braase (thirty-six years old), linebacker Don Shinnick (thirty-three), and cornerback Lenny Lyles (thirty-two). He also knew that left end Bubba Smith took an aggressive up-field rush, which left him vulnerable to traps and draw plays.

Namath was a master at this sort of dissection. As Jets linebacker Larry Grantham said: "I don't see how any team can defense Joe. He always hits you where it hurts."

Namath made headlines even before the Jets arrived in Miami. He told reporters that, in his opinion, there were at least five AFL quarterbacks who were better than Baltimore starter Earl Morrall. Namath included himself among the five, along with his backup, thirty-eight-year-old Babe Parilli.

This caused quite a stir, inasmuch as Morrall was the top-rated passer in the NFL that season. He took over as the Colts' starter when Johnny Unitas went out with an arm injury, and he played so well that Shula stayed with him even after Unitas recovered.

Asked to respond, Morrall said: "[Namath] is getting newspaper space, and that's what he's after, isn't it? Maybe he represents the kind of athlete the coming generation wants. I hope not."

During Super Bowl week, Namath exchanged words with Colts kicker and defensive end Lou Michaels at a Fort Lauderdale nightspot. What started as some harmless needling heated up when Namath told the six-foot-two, 250 pound Michaels: "What do you know? You're just a kicker."

"You've got a big mouth, boy," Michaels snarled.

At that point, Namath recalls, "a lot of guys in tuxedos stepped in to cool things down." Nothing happened, really, but it made headlines in the papers the following day.

Then came Thursday night—the night that forever shaped the legend of Joe Namath.

Namath went to the Miami Touchdown Club dinner to receive its Player of the Year award. As he walked to the podium, a heckler—one who obviously wore NFL colors—shouted: "Hey, Namath, we're gonna kick your (expletive)."

"I got a little hot," Namath said, looking back. "All week I read about how great the Colts were and how we didn't belong on the same field with them. We were the team from the Mickey Mouse league. We weren't legit, all that garbage. I was tired of it.

"I said, 'Wait a minute, pal. I've got news for you. We're going to win this game. I guarantee it.'

"I didn't plan it. I never would have said it if that loudmouth hadn't popped off. I just shot back. It was simply a gut reaction."

Jets head coach Weeb Ewbank did not hear about it until the next morning, when he saw the *Miami Herald* headline: "Namath Guarantees Victory."

Ewbank was stunned. He had played along with the underdog role all week and instructed his team to do the same. The idea was to lull the Colts into thinking the game would be as easy as the odds makers predicted.

Deep down, Ewbank knew otherwise. He had seen the films. He knew the Colts could be beaten, but he felt that making the NFL champions overconfident only improved the Jets' chances. Everything was going fine until Namath opened his mouth Thursday night.

"I was upset with Joe," Ewbank said. "I said, 'Shula will use it against us. He'll have his players all riled up.' Joe said, 'Coach, if they need press clippings to get ready, they're in trouble.'"

The game took on sociological overtones. This was January 1969. The Vietnam War had divided the country. In August, Woodstock would define a generation. The two teams were cast as metaphors for their time. The Jets, epitomized by Namath, were young and rebellious. The Colts, with their crew-cut quarterbacks and NFL pedigree, were establishment.

"We took pride in being the rebels," Namath said. "A lot of our guys had long hair and mustaches. Before the game, [AFL president] Milt Woodard sent a letter ordering us to shave. He wanted to clean up our image. We never heard about it until after the game. Weeb never posted the letter. He knew we wouldn't go along with it."

The game played out just as Namath had expected. The Jets' underrated offensive line handled the Baltimore front four, and Namath, calling most of his plays at the line, used the power running of fullback Matt Snell to control the game.

Flanker Don Maynard had a hamstring pull, but no one outside the Jets family knew it. Namath used Maynard as a decoy, allowing split end George Sauer to work one on one against cornerback Bob Boyd. Sauer caught eight passes for 133 yards. Maynard had no receptions, yet by simply lining up on every play and drawing the coverage to his side, he played an integral part in the victory

Morrall threw three interceptions before Shula lifted him in the second half. Unitas came off the bench, trailing 13–0. It went to 16–0 before Unitas led the Colts to their lone touchdown with 3:19 remaining in the game.

The Jets, playing with poise and precision, made good on Namath's guarantee. They brought the AFL its first world championship. The banner headline in the *Baltimore Sun* the next day read: "Upset of the Century."

Namath's numbers were relatively unspectacular—seventeen completions in twenty-eight attempts for 206 yards—but he was such a commanding figure, with his play calling and leadership, that he was voted the game's Most Valuable Player. He is the only quarterback in Super Bowl history to win the MVP without throwing a touchdown pass.

"I give Namath all the credit in the world," Shula said. "He backed up everything he said. We killed teams with our blitz all year, but Namath got rid of the ball so fast that even when one of our rushers came free, he still couldn't get to Namath in time."

"I watched the game from Carroll Rosenbloom's box," said Tex Schramm, the president of the Dallas Cowboys, referring to the late Colts owner. "It was a quiet place, let me tell you.

"We couldn't believe what was happening. We kept thinking Baltimore would turn it around. We waited and waited, and then the game was over. For the [NFL] diehards—and I was certainly one of them—that game was like a punch in the stomach."

Lamar Hunt went to the Jets locker room to offer his congratulations. NFL Commissioner Pete Rozelle found Hunt in the crowd and shouted in his ear: "This is the best thing that could have happened."

"Pete saw the big picture," Hunt said. "The merger was in place; the leagues were coming together, and with the Jets winning, we now had a horse race. People knew the AFL was for real."

"That game wasn't about money or individual honors; it was about respect," Namath said. "We didn't get any respect before the game. Our league didn't get any respect, period. When we won, we felt like we won for a whole lot of people, not just ourselves.

"We returned to the hotel, and Buck Buchanan and Willie Lanier [of the Chiefs] were waiting for us. They wanted to say thanks. I saw John Hadl [San Diego's quarterback] that night. John told me what it was like, sitting in the stands, watching us win. He said he had tears in his eyes.

"You ask me how much that game meant? That's how much it meant."

For the Jets, the magic proved fleeting. They were beaten in the playoffs the following year by Kansas City, 13–6, starting a steep decline that lasted for more than a decade.

The championship nucleus was broken up by age and injury. Ewbank stepped down following the 1973 season. Namath was sidelined with one major injury after another. He had five knee operations and was so stiff-legged under his tape and protective braces that he resembled a man playing on stilts.

"Namath was like a ghost from the waist down," said NFL Films President Steve Sabol. "It was as if he had no legs. If you look at film of his throwing motion, it was all upper body. He spun like a gun turret when he released the ball."

Namath was an easy target playing behind the Jets' patchwork line. Under a heavy rush each week, he took a terrible pounding. As the losses mounted, the fans began to boo. By 1976, Namath had become a forlorn figure, throwing sixteen interceptions to four touchdown passes in a 3–11 season.

The following year, Namath was released by the Jets. The team had another young quarterback from Alabama, Richard Todd, and the plan was to rebuild around him. Namath signed with the Los Angeles Rams, hoping he could manage one last hurrah. He struggled through four starts, then was replaced by Pat Haden.

"I knew it was time to quit when I found myself getting bored on the practice field," Namath said. "I didn't play the second half of that season. I was watching practice, and I was bored. I said, `I don't belong out here anymore.'"

Namath retired following the 1977 season to pursue a career in TV. He did some acting and worked as a football analyst. He also performed in stage productions such as *Damn Yankees*, *The Caine Mutiny Court Martial*, and *Sugar*, the theatrical version of the Billy Wilder film *Some Like It Hot*.

He was inducted into the Pro Football Hall of Fame in 1985 after being passed over in his first two years of eligibility. The knock against him at the time was his statistics. His career passer rating was a mediocre 65.6. He threw 220 interceptions compared with 173 touchdown passes. He had only three winning seasons in twelve years with the Jets.

To some critics, Broadway Joe was a media creation who had one shining moment and little else.

Nonsense, answers John Madden.

"If ever there was a Hall of Fame quarterback, it was Joe Namath," Madden said. "There are some guys whose numbers don't matter. You don't have to count up Lawrence Taylor's tackles to know he's a Hall of Famer. He just is. You saw it when you watched him play. Same thing with Namath.

"When you played against Namath, you knew you were playing a Hall of Famer. The whole game—everything you did, everything they did, offense, defense—it all revolved around him. He was the guy.

"I watch Dan Marino, Jim Kelly, even Joe Montana, and it's obvious they patterned themselves after Namath. The way they move, the way they throw the ball, it's like watching Namath. He influenced a whole generation of young quarterbacks, guys who have gone on to take teams to the Super Bowl. That's an impact player."

"Joe didn't play for stats; Joe played to win," Don Maynard said. "I see quarterbacks today throw four-yard passes on third [down] and fifteen [yards]. It goes into the books as a completion; it looks good in the stats, but it don't accomplish a damn thing.

"I never saw Joe throw a ball short of the sticks. If he needed twelve yards for a first down, he threw it fifteen. When he got inside the twenty, he went for the end zone. He got some balls picked off, but he also made a lot of big plays that won games."

Namath's fans—and they far outnumber his detractors—sometimes wonder, "What if?"

What if Joe had played his whole career on two sound knees? What if he had played for a team that was built to last rather than the Jets who fell apart in the 1970s?

Namath claims he never gives it a second thought.

"Things turned out well enough for me," he said. "I'd have to be a real jerk to say, 'If only this, if only that.'

"I would've loved to win five Super Bowls, but to win one was more than most guys. Ever since Little League, my dream was to win a world championship in something. I got that chance with the Jets and won The Game. We touched a lot of people's lives.

"I can't tell you how many times I've had people tell me they used our win in the Super Bowl as a motivating force. A lot of times it is a high-school or college coach who says he showed his team the film or told them the story. Sometimes it's a teacher who talked about it class. The moral is the same: If the Jets did it, you can do it.

"We sent a message to all the underdogs out there—in sports, in business, in life in general—that if you want something bad enough and you aren't afraid to lay it on the line, you can come out on top. That is an important message, because if people don't have hope, really, what do they have?

"People sometimes ask me, `What would you have done if you had lost that game?'" Namath said. "Honest to God, I never even thought about that at the time. I'm sure I would have taken a lot of abuse, especially in the press, about my guarantee. But I never gave it a second thought, because I was sure we would win.

"But if we had lost, I would not have run away and hid. I wouldn't have let it ruin my life. I would've come right back firing the next season. I loved the competition; that's why I played. The celebrity part was fun, I won't deny that, but the highlight of my week was game day. Strapping on the gear and playing, I lived for that.

"People have said, `Gee, all those injuries must have been hard on you.' No, what was hard was losing. I went into every season thinking we would win, but we just didn't have the players in the `70s. The turnover was unbelievable. There were times in the huddle, I'd look up and see linemen I'd never seen before. It's hard to win that way."

Anyone who comes looking for the old Broadway Joe today will be disappointed. He has mellowed to the point where he sometimes wonders if he is boring. He is warm and soft-spoken with no hint of pretense. His house has few reminders of his football career. Mostly, it is decorated with photographs of Jessica and Olivia.

On a warm November evening, Namath was minding the two girls while Tatiana shopped. Jessica was watching *Punky Brewster* in the next room while Olivia curled up in her father's arms. It was quite a scene: Broadway Joe talking about Super Bowl III ("Bubba Smith was lined up over there, just waiting to tear my head off") while gently stroking his daughter's brown hair.

Jessica has seen her father shake enough hands and sign enough autographs to know he is someone famous, though the origin of his fame remains a puzzle. He has told her that he played football. Big deal, she says; kids down the street play football.

Tatiana recalls Jessica rushing into the kitchen one day and shouting: "Daddy is on TV."

"Oh, good," Tatiana thought. "It must be a replay of the Super Bowl, and Jessica will finally get to see what it was that made her father famous."

It turned out to be a *Brady Bunch* rerun, with Namath doing a cameo, giving football tips to the boys. Jessica was impressed just the same.

"They will hear about the Super Bowl soon enough," Namath said of his daughters. "They will hear about it a million times. There is no need for me to bore them with it now."

But what will the girls think when they learn their father wasn't simply a football player but Broadway Joe, with his roguish past?

"I'm comfortable with that image," Namath said. "I still like it, even though it doesn't apply anymore. It was fun. Half the stories they told about me were made up or exaggerated anyway.

"I still remember how I got the name. My rookie year, there was a magazine cover with me standing on Broadway. We came back from practice one day, and there was a copy of the magazine in each player's locker. I guess the Jets' public-relations department put them there. I thought, `Uh-oh, how are the guys going to react?'

"We had a tackle named Sherman Plunkett who weighed about 350 pounds, and he had the locker right across from me. He looked at the picture and got this big smile on his face. He said, `Look at that, ol' Broadway. Broadway Joe.' That was how it started.

"All these years, I've never seen anyone say that name and not smile. There is something about it that just seems to make people feel good. I like that, you know, I really do."

Epilogue: The evening I spent at Joe Namath's Florida home was one of the most fascinating experiences of my journalistic career. We talked for almost four hours, and Namath spent most of the time with his daughter, Olivia, sleeping in his arms. It was clear that Namath was devoted to his family.

I was saddened when, a few years later, the marriage fell apart and Tatiana took the girls to California. Battling loneliness and depression, Joe resumed drinking. His problems became public in December 2003, when he was visibly intoxicated during an interview on ESPN. A few weeks later, Namath went into treatment for his alcoholism. He successfully completed the program and in 2006 wrote a best selling book about his life.

*Originally published in the Super Bowl XXVIII program, January 30, 1994.

Best of All Time? Bird's Genius Puts Him in Rarefied Air*

Larry Bird is, by his own definition, "a slow white boy who can't jump." And if you only saw him practice, you might agree.

Running sprints with his Boston teammates, he looks like a giraffe among gazelles. His stride is choppy, almost ponderous. His green sneakers hit the gym floor with a polka-like thud.

The other Celtics move swiftly and gracefully, covering the base-line-to-baseline distance with no apparent effort. They laugh and play tag. Bird, head down, arms pumping, labors to keep up.

If you didn't know better, you might figure the pale blond in the sweaty T-shirt was the tenth man on the roster. Surely, he works like a tenth man, coming out early to stretch, staying after to shoot fouls.

But this is Larry Joe Bird, at twenty-eight generally considered the best all-around player in pro basketball today, and arguably the greatest ever.

A sweeping statement, to be sure, but one heard more often each day as Bird closes in on his second consecutive NBA Most Valuable Player award and world championship. The Celtics lead the Sixers, 1–0, going into tonight's second game of the best-of-seven Eastern Conference finals.

"Larry is the best player in the world; probably the best in our solar system," said Detroit's All-Star forward, Kelly Tripucka.

"Bird is so far above everyone else he's in a different century," said Cleveland Cavaliers coach George Karl. "He sees the game on the floor the way I do after four [film] viewings. That's scary."

San Antonio Spurs coach Scotty Robertson agrees. "That Larry Bird is so damn good, he's making a farce of the game," Robertson said.

In the past, experts qualified their praise of the six-foot-nine, 220 pound forward. Some called him the "most dominant non-center" in NBA history. They thought it unfair to compare him to the likes of Wilt Chamberlain, Bill Russell, and Kareem Abdul-Jabbar.

Others called Bird the "most complete player" since Oscar Robertson, a superstar who could do more things well—shoot, pass, rebound, play defense—than anyone else.

But today, in the opinion of many NBA types, the slow white kid from French Lick, Indiana, has climbed to a plateau all his own.

"I've never seen anyone better," Karl said after Bird scored 104 points in three playoff games as the Celtics buried the Cavaliers.

"Wilt and Russell played most of their careers against smaller centers. They were really only tested when they went against each other.

"Oscar? I only saw him late in his career. By then he was a nice player, but he wasn't a dominant player like this guy.

"And given the choice between Kareem and Bird, I'd take Bird. He rebounds like a center, passes like a point guard, shoots lights out from twenty feet.

"Besides all that," Karl said, "he's a killer. He'll do anything to win."

Hall of Famer Bob Cousy saw all the greats in his eighteen NBA seasons as a coach and player, yet Cousy, the Celtics' TV analyst, says flatly: "Bird is the best who ever played this silly game."

Bird himself wants nothing to do with the argument. In fact, he wishes it would go away.

He has been compared all his life—first to his basketball-playing brothers, then to Celtics legend John Havlicek, now to the whole of civilization—and he is both weary and baffled.

"What's the point of comparing?" Bird said one recent afternoon. "I do what I do; it's either good enough or it's not. I'm concerned with one thing, and that's helping the team win. Boring as that sounds, it's the truth.

"I'm not going to sit here and tell you I don't think I'm any good. I know I'm one of the top players today, but I'd hate to say I'm better than Moses [Malone] or Julius [Erving] or Jerry West. What would it prove if I did?

"I'd rather do what I've done all along," Bird said, "and that's let my game do the talking."

This season, Larry Bird's game has spoken volumes. What is most compelling is that he actually has improved on last year's MVP performance.

He led the league in minutes per game (39.5), finished second in scoring average (28.7), finished second in three-point percentage (.427), finished sixth in free-throw percentage (.881), and finished eighth in rebounding (10.5).

He also established personal bests in points (2,295), field-goal percentage (.522), assists (6.6), and blocked shots (98). He had twenty or more points in sixty-six regular-season games. He had thirty or more points in thirty-eight games; forty or more in nine.

Bird scored a club-record sixty points in a 126–115 win over Atlanta (March 12). He won consecutive games against Portland and Detroit with shots at the buzzer (January 27, January 29). He hit more three-point field goals (fifty-six) than nine NBA teams. That's right, nine teams.

"He is the MVP of our league now," Dallas coach Dick Motta said, "and twenty years from now, I think he still would be in the top five. His game will withstand the test of time."

Asked whom he would select to the NBA's East All-Star team, Detroit Pistons coach Chuck Daly said, "Bird, Bird, Bird, Bird, and Bird." No one saw fit to quarrel.

"Yeah, this was probably my best season," Bird said, watching the rain lash against a hotel window. "I base everything on consistency, and I was pretty consistent right through. I shot 52 percent, which is good for me.

"I have to give a lot of the credit to K. C. [Jones, the Celtics' coach]. He gave me the green light on offense. I had a green light under [previous coach] Bill Fitch, but it wasn't what you'd call dark green. I couldn't just fire away if I got hot.

"K. C. is more a player's coach," Bird said. "He has faith in my judgment. He knows I'll make the right decision most of the time. If I force a shot now and then, he understands. K. C. has given me the latitude to do more things with the ball.

"But that won't mean anything if we don't win the title again. I'm a bottom-line guy. What made last year satisfying wasn't the MVP award; it was winning the championship. If we hadn't won that seventh game against [Los Angeles], that [MVP] trophy wouldn't have meant diddly.

"So all this talk about the greatest this and that don't even enter my mind," Bird said. "We've reached one level—we finished the season with the best record [63–19]. Now we have to take it one series at a time until we get back to where we were this time last year.

"Everyone has made such a big deal out of this so-called jinx. [No NBA champion has repeated since the 1968–69 Celtics.] I'd like to win it just to bury all that and prove this team is something special. It won't be easy. I know that already."

The Celtics' chances would be better if Bird were healthy, but he is not. His right (shooting) elbow bothered him the second half of the season, and the condition has worsened in the playoffs.

The inflammation was first diagnosed as bursitis, but later tests revealed bone chips in the elbow. Bird played with the swelling, but he was unable to go on when the elbow locked and he couldn't get full extension on his shot.

He missed game three of the Cleveland series (Boston lost, 105–98), then he returned wearing an elbow pad and scored thirty-four points in game four. The Celtics won, 117–115.

Bird didn't miss a start in the Detroit series—he scored forty-three, his career playoff high, in game five—but his attorney, Bob Woolf, said it was a struggle all the way.

"The pain is excruciating," Woolf said, "but Larry would never admit it. These are the playoffs.

"When Larry went to the Final Four with Indiana State, the word was he had a sore thumb. When the tournament was over, someone asked how the thumb was. Larry said, 'Broke.' He never complained, never made excuses.

"The man has a toughness like no athlete I've ever known."

"For me," Bird said, "the worst pain is missing a game. The night I didn't play against Cleveland was awful. I couldn't even watch on TV. I got so frustrated with what was happening I switched over to a movie.

"I made up my mind: I'm going to do whatever it takes to play the rest of the way. If I can go at all, I want to be out there."

The doctors feel that Bird's latest injury is a direct result of the way he plays: diving for loose balls, taking the charge, hitting the floor after rebounds. He has done this since his days at Springs Valley High School, so it's no wonder his body is breaking down.

"I remember when I was a rookie," Bird said, "[veteran] players would say, 'If you don't slow down, you'll pay for it.' I didn't understand then, but I do now. These [physical] things crop up more often and hang around longer.

"But I can't change the way I play. I might not feel 100 percent, but when they toss the ball up, I'm going to go hard. The day I start coasting, I'll know it's time to get out."

To underscore Bird's point, it is worth noting this interview took place in trainer Ray Melchiorre's hotel room. The All-Star forward had his right elbow plugged into a high-voltage stimulator, his post-practice companion of the past two months.

The machine came with an arm wrap similar to that on a blood-pressure gauge. Melchiorre put that around Bird's swollen elbow, flicked a switch, and the wrap began expanding and contracting, working the muscles in the area, calming the nerves.

Normally, Bird can't sit still for longer than ten minutes, and this treatment lasts an hour. Bird does his best to pass the time, talking and watching TV, but his impatience is obvious. His feet tap the carpet the entire sixty minutes.

The day before Bird had made a few statements that had incensed the Cleveland fans. They had chanted "We Want Bird" during the final minutes of game three. A newsman playfully asked Bird for his reaction.

"They don't want me," Bird said sharply. "They don't want no part of me. It shows they don't know much about basketball if they're calling for me. Well, I'm going to throw both barrels at 'em."

On this particular afternoon, the Cleveland media were coming after Bird with a vengeance. One disc jockey was giving away albums to listeners who called in to say, "I hate Larry Bird."

"These [fans] will be all over you tonight," Melchiorre said, glancing at the local paper with its banner "Bird Blasts . . ." headline.

"I hope so," Bird said with a smile. "It'll be more fun to beat 'em. I'm ready. I wish we could play right now."

It is this quality—call it desire, determination, whatever—combined with uncanny court sense that has enabled a player with ordinary physical attributes to become the best in the NBA.

No less an authority than Boston Celtics president Arnold "Red" Auerbach calls Bird "the most intense player ever to wear the Celtic uniform."

Think about that for a moment. Auerbach is saying Bird plays with more intensity than any man who suited up on fifteen NBA championship teams. How could anyone play with more intensity than Bill Russell, Dave Cowens, and John Havlicek?

"I never thought I'd see it," Auerbach said, "but time moves on. It's like they say, records are made to be broken. Players come along and exceed things you never thought possible. Bird has done that.

"Night after night, he plays harder than anyone I've ever seen. People ask how I could pay anyone that kind of money [$2 million a year]. I say, 'Have you ever seen the guy play?' Larry earns every cent."

"Larry encompasses everything that team basketball is about," K. C. Jones said. "He has great confidence in himself, and he has the cockiness and brains to go with it."

What Boston management sees as intensity and healthy cockiness looks a little different from the other side of the court. Many NBA coaches and players talk about the harsh edge that lately has become a part of Bird's game.

"I respect [Bird's] ability," said one NBA coach who asked not to be identified, "but I don't like the way he plays. He's sneaky dirty."

Bird was never a pushover. In his second NBA season, Fitch referred to him as "one of the meanest SOBs in the league." If you try to bully Larry Bird, Fitch said, "you picked the wrong guy."

Fine. No one questioned Bird's right to stake out his place in the NBA. Like most high-salaried rookies (he came in at $650,000 a year), Bird was tested by the hatchet men and proved he could cope. That's part of the ritual.

But now Bird seems quicker to shove and snarl, to jab his finger in the face of a startled opponent, as he did with Phil Hubbard in Cleveland. "I'm comin' at you all night long," Bird told Hubbard.

"Larry was just firing himself up," Auerbach said, dismissing the incident with a wave of his cigar. But is it that simple?

Who could forget the November 9 rumble in Boston, when Bird and the 76ers' Julius Erving exchanged shoves, then punches. Both benches emptied, and Bird and Erving were fined $7,500 apiece, the second largest individual fines ever handed out by the NBA.

The incident shocked many fans who considered Bird and Erving above that sort of thing. It was like seeing Wayne Gretzky and Mike Bossy slugging it out in the Stanley Cup finals.

Besides, Bird and the Doctor do all those chummy Converse and Spalding ads together. They're buddies, right? Uh, well . . .

"We're friendly," Erving said, "but we're not what I'd call friends. I admire Larry greatly as a player, but on another level, I have trouble dealing with some of the things he does.

"There's a lot of cockiness to his game now, more than there used to be. He mouths off and tries to intimidate. I heard he told [Detroit forward] Terry Tyler, 'The coach must not like you, asking you to guard me.' Then he stuck his finger in Hubbard's face.

"Those are pretty crass moves," Erving said, "but that's the Boston influence. He's up there with M. L. [Carr] and Cedric [Maxwell], guys who talk a lot of junk. Personally, I don't think Larry needs that. He's too good for that."

Even Woolf, Bird's neighbor and closest friend in Boston, concedes the Doctor has a point.

"It's true," Woolf said. "Larry is more vocal than he used to be. I've seen him do some things [this season] that made me wonder. . . . I haven't come out and asked him. I think it all comes back to his great intensity.

"He's coming off an MVP season. He wants to show that, unlike a lot of superstars, he won't let down. He wants that second [consecutive] championship, too. Larry is a driven young man. He has been from day one.

"The incident with Hubbard," Woolf said, "you have to remember [Bird] was upset about his injury and missing that game. The incident with Julius was a spontaneous thing. I know how much Larry respects Julius. He regretted it; he said so."

"I know I regret it," Erving said. "But I still feel Larry was the instigator. He was upset over a call, and I was his emotional outlet. I guess he felt he could do whatever he felt like doing in his [home] arena.

"I tried to be cool, but at the same time I knew I couldn't back down. I learned that lesson my rookie year. You back down in November, and people are walking on your head in February. But it's over. I'd like to forget it."

"In your opinion," a visitor asked, "is Bird a dirty player?"

Erving thought a moment.

"I don't think Larry goes out of his way to play dirty," he said. "But I think he'll do anything he has to do to get the upper hand. This whole [cocky] thing figures in there.

"Does he have to do it? Only Larry can answer that."

"I play hard all the time," Bird said. "I guess people interpret that different ways. If I'm still diving for loose balls with a fifteen-point lead, maybe they think I'm showing the other team up. I'm just playing the only way I know how.

"Talking? I don't talk any more than anybody else. People said I ran up the court saying, 'Forty-two to six' to Julius [their point totals] before we had our scuffle. That's not true. I have too much respect for Julius to do something like that.

"That fight was just something that flared up in the heat of battle," Bird said. "The Philly–Boston series brings those emotions to the surface. It didn't mean I hated Julius. The press made a bigger deal of it than it was.

"Growing up, I had fights with my brothers on the court all the time. They'd do something I didn't like, I'd say something, next thing you know we were going at it. But they were still my brothers, I loved `em. It's the competition. The NBA is like that every night.

"Julius has been around long enough, he knows that. I like him. I like his family. But if he tries to take my [championship] ring away, we're liable to be at it again. Nothing personal, but that's the nature of the business."

More precisely, that's the nature of the Bird.

Epilogue: Larry Bird retired in 1992 after a thirteen-year NBA career. He was head coach of the Indiana Pacers from 1997 to 2000. He later became president of basketball operations. He stepped down in 2022.

*Originally published in the *Philadelphia Daily News*, May 14, 1985. Reprinted with permission by Philadelphia Newspapers, LLC.

Climbing Capitol Hill*

Last November, more than one hundred financial and political leaders from the United States, Europe, and Japan gathered in Washington, D.C., for a summit on world economics.

The conference, which attracted the best and brightest of currency scholars, was cosponsored and chaired by Senator Bill Bradley (D–N.J.) and Representative Jack F. Kemp (R–N.Y.).

Bradley and Kemp, two men on the cutting edge of tax reform in America. Rising stars in their respective parties. "Potential presidential candidates," as seen by *U.S. News and World Report*.

One is a former professional basketball player; the other is a former professional football player.

Jocks, in other words.

Bradley, forty-two, was an All-America at Princeton, a Rhodes scholar, and later a ten-year pro with the New York Knicks. In 1984, he was reelected to the Senate with a staggering 67 percent of the vote over Republican Mary Mochary.

Kemp, fifty, quarterbacked the Buffalo Bills to back-to-back American Football League championships (1964–65). Now in his eighth term, Kemp is the third-ranking Republican in the House of Representatives.

"They have this city's attention," said Robert Goodman, a Washington-based political consultant. "When they talk, people listen. You don't hear the old `jock' jokes anymore."

Said Lee Atwater, deputy director of the 1984 Reagan for President campaign: "Athletes might well be the new American heroes . . . [men] who can transcend party loyalties."

There was a time when we would have laughed at the notion of an ex-athlete in government, probably with good cause.

Johnny "Blood" McNally, a Pro Football Hall of Fame halfback, was soundly defeated in his 1940s bid for county sheriff in his native Minnesota.

"No one took me seriously," McNally said later.

His platform? Among other things, a return to honest wrestling. Jock politicians have come a long way since then.

Former Olympic decathlon champion Bob Mathias (R–Calif.) was elected to four terms in Congress. Former Phillies pitcher Jim Bunning was a state senator in Kentucky and ran for governor in 1983.

Former La Salle basketball great Tom Gola was elected to the Pennsylvania legislature in 1966, then won the race for Philadelphia city controller four years later.

"The name helps, no question about it," said Gola, now retired from politics and working for the Valley Forge Investment Corporation.

"You'd be surprised how many [voters] step into the booth and don't know anything about the candidates. They look at the list, and if they recognize your name—whether it's for sports or whatever—chances are they'll vote for you.

"Of course, once you get into office, you have to perform. You can't get by on your jump shot. You have to know the issues; you have to know which buttons to push and when."

That is where Bradley and Kemp stand out. While they might have won election with their names, they have grown into formidable politicians. There isn't much that goes down on Capitol Hill that they don't influence in some way.

Bradley is the ranking Democrat on the Senate Finance Committee. Kemp is chairman of the House Republican Conference. Kemp was also an active congressional delegate to the Strategic Arms Limitation Talks in Geneva from 1979 to 1981.

They have co-written their parties' proposals for tax reform: the Democrats' Bradley–Gephardt plan (written with Representative Richard Gephardt of Missouri) and the Republicans' Kemp–Roth bill (written with Senator William V. Roth of Delaware).

Last year, when the *Today* show wanted two political heavyweights to appear the morning after President Reagan's State of the Union address, the call went out to Bill Bradley and Jack Kemp.

The *Congressional Almanac* notes that Bradley "brings impressive assets to a campaign, a record of distinction [and] a genuine philosophy on issues different in emphasis, but not very different in substance from traditional Democratic liberalism."

Of Kemp, political consultant Raymond Strother said: "He seems to have the right message at the right time. . . . The country is looking for change, and Kemp represents the best the Republicans have to offer."

The *Congressional Almanac* agrees: "There is no reason why [Kemp] should not run for president, and be taken as a serious candidate."

But a former football player in the White House? What does that say about the U.S. political process in the `80s? What does it say about us, the voters?

Nothing new, really. It says we are capable of voting for images rather than issues, throwing our support behind candidates we "like" for reasons that have little or nothing to do with their politics.

We voted in military heroes (Dwight Eisenhower) and movie stars (Ronald Reagan), why not an athlete? Think about it. What's the film role we associate most often with Ronald Reagan? George Gipp, a football player.

We live in a society in which sports is one of few common denominators. Three of the top six, five of the top ten rated TV shows of all time are sporting events. Doug Flutie throws a last-second touchdown pass, and 40 million Americans leap from their chairs and say, "That guy's a winner."

Walter Mondale, with all his money and political know-how, couldn't come close to doing what Flutie did with one sixty-yard heave of a football. Mondale only could talk about leadership. Flutie demonstrated it in a way that both hard-hat and Main Liner could understand and admire.

An athlete builds credibility with his performance because we know it is something real. It is not a thirty-second TV spot that was written, rehearsed, and re-dubbed a dozen times until it came out just right. The athlete puts it all on the line every time out.

Come to think of it, that is not bad training for a career in politics.

An article in the *Washington Weekly* noted: "Perhaps it's because professional sports are so much like big business, and that big business is so much like the media, and the media are so much like politics.

"But for whatever reason, the transition from locker room to Oval Office seems very reasonable these days. . . . There was a time when political accomplishment brought fame. Now the process has been reversed."

The ex-athlete has a natural rapport with the TV audience; the networks and advertisers realized that long ago. Today, jocks are all over the tube as play-by-play men, color analysts, commercial spokesmen, and actors.

It stands to reason that, if these guys can sell beer and flowers, they can sell themselves in this age of electronic politics. Put the name on the screen, jog the memory a little, and watch the campaign take off.

When Bill Bradley announced his candidacy for the 1978 New Jersey Democratic Senate nomination, he was received coolly by many political insiders.

One newspaper analysis dismissed Bradley as "a well-intentioned dilettante whose grasp of politics, nurtured in the ivied cloisters of Princeton and Oxford, tends to be academic, theoretical, clinical and detached."

Then Bradley did a TV ad that showed him wadding up a piece of paper and hook-shooting it through a hoop over a wastebasket. Without saying a word, it recalled Bradley's glory days at Princeton and his two NBA titles with the Knicks.

Dilettante, hell. This was the All-American Boy. Bradley won the Democratic primary with almost twice as many votes as the other two candidates, Richard Leone and Alex Menza, combined.

"When a public figure has an identity outside of politics, like Kemp and Bradley, it gives them additional credibility," said Mac Carey, who worked as press secretary for Jeff Bell, Bradley's opponent in the `78 Senate race.

"The public is more likely to believe them because they are not just another lawyer or businessman or politician on the make."

"People still vote for people," Robert Goodman said. "You have a few who vote for a party, and a few who vote on the issues, but they're the minority. Most people vote for what they see. They vote for the man.

"If they like that guy to begin with—if they associate him with something like an Olympic medal or a Super Bowl—that's a plus. Most candidates spend months shaking hands, trying to become known. They might succeed, they might not.

"Kemp and Bradley are known," Goodman said. "They have what amounts to a half-mile jump in a two-mile run."

Of course, a name alone is no guarantee of success.

John Glenn entered the 1984 presidential race at a time when *The Right Stuff* was opening in theaters across America. The film was splendid, and Glenn (played by actor Ed Harris) came off as the most admirable of the seven original U.S. astronauts.

A national magazine called it "the movie that could make a president." But the Glenn campaign never got off the ground in the primaries, collapsing due to a shortage of funds and lack of organization.

The campaign was such a disaster, in fact, it took *The Right Stuff* down with it. The film flopped at the box office, polls revealed, because people thought it was a political movie and stayed away.

That is how volatile the equation can be. It is great to have a name, but only if you have the right stuff—money, staff, and game plan—to back it up. If things go sour, a name can actually work against you.

"What happens," said Neil Oxman, a Philadelphia-based political consultant, "is it allows the other side to turn that [name] around. 'The Right Stuff,' for example, becomes 'The Wrong Stuff.'

"If an athlete like Kemp or Bradley were to stumble in a campaign, it would leave him open for the stereotypes about playing without a helmet and so forth. Fame can cut both ways. It's not a free ticket to election.

"But Kemp and Bradley have handled themselves well," Oxman said. "They know the issues, they paid their dues on the Hill, now they're leading the fight for tax reform. You don't see the jock references anymore.

"It's no longer 'former basketball star Bill Bradley' and 'former quarterback Jack Kemp.' They established an identity beyond that. But they still wear those championship rings, you know, just to remind us."

At a glance, it doesn't appear Bill Bradley and Jack Kemp have a whole lot in common.

Bradley was a truly great college athlete; Kemp set no worlds afire at California's Occidental College. Bradley was a Rhodes scholar; Kemp was a physical-education major.

Bradley made it big in New York City; Kemp lasted one season with the NFL's Giants and was released. Success came easily to Bradley and not so easily to Kemp, who was cut by three teams and was claimed for the waiver price, $100, by Buffalo in 1962.

"Only the bottom line was the same," Kemp said. "We both went out winners."

Politically, they belong to different parties and have differing views on the role of government.

Bradley believes in a woman's right to choose an abortion; Kemp is opposed. Kemp is a supporter of the MX missile; Bradley is not. Kemp applauded the president's actions in Grenada and Libya; Bradley did not.

The two men found agreement, finally, in tax reform, and each wrote bills that would substantially lower rates and close loopholes.

Their programs differed in detail, but they were similar in philosophy. Simply put: The average Joe has been kicked around long enough. It is time to crack down on rich folks and their tax shelters.

This was a cause Bradley espoused even while he played pro basketball. In his 1976 book *Life on the Run*, Bradley wrote: "It has been claimed that pro sports does everything from insuring community pride to contributing to social stability. Predictably, the men who write [tax] laws are only too eager to . . . provide [team] owners with loopholes big enough to drive a Sherman tank through."

Kemp's bill, which was eventually signed into law by the president, didn't cut quite as deeply as Bradley–Gephardt, but it cut enough to have a few GOP fat cats wailing on the White House fence. And that wasn't such a bad thing for the party.

"Politically, it had great value," consultant Charles Black, a former Republican National Committee staffer, told the *New York Times*.

"The Republican Party since [Herbert] Hoover had been viewed as the party of the rich and 'big business.' After Watergate, the corruption image was added into it.

"Of the first 10 things people thought about Republicans, eight or nine were negative. It didn't take a genius to see the way to shake our terrible image was to take Kemp's bill and his rhetoric and spread it to the party's candidates."

Representative Newt Gingrich, of Georgia, calls Kemp "the first Republican in modern times to show it is possible to be hopeful and conservative at the same time."

"I've heard that," Kemp said during a recent interview, "and I take pride in it. It bothered me that so many people saw our party as anti-growth, anti-hope. That isn't what we're about. It's sure as heck not what I'm about.

"I've tried to make some changes in the tax structure, not because I thought it would further my career, but because it made sense. All these years we [in government] have been subsidizing unemployment and taxing work. We've been going backwards.

"We're on the right track now," Kemp said. "It's interesting that Bill [Bradley] and I would find ourselves allied on this issue. I don't think you could say it has anything to do with our [athletic] backgrounds. This is more philosophical.

"Bill is a good friend; I have great respect for him. Whenever I'm asked who is emerging as a force in the Democratic Party, I always mention Bill. I think he stands head and shoulders above the rest of the liberal wing."

Most experts surveyed agree Bradley is presidential material, but not just yet. Bradley himself deflects the question.

"I'm only interested in one thing," he said, "and that's doing the best job I can for the people of New Jersey."

Bradley's schedule supports that. He spends almost all his time shuttling between his offices in Washington and Union, New Jersey. He invented the "walking town meeting," where he visits a factory or shopping mall unannounced to ask people, "What's on your mind?"

Kemp, by contrast, flies all over the country making speeches and raising money. You're as likely to find him in, say, New Orleans as in his 31st Congressional District, which includes Niagara County, with Erie, Buffalo, and Rochester, New York.

Kemp has added several experienced lieutenants to his staff, including John Maxwell, who just happens to have experience running senate campaigns in Iowa, site of the first presidential caucus.

And wasn't it interesting to see Kemp address a Republican gathering in Concord, New Hampshire, last month? New Hampshire will be the site of the first primary after the caucus. (And there was a "Kemp 88" ice sculpture on display.)

"Kemp is running his butt off," Neil Oxman said. "Can he beat [Vice President George] Bush for the nomination? Possibly."

Edward S. Rollins, who ran the president's last campaign, favors Bush in '88 but admits, "If the vice president chose to run and asked me to run his campaign, the candidate I would least like to run against is Jack Kemp."

Why?

"Kemp is more like a regular guy," said Scott Miller, a New York political adviser. "Bush leaves people cold. Put 'em side-by-side on TV, and Kemp would blow Bush away."

Ask Kemp about the '88 presidential bid and he shifts in his leather chair and smiles. He says nothing is decided yet, but his eyes look like two campaign buttons. Make no mistake, Jack's in the race.

"I'm interested," Kemp said, "but I'm not obsessed with the presidency. If the time comes and I feel it's do-able, I'll take a shot. It would be a challenge. I've always enjoyed challenges."

Would the challenge of winning a presidential election compare to leading the underdog Bills past the San Diego Chargers for their first AFL title in 1964?

"There are similarities," Kemp said. "You have to look ahead in both. If you make a mistake, you learn from it, but you move on. You can't dwell on the past. The next snap is what counts.

"A quarterback and a candidate are both required to make tough decisions, and you can't hold up a wet finger to see which way the wind is blowing, either. You have to go with your gut feeling, then have the courage to stick with it.

"Dealing with the press," Kemp said, "that's part of it, too. As an athlete, especially a quarterback, you have to let that [criticism] roll off your back. My [political] colleagues feel editorial writers are tough. I tell them they ought to spend twelve years on the sports page. That's tough.

"One thing is very much the same: You have to win," Kemp said. "Whether it's politics or football, winning is like shaving. . . . You do it every day, or you wind up looking like a bum."

Would Kemp use his football career as part of his campaign? Would he weave film of his touchdown passes into his TV commercials? It would be such a natural: "Vote Jack Kemp for America's Quarterback."

Kemp laughed. "It wouldn't work," he said. "The other side would come out with films of my fumbles and interceptions. They'd say, `Do you want this man as your president?'

"I think I'll stick with tax reform."

Epilogue: In 1996, Jack Kemp was the Republican Party's vice-presidential nominee, running on the ticket with Senator Bob Dole. They lost in a landslide to the Democratic incumbents Bill Clinton and Al Gore. In 2000, Bill Bradley ran in the Democratic presidential primary but lost the nomination to Gore.

*Originally published in the *Philadelphia Daily News*, June 10, 1986. Reprinted with permission by Philadelphia Newspapers, LLC.

Abolition of Boxing Wouldn't Be Jake*

Jake LaMotta didn't pay much attention to the recent congressional hearings on boxing. He said he heard all that stuff before.

And the former middleweight champion wasn't surprised to learn Dr. George Lundberg, president of the American Medical Association, has called for the abolition of the sport. Jake has heard all that before, too.

"Boxing has always been a political football," LaMotta, sixty, was saying the other night, before he dusted off his comedy act at Palumbo's.

"They have these hearings; they appoint commissions to investigate the game; they get a few headlines, then it all goes away. A year or two later, it comes back. Different guys, different commissions, same results.

"The trouble is, the people who are running these things are politicians and doctors; they don't know anything about boxing. They don't know what goes on in the back rooms; they don't know how deals are made, so all they can do is talk about change.

"There's no question the sport should be federally regulated," LaMotta said. "It's the only sport that doesn't have a clear-cut authority . . . one office or one commissioner who says, 'This is OK' and 'That ain't OK.' If you don't have that, you're gonna have abuses.

"Boxing is also the only sport that doesn't have a pension plan. I tried to start one years ago, but I got blackballed. The managers and promoters didn't want any part of it. They want to slice up the pie their way. If the fighter suffers later, too bad.

"Boxing is a tough business, but it's not bad in itself. Regulate it, put the right men in there to run it, and it'll be OK. These people who want to abolish boxing. . . . They don't know what they're talkin' about."

But what about the kids who are killed in the ring? What about Duk Koo Kim, the Korean who died following his savage fight with Ray "Boom-Boom" Mancini last year?

"People die driving their cars. Does anybody want to outlaw driving?" LaMotta said. "Construction workers die falling off buildings. What are we gonna do, stop putting up buildings? You can't regulate life and death. It would be nice if we could, but we can't.

"It happens in all sports. More kids die playing football than boxing. And how many guys get killed in automobile races? Nothing's said. But a fighter gets killed, and the next day everybody's screaming brutality. It was the same way when I started [in 1941].

"Personally, I don't think the risk is as great now as it was back then. Today, they stop a fight the first time a guy gets in trouble. Sometimes I think they jump in too quick; they don't give a guy a chance to come back.

"I don't know if I could fight today. I was the type who took a lot of punishment. Move inside, take a couple shots to land one. I wore guys down, won in the late rounds. I might have to change my style now. Other guys, like Sugar Ray, would be great in any era."

LaMotta is referring, of course, to the original Sugar Ray. Robinson, that is—not Leonard. LaMotta is quite specific about that.

The Bronx Bull has an intimate knowledge of Sugarman I because they fought six times in a nine-year period (1942–51). Jake fought Sugar Ray more often than anybody, if you don't count his five wives.

"I fought Sugar Ray so many times, it's a wonder I don't have diabetes," LaMotta says in his routine.

LaMotta won one; Sugar Ray won the rest, including a bloody thirteenth-round technical knockout that ended Jake's reign as middleweight champion in 1951. Three decades have passed, and LaMotta still says he hasn't seen a better fighter than the one who lifted his crown that night.

"Fast, smart, tough," LaMotta said. "The experts say Ray Robinson was the best fighter, pound-for-pound, who ever lived. I have to go along with that.

"We had some great fights. We brought out the best in each other. Contrasting styles, like the bull and the matador. Put those six fights together today and we could make $100 million. I could live real nicely on that."

Jake LaMotta had 106 professional fights. He won eighty-three and lost nineteen, with four draws. He figures he made $2 million in his career. His biggest payday was $75,000 for his title match with Robinson.

"Just about covered my medical bills," LaMotta recalls, smiling.

This is a different era, LaMotta points out. A kid wins ten fights today and he's on TV, pulling down a half-million dollars while Don King and Bob Arum measure his waist for a championship belt.

LaMotta went eight years, eighty-eight fights, before he got his title shot. Even then, Jake had to dump a fight to Billy Fox to satisfy the mobsters before they would put him in with the champion, Marcel Cerdan.

"That's the way they did business back then," LaMotta growled. "Sure, it made me mad, but what was I gonna do, keep getting my brains punched out for nothing?

"Today, kids come up fast and make good dough. TV's had a big impact. Good and bad. I don't begrudge these young guys the money. If they can make it, more power to 'em.

"My point is, they're being brought along too fast. They don't have enough fights to really learn anything. They don't fight all the four-rounders and six-rounders like we did. They don't serve that apprenticeship.

"That's why I can't compare today's fighters with the fighters forty years ago. Sugar Ray Leonard was a real talent. He reminded me of the other Sugar Ray, and I can't pay nobody a higher compliment, but I can't compare them.

"Ray Robinson had one hundred fifty pro fights. . . . He was the finished product. Leonard had nowhere near that experience. Leonard should just now be hitting his stride. As it is, we'll never know how good he could have been."

Jake LaMotta turned pro in March 1941. He had twenty fights that first year. He had five bouts in April alone. He fought three guys—Stanley Goisz, Lorne McCarthy, and Monroe Crewe—in eleven days.

"I liked stayin' busy," he said.

He fought Ray Robinson twice in three weeks. He had two more fights in the three weeks after that. If you saw his stunning film biography, *Raging Bull*, you know Jake paid his dues.

"That movie has done great things for me," said LaMotta, who lives in Manhattan when he isn't busy on the nightclub and talk-show circuit.

"I tell people I lost my title in 1951, and I won it back thirty years later when *Raging Bull* came out.

"People come up to me now, call me `Champ.' It's a nice feeling to be back on top after all these years. I've had people approach me tonight and say, `Hey, Jake. I saw you fight so-and-so at the Garden.' They remember better than me sometimes.

"I took a lot of hard knocks in the fight game, but, yeah, I'd do it all over again," said LaMotta, who has trimmed down from a bloated 220 pounds to 180 for his show-business comeback.

"Boxing was good to me; it was good to a lot of guys. I use the example of me and Rocky Graziano. We grew up in the same neighborhood on the Lower East Side. It was a tough place. You had to fight to survive.

"Rocky and me, we had to steal to get by. But we agreed, we'd only steal things that began with the letter `A,' like A bike, A car, A TV set. That's how we wound up being sent to A reform school together.

"But we turned to boxing, and look what happened. We both won the middleweight championship; we had movies made about our lives. Rocky's an actor; I'm doing my comedy, and we still live a block from each other uptown. We've done OK.

"I look back on where I came from," Jake LaMotta said, "and I see where I am today, and I can't say too much bad about boxing.

"Let these people in Washington talk all they want. They don't know. Rocky and me, we can tell `em a few things."

*Originally published in the *Philadelphia Daily News*, February 22, 1983. Reprinted with permission by Philadelphia Newspapers, LLC.

For Magee, Winning's a Science*

It was 5 A.M., and the lights were on in the gymnasium at Philadelphia College of Textiles and Science.

That could only mean one thing.

Herb Magee was shooting 'em up again.

At 5 in the morning, 5 in the afternoon, Philly time, Miller time, any time, it doesn't matter. If Herbie is awake, chances are he is shooting a basketball.

"Herbie is one of my best friends, but the guy is definitely weird," said Jim Boyle, Magee's former teammate at West Catholic High School, now assistant coach with the NBA's Denver Nuggets.

"I mean, he's fifty years old and still shooting jump shots. That seems a little strange to me."

On this particular morning, Magee arrived at Textile's East Falls campus before dawn to unlock the field house for basketball practice, which was scheduled for 6 A.M.

Magee, Textile's all-time leading scorer, now entering his twenty-fifth season as head coach, opened the door and flipped on the lights, then shot around for twenty minutes while waiting for his players to arrive.

He started with bank shots, then baseline jumpers, gradually working his way beyond the three-point line. He knocked down ten, fifteen, twenty shots in a row.

As the players straggled into the gym, many of them still half asleep, they could hear the familiar sound—*swish, swish, swish*—and they knew it was the coach.

No one else shoots like that—certainly, not before the sun comes up.

"I'm just messing around," Magee said, slouching around the court in his white Textile shirt and red sweat pants.

Swish.

"Getting loose . . . "

Swish.

"Killing time . . . "

Swish.

Like Jim Boyle said, Herbie is not your typical fifty-something basketball coach.

He wasn't your typical All-America player, either. He was too small and too frail to be recruited by the Big Five schools, so he wound up at Textile, and the rest is history.

He averaged twenty-four points a game as a five-foot-ten, 150 pound guard, and he was drafted by the Boston Celtics in 1963. Magee passed up his shot at the NBA to stay at Textile as an assistant coach under Bucky Harris.

In 1967, Magee succeeded Harris as head coach, and now he is knocking on the door of five hundred career wins.

Magee's coaching record at Textile is a glossy 486–200, a .708 winning percentage. He ranks twenty-third among active college coaches in victories, fourth among all Division II coaches. He keeps grinding out those twenty-win seasons: He has seventeen of them in twenty-four years on the job.

"Herbie is an excellent coach in every respect," said the Sixers' Jim Lynam, who grew up with Magee in West Philadelphia and played alongside him in the West Catholic backcourt.

"He relates well with his players; he is a great teacher, and he gets the maximum out of his teams.

"I'll be honest: One of the first things I did when I got the [coaching] job at St. Joseph's [in 1978] was to take Textile off our schedule because the game was a headache I didn't need.

"I wouldn't get any pats on the back for beating Textile, but I knew Herbie's kids were always capable of springing the upset. I told him, `We're friends and all, but I've got to drop you.'

"Herbie understood," Lynam said. "He knew I was really paying him a compliment."

Indeed, Textile might be a small school (enrollment of 1,812), but it is a force to be reckoned with in basketball.

The Rams have suffered just two losing seasons since 1952, and they won the NCAA College Division championship in 1970 with Magee as coach. The title team won twenty-eight games in a row, with the average margin of victory a whopping 24.5 points.

Last season, Textile finished 24–8 and advanced to the Division II Elite Eight before losing.

With four starters back, including the willowy six-foot-six senior forward Randy Stover, the Rams appear poised for a monster season as they venture into a new conference, the New York Collegiate Athletic Conference.

If all the pieces fall into place, if Stover has another big year and six-foot-eight senior Damon Rountree comes through at center, Textile could make another run at the national championship.

Along the way, Magee expects to pick up career win number five hundred (that's the good news) and see his school scoring record finally fall (that's the other news). Stover needs 495 points to break Magee's mark (2,235), which has stood for almost thirty years.

"People who know me have said that when Randy gets close to the record, I'll probably bench him," Magee said with a smile. "I wouldn't do that. My ego's not that big.

"But I have told Randy, `If they were counting three-pointers back when I played, forget it, I would've put that [scoring] record outta sight.'"

For all of his accomplishments as a player and coach at Textile, Herb Magee is best defined by his exploits as a West Philly schoolyard player.

Hardly anyone talks about Herbie scoring fifty points against Wilkes College and lighting up Kings College for forty-four. Mostly, they talk about the games he played at B Street and Wyoming Avenue, 4th and Shunk, and the Sherwood Recreation Center at 56th and Christian.

The Philly playgrounds—that was where Magee really put on a show, sometimes playing in three leagues at the same time, shuttling between two games in the same night, playing a half at, say, Sherwood, then driving to Kingsessing, at 50th and Chester, to another court and playing a second half there. He usually finished as high scorer in both games.

"Herbie was a legend. I'm not exaggerating," Boyle said. "Jimmy [Lynam], Herbie, and I would go all over, looking for pickup games. The three of us would take on all comers, and Herbie knocked their socks off.

"One time we played some guys from St. James and Chester [high schools], three on three. Jimmy and I were . . . freshmen at St. Joe's; Herbie was at Textile. The other guys could play, too, so this was serious ball. First team to score ten baskets wins.

"First game, Herbie takes every shot for our team, hits ten out of ten, and we win. Now we play the other team. Same rules, same result. Herbie takes every shot, hits ten out of ten. We've played two games, and nobody else has touched the ball. Unbelievable.

"So what do you think Herbie does? He says, `That's enough, I'm leaving,' and off he goes. I was ticked because I wanted to keep playing."

Why did he leave?

"Because he knew it would add to the legend," Boyle said. "The guy hit twenty straight jumpers. I've played in a thousand games and never seen a guy have a run like that. Herbie knew the coolest thing to do in that situation was just walk away.

"It worked, obviously, because here I am still talking about it thirty years later."

"I don't remember the game, but that sounds like me," Magee said, kicking back in his Textile office. "I was cocky. I knew I could shoot, and I knew there weren't many guys around who could stop me.

"A guy once bet [Lynam] that so-and-so could hold me under twenty points in a summer game. Jimmy took the bet for $20, which was probably all the money he had in the world.

"We played the game, and, of course, Jimmy was feeding me the ball like mad. I had twenty points in the first ten minutes. I finished with fifty. It was so easy, it was like stealing.

"I loved those days," Magee said wistfully. "Hanging out in the schoolyard, playing ball all the time—that was the most fun in the world.

"Jimmy, Bo [Boyle], and I would go to a court in Overbrook, and there would be Wali Jones and Walt Hazzard. We'd go someplace else and run into Hubie White, Billy Hoy, John O'Reilly [Mount St. Mary's All-America], Sonny Hill, guys like that.

"That's what made me a player. I loved the game so much, I couldn't stand the thought of not playing, so I pushed myself to keep up. And if you could keep up with those guys, Jack, you could play."

With his lack of height and spindly frame, Magee knew the only way he could make it in basketball was to develop an outside shot. So he worked on it.

Magee practiced every day, taking five hundred shots from various points on the floor and marking the spots where he missed. Then he shot again from those troublesome spots until he made, say, twenty in a row.

Magee developed into one of the city's most prolific schoolboy scorers. His dream was to play for Jack Ramsay at St. Joseph's, but he never received an offer. The Hawks recruited his West Catholic teammates, Lynam and Boyle, but not him.

"I was crushed," Magee recalled.

"It was a size thing," Lynam said. "I wasn't big, but I had a decent frame. Herbie was like a rail. He weighed 130 pounds when we were seniors [at West Catholic].

"Jack has said that not recruiting Herbie was one of his biggest mistakes. If he had kept the two of us together [in the backcourt], I know we would have done very well."

Instead, Magee wound up at Textile, a small school that didn't even have its own gymnasium at the time. He was steered there by his uncle, the Reverend Edwin Gallagher, who was appointed guardian of Magee and his three brothers after their parents died two years apart.

Magee did not enjoy his freshman year. He was taking thirty hours of class a week and commuting to basketball practice at Mann Recreation Center, on 5th and Allegheny streets. A campus field house was built the following year, and the quality of basketball life improved. Magee began piling up the points, and the Rams rolled to fifty-nine wins in seventy-one games over the next three seasons. Magee was named to the small-college All-America team twice.

The Celtics selected him in the seventh round of the 1963 NBA draft, but Magee took one look at the Boston roster—the guards were Sam and K. C. Jones and a kid named Havlicek—and decided to accept Harris's offer to stay at Textile as assistant coach.

"Now I wish I had given it a shot," Magee said. "I don't think I would've made it, but how often do you get a tryout with the Celtics? I know I would've wound up back here anyway, but it would've been a neat experience just practicing with all those Hall of Famers, even if it was only for a few weeks."

On balance, Herb Magee is a very happy man.

The regret he feels for not taking a flier at the NBA is little more than an occasional twinge, and he doesn't resent the fact that he still is coaching at Textile—small time, some would say—after all these years.

With his record and reputation as a shooting instructor, you would have thought some big-time program would have hired Magee by now.

But the truth is that Herbie is quite comfortable. He is the most recognizable figure on the Henry Avenue campus. Said former assistant coach Al Angelos: "Herbie is Mr. Textile. I can't imagine the school without him, and vice versa."

Magee interviewed at Villanova during the 1973 coach hunt that ultimately went to Rollie Massimino. Later, he was approached by Rutgers University, but he wasn't that interested. Divorced and the father of two girls, Magee did not want to leave Philadelphia.

When St. Joseph's called him in 1978, Magee asked one question: "Is Jimmy [Lynam] a candidate for the job?"

The answer was yes.

Magee told them: "Then why would you talk to me or anyone else? Jimmy's your man." (Lynam was hired shortly thereafter.)

Magee still receives occasional feelers, but he isn't likely to abandon his cozy niche at Textile. He coaches basketball in the winter and golf in the spring. He also teaches a physical-education class.

Magee spends his summer touring basketball camps as a shooting coach. He has an instructional video aptly titled *Swish*. He is available for individual tutoring by the hour. Among his pupils: Charles Barkley and former Sixer Tim McCormick.

"I can't believe how lucky I am to be doing this for a living," Magee said. "I'm probably having more fun now than I've ever had.

"This is my twenty-fifth season, and I could hardly sleep last night. I was out of bed at 3 A.M., and I was here at 4:30. Practice wasn't until 6, but I couldn't wait to get started.

"My heart is here," Magee said. "You hear those St. Joe's guys—Lynam, Boyle, [Jack] McKinney, that bunch—talk about the Hawk blood running through their veins. That's how I feel about Textile.

"Things happen at a school like this that just don't happen at other places. Crazy things."

For example . . .

"It's the first day of tryouts a few years ago," Magee said. "We've got thirty kids scrimmaging on two courts, running up and down. I'm walking around, seeing who can play and who can't.

"I spot this kid who has [Bermuda] shorts under his gym shorts, and they're hanging down to his knees. I think, 'What's this, a joke?' Then he hits a couple jumpers and takes it to the hoop, bam. My jaw drops.

"I figure I've got a great discovery. I pull the guy off to the side and say, 'What year are you in?' He looks at me like, 'What are you talking about?' I say, 'Are you a freshman?' He says, 'No, I work in a laundry.'

"It turns out the guy was waiting for the 'A' bus on Henry Avenue and saw the gym door open. He walked in and got in the scrimmage. He thought it was a pickup game.

"I said, 'Uh, this is a college team. We're practicing.' He said, 'Oh, OK,' and left.

"That kind of thing never happens to Bobby Knight at Indiana. I doubt that it ever happened at Pauley Pavilion [at UCLA]. But here, anything goes."

One thing Textile has in common with both Indiana and UCLA is that it has won a national basketball championship. It was on the Division II level, but it was an NCAA championship just the same.

Magee still has the 1970 team photo hanging in his office. Jim Lynam's kid brother, Mike, was a guard on that team. John Pierantozzi, the star forward, now works in the admissions office at Textile.

"A very special group," Magee said, looking at the photograph. "We beat American International in the [NCAA] quarterfinals by forty-eight points. Forty-eight points."

This season, Magee has a team that some experts believe is even more talented than the class of '70. Some Textile fans have started warming up the "We're Number One" chant, and the season doesn't begin until Saturday, when Wilmington College visits Althouse Hall.

"This team could be very good, but time will tell," Magee said. "We have talent, but will these kids put it all together the way that team did? I don't know yet.

"Pierantozzi, [Jim] McGilvery, and [Carlton] Poole intimidated other teams with their mental toughness. They'd get a team down by six, and the next thing you knew, [the lead] was sixteen. They had a killer instinct. They put people away.

"It's a helluva climb to the top, I know that. In '70, we breezed through the tournament, won every game by double figures. I told [assistant coach] Gary Rupert, 'This is easy. We'll win this thing every year.'

"That was twenty years ago," Magee said, "and we haven't won it since. Shows how smart I was."

This season, Herbie takes—what else?—another shot.

Epilogue: In 2022, Magee retired after fifty-four years as coach at the school that was renamed Thomas Jefferson University. He won 1,144 games. He was inducted into the Basketball Hall of Fame in 2011.

*Originally published in the *Philadelphia Daily News*, November 19, 1991. Reprinted with permission by Philadelphia Newspapers, LLC.

"I'm Not a Whiner"*

The early-morning smog was just starting to burn away, and the backstretch at Santa Anita Park was coming to life.

Grooms led horses to and from the track, trainers and owners huddled along the rail, handicappers mingled and sipped coffee as the thoroughbreds went through their workouts.

On the clubhouse patio, overlooking the scene as usual, sat Bill Shoemaker, the winningest jockey of all time, now confined to a wheelchair, the result of a near-fatal car wreck last April.

Shoemaker arrived at the track before dawn, checking on the thirty horses in his stable. He is a full-time trainer now, and he hopes someday to join the legendary Johnny Longden as the only men to both ride and train Kentucky Derby winners.

That is one of the dreams that keeps the sixty-year-old Shoemaker going. The other?

"I want to get out of this chair and walk," Shoemaker said. "It may take a year or two years, but I'm going to keep working at it."

As a jockey, Bill Shoemaker beat long odds on many occasions, but this is the toughest ride of his life. It has been almost a year since he flipped his Ford Bronco into a canyon in nearby San Dimas, California, and wound up with three crushed cervical vertebrae.

Today, Willie the Shoe is a quadriplegic, with virtually no feeling below his neck. He has slight movement in his right hand, but that's all.

The man who rode four Kentucky Derby winners now gets around in a sip-and-puff wheelchair that he operates by blowing into a plastic straw placed near his mouth.

"I rode in forty thousand races and had plenty of falls; I never got a spinal injury," Shoemaker said. "Then a car gets me. You never know."

Shoemaker always was a diminutive figure at four-foot-eleven and 95 pounds, but he seems even smaller and more fragile now, sitting with a wool blanket across his lap, his tiny hands resting, doll-like, on the arms of his wheelchair.

It would be unbearably sad if it weren't for the piercing look in Shoemaker's eyes. It is a look that puts all visitors on notice: If you want to talk horses, fine, pull up a chair. But if all you have to offer is pity, forget it, Shoe isn't interested.

A sample conversation . . .

"Does it take a special kind of courage to keep going?" a visitor asked recently.

"No," Shoemaker said flatly. "You just do it."

Wheeling around the barn, Shoemaker is all business. He calls every shot, and he is visibly irritated when an exercise rider takes a horse out too slowly or a stable hand is careless with a rake. Shoemaker insists on things being done right.

"Bill is a perfectionist; that's what made him such a great jockey," said Harry Pariotta, who owns two of the horses in Shoemaker's stable. "That's what will make him a successful trainer."

So far, Shoemaker's barn has only one real star: Fire the Groom, a speedy mare who won the 1991 Santa Anita Breeders' Cup. But Shoe claims to have several nice colts coming along. So if you are tempted to feel sorry for him, well, don't.

"I'm alive, and I'm doing what I want to do," Shoemaker said, watching intently as two of his horses galloped down the backstretch. "I don't think I've got it so bad. There are lots of people worse off than me.

"My greatest fear was that I'd be hooked up to some machine the rest of my life. That's what the doctors said. They told me I'd be on a ventilator because I'd never be able to breathe for myself. But here I am, back at work.

"Now if we can just find a winner out here," Shoemaker said, surveying the track, "everything will be dandy."

The saddle was Bill Shoemaker's home for forty-one years. He mounted 40,350 horses and won 8,833 races. His total purses added up to a staggering $123 million.

There have been other great jockeys—Longden, Eddie Arcaro, Angel Cordero, and others—but the Shoe was in a class all by himself.

He began as a fourteen-year-old cleaning stalls at a ranch near his home in Fabens, Texas. He had his first ride at eighteen, and he was voted into the Racing Hall of Fame at twenty-seven, yet he continued to ride for another three decades after that.

Asked why, Shoemaker said simply: "I loved it. I felt like it was what I was born to do."

He won four Kentucky Derbys, five Belmonts, and two Preakness Stakes. He won his last Derby in 1986 aboard a 17:1 shot named Ferdinand.

Shoemaker rode perhaps his finest race that day, coaxing the skittish colt through a narrow opening on the final straightaway. At fifty-four, Shoe was the oldest rider ever to win the Derby.

Wrote columnist Red Smith: "Shoemaker is an athlete's athlete. If he were six feet tall and weighed 200 pounds, he could beat anybody at anything."

Shoemaker retired as a jockey in February 1990, following a nine-month farewell tour that barnstormed from Australia to Oklahoma. He took his final

ride at Santa Anita—finishing fourth on a horse named Patchy Groundfog—
and settled into his new life as a trainer.

Fourteen months later, Shoemaker's world was turned upside down.

On the evening of April 8, 1991, Shoemaker was driving home after playing golf at the Sierra La Verne Country Club when his 1990 Ford Bronco
veered off the road and tumbled down a fifty-foot embankment.

Shoemaker claims he was reaching for his cellular phone when he lost control of the car. However, a blood test conducted after the crash showed his
alcohol level (.13) was above the legal limit.

Shoemaker said he had two beers at the country club. He insists he was
not drunk at the time of the accident. Police chose not to file charges against
Shoemaker, probably feeling he suffered enough in the crash.

Witnesses reported that Shoemaker's car hit a beam on the side of the road
and rolled down the steep hillside, finally coming to rest on its wheels on an
access road near the Orange County Freeway.

When paramedics arrived, they found Shoemaker slumped over the steering wheel. He had stopped breathing, but he was revived by mouth-to-mouth
resuscitation on the scene. He was rushed to the Centinela Medical Center in
Inglewood, where surgeons discovered his massive spinal injuries.

Shoemaker's head was braced in a metal halo, and a tube was inserted in his
trachea. He was hooked to a ventilator, which allowed him to breathe.

Shoemaker couldn't feel anything below his neck, and he couldn't speak for
several weeks because of all the hardware in his throat.

"There were times when I felt more dead than alive," he said, looking back.
"For a while, I didn't think I would make it. But I never gave up."

"Shoe is a fighter; he always was," former jockey Ron Turcotte said
on learning of the accident. "He has always known how to put the good
things in his mind and leave the bad ones behind. Somehow, Shoe will be
all right."

Shoemaker's wife of thirteen years, Cindy, and their ten-year-old daughter,
Amanda, saw him through the ordeal. Amanda stayed at her father's bedside
for hours, reading him the hundreds of get-well messages that arrived at the
hospital each day.

In late April, Shoemaker was flown to the Craig Rehabilitation Center near
Denver. It is the same facility where Mike Utley, the Detroit Lions' offensive
lineman, spent the winter rehabbing his injured spine.

Shoemaker was there for six months with attendants massaging and stretch-
ing his muscles every day and gradually easing him off the ventilator so he
could breathe for himself again.

The whole time, Shoemaker kept up with things at Santa Anita. His assistant, Paddy Gallagher, filmed the daily workouts and transmitted them to the
hospital via satellite dish. Shoemaker would study the tapes, then confer with
Gallagher by phone.

"I'd love to say it was Amanda and I that Bill wanted to come home to, but the backstretch is really what he loves," Cindy Shoemaker told Tim Layden of *Newsday*.

She wasn't kidding.

In October, Shoemaker returned to Santa Anita, riding in a customized blue Plymouth Voyager van. The vehicle has an electronically controlled side door that unfolds into a ramp for Shoemaker's wheelchair.

Two physical therapists, Larry Cox and Alvin Lewin, take turns driving the van and tending to Shoemaker, feeding him bits of muffin and giving him sips of coffee while he watches his horses work in the early-morning chill.

"This is probably what kept me going, thinking about the track and getting back with the horses and the people," said Shoemaker, staring off past the barns toward the majestic San Gabriel Mountains.

"Seven months away from here was such a long time. When I first came back, I was pretty weak. I'd be worn out after an hour in the morning. But I've got a lot of my strength back. I can go right through the morning and feel fine.

"In the hospital, I had two bad days for every good one," Shoemaker said. "Now I rarely have what I'd consider a real bad day.

"I've surprised the doctors with what I've been able to do. I can move this [right] hand, which I couldn't do a few months ago, and when the boys [Cox and Lewin] massage me now, I can feel things in my arms.

"I met this fellow in the hospital who also was paralyzed from the neck down," Shoemaker said. "He walked out of the place, so it can happen. That's the attitude I'm taking. It can happen."

Shoemaker's office, located off the barn, is lined with photographs. There are pictures of Shoe embracing Cindy and Amanda. There are pictures of Shoe in his old silks, smiling in the winner's circle.

It is a poignant contrast to see Shoemaker now sitting stiffly in his wheelchair, surrounded by these images from the past. He claims it doesn't bother him.

"They are nice memories," he said. "They'll always be nice memories."

If there is pain, Shoemaker keeps it to himself. He was quiet and hard to read in the best of times, friends say, so it is not surprising he is reluctant to open up now.

A conversation with Shoemaker is a bit like a tour of the Louvre: He allows you to see certain things, but he keeps other areas roped off. His eyes let you know when you have stepped across one of the ropes.

"I've talked to him a few times," said Eddie Arcaro, Shoemaker's longtime friend, "but how many times can you say, `I'm rooting for you'? After a while, he just clams up on you.

"You're never going to know how he really feels. I promise you that."

Shoemaker's stoic toughness is legend in racing. At fifty-five, he underwent knee surgery and was riding again in two weeks. In 1955, he was carried off the plane in Louisville (again, a bad knee), yet he insisted on riding in the Derby. He won aboard Swaps.

Once asked to describe himself, Shoemaker said: "I'm not a whiner."

That is how he has treated the past eleven months. He has thrown himself into his work and refused to dwell on the past.

"Being a competitive person has helped me, I'm sure," Shoemaker said as his van slowly made its way through the stable area.

Everyone recognized the blue van and the familiar figure in the shotgun seat. Dozens of riders and grooms waved and shouted, "Hey, Shoe." Shoemaker, unable to wave, simply smiled back.

"All my life I made up my mind to do things, and I did them," Shoemaker said. "I'm a fighter. Too many people give up."

"Do you feel bitter about what happened?" someone asked.

"What for?" Shoemaker said. "It happened; there's nothing I can do about it. All I can do is take this [situation] and do the best I can with it.

"The big thing is it doesn't keep me from doing my job. I still come to the track and train my horses. I know the business; I know what to look for.

"The only thing is, I can't get on a horse and ride it myself. I used to enjoy working my horses once in a while, getting a feel for what they could do, but I can do the same job [training] without it."

"Is it hard . . . not being able to ride anymore?" he was asked.

"No," Shoemaker said, matter-of-factly. "I rode a long time. I rode plenty.

"[Training] is a different challenge. I like it. I get more satisfaction out of winning now than I did when I was riding.

"As a trainer, you develop the horse, you bring it along, you pick its races. All the jockey does is ride it."

"If you don't miss riding, what do you miss?" a visitor asked.

"I miss not being able to do things for myself," Shoemaker said. "Getting dressed. Getting washed. Brushing my teeth. Other people have to do that for me. It gets hard sometimes, but I manage.

"Look around," he said. "I've got a lot to live for."

Epilogue: Willie Shoemaker retired from training horses in 1997. He died on October 12, 2003, at age seventy-two. He never did get out of his wheelchair.

*Originally published in the *Philadelphia Daily News,* March 18, 1992. Reprinted with permission by Philadelphia Newspapers, LLC.

OPINION

Phillies Are Rose-less and Red-faced*

In a week when the Consumer Price Index broke 200, a week when we learned the dollar is now worth half of what it was worth in 1967, Phillies president Ruly Carpenter declared war on baseball inflation.

Carpenter put Pete Rose, the caviar of free agents, back on the shelf and wheeled his empty shopping basket to next week's winter meetings in Orlando, Florida. After a month of talking about what Rose would mean to his team, Carpenter decided the future Hall of Famer is too expensive for his tastes.

The end came yesterday in a brief meeting at Carpenter's Delaware estate. Rose spelled out the offers he had received in Atlanta, Kansas City, and St. Louis, and Carpenter folded his hand like a penny ante poker player staring at a $10 raise. The Phillies called a press conference and announced they were withdrawing from the run for the Rose, a race they seemingly had won a week ago.

The Phillies appeared shocked by the sudden reversal like they had just blown a ten-run lead with two outs in the ninth. Actually, the Phillies have just completed a rare baseball hat trick. They blew a five-game lead in September, blew the National League playoffs in October, then blew the Pete Rose caper in November.

Meanwhile, the New York Yankees spent over $2 million for Tommy John and Luis Tiant, and any day now they are expected to sign Cy Young and Christy Mathewson. That's the way George Steinbrenner operates. The Yankees have won two straight world championships, and Steinbrenner's two big free-agent investments—Reggie Jackson and Goose Gossage—have repaid him handsomely.

Instead of gaining on the Yankees, the Phillies have lost ground. For a while there, Ruly Carpenter was browsing in Tiffany's, but now he's back at Kmart. Ruly wanted to sign either Rose or Tommy John, and they both expressed interest in coming to Philadelphia. Ruly checked the price tags and purchased neither.

The Phillies come out of this Pete Rose fiasco looking pretty silly. Paul Owens and Danny Ozark have talked openly about how badly the Phillies need a player with the fire, the spark of a Pete Rose. They spoke—indirectly, of course—about how Rose would give their stable of brooding young sulkers an example of how a professional approaches the game. (Owens said Rose would "show us how to win.")

Basically, the Phillies talked themselves into a corner. They told their fans, "We need a leader, and this guy is it." Rose is gone now, so what do they do? Do they pretend the old problems, the cliquishness, will miraculously go away? Do they predict a leader will suddenly arise in their midst? The Philadelphia fans aren't that naive.

For weeks now, the fans have been drawing mental pictures of Pete Rose in a Phillies uniform, sliding head first into home plate, bowling over Johnny Bench in the bottom of the tenth. They aren't going to take this news very kindly. After three straight playoff blowouts, the fans are running out of patience, anyway. Unless Owens recoups with a dramatic trade at the winter meetings—getting, say, a Rod Carew—Bill Giles will need a comeback by Karl Wallenda to sell tickets for opening night.

Carpenter claims he will not sign Rose because it would distort the club's salary structure. That's nonsense. What could be more distorted than a third-string catcher like Barry Foote earning $120,000 a year? Pete Rose is an all-time great. His forty-four–game hitting streak made him the focus of more national attention than any athlete in decades. Besides, he is more than just a player; he is an attitude. He is a pulse in your clubhouse. He is a statement about your organization.

He might be thirty-eight years old, but don't be misled. He slashed out 198 hits last year. Larry Bowa led the Phillies with 192. Rose would have been the best leadoff hitter the Phillies have had since Richie Ashburn, and his frantic sprints from first to third would have had the blue-collar stiffs from Kensington pounding each other on the back and splashing their dollar beers all over the upper deck.

And name one Phillies player who could rightfully complain about Rose taking home a fatter paycheck? Could Mike Schmidt complain? Schmidt earned a half-million dollars last year, batted .251, and took infield practice the way your three year old takes castor oil. Could Bake McBride complain? Pete Rose hit safely in forty-four straight games. Shake-and-Break can't even play in forty-four straight games.

Greg Luzinski and Larry Bowa couldn't complain, because they led the movement to bring Rose to Philadelphia.

If any of the Phillies griped about Rose's salary, he could have pointed to his .310 career batting average. If that didn't work, he could have flashed his two World Series rings. The point is, if the Phillies had to pay Rose a million dollars a year, you know he would have given a million dollars' worth of effort. And he would have made that team take off.

I don't know what made Carpenter think he could steal Rose so cheaply, anyway. You aren't going to sneak the Hope Diamond out of an auction for petty change, not when you are surrounded by dashing yachtsmen like Ted Turner. I guess Carpenter underestimated Pete's appetite for money.

Oh well, Ruly had his shot to bring a hunk of Cooperstown to Philadelphia and maybe win a National League pennant at the same time. He booted it.

Add that to the three playoff losses and maybe we'll have the Phillies slogan for 1979: "We Owe You Four."

Epilogue: A week after this column appeared, the Phillies signed Pete Rose for $3.2 million over four years. *Philadelphia Magazine* credited me with making the deal happen, as if team president Ruly Carpenter read my column and grabbed his checkbook. I doubt that, but if I played even a small part in the signing, I'm glad, because I do believe Rose was the key to the Phillies' winning their first World Series in 1980.

*Originally published in the *Philadelphia Bulletin*, December 1, 1978.

Woody Hayes Doesn't Merit an Appreciative Audience*

Late arrivals were standing four deep in the hallway outside the Racquet Club banquet room yesterday. Most were balancing on their tiptoes; others were standing on chairs, and they were all straining for a glimpse of the head table.

All the seats inside were filled, and the waitresses could hardly squeeze through to clear away the dishes. People were lining the walls, wedging themselves into doorways, coiling themselves around pillars just to hear the guest speaker at the Maxwell Club football luncheon.

More than 350 people, a Maxwell Club record, turned out to hear Woody Hayes lecture on American military history, the rise of Lenin in the Communist Party, the future of Soviet agriculture, the evils of the news media, and, of course, winning football.

When we last saw Woody Hayes, he was delivering a right uppercut to the throat of Clemson's Charlie Bauman, a middle guard from Runnemede, New Jersey. Bauman had just committed the heinous crime of intercepting an Ohio State pass to wrap up a Clemson win in the 1978 Gator Bowl.

Ohio State's president, Harold Enarson, fired Hayes the next morning, piously citing the nationally televised punch as the reason. People close to the scene sneered at the official statement. They believed the university hierarchy had been looking for a tactful way to unload the sixty-five-year-old coach all season.

Not because of Woody's repulsive behavior, mind you, but because his Buckeyes were a disappointing 7–4–1, and they had lost their once firm grip on the Big Ten title. Woody had been slapping people around for years, but he kept his job as long as he won. Woody would slug a photographer, and the Ohio State folks would chuckle and say, "That's ol' Woody for you."

But then the alumni started missing those midwinter trips to Pasadena, and their patience wore a trifle thin. Woody gave his bosses an easy out by slugging Bauman, and they jumped at it. Today, the Buckeyes are 8–0 under new coach Earle Bruce, ranked third in the country, and everyone in Columbus is feeling greatly relieved.

But Woody did not go into hiding after the ugly spectacle in Jacksonville. He figured if Richard Nixon could sell his memoirs for a million bucks, there had to be a market for him somewhere. So he went on the banquet circuit, selling his shrill brand of hypocrisy and hard-line patriotism to the highest bidders.

Yesterday, Woody brought his act to Philadelphia and the Maxwell Club—an organization that supposedly stands for high principles in athletics—and he filled the Racquet Club to overflowing. They welcomed Hayes warmly, and they applauded his remarks vigorously, and all the while, you couldn't help wondering why these men and women suddenly found poor sportsmanship so admirable.

Woody Hayes tries to come off like a philosopher, but he sounds more like a crotchety old man waving his cane and shouting at the world from his front-porch swing. He tried to impress his audience with his vast knowledge of history, yet he blamed Watergate on "that traitor Ellsworth." He meant Daniel Ellsberg.

He talks about how much he admires young athletes, yet I remember watching him grab one of his players by the face mask, then slug him across the head after the player missed a tackle in the 1973 Rose Bowl. People in Ohio say Woody represents the American Way. I suppose that's true if the American Way means pounding your chest in victory and slinking out the back door in defeat.

Woody Hayes has been a head coach for thirty-three years, yet he has never understood what coaching really means. He has won more than two hundred games, yet he has never really learned how to win.

Yesterday's address was a typical piece of pompous rambling. Here's a guy who couldn't teach a quarterback how to throw a forward pass, and all of a sudden he is able to chart the course that will lead our nation through a time of crisis. Naturally, football is his analogy for life.

"There are things you learn when you play football," he said. "First, you learn to get hit, get up, and go once more. Second, you learn to go together. In football, somebody will pick you up by the pads, smack you on the butt. This country seems to have forgotten that."

Hayes then launched into one of his many digressions. "Did you know," he said, "that since World War II, only one president has left office with more than 27 percent national popularity? It was Dwight Eisenhower. All the rest had 27 percent [approval] or less. Why? I'll tell you why. It's because every time the president goes on TV to give the nation a pep talk, as soon as he's done, there is some guy [TV reporter] with his hair fixed just so, who comes on and tells you what the president 'meant' to say or what he 'should have' said.

"Everybody wants to call the signals," Hayes said, shaking his fist. "Imagine if that happened in football. The quarterback would call the play; the team would come to the line; and the split end would yell, 'No way we're running off tackle. Throw me the ball.' Then the guard would say, 'No, run it over my side.' Then somebody else would jump in, then somebody else, and before you ever got the ball snapped, the referee would be throwing that ugly yellow flag.

"That's what's wrong with this country: Everybody wants to call the plays.

"I talked to some agricultural teachers awhile back," he said. "I told them, 'If you want to do your students a favor, teach them about the Russian agriculture. Tell them how the Russians have to buy 25 million tons of wheat from us every year.' Why? Because they're lousy farmers, that's why.

"Herbert Hoover started selling wheat to the Russians so they wouldn't starve. The same as Douglas MacArthur gave the Japanese food after World War II. The same as the Marshall Plan kept the Germans alive. But you don't read about that in our history books. No, they would call that chauvinism."

In the midst of all this red, white, and blue oratory, Hayes never did address the matter of Charlie Bauman. At least, he did not address it directly. He brushed by it with a story he told about meeting an Ohio State football player on campus recently.

"I asked him, 'How are you doing in class?'" Hayes said. "He said, 'I'm having trouble with math. I never had calculus before.' I told him to see a tutor. I told him not to wait another day. As I was leaving, I said, 'Now don't forget to do that.' I punched him like this [playfully]. I'm sure glad there were no photographers around."

In other words, the photographs of this innocent gesture would have moved on the national wires, and Hayes would have once again been wrongly accused of assault. In other words, the press has persecuted Woody all these years. Tell that to the ABC cameraman who tried to take a shot of Hayes two years ago and had his lens shoved back into his eye.

Hayes concluded his remarks with a telling story about his favorite historical figure, General George Patton.

"Momentum, that's what Patton developed at Normandy," Hayes said. "The Germans fell back and tried to regroup, and when they did, Patton hit them like a ton of bricks. You know who released the news that Patton was in command at Normandy? The Germans released the news.

"You know why? Because they thought the bleeding hearts back in this country would demand that he be recalled because he had already slapped that soldier in Sicily. But they didn't call him back. You know why? Because he was winning, that's why."

The audience applauded loudly. Not for General Patton, but for General Woodrow Hayes, the field marshal of Columbus, Ohio, who became a legend by mistaking a game for a world war, ill temper for courage, and profanity for leadership.

Hayes finished his speech, and several reporters approached to ask questions. He declined all interviews and fled toward Walnut Street. His friend General Patton would have called it cowardice in the face of the enemy.

Epilogue: Woody Hayes died on March 12, 1987. Richard Nixon delivered the eulogy at his funeral.

*Originally published in the *Philadelphia Bulletin*, October 30, 1979.

The Real World of Professional Football*

They are lecturing us on pro football now—the columnists, the editorial writers, the essayists who have tired of the theater, and the radical chic.

They are coming forward with their views on the NFL players' strike. They are picking apart the players and their salary demands, all the while suggesting how preposterous the whole thing is.

They insist on pointing out that pro football is "just a game," as if it were something played in short pants and knee socks, with cups of fruit punch being dispensed between downs.

Pro football is nothing like that, of course. Pro football is scarred knees and heat prostration and shots of Novocain at halftime. Pro football is a man talking about being old at twenty-seven.

The people who scoff at the players' union understand none of this. Their grasp of the game runs as deep as a Phyllis George interview or a LeRoy Neiman painting, which is to say, not very deep at all.

The essayists never have stood on the sidelines and heard what goes on when the ball is snapped. The grunts, the moans, the screams of pain.

They never saw an NFL team fly home from a game. Players on crutches hobbling up the steps. Players with ice packs taped to their shoulders and knees, washing down pain pills with their allotted two beers.

They never looked into the eyes of a 270 pound defensive lineman as he was lifted, crying, into the back of an ambulance outside a losing locker room.

If they had, maybe they'd understand what the hell the NFL players are talking about and why they're not playing this weekend.

Pro football is a great game but a cruel business. That's what the NFL Players Association is telling us, and it's true.

Every week, literally dozens of players are seriously injured. I'm talking about broken legs, broken ankles, dislocated hips, the kinds of things most people get only if they wrap the family car around a telephone pole.

In football, it's a matter of course. After each game, the teams hand out a medical report along with the final statistics. The torn ligaments are tallied up every bit as routinely as the first downs.

The casualties are sent to the repair shop; new bodies are brought in to take their place, and the machine grinds on. If that sounds rather callous, it's because it is.

"Pain is part of the contract," former St. Louis safety Larry Wilson once said. He was right.

Every time I hear someone talk about these NFL players living in a kid's world, I recall the sight of Wally Henry following a 1980 Eagles game. He had a bandage wrapped around his waist, and he was wincing as he buttoned his shirt.

Henry had just taken an enemy helmet flush in the back. He thought he had a few cracked ribs. He was afraid maybe one of them had punctured a lung. He was going to the hospital for X-rays.

"I'm not gonna sleep too much tonight, I know that," Henry said.

The next morning, we got the word. Wally Henry was admitted to the hospital with a ruptured spleen. He had the spleen removed, and he came back the next year to lead the Eagles in kickoff and punt returns.

Last year, Wally Henry fumbled two kicks in the NFC playoff loss to the New York Giants. The fans booed him, the press buried him and the head coach signed a half-dozen rookies to take his job.

This year, Wally Henry was released, then recalled when John Sciarra was injured in the league opener. It marked the fourth time in five years that Dick Vermeil fired Henry, then brought him back.

Now Wally Henry is out on strike. His NFL career shows five seasons, four pink slips, four recalls, two busted legs, a ruptured spleen, a near-nervous breakdown, and a strike.

If that's your definition of a kid's world, then you have a strange idea of adolescence.

Pro football is not glamorous, and it's not fantasyland. It's not a place to hide from growing up.

It's a place where a gifted athlete can earn good money, but only for a short time and at a steep price.

A physicist once figured that a collision between a 240 pound lineman who runs the one hundred in eleven seconds and a 200 pound back who runs a ten-flat generates sixty-six thousand inch-pounds of kinetic energy.

That's enough to move sixty-six thousand pounds, or thirty-three tons, one inch. It's also enough to rip an arm from its socket, shatter a knee beyond recognition, or, in some cases, cripple a player for life.

Several years ago, I covered a New England Patriots game and interviewed wide receiver Darryl Stingley. Stingley had a big day. Two touchdown catches, including a leaping, fingertip classic that bordered on the miraculous.

Stingley was a delightful fellow. Bright, witty, articulate. I remember thinking this was a man with a great future, a man who could leave football and be a success in almost any line of work.

The next time I saw Darryl Stingley was the opening game of the 1979 NFL season. He was being gently wheeled onto the Schaefer Stadium elevator by two hospital attendants.

Thirteen months had passed since Darryl Stingley was paralyzed in a pre-season game at Oakland, yet this was his first trip back to the Patriots' complex.

The New England management gave Stingley a job in the player personnel department, which was nice. The Foxboro fans gave him a five-minute standing ovation, which also was nice.

But the fact remained, pro football put Darryl Stingley in a wheelchair. In a matter of twenty seconds, his whole world was turned upside down for all time.

It's the specter that hangs over every player when he comes across the middle or lowers his head to make a tackle. It's the grim reality that makes the player gnash his teeth every time the owners tell him he's asking for too much money.

There are no guarantees in pro football. A career could end on any given play, and that fear is never far from the players' minds.

"When you come right down to it," Merlin Olsen once said, "your life is at stake out there.

"I'm not a weak man, and I've had quarterbacks bent under me in such a way that I'd only have to twist them a little to end their careers. I don't do it because I don't want to, and I don't want it done to me."

Joe Klecko, the New York Jets' All-Pro end, went down in last week's game at New England. Tackle Brian Holloway rolled over Klecko's right leg. He dislocated the knee and ruptured the patella tendon.

Joe Klecko knew it was bad: He heard it pop. So did the players around him.

"It's amazing when you sit there on the field," Klecko said. "Everything goes through your head. I was thinking about where I was gonna get a truck-driving job next year.

"I was worried. It's something that worries me a lot. . . . There's a lot of fear in any injury. Especially in this game. Knees aren't made for it."

Knees aren't made for it. Neither are backs, ankles, big toes, or anything else.

Check the medical files of most NFL players and you'll find joints held together by wires, pins, and staples. These are ugly mementos of their careers that will linger forever.

Is it any wonder former Redskin halfback Larry Brown, thirty-five, cannot play racquetball? Is it surprising former Cowboy tackle Bob Lilly, forty-three, has trouble straightening up on damp winter mornings?

Pro football gives, but it also takes away. For every ex-player with a Super Bowl ring, there are a dozen who can't jog to the mailbox and back.

The next time you think the players are asking for too much, consider how you would feel, hearing your knee tear apart, and wondering what you were gonna do for a living the next year and the year after that?

Think about that Sunday afternoon when the TV screen is blank. Maybe then it will all make sense.

Epilogue: The 1982 strike shut down the NFL for two months. The teams returned in late November, and the Eagles were never the same. They lost four games in a row and missed the playoffs for the first time since 1977. Dick Vermeil resigned as head coach at the end of the season.

*Originally published in the *Philadelphia Daily News*, September 23, 1982. Reprinted with permission by Philadelphia Newspapers, LLC.

A Sense of Perspective*

At 8 P.M., the seventy-year-old Ronald Reagan lay in a Washington hospital with a bullet hole in his chest. His press secretary was still in the operating room, fighting for his life.

A Secret Service man was shot; so was a District of Columbia cop. At the White House, a vice president, a man we hardly know, fumbled for the rudder of our listing nation.

We sat numbly in front of our color TVs, watching the Apocalypse of American politics. We saw a sidewalk littered with bodies; we saw men waving submachine guns; and we shuddered with the awful memories of Dallas, 1963, and Los Angeles, 1968.

Surely, it was a night to pause and reflect on just where we're going. It was a night to bow our heads and hold hands and try to pull this sick society together before it's too late.

Wearing green ribbons just isn't good enough; we know that now. What's wrong with our country goes far deeper than our lapels. We should look in our souls now for hard answers.

Ah, but they cranked up the Great Fun-and-Game Machine, anyway. Yessir, just moments after they showed us James S. Brady bleeding on the street, they brought the Indiana and North Carolina basketball teams dribbling onto our TV screens.

The show, after all, must go on.

This was the NCAA championship game, and that, you understand, is really big stuff. A bullet had just missed the president's heart. The nation's capital was spinning on its edge. But so what? We had to find out how Bobby Knight would defend against Carolina's Al Wood.

Oh, the NCAA acknowledged the events of the day. It moved the starting time back fifteen minutes and added a special pre-game prayer. The NBC-TV folks made sure they had a close-up of a tearful Carolina cheerleader. They made every attempt to tell you how sorry they were.

Then the national anthem ended, and the 18,276 fans cheered, and the game began. Within a minute, the bands were blaring, the fans were hurling profanities at the officials, and ten kids in sneakers went about settling an issue that should have mattered to no one.

That game should have never been played last night. Anyone with any sense of decency realizes that.

To see men in responsible positions, leaders in our academic community, simply shrug off what happened yesterday afternoon and hang out the "Open for Business" sign raises moral questions of frightening proportions.

All this time, we've been making fun of Hollywood. We've called it Tinseltown, the Land of Make-Believe, the playground of egocentric yachtsmen and dimwitted blondes.

But last night, Hollywood had the good sense to postpone its Academy Awards ceremony. The NCAA did not. The jock community slipped behind the Screen Actors Guild in the reality sweepstakes. But I guess we all saw it coming, didn't we?

Sports have grown beyond all rational bounds in this country. Over the years, we have hyped the college basketball championships into such a huge event that it was easy for the NCAA brass to decide that last night's game should be played. They had that vast TV audience to consider, not to mention all that advertising revenue.

Wayne Duke, chairman of the NCAA basketball committee, met with the press shortly before 8 P.M. and announced the game would go on. He said the committee met at halftime of the consolation game to discuss a possible postponement of the championship game. They met again after the consolation, and on hearing that the president was out of surgery, they decided to play.

He emphasized the television network had absolutely no input into the decision. There was a considerable throat clearing and foot shuffling over that one. Since when did TV have nothing to say in these matters?

Duke made it all sound very reasonable; bureaucrats are good at that. He said the tournament officials were not even aware the president had, indeed, been hit until after the Spectrum doors had opened (at 3:30 P.M.) for the third-place game.

"The initial indication was that he was not injured except for a bump while being moved into his presidential limousine," Duke said.

What's the difference? We are talking about an attempt on the life of a president here. This isn't some kid tossing a rock at the White House window. This is a national trauma, an event that, in any fashion, takes precedence over a college basketball game.

If the NCAA had any sense of responsibility, it would have at least held up the program until it had a clear picture of just what took place in Washington, D.C. Better yet, it could have announced a postponement right then and there.

The fact that Duke and his lieutenants let the Spectrum fill with spectators, then let the matter drag through the consolation game with no decision being reached is ridiculous. The ultimate decision to play, of course, was an affront to any person who doesn't have pompoms for brains.

There are those who argue that a postponement would have been impractical. After all, the Spectrum is booked for tonight, with the 76ers playing the Indiana Pacers. Then there is the matter of out-of-towners with hotel reservations and airline connections that won't hold past today.

OK, why not just call the whole thing off? Just name Indiana and North Carolina co-champions. Put it in the record book with an asterisk. You might say it's unfair to the players. I say it's unfair to make these kids play under such extraordinary circumstances.

If they had called off last night's games, it would have given the NCAA basketball tournament a credibility unique in today's sports world. It would have allowed this group to stand apart from the National Football League, which decreed that all games would be played the Sunday after John F. Kennedy was killed in 1963.

I had hoped our sports leaders had learned from the NFL's unfortunate decision—and the criticism it invoked. Apparently, Wayne Duke and company did not. And their last-minute memorial ceremony only made them appear hypocritical, not concerned.

The whole time we were looking at those solemn faces during the national anthem, we could hear the cash register ringing in the background. It's a memory we will probably associate with the NCAA championship from now on. It's a blemish that won't rub off.

I'm not surprised the coaches and athletic directors went along with the decision to play. After all, they are the ones who recruited these players, built these little empires in sweat socks, striving all the while for this one ultimate moment.

What disappoints me is that the two university presidents did not get together and agree it was in bad taste to play basketball on a night like this. They are educators and, therefore, men who should possess some sense of balance.

However, they saw fit to go along with Wayne Duke and the wahoos. It's a decision they will now have to live with—hopefully, not easily.

Two newsmen found Dr. John Ryan, the Indiana University president, in the crowd at halftime. One reporter asked Ryan if this situation was not essentially the same as that involving President Kennedy in 1963. Back then, most colleges canceled their football games.

"No, this is entirely different," Ryan said. "Mr. Kennedy was killed."

I guess that's what our country has come to. You have to kill the president before they lock up the basketballs and turn off the gymnasium lights. Put a bullet in his chest and we can get by with a moment of silence.

They say sports are a reflection of our society, and sadly, that's true. What we learned about ourselves last night is that Isiah Thomas is a more compelling prime-time story than a president with a tube through his lungs.

Our perspective is totally out of whack, folks. If this fiasco accomplishes nothing else, perhaps it will drive that point home to some people.

It made the point with me. I felt embarrassed sitting in the stands last night, shouting questions about slain presidents over the slide trombones of the Indiana band.

I walked through the Spectrum, listening to the crowd and all the while recalling those horrible pictures of Jim Brady, face down on the sidewalk, blood streaming from his forehead. It's a feeling that will haunt me for quite awhile.

I left the Spectrum early. I heard that Indiana won, and that Bobby Knight, that paragon of American virtue, left with the grand prize.

Good. I can't think of anyone who deserves it more.

Epilogue: That night marked the only time in my life that I walked out of an event I was assigned to cover. I knew what I wanted to write, and it didn't have anything to do with basketball.

*Originally published in the *Philadelphia Daily News*, March 31, 1981. Reprinted with permission by Philadelphia Newspapers, LLC.

NFL Should Sack Tose*

The barons of the National Football League met for five hours yesterday, discussing what to do with their bumbling comrade, Leonard Tose.

When the session ended, Commissioner Pete Rozelle said that a committee had been established to explore ways to refinance the Eagles and bail Tose out of his latest case of the shorts.

Rozelle said this committee had forty-five days to research the matter and draw up a proposal. With Tose at his side, the commissioner said he was "confident" everything would work out just fine.

Rozelle assured everyone the Eagles would remain in Philadelphia. Tose made it clear he would stay on and run the show.

The committee was left to work out the estimated $14 million in particulars.

The whole scenario came off very nice and friendly. The way Rozelle acted, you would have thought the Eagles' owner was a candidate for NFL Man of the Year, not a tapped-out playboy coming around shaking a tin cup.

"Are you bailing out Leonard Tose or the Eagles?" someone asked.

"Leonard Tose is the Eagles," Rozelle responded. (The Philadelphia fans will be gnashing their teeth over that one for a while, commissioner.)

Rozelle said there "was a very good tenor" in the meeting room. In other words, no one threw an ashtray at Leonard and lawyer–daughter Susan Fletcher, although a few hard-line NFL bosses probably wanted to.

Tose said he was gratified by the support he received from the other twenty-seven club owners.

"They expressed confidence in me," Tose said.

My question is simple: Why?

At this point, what is there about Leonard Tose that would inspire confidence, or trust, in anyone?

Here is a man who has proved he can't run a business, can't handle a buck, and apparently can't tell the truth. This is a man who last week tried to move one of the NFL's best franchises and didn't bother to notify anyone.

These same twenty-seven club owners awoke last Tuesday to find the Philadelphia Eagles, an NFL cornerstone since 1933, mounted on a pushcart and pointed toward Phoenix, which is midway between Los Angeles and nowhere.

Don't these businessmen think there is something, well, less than honorable about the way Tose and Fletcher conducted themselves in that whole affair? Don't they feel at all compromised?

And consider for a moment the damage, public relations and otherwise, that already has been done.

In one week, Tose and his daughter: (1) betrayed and alienated one of the NFL's best markets; (2) added to the league's image problem ("Carpetbagging for Fun and Profit"); and (3) used their threatened move to shake down City Hall.

Tose and Fletcher have been loudly denounced from Strawberry Mansion to Capitol Hill.

They have a U.S. senator, Arlen Specter (R–Penn.), working overtime on a bill that would make an owner prove he is losing money at the box office before he can move his franchise.

You can bet other owners get real nervous when U.S. senators start talking about bills like that. They can thank the Eagles' brass, not Al Davis or Robert Irsay, for sounding the general alarm.

Tose and Fletcher have turned off sports fans with their disloyalty and irritated non-fans with their greed. They stuck a gun in Mayor Wilson Goode's back and said, "Give us our skyboxes, or else . . ."

Simply put, Leonard and Daughter Dearest fell $42 million in debt, tried to sneak out of town, and were caught; then, instead of acting contrite (or at least embarrassed), they said, "OK, Mayor, gimme . . ."

And the NFL owners still want to do business with people like that? It makes you think the United States Football League might have a chance, after all.

I can't think of another corporate body in this or any other country where Leonard Tose would survive, much less prosper.

Most review boards would check his credit rating and say, "Sorry. . . . Next." A hearing such as the one conducted yesterday would last, oh, five minutes.

But Tose goes before the NFL, IOUs sticking out of his pockets, and the commissioner reports, "No, no one was mad."

Well, someone should have been mad. Tose and Fletcher have fumbled the ball in a very big and very public way.

You have to realize, the Philadelphia Eagles are not exactly a run-down commodity. This is a blue-chip franchise with fifty thousand–plus season tickets and TV millions falling like snowflakes through the skylight.

Tose took it over in 1969, and while the league enjoyed its most profitable decade and the Eagles went to the Super Bowl, the man in charge managed to lose his ruffled shirt and cuff links.

It is hard to believe any business executive could be that incompetent; it's even harder to believe his partners in the industry would turn around and give him another chance.

This newly appointed committee has forty-five days to come up with a solution to the latest Tose embarrassment. I can suggest one right now: Get rid of him.

What's to review and evaluate? After all this time, the NFL doesn't know the man?

Let the league take over the franchise for the time being, until new owner-ship can be found to keep the Eagles both alive and solvent in Philadelphia.

Anything else, any lifesaver plan that includes Tose and Fletcher staying on, is a waste of time.

They won't provide the stability the organization needs, and what's more, they will leave the team with zero credibility in the community.

Can you see Leonard and Susan telling the Eagles' fans, "Hey, gang. We need your support in `85"? They would have a better chance selling Toyota stock in Detroit.

If Rozelle is serious about saving the Philadelphia Eagles, he has to start with new ownership. Maybe that's what will happen when this forty-five–day review is completed and the financial statements are sorted out.

Maybe the league will buy Tose enough time to meet his Crocker Bank note, but only with the assurance that he sells the franchise to a suitable inves-tor within a year. That way, Tose gets out in one piece, and the NFL is rid of him for good.

All I know is, if I had a neighbor who kept blowing his money and he came around and asked for another $50, I'd say no. That may be reducing NFL eco-nomics to the lowest common denominator, but it makes sense.

If the NFL rushes in to save Tose and Fletcher here, either with a loan from the other owners or a fresh bank note, it is establishing a dangerous precedent.

It is, in effect, telling its members, "It's OK to run your team into the ground. Don't worry about your debts. Just call a meeting. We'll bail you out."

Wouldn't it make more sense to weed out the bad owners and build the league around men who have some smarts and integrity?

If the NFL lets Tose and Fletcher off the hook here, it is making a mistake. The league is quick to discipline its coaches and players. The time has come to apply the same standards to its owners.

Epilogue: Leonard Tose's debts eventually forced him to sell the Eagles to Nor-man Braman in 1985. Tose's compulsive gambling left him virtually penniless. He died on April 15, 2003.

*Originally published in the *Philadelphia Daily News*, December 19, 1984. Reprinted with permission by Philadelphia Newspapers, LLC.

Flyers' Shining Moment Tarnished before Game*

The Flyers painted a hockey masterpiece at Montreal's Forum last night. Too bad they had all that graffiti scrawled across it.

They played a splendid game, clawing back from two goals down to finally break the Montreal Canadiens, 4–3, and advance to the Stanley Cup finals. That was the happy ending, but that is not what people will remember.

What people will remember, basically, is a lot of grown men acting like children. And not particularly bright children, at that.

This will go down in Stanley Cup lore as the night when a silly superstition turned into a sillier spectacle. The players called it a mind game. If it was, the principals came unarmed.

The Flyers and Canadiens concluded last night's pre-game skate with a brawl that lasted fifteen minutes. The only thing sorrier than the fight itself was the rationalization afterward. No one on either side would admit he did anything wrong.

"They started it," the Flyers' Ed Hospodar said, pointing down the hall at the Canadiens.

"I didn't know Hospodar would do anything like that," Montreal's Claude Lemieux said, tossing the blame right back.

Meanwhile, the Forum crowd saw forty hockey players—many only half-dressed—streaming back from the locker room to push and shove each other around the ice. It was ugly, cheap, and hazardous to their health. Mostly, it was just plain stupid.

Flyers captain Dave Poulin was there with a broken rib. Defenseman Doug Crossman had removed his skates for sharpening. He came slip-sliding into the fray in his shower slippers. That's a good way to have your toenails clipped, toes and all.

"I looked around and said, `What am I doing here?'" Crossman said later. "I had never seen a fight before a game. It must have looked pretty foolish."

Yes, it did. Hall of Famer Jean Beliveau, now the Canadiens' senior vice president, watched the TV replay and shook his head. He looked more disgusted than angry.

"Wrestling," Beliveau said. "Roller Derby."

No, it's the Stanley Cup semifinals. Sad, isn't it, when you can't tell the difference?

Last night's brawl actually began a week ago. It started with a superstition, which should rank among anyone's bottom five reasons for going to war, but remember, this is the NHL.

Claude Lemieux has this thing about finishing his pre-game warm up by shooting a puck into the other team's empty net. It is, like most pre-game rituals, innocent enough.

The last two games in Montreal, the Flyers' Ed Hospodar and Chico Resch teased Lemieux, turning the net around so he couldn't have his good luck shot. The Flyers also won those two games to take a three games to one lead in the series.

On Tuesday at the Spectrum, Resch spun the net again, but Montreal's Chris Chelios turned it back around so Lemieux could bank in his shot. The Canadiens won that game, 5–2, and Lemieux scored a goal.

You see the pattern? Don't call it coincidence, folks. That would make too much sense.

With the Canadiens facing elimination, Lemieux considered it an absolute must to hit the empty net before last night's game. Hospodar and Resch, the Flyers' Batman and Robin, were equally determined to stop him.

The entire series, after all, was hanging in the balance. Well, wasn't it? Hospodar thought so.

"If it's that important to Lemieux, then it's important," Hospodar said. "Everyone is looking for a little edge."

So began the hide-and-seek routine. The horn sounded, ending the warm-up period. Most of the players left the ice. Hospodar and Resch lingered in the Flyers' end. Lemieux, Shayne Corson, and Patrick Roy dawdled near their bench.

Finally, the Montreal players appeared to tire of waiting. They went up the hallway toward their locker room. Hospodar and Resch left, too, their mission seemingly accomplished.

Suddenly, Lemieux and Corson dashed back onto the ice with a puck and headed for the Flyers' net. Hospodar and Resch rushed out to intercept them.

Corson flipped the puck into the net as Resch threw his stick in a vain attempt at a save. At this point, the whole charade still appeared playful. Then Hospodar caught up with Lemieux and started throwing punches. That's when the alarm was sounded.

"The stickboy ran in here," Poulin recalled. "He said Eddie was in a fight. Most guys had their shirts and pads off. We rushed back out. I don't think any of us expected it to go on as long as it did."

It went on and on, with a shirtless Dave Brown squaring off against Chris Nilan, with Don Nachbaur slugging Larry Robinson, with Daryl Stanley battling John Kordic. All this macho posturing over a pre-game routine.

The three game officials were still suiting up. They didn't arrive on the scene for another ten minutes. There was no one on the ice to restore order.

"I've never seen anything like it," said Robinson, a sixteen-year veteran. "I hope I never see anything like it again."

"I just thought he [Hospodar] would try to stop the puck," Lemieux said. "I didn't know he'd do anything like that. It was completely stupid."

Ed Hospodar sat in the corner of the dressing room, fully dressed, sipping a beer while his teammates celebrated their Wales Conference championship.

The defenseman had not played in the game, just as he had not played the entire series.

Hospodar was a scratch in fourteen of nineteen post-season games. Maybe he was suffering from adrenaline buildup. Maybe he was looking for some way, any way, to contribute to the Flyers' cause, and that's why he went after Lemieux last night.

Hospodar said he was simply "defending" the Flyers' half of the ice. But after the warm ups? After the players leave the ice, the rink belongs to the Zamboni driver, not the players.

Why didn't Hospodar simply let Lemieux go? If the guy wants to carry out his silly pre-game act, let him. What difference does it make?

"He had no business coming in our end," Hospodar said. "Maybe what I did wasn't right, but what he did wasn't right either. As it was, he didn't put the puck in the net [Corson did], and we won the game. So maybe we got a little edge on him."

The scary thing is, Hospodar sounded like he really believed it.

The NHL will review last night's fiasco and no doubt hand down fines and suspensions. Hospodar probably will be suspended for the start of the championship round against Edmonton, not that he figured to play anyway.

The Flyers are fortunate they did not sustain any new injuries in last night's rumble. Imagine losing a Mark Howe or Rick Tocchet for the Stanley Cup final because they were stepped on in that burlesque act?

It is too bad the tag-team match will overshadow a superb series in which the Flyers swept three games in the Forum. They actually had cleaned up their league-wide image. They had just three fighting majors in the last series against the Islanders.

Last night, the old Broad Street Bullies label was back in place.

"I guess you'd have to say both [teams] reacted in a childish way," said Resch, a longtime critic of hockey violence. "But it was an emotional evening."

"I don't think we set the best example for the kids who were in the stands," Crossman said. "Hopefully, we'll stick to hockey against Edmonton."

Hopefully.

Epilogue: The Flyers lost the Stanley Cup finals to Edmonton, four games to three.

*Originally published in the *Philadelphia Daily News*, May 15, 1987. Reprinted with permission by Philadelphia Newspapers, LLC.

Working Up a Strong Hate*

$\mathbf{Y}$esterday, for the first time in my life, I hated pro football. I hated what I saw outside Veterans Stadium, and I hated what I saw inside. I hated what the game had become.

I watched dozens of men and women—regular, everyday folks—bumped and shoved away from the stadium gates by toughs in union jackets. I saw kids in Eagles T-shirts frightened to tears as they walked through the picket line on Broad Street.

I hated the way so many foul-mouthed bullies used pro football as an excuse to throw their weight around. I hated the way they sneered into the TV cameras and made the NFL players' stand look like a pep rally for punks and troublemakers.

I hated seeing twelve days of orderly protest by the Eagles' veterans smeared by the actions of a few union jugheads who didn't know when to quit. I hated seeing picketers spit on cars and pelt them with eggs, knowing it was the striking players who would have to answer for it.

I hated what was taking place inside the barricades, too. A handful of people (4,074) watched two pickup teams—one called the Eagles; the other, the Chicago Bears—play a game that scarred the image of pro football in this blue-collar town.

I hated the fact they were selling programs with the Bears' Dan Hampton and Otis Wilson on the cover when Hampton and Wilson were in Chicago, wearing picket signs. I hated the fact Mike Quick was featured on pages thirty-five and thirty-six when he was sitting glumly on a folding chair outside Gate A.

I hated the fact that Philadelphia fans were denied one last look at Walter Payton, the game's all-time leading rusher. They got Sean Payton, a free-agent quarterback, instead. Feel free to laugh the next time Pete Rozelle talks about the NFL's commitment to a first-class product.

I hated the carnival atmosphere that surrounded the whole affair: the politicians making speeches, the rock singers on the flatbed trucks, the teamster convoy lined up, air horns blasting. I hated the way every loudmouth in town wanted to use the game as a soapbox.

I especially hated owner Norman Braman tossing the post-game blame around like confetti without getting any on himself.

Braman blamed the players for "opening a bottle and letting the devil [union support] fly out." He blamed the police for not controlling the pickets, and he blamed the media for inflaming the situation. He blamed everyone except his fraternity of NFL owners, which seemed like a glaring oversight.

None of this would have happened if the owners had not insisted on playing these stupid "replacement" games.

Braman and his cronies knew they were lighting a quick fuse when they brought in scab teams two weeks ago. Yesterday, he piously expressed shock and dismay when the collective labor explosion rattled his castle gates.

Who is Norman Braman trying to kid, anyway?

Does he really think you can double-dare the unions in a town like Philadelphia and skip blithely away? Did he really think his veteran players would pass this 1987 season off to the scabs as though it were a baton in a relay race?

Strikebreaking is an ugly business; it has been since the days of the Molly Maguires, and yesterday Braman got all the ugliness he and the other owners bargained for.

The players, meanwhile, got more than they bargained for when they asked the other local unions to support them. The thuggery on the picket line probably hurt the Eagles' veterans more than the 35–3 loss they inherited from their bumbling scabs.

Not all the union picketers overreacted yesterday—only a radical handful was involved—but it was enough to make the network news and leave a bitter aftertaste in what was otherwise a watershed afternoon for John Spagnola and his striking players.

The Eagles did what they set out to do, turning a virtual sellout into a ghost town and showing Norman Braman he can't force an Alpo game down the throats of his season-ticket holders. The union game plan worked perfectly, except for the goon tactics on the gate.

The players did what they could to keep things under control outside the stadium. Gerry Feehery, Reggie White, Michael Haddix, Kenny Clarke, and Joe Conwell were a few of the players who walked around, urging the union pickets to stay cool and lay off the rough stuff.

Some pickets took their advice; others did not. Those that did not should have stayed home. The players would have won without them yesterday, and they would have won more nobly. As it was, several Eagles left shaking their heads, wishing the whole nightmare would just go away.

"It was a long, hard day," said linebacker Garry Cobb, the last of the pickets, as he prepared to leave around 3:40 P.M. "You'd walk one place, and it would be like a party. You'd walk to the next [gate], and you'd find a skirmish.

"It was like riding a roller coaster. Now it's over, and I just feel empty. . . . I really think we would have beaten the [real] Bears today. Of course, we'll never know."

Very few Eagles bothered to keep track of yesterday's game as they patrolled the picket line. They walked among the other demonstrators, talking, signing autographs, and posing for pictures. They walked past transistor radios and portable TVs without a second look.

"Your team is losing, 14–3," someone called to Spagnola as the game droned into the second quarter.

"That's not our team," Spagnola replied. "Our team is out here. That game doesn't even exist."

Safety Andre Waters agreed. "I wouldn't even look at that mess [on TV]," he said. "I'm afraid I might go blind. I wouldn't listen to it for fear I'd go deaf. Nothing there worth watching."

"But the result still counts on your record," someone said. "Aren't you rooting for them, just a little bit?"

"I'd like to see `em fumble fifteen times and throw twenty interceptions," Waters said. "I'd like to see `em look as bad as possible. But then, yeah, I guess I hope they find a way to win. For our sake, not theirs."

Quick sat on a folding chair, autographing picket signs. He couldn't figure out what smelled worse: the droppings of several nearby police horses or the sham game going on inside the stadium.

"What's the score now?" Quick asked.

"Twenty-eight to three," he was told.

"I didn't expect any better," Quick said. "I'm a little surprised the [Chicago] scabs could score that many points, though. I hope when they finally settle this, they agree to wipe these games off the books. Everyone knows they're a farce."

Just then, a late-arriving fan walked through the gate, past the union picket line that had pretty much disbanded. The man stopped on his way into the stadium to pat Quick on the shoulder and say hello.

"Don't talk to me," Quick said. "The real fans are out here. There's nothing to see in there."

The man kept walking. Quick shrugged.

"People are going in to see the helmets and jerseys," he said. "To some people, I guess, that's pro football. But it's a minority. We've proven that today."

It was, in a strict union sense, a win for the striking Eagles. They remained united on the picket line, and so did their scheduled opponent, the Bears. "If every [NFL team] had the character these two teams have," Spagnola said, "this strike could be over by now. And we would have won."

The stadium was empty, and Braman's replacement team—the team he promised would be "competitive and exciting"—was a ragged embarrassment. But in the end, it was a day that dragged everyone down into the same dark hole and left them there to ponder, sadly, what might have been.

"All I can think of," tackle Joe Conwell said, "is, say, we were 2–1, and the Bears were 3–0 coming into this game. The stadium was sold out. Buddy [Ryan] going against [Mike] Ditka. Imagine what this place would have been like.

"This is the kind of day you work all your life [as an athlete] for. This is one of those days you talk about for twenty or thirty years after. You remember how it sounded, how it felt, how it went play by play."

Conwell and the other Eagles will remember yesterday, but they will remember it for the game that wasn't. And for that reason, they will probably hate it, too.

Epilogue: The decision to play regular-season games with strikebreakers remains one of the most shameful chapters in NFL history. The Eagles' replacements lost all three of their games, and while they are listed in the team's all-time roster, each of their names is marked by an asterisk. In the press conference following the loss to Chicago, I asked Eagles owner Norman Braman: "What was accomplished by playing this game?" I'm still waiting for an answer.

*Originally published in the *Philadelphia Daily News*, October 5, 1987. Reprinted with permission by Philadelphia Newspapers, LLC.

Afterword

Sportswriters and broadcasters live in a world of numbers. *Earned run averages, turnover ratios, shooting percentages, red zone efficiency. . . . Wins Above Replacement, Defense-adjusted Value Over Average, Pitches Per Plate Appearance. . . .*

Numbers, numbers, and more numbers.

When I announced my retirement from full-time writing and broadcasting in May 2022, I tallied up *my* numbers:

- Fifty-three years spent working in sports media
- 844 Eagles games, not counting pre-season
- More than 2,500 shows on WIP Sports Radio. That's 10,000 hours spent talking to Murray from Mayfair, Butch from Manayunk, Neal from the Northeast, and all the other callers to sports talk radio.

After all those years and all that talk, here is the bottom line: six world championships—two each for the Flyers and Phillies, one each for the Sixers and Eagles—and six victory parades, which add up to 12 million people hugging and cheering, laughing and crying, sharing in a special joy that allows us all to stand a little taller and closer together.

Those are the numbers that matter. The analytics cult sees games as data. They point to new-age metrics that would have you believe winning is a computer science. But if it is all about numbers, how do you explain the 2022 Phillies, who barely made it into the expanded National League playoffs, yet went all the way to the World Series?

You won't find the answer in numbers because this isn't about what you measure; it's about what you feel.

The Phillies found a special magic, a shared belief that for all their defensive lapses and late-inning meltdowns, they could salvage a season that appeared lost. They developed a winning chemistry that lit a fire in Philadelphia. When MVP Bryce Harper said, "We're all a family here," he wasn't just talking about a baseball team. He was talking about the entire city.

In seventy-two hours, the Phillies won games three and four to close out their playoff series against Atlanta, and the undefeated Eagles rolled over the Dallas Cowboys, 26–17, at Lincoln Financial Field. All three games were played in South Philadelphia, but the joy was felt in every neighborhood from Fishtown to Chestnut Hill.

Red October, they called it, with a splash of Eagles green.

Wrote Jason Gay of the *Wall Street Journal*, "Philadelphia feels like the place to be in sports at the moment. It's certainly not those deadbeats in New York or Boston or Los Angeles. Not even Tuscaloosa can make a claim. I have all the evidence I need. Philadelphia is the sports capital of the universe."[1]

I've seen it before. Indeed, I lived it. I was there for all six championship parades: I covered the first one in May 1974, when the Flyers won the Stanley Cup, and I covered the last one in February 2018, when the Eagles won the Super Bowl. One day was brutally hot and the other was brutally cold, but no one cared. It was a time to celebrate.

After that Super Bowl, there were stories about people going to cemeteries and draping green jerseys over the headstones of their loved ones. At the parade, there were people carrying urns with the ashes of family members who would have wanted to be there, and so they were.

That emotion is what kept me going for fifty-three years. It kept the words flowing in my newspaper column, in my books, and on radio and TV. I felt like I had the greatest job in the world. Certainly, there is nothing I would have rather done. That's why it was hard to walk away.

I thought about retirement for almost a year. I was in good health, but I was also aware that when I walked into the press box, I was surrounded by people who were young enough to be my grandchildren. We joked about it—the fact that I still don't have a cell phone came up often—but there was a certain truth to it. I was an old timer in a young man's game.

I understood there was value in my fifty-plus years of experience. I had seen a lot. I brought perspective. If a young player put together a few dazzling games—say, Carson Wentz in 2017—and younger media voices would start proclaiming it the stuff of all-time greatness, I could restore order by saying, "Well, there was a guy named Norm Van Brocklin. . . ."

In other words, what's the rush? Let's wait awhile before we put our latest hero on a pedestal.

I was the time capsule that kept the hot takes fraternity honest. When talk-show hosts referred to Ben Simmons as a "generational player," I asked, "What about Julius Erving and Michael Jordan? What were they?"

There was so much contrived debate—is Tim Tebow the greatest college football player ever?—so I tried to keep things real. I didn't mind doing that.

But there was no escaping the fact that the business was changing, the games were changing, and I was falling out of step. I began losing interest in pro basketball: the game was nothing but three-point shots and dunks. I didn't like what I saw in major league baseball either. It was an endless parade of interchangeable pitchers trudging in from the bullpen. Nine-inning games ran into the eleven o'clock news. Some nights I was bored stiff.

Major league baseball tried to speed things up by introducing a pitch clock for the 2023 season, and while it did shorten the games, it felt weird to me. For more than a century, one of baseball's charms was that it was the only game *without* a clock. Now, *sigh* it has one.

The younger people in the business accepted it. OK, the games have changed. So what? When I went on the radio and complained about the new rules—like starting extra innings with a gift runner on second base—I felt like a cranky old man telling the neighborhood kids to get off his lawn. I decided it was better to just step away.

On Sunday, May 8, 2022, I announced my plans to retire at the end of the month. I talked about wanting to spend more time with my family; watch my granddaughter Haley play field hockey; and watch my grandsons, Emmet and George, play their first season of organized football.

"I love the people I worked with and I'm proud of what we built," I said on WIP, "but I feel it is time to go. I'm healthy, I'm happy, but I'm also seventy-five years old. It's time. Really, it's that simple.

"I grew up wanting to be a writer and hoping to be involved in sports. I've seen it all come true. It was great, but even great things run their course. I've run mine."

Instantly, the phone lines lit up. Listeners began calling in with stories about various shows my cohost Glen Macnow and I had done over twenty-one years. I choked up several times.

When I got home, my email inbox was full. One name jumped out at me immediately.

Mike Schmidt.

What?

I clicked on the email and, sure enough, it was *that* Mike Schmidt. He was in town to broadcast the Phillies game that afternoon. He listened to our show on his way to Citizens Bank Park.

"I wanted to offer my congratulations on your amazing career as a sports analyst/expert in the great city of Philadelphia," he wrote. "You may remember my occasional difficulty with the media during my playing days. Well, now that I'm a member of the media I have a much different perspective.

"I remember how you seemed to stand in the rear of the media crowd around my locker asking more poignant questions and writing on specific issues. I have been away from the Phillies, Sixers and Eagles world of sports for a while but I know you have become a well-respected Eagles expert and the Eagles fans will miss you.

"You truly made your mark on Philly sports. I wish you the best in your retired life."[2]

I read the email several times to let it sink in. I had not spoken to Mike in more than twenty years. The last time I saw him was in 1995, the year he went into the Baseball Hall of Fame. I sat down then with Mike and Rich Ashburn, who was also going into the Hall that summer.

We did a ninety-minute interview for a piece I was writing for the *Daily News*. It was a wonderful afternoon—Schmitty and Whitey, two old friends, two all-time greats, kicking back and talking baseball for an audience of one. Lucky me.

It was the most open and relaxed I ever saw Mike Schmidt. I covered his entire eighteen-year career. For most of those years, he was aloof and distant. Earlier in this book, I talk about the hostile atmosphere in the Phillies clubhouse. Many players were openly antagonistic toward the media. Angry words shot back and forth almost every night.

Mike wasn't like that, but he wasn't exactly welcoming either. After games, he often answered questions while staring into his locker. He didn't snarl at reporters the way some of his teammates did. He just seemed bored. He rarely looked us in the eye. Mostly, he gazed off into space.

That's why I was surprised by his reference to me "standing in the rear of the crowd." I would not have expected him to notice such a thing, but it was a good observation.

I did tend to hang on the outer edge of the media circle. I wasn't using a tape recorder, so I didn't have to get in anyone's face. With a pen and notepad, I could do my job from a distance.

I found it fascinating that Mike Schmidt kept a mental book on the media in much the same way as he did on opposing pitchers. All those years, he barely seemed to know our names, yet he was taking notes on where we stood and what we asked. I never would have known.

Several weeks after I announced my retirement, the Phillies invited me to throw out the first pitch at a home game. Initially, I turned it down. I thought first-pitch ceremonies were a waste of time. Usually, it was a pandering politician or disc jockey looking for a photo op. Most of the time, the fans didn't even bother to look up from their nachos.

But my granddaughter Kaitlyn heard about the invitation and said, "Pop, you *have* to do this." So I agreed.

I slipped on a Phillies jersey with the number 27, the number worn by my favorite player in the 1960s, pitcher Jack Baldschun. As I walked onto the field, public address announcer Dan Baker introduced me by saying, "No sportswriter in the city's history was more admired, respected, or loved."

The ovation was louder and longer than I had expected.

It was a gorgeous Sunday afternoon, and a big crowd turned out to see the California Angels with Mike Trout and Shohei Ohtani. I looked at the cheering fans, many of whom were standing, and as my face appeared on the Phanavision screen, I mouthed the words, "Thank you." It was a far more emotional moment than I had imagined.

I threw the ceremonial pitch to a crouching Phillie Phanatic—thankfully, I didn't bounce it—waved, and walked off the field.

Later, I was invited to the broadcast booth to join the TV crew. Mike Schmidt was there, along with play-by-play man Tom McCarthy and former Phillie John Kruk. I thanked Mike for his thoughtful email.

"You were always fair," he said. "Even when you were critical, I thought you were fair."

"Some writers just want to rip you," Kruk said.

Mike had spent enough time in the press box to see the disconnect between the media and the athletes they cover. They are involved in the same game, but they see it through different prisms.

"Up here, the game looks easy," Schmidt said. "Down there, it's hard."

He is right. Down there, it's hard. Even for a guy who hit 548 home runs and won three MVP Awards, it is hard. It is true of every third baseman, point guard, quarterback, and prize fighter. It is a merciless stage they perform on. We should never lose sight of that.

I didn't think my retirement would cause much of a stir. I thought there might be a few newspaper articles, a handful of cards and letters, and nothing more.

"No, it will be a big deal," my wife, Maria, said. She was right.

Mail poured into the TV and radio stations. NBC Sports did a thirty-minute special with video tributes from former Eagles coaches Andy Reid and Doug Pederson. Pederson referred to me as the "Godfather of Philly Sports," which cracked up everyone in the studio. NFL Films did a profile on my career.

Eagles owner Jeffrey Lurie issued a statement saying, in part, "Ray Didinger spent more than five decades telling the story of the Philadelphia Eagles and bringing our team into the homes of Eagles fans everywhere. . . . [He] is a consummate professional who analyzed the game with tremendous passion and thoughtfulness. . . . On behalf of our organization and Eagles fans around the world, we congratulate Ray on a tremendous career and wish him all the best in retirement."[3]

A friend sent me a photograph of a highway sign on Route 222 in Wyomissing. It read: "Enjoy your retirement Ray Diddy. We're going to miss you." The *Philadelphia Inquirer*'s Matt Breen wrote a long piece about my career saying: "In a city with a rich tradition of sports writing, it's hard to find a career that can match his."[4] It was a lovely send off, much more than I had anticipated.

Chuck Zacney, who owned Preakness- and Belmont-winner Afleet Alex, named his new two-year-old racehorse after me. Chuck, a big Philly sports fan, bought the colt as I was retiring, and he decided to name him Didinger. The horse finished in the money in his first five races, including an eye-popping thirteen length victory at Parx in Northeast Philadelphia.

Maria saved the track announcer's call: "Didinger is pulling away, showing off his speed." Trust me, it's the only time you will ever hear the words "speed" and "Didinger" in the same sentence.

Many thoughts crossed my mind in the weeks leading up to my final show at WIP. Program director Rod Lakin spoke with Glen and me about how to handle it. We decided to make the next-to-last show a going-away party. Maria would join us in studio with our son, David; his wife, Christine; their two girls; our daughter, Kathleen; her husband, Scott; and their two boys, ages nine and eleven.

It was a fun three hours with old friends checking in. Dick Vermeil called from his winery on the West Coast. Jim Gardner, the legendary news anchor whose career was also winding down, phoned in his good wishes. Seth Joyner, Ike Reese, and Fran Dunphy stopped by. Former governor Ed Rendell delivered a proclamation from Mayor Jim Kenney declaring it "Ray Didinger Day" in Philadelphia.

The highlight was Lakin wheeling in a cake in the shape of a yellow legal tablet, my trademark after years of dutiful note-taking on the Eagles postgame show. We ate cake, swapped stories, and had a rollicking good time.

The final show on Sunday, May 29, 2022, was a different story. Glen and I agreed it should be just the two of us in the studio. Nothing was scripted. We didn't rehearse. We barely even talked before we went on the air. We wanted to save the emotion for the show.

As producer Moshe Kravitz counted us down—"five seconds to air, four, three, two . . ."—it became real to me. This is it. This is *really* it—the last show. I had no idea where we were going. I only knew that in three hours it would be over.

During the pandemic, Glen and I created a feature called "Tell Us Your Story," a one-hour interview, the sort of thing radio rarely does anymore. It was a way to fill airtime until the sports world reopened, but it became so popular that the listeners asked us to keep it going. We wound up doing 108 interviews with guests including Jay Wright, George Foreman, Al Michaels, Mike Eruzione, Dawn Staley, Franco Harris, and Bobby Clarke.

For the final show, Glen turned the focus on me. It was: "Ray, today it's *your* story." We talked about my growing up in Southwest Philadelphia, hanging out at my grandfather's bar, Ray's Tavern.

We touched on my childhood over the years: stories of me watching the Phillies on the black-and-white TV and talking sports with those gruff, blue-collar guys who were like family. I told the stories in passing, flashing back to a particular incident like the December day in 1968 when the fans threw snowballs at Santa Claus.

I was there watching the Eagles close out that miserable 2–11–1 season. My mother was next to me wearing the "Joe Must Go" button she purchased from a vendor outside Franklin Field. After five years of watching Joe Kuharich coach her beloved Eagles into the gutter, Mom joined the movement calling for his ouster.

Glen and I sprinkled those stories across our many shows over the years, but for the final show, those memories became the entire three hours. Glen saw it as a straight line from Ray's Tavern to my career in sports journalism. He said once listeners understood that, yes, I really could spell Alex Wojciechowicz when I was six years old, the rest of my life story made sense.

All those games, all those yellow tablets, that was my destiny.

Our conversation took me back to a simpler time when the games belonged to the working men who filled the stools at Ray's Tavern. They drove trucks, pumped gas, and did shift work at General Electric, but that wasn't how they defined themselves. Their work was what they did—that's what paid the bills and fed the kids—but what they lived for, what they talked about, was sports.

If the Phillies won the previous night, the guys at Ray's were having a good day. If the Eagles won the previous Sunday, the guys were having a good week. I grew up watching games through their eyes. The truth is I never stopped watching games through their eyes.

I came to realize these games were more than just games; they impacted people's lives. I didn't know if it was true everywhere, but it was true on Woodland Avenue, and when the Phillies blew the pennant in 1964, Ray's was where they came to mourn. They pulled the plug on the jukebox when the Phillies fell out of first place in October, and they didn't plug it back in until Christmas.

When I became a sportswriter, I brought that awareness with me. I knew those guys waited a lifetime to see the Phillies win a World Series, so when the team made its run in 1980, I knew the guys at Ray's were glued to the TV, praying that this was the year.

The more we talked, the more I was reminded of what sports are really about. It's the human element, not the statistics we discussed so often.

There are some things numbers cannot explain; one of them is the biggest win in Philadelphia sports history, Super Bowl LII (52). The Eagles and Patriots amassed 1,131 yards of total offense, an NFL record, yet when we think about that game, what's the first thing that comes to mind? It is the Philly Special, a crazy, draw-it-up-in-the-dirt trick play that officially gained one yard. That's one yard out of 1,131 yards.

If ever a game proved sports is not all about numbers, that was the game. Tom Brady passed for 505 yards, his career high, yet he lost to a back-up quarterback named Nick Foles. The Eagles defense gave up 613 yards and the Patriots never punted, yet the Eagles won and the Patriots lost.

Feed those statistics into a computer and there is nothing that will explain "Eagles 41, Patriots 33." But that's what was on the scoreboard when the confetti fell and Philadelphia turned upside down.

Ask the guys at Ray's Tavern why the Eagles won. They'll say, "They played better," and they would be right. Sometimes it's that simple, even on a Super Bowl Sunday.

That day, my son, David, and I shared a tearful hug on the Eagles postgame show. David was at the Super Bowl as a cameraman for NFL Films. His assignment was to shoot Foles, who was wired for sound. David got the now-famous shot of Foles asking Doug Pederson: "You want Philly Philly?" The coach thought a moment and said, "Yeah, let's do it." It is now football history.

After the game, David found our broadcast location. The host, Michael Barkann, waved him onto the set. With all of Philadelphia watching on live TV, David and I celebrated the Eagles' victory with a father-son hug.

It was the one time in fifty-three years that I took off my press credential and allowed myself to be a fan. We put our arms around each other, and it was like we put our arms around all of Philadelphia.

People still talk about it because at that moment they were hugging someone too.

In March 2022, the Maxwell Club presented me with the Reds Bagnell Award for contributions to the game of football. It is a prestigious honor with a list of recipients that includes Pete Rozelle, Don Shula, and Dick Vermeil.

As I sat on the dais in my tuxedo, flanked by Heisman Trophy–winner Bryce Young and Eagles Hall of Famer Brian Dawkins, I thought, "Can it get any better than this?" Answer: Probably not.

Our WIP show was doing very well and Eagles Postgame Live was pulling in big numbers on NBC Sports Philly, and I saw an opportunity to go out on a high note. Why hang around and wait to get shoved out the door like so many of my media colleagues? Here was a graceful exit. Why not take it?

I didn't say anything about retiring when I accepted the Bagnell Award, but my mind was made up and I felt good about it. Still, there was the matter of getting through that final show.

Over the years, Glen and I had done shows from car dealerships, race tracks, supermarkets, and hoagie shops. It was always fun, even when we went home smelling like cigarettes and onions. But in all that time, I didn't fully appreciate the effect our show had on people's lives.

I thought we were just two guys talking sports, talking TV and movies, and wondering aloud if Ben Simmons would ever shoot a three-pointer or if Jalen Reagor would ever make a play. I thought it was innocuous chitchat, fun but inconsequential. Glen knew better.

He understood what we had wasn't an audience, it was an extended family. These were people who invited us into their homes and let us ride with them when they drove their kids to Little League. We kept them company when they cut the grass and walked the dog. When they called the show, it was like they were calling a neighbor or a friend.

I didn't get it until I announced my retirement and the letters began pouring in, all telling personal stories. They came from all over, total strangers saying I was a big part of their lives. Several referred to me as a surrogate sports father, a guy who talked sports with them just like their real father did once upon a time.

"We never met," they would say, "but I feel like I know you."

They thanked me for what I had given them. All I could think about was what they had given me. For fifty-three years, they helped me live my dream. Their passion as the best sports fans in America lifted my words and gave them resonance.

I received dozens of letters from women thanking me for teaching them the intricacies of football. Now they can actually sit with their husbands on Sunday and watch the game.

"You probably saved some marriages," Glen said.

Imagine that.

As we came to the end of our final show, Glen allowed me to have the last word.

"I'm leaving WIP, but I'm not leaving Philadelphia," I said. "This is my home. It will always be my home, so if you see an old guy in a St. James sweatshirt walking a bulldog through Rittenhouse Square and you feel like talking about Jalen Hurts or Joel Embiid, don't be shy. Come over and say hi. I'll never tire of the conversation. In fact, I'd welcome it.

"Your expressions of support have meant so much, and I thank you with all of my heart. I wish you and your families health, happiness, and more Super Bowl parades. I'll see you there."

That's how it ended. When I looked up, Glen had tears in his eyes. So did I.

I packed up my yellow legal tablets and headed for the elevator. Unlike the day before when there were dozens of people partying and wishing me well, now the building was deserted. Glen stayed to host the Phillies pre-game show, so I rode the elevator alone.

I waved goodbye to the security guard in the lobby and began the six-block walk to our apartment. As I crossed Walnut Street, a SEPTA bus slowed and the driver opened his window. He called out: "Hey, Diddy, we're gonna miss you." I smiled and waved.

My retirement never really fit the textbook description. There were more interview requests, podcasts, book signings, and charity events. I vowed to answer every person who sent a card or letter wishing me well. That alone took six weeks.

Then came the giddiness of October with the Phillies making it to the post-season for the first time in eleven years and the Eagles getting off to the best start in franchise history. It was a wonderful time in the city. Everywhere you looked, there were people of all ages wearing Phillies caps and Eagles jerseys.

One night over dinner Maria said, "You know, they'll be calling. They'll want you to come back." I laughed.

The next morning, the phone rang. It was Michael Barkann calling from NBC Sports. The Eagles were a lock to make the playoffs, he said. He asked if I'd consider coming back for the network's post-season coverage.

As a former reporter herself, Maria understood the Eagles were on a historic trajectory. If I wanted to climb aboard the Super Bowl express one more time, she was OK with it.

WIP called a week later asking the same thing. Soon, I was setting the alarm to wake up and call into Angelo Cataldi's morning show and talk about the team's record-setting season. No one saw it coming—a 14–3 record, the best in the NFC—but that's what made it such fun.

"You've been following this team for years," Angelo asked. "Is this the best team in Eagles history?"

They had just crushed the New York Giants and San Francisco 49ers in the NFC playoffs. They were favored over Kansas City in the Super Bowl. The Philadelphia police were already greasing the poles on Broad Street, anticipating a victory parade.

"If they win the Super Bowl, yes, they will be the best team in franchise history," I said. "But they have to win the game."

On Super Bowl Sunday, the Eagles saw a ten-point lead evaporate in the second half. With eleven seconds left, Harrison Butker kicked a twenty-seven-yard field goal to give the Chiefs a 38–35 victory. It was a thrilling game with heroic performances by quarterbacks Jalen Hurts and Patrick Mahomes, but to Philly fans it was one more heartache in a collection that dates back generations.

The next day, a man stopped me on the street. "Why does this always happen to us?" he asked.

"It doesn't *always* happen," I replied.

"It feels like it," he said, walking away.

Maria and I love living downtown. One of the things I like best is our unobstructed view of Franklin Field. Our apartment is on the fifteenth floor facing west, and on a clear day I can almost count the bricks in the stadium walls.

My boyhood hero, Tommy McDonald, said he enjoyed going back to Franklin Field now and then. He scored the biggest touchdown of his Hall of Fame career there helping the Eagles defeat Green Bay in the 1960 NFL championship game. He never let go of that memory.

Even when the stadium was empty, he said, the sight of the wooden bleachers and old façade gave him chills.

"I can hear the crowd," he said. "I can hear the cheers. It's like this echo."

Every morning, I look out my window and I see Franklin Field.

And, yes, I hear it too.

NOTES

1. Jason Gay, "In Praise of Philadelphia, Sudden Paradise of Sports," *Wall Street Journal*, October 31, 2022, https://www.wsj.com/articles/philadelphia-eagles-phillies-union-11667221966.

2. Mike Schmidt to Ray Didinger, "Congratulations," email message, May 8, 2022.

3. Jeffrey Lurie, "Statement from Eagles Owner Jeffrey Lurie," statement, May 8, 2022.

4. Matt Breen, "After 53 Years, Ray Didinger Retires from a Career That's Hard to Match," *Philadelphia Inquirer*, May 28, 2022.

Index

The photo section is indicated by numbers *p1* to *p6*,
which is found in the middle section of the book.

Ray Didinger was the first print journalist inducted into the Philadelphia Sports Hall of Fame. As a columnist for the *Philadelphia Bulletin* and the *Philadelphia Daily News*, he was named Pennsylvania Sportswriter of the Year five times. In 1995, he won the Dick McCann Award for long and distinguished reporting on pro football, and his name was added to the writers' honor roll at the Pro Football Hall of Fame. He also won six Emmy Awards as a writer and producer for NFL Films. He has authored or coauthored twelve books including *The Eagles Encyclopedia* and *Finished Business: My Fifty Years of Headlines, Heroes, and Heartaches* (both Temple) and *The Ultimate Book of Sports Movies*. He was a talk show host on 94WIP Sports Radio and a football analyst for NBC Sports Philadelphia for more than twenty-five years.